INTRODUCTION TO PRAKRIT

PANJAB UNIVERSITY ORIENTAL PUBLICATIONS.

INTRODUCTION TO PRAKRIT

BY

ALFRED C. WOOLNER.

M.A. (OXON), C.I.E. F.A.S.B.,

PRINCIPAL OF THE ORIENTAL COLLEGE, LAHORE

GYAN

Published by

Gyan Publishing House
5, Ansari Road
Daryaganj, New Delhi-110002
Phone: 011-47034999, 9811692060
E-mail: books@gyanbooks.com

Distribution Network
gyanbooks.com
India, USA, Canada, UK, Australia, France

ISBN : 978-81-212-2532-8 (HB)
First Published, 1928

2nd Impression 2021

Printed at: Gyan Press, Delhi.

Introduction to Prakrit
Author: Alfred C. Woolner

PANJAB UNIVERSITY ORIENTAL PUBLICATIONS.

INTRODUCTION TO PRAKRIT

BY

ALFRED C. WOOLNER.

M.A. (*Oxon*), C.I.E., F.A.S.B.,

PRINCIPAL OF THE ORIENTAL COLLEGE,

LAHORE.

PUBLISHED

BY THE

UNIVERSITY OF THE PANJAB,

LAHORE.

(*Second Edition.*)

CALCUTTA:

PRINTED AT THE BAPTIST MISSION PRESS.

1928.

Ganthaārena ṇiaguruṇo Siri-

ARTHUR ANTHONY MACDONELL

-ācāriaṇarindassa Baïllatitthatthassa

ṇāma

savvāiṃ uvaaraṇāiṃ sumaria

imassa potthaassa ādimmi

sasiṇehaṃ

ahilihidaṃ.

PREFACE TO FIRST EDITION.

Degree courses in Sanskrit almost invariably include a Drama, of which a considerable portion is in Prakrit. In practice, whatever Examiners may imagine, the student reads the Sanskrit *chāyā*, which most editions provide for him on the same page. At any rate he begins that way; reading the Prakrit afterwards, noticing certain similarities, and *some* of the differences, so that he may be able to recognize a passage, with which he is already familiar in its Sanskrit form, and perhaps in an English translation. Even the more advanced student who reads the Prakrit as it comes, at the slightest check looks down at the 'shadow.' Consequently few students have any definite knowledge of any one of the Prakrits. One cannot blame them. The editions they use are often incorrect in the Prakrit portions, and there is no convenient book of reference in which they can find definite rules. **One object** of this *Introduction to Prakrit* is to provide students with a guide for the more attentive and more scholarly study of the Śaurasenī and Māhārāṣṭrī passages in their Sanskrit Plays.

The **main object** however is to assist the student of the History of the great **Indo-Arayan Language** from Vedic times to the present day. The Indian student starts with an intimate knowledge of at least one **modern** Indo-Aryan language. In the Sanskrit he learns at school, he becomes familiarised with the stereotyped literary form of the ancient language If he studies Sanskrit in the University, he will discover that the Vedic language represents a still more ancient stage of

Indo-Aryan. For this there are accurate texts, and many works of reference available.[1]

The **middle** stage has been comparatively neglected. In India itself, the mediæval Prakrits are in a more real sense *dead* languages, than is Sanskrit itself. Outside India scholars have found in Pali, the language of the oldest Buddhist Scriptures, a convenient representative of this stage. The student of Indo-Aryan Philology needs a clear view of the main characteristics of the different Prakrits. It is hoped that this work may prove useful for this purpose.

Method of Study. Perhaps the best plan is to begin with the thorough study of *one* dialect, afterwards comparing others with this as a standard. This was the method of the Indian grammarians who took Māhārāṣṭrī as their standard. But the only *prose* extant in Māhārāṣṭrī was written by Jains, and that not in the same dialect as the songs in the dramas. There are excellent aids to the study of Pali, but Pali is too archaic to make a good central point, and it is a separate *subject* in our curricula, and generally regarded as appropriate only to students of Buddhism. Moreover the Sanskrit student does actually first come into contact with Prakrit in the plays, and most of it is Śaurasenī. For this, among other reasons, it has been thought desirable to present a general view of the subject, with special stress on Śaurasenī and Māhārāṣṭrī.

The student making use of this book is advised to read the general sections, and to study the chapters on Phonetics and Grammar with special reference to the two main Dramatic

[1] Particularly recommended: A Vedic Grammar for Students by Prof. A. A. Macdonell, Clarendon Press, 1916.

Prakrits. The more important examples are printed in bold type and may be memorised. The Extracts 1 to 14 should then be thoroughly mastered, and the knowledge acquired applied to any play the student may be reading.[1]

The next step will be more philological, consisting in the comparison of the several stages and dialects as far as they are described in Chapters IV to X, and illustrated in Extracts 15 to the end.[2]

The specimens of Pali and of old Prakrit are intended as inducements to further study.

Modern forms have been occasionally quoted to show the historical continuity of words from ancient times. The student should be able to connect up a much larger number of forms from his mother tongue.

The Index is intended partly for convenience of reference, and partly to provide an instrument by which one may test one's ability to explain forms, and to recognize them out of their context.

Transliteration. The Roman script has been used for several reasons. Over a dozen years of teaching experience has convinced the writer that the slovenly spelling, so prevalent in both Roman and Devanāgarī scripts, is partly due to the fact that Hindi and Sanskrit are written in the same script, but with slightly different sound-values. A word written in Devanāgarī may be pronounced as in Sanskrit or as in Hindi, e.g.—**भगवान्**, as *bhagavān* or as *bhagvān*, **धर्म** as *dharma* or *dharam*,

---

1 If he will read a play for the sake of these two Prakrits only, let him choose Karpūramañjarī (Konow's Edition).

2 The most interesting play for variety of dialect is the Mṛcchakaṭikam.

सामवेद as *sāmaveda* or *sāmved* and so on. Confusion is increased if the student has to distinguish a Prakrit pronunciation when the spelling is identical with that of a modern word.

Another reason is that the Roman script being more atomic than Devanāgarī has advantages for stating phonetic laws in English.

Moreover any Indian student who aims at keeping abreast with modern scholarship should make himself thoroughly familiar with the use of this script. To make use of many books of reference, and Oriental Journals, it is almost as important to him, as Devanāgarī to the Western scholar.

These reasons seemed to outweigh the disadvantages of increased labour in proof-reading, and the initial feeling of unfamiliarity with Sanskrit in this guise that may be experienced by the beginner.

On doubtful points, such as derivations where "Doctors disagree," the authority of Pischel has generally been followed. Controversy has generally been avoided, and where any reference has been made to rival theories or matters of dispute, it is only to suggest to the student fields of enquiry that still await his enterprise.

Apart from facilitating the study of the Indian Drama, and of Indian Philology, it is hoped that this little book may lead some of our students and graduates to take an interest in the great field of Indian thought and literature that lies outside the Sanskrit circle. Without some knowledge of this, it is impossible to obtain an adequate idea of the life of mediæval India.

A. C. WOOLNER.

Gulmarg,
1917.

PREFACE TO SECOND EDITION.

The first edition was issued during the Great War. Proofs were read in intervals snatched from Civil and Military duties combined. In this second edition a number of misprints has been removed. In the meantime important contributions have been made to the history of the Indo-Aryan languages. The Chapters on Classification and Literature have been brought more up to date. Since this book first appeared there has been an increased interest in Prakrit in the Indian Universities and the general level of knowledge has risen. More attention is being given in several Universities to the history of the Indian languages. In view of this something has been said of Early Prakrit represented by Aśoka's Inscriptions and late Prakrit represented by Apabhraṃśa.

For reading the proofs and seeing the second part through the press, I am much indebted to my friend and colleague, once a pupil, Dr. Banarsi Das Jain, M.A., Ph.D., now Lecturer in Hindi at the Oriental College, who has also made a number of useful suggestions.

A. C. WOOLNER.

Oriental College,
LAHORE.
1928.

TABLE OF TRANSLITERATION.

Vowels.

अ	a	आ	ā	इ	i	ई	ī	उ	u
ऊ	ū	ए	e	ओ	o				

For Sanskrit add ऋ ṛ, ॠ ṝ, ऌ ḷ, ऐ ai, and औ au.

Note 1. अइ and अउ in Prakrit should strictly be written aï and aü to distinguish them from the Sanskrit diphthongs ऐ ai, औ au; but as the latter do not occur in Prakrit the dots can be omitted without any ambiguity, e.g. uttarai 'he crosses' can only represent उत्तरइ.

2 ए and ओ in Prakrit sometimes represent short vowels. When distinguished these are written ĕ and ŏ (*vide* § 61).

Consonants.

क्	k	ख्	kh	ग्	g	घ्	gh	ङ्	ṅ
च्	c	छ्	ch	ज्	j	झ्	jh	ञ्	ñ
ट्	ṭ	ठ्	ṭh	ड्	ḍ	ढ्	ḍh	ण्	ṇ
त्	t	थ्	th	द्	d	ध्	dh	न्	n
प्	p	फ्	ph	ब्	b	भ्	bh	म्	m
य्	y	र्	r	ल्	l	ळ्	ḷ	व्	v
श्	ś	ष्	ṣ	स्	s	ह्	h.		

Visarga (not used in Prakrit) ḥ.

Anusvāra ṃ.

A nasalised vowel is represented as in ā̃, ū̃.

Note 1. Sanskrit न् n is generally represented in Prakrit by ण् ṇ, but the dental n may occur before another dental, e.g., danta as in Sanskrit. This, however, is often written दंत daṃta. In Jain works the dental n is frequently written at the beginning of words.

2. Similarly other nasals are often represented by anusvāra.

पंच paṃca for pañca
संख saṃkha for saṅkha
दंड daṃḍa for daṇḍa
जंबु jaṃbu for jambu

but see § 35.

3. For the weak ẏ see § 9. Note.

4. Hindi ड़ is represented by ṛ, cerebral ळ by ḷ. In practice this causes no confusion with the vowels ऋ ṛ and ऌ ḷ. The letter ड ḍ was probably pronounced as a cerebral ṛ long before the diacritical dot for ड़ was devised.

5. In general it should be understood that transliteration is merely the substitution of one set of symbols for another, and does not tell us anything more about the pronunciation. It is quite possible that च ca was pronounced something like *tsa* in Māhārāṣṭrī as in modern Marathi, and that in Magadha श a was pronounced as Bengali renders it to-day. Even if so, we may feel sure that a Midlander would use his own sounds in pronouncing either Prakrit.

CONTENTS.

PAGES

PREFACE v

TABLE OF TRANSLITERATION xi

CORRECTIONS xvii

PART. I.

CHAPTER I: SUBJECT DEFINED.
Three periods of Indo-Aryan speech—Three stages of the middle period—Various uses of the word Prakrit 1–4

CHAPTER II: PRAKRITS.
Enumeration of the more important literary Prakrits 4–7

CHAPTER III: GENERAL CHARACTER OF PRAKRIT.
Remains synthetic—Grammar simplified—Phonetic changes—assimilation—Parallel of Romance languages 7–10

CHAPTER IV: PHONETICS. SINGLE CONSONANTS.
A. Initial §§ 1 to 8.—B. Medial §§ 9 to 28.—C. Final § 29 10–17

CHAPTER V: COMPOUND CONSONANTS.
Assimilation § 33—Two Mutes § 34—Nasal and Mute § 35 – Mute and Sibilant § 38—Semivowel and Mute § 42—Two Nasals § 46—Nasal and Sibilant § 47—Nasal and Semivowels Sibilant and Semivowel § 49—Two Semivowels § 50—Svarabhakti § 57 17–24

CHAPTER VI: VOWELS.
Substitutes for ṛ § 60 – for ai, au § 61—Change of Quantity § 62—Lengthening § 63—Shortening § 67—Vowel for Vowel § 69—Omission of Vowels § 74—Samprasāraṇa § 75—Epenthesis § 76 25–30

CHAPTER VII: SANDHI.
A. Consonants § 77—B. Vowels § 80 .. 30–32

PAGES

CHAPTER VIII: DECLENSION.
A stems § 86—**I** stems § 88—**U** stems § 90—Feminine declension § 91—Variants § 92—**Ṛ** stems § 96—**AN** stems § 98—**IN** stems § 100—**AT** stems § 102—**S** stems § 104—Pronouns § 106—Numerals § 112 32–43

CHAPTER IX: CONJUGATION.
Indicative § 114—Imperative § 116—Optative § 117—Future § 118—Passive § 119—Causatives § 120—Participles and Infinitive § 121—Gerund § 122—Irregular Verbs § 123—Past Participles § 125—Irregular Indicatives § 126—Irregular Futures § 134—Irregular Passives § 135—Infinitives § 136—Gerundives § 137 .. 43–58

CHAPTER X: CLASSIFICATION OF PRAKRITS.
Māgadhī—Dialects of Māgadhī—Ardha-Māgadhī—Jain Māhārāṣṭrī—Jain Śaurasēnī—Geographical classification—Paiśācī—Old Prakrit (Aśokan, Pāli, Aśvaghoṣa)—Apabhraṃśa .. 59–80

CHAPTER XI: PRAKRIT LITERATURE.
Jain Literature—Ardha-Māgadhī *aṅgas*—Jain Māhārāṣṭrī — Kāvya :—Setubandha — Gauḍavaho — Hāla — Dramatic Prakrits — Prakrit Grammars 80–92

PART II.

Extract No. 1. Śaurasenī. Ratnāvalī—(Dialogue)—*Translation* 93–95

„ „ 2. Śaurasenī. Ratnāvalī—(The Picture) —*Translation* 95–98

„ „ 3. Śaurasenī. Śakuntalā—(Vidūṣaka) —*Translation* 98–101

„ „ 4. Śaurasenī. Śakuntalā—(Before the King)—*Translation* 101–104

„ „ 5. Śaurasenī. Karpūra-mañjarī—(Heroine and Tunnel) .. 104–108

„ „ 6. Śaurasenī. Same Play—(Puns) .. 108–109

„ „ 7. Śaurasenī. Mṛcchakaṭikam—(Scene with the child) 109–112

„ „ 8. Śaurasenī. Same Play—(Jester admires the door) 112–114

		Pages
Extract No.	9. Māhārāṣṭrī. Verses from Sattasaī of Hāla	114–119
,, ,,	10. Māhārāṣṭrī. Five Songs from Śakuntalā	119–121
,, ,,	11. Māhārāṣṭrī. Three Verses from Mṛcchakaṭikam	121–122
,, ,,	12. Māhārāṣṭrī. Six Verses from the Camphor Cluster	122–124
,, ,,	13. Māhārāṣṭrī. Ratnāvalī—One Song and Three Verses	124–125
,, ,,	14. Māhārāṣṭrī. Setubandha—Building the Causeway—Rāma's head—Sīta's lament—Return to Ayodhyā—*Translation*	125–134
,, ,,	15. Jain Māhārāṣṭrī. Maṇḍio the Robber—*Translation*	134–139
,, ,,	16. Jain Māhārāṣṭrī. Domuha—King Doubleface—*Translation* ..	139–145
,, ,,	17. Jain Māhārāṣṭrī. Kakkuka Inscription—*Translation*	146–151
,, ,,	18. Jain Māhārāṣṭrī. Kālakâcārya—Story of the Shāhī—*Translation*	151–156
,, ,,	19. Ardha-Māgadhī. Udāyaṇa—*Translation*	156–161
,, ,,	20. Ardha-Māgadhī. Uvāsagadasāo—Saddālaputta the Potter—*Translation*	161–168
,, ,,	21. Ardha-Māgadhī. Kalpasūtra—The King's Toilet—*Translation* ..	168–177
,, ,,	22. Māgadhī. Śakuntalā. Fisherman and the Police	177–180
,, ,,	23. Māgadhī. Mṛcchakaṭikam. Sthāvaraka on the roof	180–181
,, ,,	24. Māgadhī. Same play. The King's brother-in-law	181–183
,, ,,	25. Māgadhī. Same play. Śākārī verses	183–184
,, ,,	26. Māgadhī. Lalita - Vigraharāja. Two Turushka Prisoners and a Spy	184–187

		Pages
Extract No. 27.	Āvantī and Dākṣiṇātyā. Mṛcchakaṭikam. Vīraka and Candanaka	187–189
„ „ 28.	Pravacanasāra	190–191
„ „ 29.	Bhāsa.	191–195
„ „ 30.	Early Prakrit. Aśoka. ..	195–198
„ „ 31.	Pāli. Jātaka (308).	198–200
„ „ 32.	Pāli. Jātaka (339).	200–202
„ „ 33.	Pāli. Mahāvaṃsa.	202–205
„ „ 34.	Old Prakrit. Hāthīgumphā Inscription	205–208
„ „ 35.	Late Prakrit. Apabhraṃśa ..	208–209
Index of Examples		211–230
Students' Bibliography		231–235

CORRECTIONS.

Page 4, note 2, l. 2, *for* XIXth *read* XIth.
,, 8, l. 26, *for* Vappaïrāā *read* Vappaïrāa,
for Vākpatirājā *read* Vakpatirāja.
,, 9, l. 17, *for Śrithriá read *Śṛthirá.*
,, 10, § 1, *for yadī read yadi.*
,, 12, § 12, *for* Kirada *read* Kirāda.
,, 13, § 13, *for yutha read yūtha.*
,, 15, l. 1, *for* ṇāvia *read* ṇāvida.
,, ,, (23), *for* ḷ *or* ḷ *read* l *or* ḷ.
,, 20, l. 17, *for* tshii *read* thii.
,, 29, § 72, l. 2, *for* viaṅā *read* viaṇā.
,, 31 l. 2, *for* aniga-m- *read* aṅga-m-.
,, ,, § 79, l. 1, *for* number *read* member.
,, ,, § 80, *for rājârṣi read rājarṣi.*
,, 34, § 90, *for* vauṃ *read* vāuṃ.
,, 36, § 92, (v) *for* davahaṇāhiṃ *read* pavahaṇāhiṃ.
,, ,, § 93 (iii), *for* risāō *read* risao.
,, ,, last line, *for mṛgatṛṣṇikāyaḥ read mṛgatṛṣṇikāyāḥ.*
,, 37, l. 1, *for rekhaḥ read rekhāḥ.*
,, 42, § 110, l. 10, *for* -iṇa *read* iṇa-.
,, 53, l. 3, *for* viṇṇāveï *read* viṇṇaveï.
,, 57, l. 3, *for* ādhappaï *read* āḍhappaï.
,, ,, l. 4, *for* vidhappaï *read* viḍhappaï.
,, 88, l. 17, *insert* been *after* have.

INTRODUCTION TO PRAKRIT.

PART I.

CHAPTER I.

SUBJECT DEFINED.

The history of the North Indian or Indo-Aryan languages may be conveniently divided into three periods—ancient, mediæval, and modern.

(i) The speech of the ancient or **Old Indo-Aryan** period is represented in literature (*a*) by the language of the Ṛig Veda, (*b*) by that of later Vedic books. To this period belonged also those spoken dialects on which were based (*c*) the poetic diction of the Epics, and (*d*) the more highly polished **(Saṃskṛta)** literary language of Pāṇini, Patañjali, and thereafter of Kālidāsa and the others down to the present day.

(ii) The mediæval or **Middle Indo-Aryan** period is represented in literature by Pāli and the Prākṛits. It comprises all the dialects from the time (whenever it was) that certain *phonetic* changes, with some variations in grammar also, had produced a language obviously different from Old Indo-Aryan, down to the time (? about 1100 A.D.) when further phonetic changes and the complete break up of the old grammar had produced a new type of language similar to that of the modern vernaculars. Our knowledge of this period has to be pieced together from a variety of records, referring to different localities and different times. These records comprise inscriptions as well as literary works. Of the inscriptions the most famous are the Edicts of Aśoka. The literature comprises the Pāli Canon of the "Southern" or Hīnayāna Buddhists, the Prākrit

Canon of the Jains, the Prākrit of Lyrics, Epics and Plays and the Prākrit grammars.

(iii) The beginning of the third or modern period has not been fixed with precision. It lies between the latest sort of Prākrit, or **Apabhraṃśa** such as that described by Hemacandra in the twelfth century, and the earliest poetry of the Old Vernaculars. The oldest poem in Western Hindi is the Prithi Rāj Rasau by Chand Bardai of Lahore (? about 1200 A.D.).

The middle period can be again divided into three stages: (1) **Old Prākrit** (or Pāli); (2) **Middle Prākrit**; (3) **Late Prākrit** or Apabhraṃśa.

(1) The Old Prākrit stage includes (*a*) Inscriptions from the middle of the 3rd century B.C. down to the 2nd century A.D. The dialect varies with time and place.

(*b*) Pāli of the Hīnayāna Canon and other Buddhist works, as the Mahāvaṃsa and the Jātakas.

In the Jātakas, or Birth Stories of the Buddha, the verses (gāthās) preserve a more archaic form of language than the prose.

(*c*) The language of the oldest Jain Sūtras.

(*d*) The Prākrits of early plays, such as those of Aśvaghoṣa of which fragments have been found in Central Asia.

(2) The Middle Prākrit stage includes (*a*) Māhārāṣṭrī, the language of the liquid lyrics of the Deccan, (*b*) the other Dramatic Prākrits, Śaurasenī, Māgadhī, etc., as found in the plays of Kālidāsa and his successors, and in the grammarians; (*c*) the dialects of the later Jain books; (*d*) Paiśācī, in which the Bṛhatkathā is said to have been composed, but which is known only from the statements of grammarians.

(3) *Apabhraṃśas* were not much used for literary purposes. They represent the stage reached by ordinary colloquial speech when the Prākrit type of speech as found in the plays was already archaic, and had been refined and stereotyped by the grammarians. By the time that Hemacandra recorded a

particular Apabhraṃśa of the West, this was probably already archaic.

This book is concerned in general with the second, mediæval, or **middle period** of the Indian language, and in particular with the **Middle Prākrit stage**, especially the Dramatic Prākrits.

Various uses of the word "Prākṛit."

Prākṛta derived from *prakṛti* has two lines of meaning: (*a*) the more precise meaning of something belonging to or derived from a *prakṛti*, that is from the original form of anything as opposed to a *vikṛti* its modification. (In Sāṃkhya Philosophy *prākṛta* means what is derived from Prakṛti, the original element); (*b*) the looser meanings of 'natural, ordinary, vulgar, provincial.'

It is probable that it was in the more general sense that '*prākṛta*' (Śauraseni '*pāüda*' Māhārāṣṭri '*pāüa*') was first applied to *ordinary common* speech as distinct from the highly polished, perfected *Saṃskṛitam.*

Grammarians and Rhetoricians of later days however explain *prākṛtam* as derived from the *prakṛti,* i.e. *saṃskṛtam.* This explanation is perfectly intelligible even if it be not historically correct. Practically we take Sanskrit forms as the basis and derive Prākrit forms therefrom. Nevertheless modern philology insists on an important reservation: Sanskrit forms are quoted as the basis in as far as they represent the Old Indo-Aryan forms, but sometimes the particular Old Indo-Aryan form required to explain a Prākrit word is not found in Sanskrit at all, or only in a late work and obviously borrowed from Prākrit.

If in "Sanskrit" we include the Vedic language and all dialects of the Old Indo-Aryan period, then it is true to say that all the Prākrits are derived from Sanskrit. If on the other hand "Sanskrit" is used more strictly of the Pāṇini-Patañjali language or "Classical Sanskrit" then it is untrue to say that any Prākrit is derived from Sanskrit, except that Śauraseni, the Midland Prākrit, is derived from the Old Indo-Aryan dialect of the Madhyadeśa on which Classical Sanskrit was mainly based.

In Europe the word Prākrit has been used (*a*) to refer to particular languages classed as Prākrit in India, e.g. Māhārāṣṭrī, or to the Prākrit passages in plays;

(*b*) Of the Middle Period of the Indian languages (Pāli and the early inscriptions forming an earlier stage were sometimes distinguished from Prākrit[1]);

(*c*) Of the *natural* spoken language as distinct from the literary learned language. In this last sense some writers[2] distinguish Primary, Secondary and Tertiary Prākrits as the natural spoken dialects of the three great periods. Out of these successive types of spoken speech grew the various literary idioms which became stereotyped or fossilised as it were, and remained in use alongside of the living and ever-changing dialects.

CHAPTER II.

PRAKRITS.

The following are the more important literary Prākrits (Pāli being excluded):—

M.	**Māhārāṣṭrī**	Dramatic Prākrits.
Ś.	**Śauraseni**	
Mg.	**Māgadhī**	
AMg.	Ardha-Māgadhī	Jain Canon.
J. M.	Jain-Mahārāstrī	
J. Ś.	Jain-Śauraseni	
(Apa.	Apabhramśa.)	

---

[1] Dr. O. Franke in his *Pāli and Sanskrit* uses 'Pāli' for the Middle Period including Inscriptions.

[2] *Vide* Article on Prākrit by Dr. Sir George Grierson in Encyclopaedia Britannica, XIXth Edition.

M. **Māhārāṣṭrī** was regarded as the Prākrit *par excellence.* Prākrit grammars gave the rules for this first. For others there were some special rules, and then "the rest is like Mahārāṣṭrī." Daṇḍin remarks (K.D.1.35): *Mahārāṣṭrāśrayām bhāṣām prakṛṣṭam prākṛtaṃ viduḥ·*

In the Drama ladies who speak Śauraseni, sing their songs in Māhārāṣṭrī. The Māhārāṣṭrī lyrics were famous far beyond the limits of Māhārāṣṭram. The same language is used for the Prākrit Epics such as the Gaüḍavaho. This language of the Deccan poets carries further than other Prākrits the principle of omitting single consonants between vowels (*vide* § 10). This is natural in a literary song-dialect, for in a song it is the melody and sentiment that matter most, the precise words or forms of words are less important. It is not to be supposed however that Māhārāṣṭri is a mere invention of the poets. It is based on the old spoken language of the country of the Godavari, and contains many features that survive as peculiarities of modern Marathi.

Ś. **Śaurasenī** was the Prākrit of the Madhyadeśa taking its name from Śūrasena the country round Mathurā ('Muttra'). This is the ordinary Prākrit of a Sanskrit drama. It is spoken by ladies and the Vidūshaka; in the Camphor-cluster (Karpūra-mañjarī) even by the king. This Prākrit is the nearest to classical Sanskrit. It arose in the same country, and is descended from the spoken language, on which classical Sanskrit was mainly based. It thus forms an intermediate stage between Sanskrit and Hindi (that is, the Western Hindi on which Literary Hindi has been based). Owing however to this close kinship with the sacred tongue, Śaurasenī was overshadowed; continually influenced by Sanskrit, it failed to make much independent progress.

Mg. **Māgadhī** is the Prākrit of the East. Its geographical centre was in the ancient Magadha not far from the land of modern Māgahī, a dialect of Bihārī. In the plays Māgadhī is spoken by low people. Dialects of Māgadhi also occur, e.g., Ḍhakkī in the Mṛcchakaṭikam. This Prākrit differs conspicuously from the others in its phonetics. स is replaced by श, and र by ल. The nominative singular of -a stems end in -e. य remains and even replaces ज. [For further particulars vide Chap. X). Where other Prākrits say *hattho*, Māgadhī has *haśte*; others *so rāā* = *so rājā*, Māgadhi śe lāā.

Jain Prākrits.

AMg. The oldest Jain Sūtras were composed in **Ardha Māgadhī**, a Prākrit based on the dialect spoken between Śūrasena and Magadha (about Oude). In its phonetic character it resembles Māgadhī in some respects. It preserves more traces of the old grammar than Śaurasenī, and shows a greater independence from Sanskrit.

J. M. The non-canonical books of the Śvetāmbaras were written in a form of Māhārāṣṭrī that has been termed **Jain Māhārāṣṭrī.**

J. Ś. The language of the Digambara Canon in some respects resembles Śauraseni and has been termed *Jain Śauraseni.*

Apabhraṃśa has been used in India (*a*) for anything diverging from Sanskrit as the standard of correct speech, (*b*) for spoken languages as distinct from literary "Prākrits," including non-Aryan as well as Aryan languages; (*c*) a literary form of any such vernacular. The only literary Apabhraṃśa described in detail by the grammarians is the *Nāgara* Apabhramśa which appears to have belonged to Gujarat. To this is said to be related the *Vrācada* Apabhraṃśa of Sindh. Ḍhakkī and some other dialectic forms of the main Prākrits are sometimes styled *apabhramśas.* If we had records of the Apabhraṃśas spoken in the areas connected with each of the main Prākrits an important link in the history of the Indian languages would be supplied. Even as it is, the tendencies of Apabhraṃśa in phonetics and grammar, help to bridge the gap between typical Prākrit and the modern languages. The number of text available gradually increases and these supplement the information contained in Hemacandra's grammar.

The use of various Prākrits in the Drama is discussed in Chapter XI on Prākrit Literature. Further details as to sub-dialects, Paiśācī dialects, the dialects used in Inscriptions, and their relationships, are given in Chapter X on the classification of Prakrits.

CHAPTER III.

GENERAL CHARACTER OF PRAKRIT.

Prākrit (including Pāli) was still a synthetic language. The ancient grammar had been somewhat simplified. The number of case forms and verbal form tends to dwindle. The Rigveda possessed a greater variety of forms than the later Vedas. Pāṇini's Sanskrit has discarded a number of forms used in the Brāhmaṇas. Pāli and old Ardhamāgadhī retain a good deal that has disappeared from the Māhārāṣṭrī and Śaurasenī of the lyrics and plays. Apabhraṃśa finally indicates the approaching dissolution of the last remnants of the old etymology. The time was approaching when a noun might have only two or three distinct endings, and the verb was reduced to little more than one tense and two participles. The ambiguity thus produced was avoided by new devices, and out of the ruins of the old language grew up the analytic languages of modern India.

Though simplified, yet the remaining Prākrit grammar is of the same type as Sanskrit grammar. There is a strong tendency to reduce all declension to one type, that of *a*-stems, and to conjugate all verbs according to one scheme, that of the old *A.* Conjugation. The Dative disappears. Nominative and Accusative Plurals tend to coincide. The Imperfect, Perfect and numerous Aorists had gone by the time of the Middle Prākrit stage. The Dual number was found unnecessary. The Ātmanepada hardly survived after the Old Prākrit stage and never in its original meaning. But it was not yet necessary to resort to postpositions or auxiliary verbs. The essentials necessary for ordinary conversation and even verse-writing remained down to the Apabhraṃśa stage. For more important work, for more exact thinking the tendency was to resort to Sanskrit. As Pāli, Ardhamāgadhī and the other Jain Prākrits successively lost the advantage of being the language of the day, or of the locality, they were unable to withstand this tendency and were eventually replaced by Sanskrit.

Apart from this simplification the main changes arising in Prākrit are phonetic. Conjunct consonants are mostly assimilated: *rakta* became *ratta* (as Latin fructu-s became Italian frutto); *sapta* became *satta* (as Latin septem became Italian sette). Some of the sounds of the old language disappear: ऋ *ṛ*, ऐ *ai*, औ *au*, य *ya* (except in Mg. and a shadowy य to bridge hiatus), श *śa* (except in Mg. where स is missing), ष ṣa and Visarga; whereas the only sounds contained in Prākrit and not recorded for Sanskrit are the short vowels ĕ and ŏ. Final consonants are avoided. Not more than two consonants can follow a short vowel, nor more than one follow a long vowel.

[For details see Chapters IV to VI.]

The cumulative effect to such changes in the case of a particular word may be such as to completely alter its appearance. "Vappaīrāā" does not immediately suggest Vākpatirājā, "oiṇṇa" is not very like *avatīrṇa*. On the other hand some words are indentical with Sanskrit and the *majority* could readily suggest a Sanskrit equivalent to anyone with a living colloquial knowledge of the classical language. This is true not only of Śaurasenī but also of the others.

From this circumstance it may be understood that the different Prākrits were mutually intelligible among the educated. A speaker of Sanskrit, whose *mother* tongue was the spoken form of any one of the Prākrits, would readily understand any of the literary Prākrits. Moreover a speaker of Śauraseni would easily learn to recognise many Sanskrit words, and even grasp the meaning of a Sanskrit sentence without being able to speak Sanskrit. In the older stage the difference was still less marked. Still further back we should find only the difference between 'correct' and 'incorrect' pronunciation, grammatical speech and ungrammatical, standard speech and dialectical—the differences between the speech of educated and uneducated people speaking substantially the same language. At this stage though differences existed the new speech had not attained a separate existence, it was not yet distinct enough to be recognized as a separate language capable of having a fixed grammar and a literature of its own.

Even in the Rigveda we find "*prākritisms*," that is phonetic variations along just those lines that were followed by the Prākrits. For instance *śithirá*="loose" instead of *śrithriá* as might be expected from the root *śrath.* From this and similar instances it is not necessary to deduce a wide difference between the language of the hymns and contemporary speech. Rather the inclusion of such "prākritisms" in the sacred texts indicates that the priests regarded them as possible forms in the same language, and were not yet conscious of any gulf between the two kinds of speech.

An interesting parallel to the history of the Indo-Aryan languages is shown by that of the Romance languages in Europe. Of several old Italic dialects, that of the Latin tribe prevailed, and Latin became the dominant language of Italy—and then of the Roman Empire. It became the language of the largest Christian Church of the middle ages, and thence the language of Science and Philosophy until the modern languages of Europe asserted their independent existence. Like Sanskrit in India, Latin was long the medium of conversation between educated men of different nations. Again, as the language of religion, Latin was always to be heard in the mouths of priests, and common people caught stray phrases of it. The mediæval quack or schoolmaster, however ignorant, must needs air his Latin.[1] Here again phonetic changes and the working of analogy have gradually simplified the old grammar until prepositions and auxiliary verbs had to be used to avoid ambiguity.

Some speculation has been devoted as to the *causes* of such changes as in India may be styled prakritic. Economy of effort, progressive refinement especially in courts and cities, softening influence of a semi-tropical climate, influence of the speech habits of non-Aryan peoples who adopted the Aryan speech—all these may have been at work both in India and in Europe.

CHAPTER IV.

PHONETICS.

Single Consonants.

§ 1. **A. Initial.** The general rule is that a **single consonant at the beginning of a word remains unaltered, except n, y, ś, and ṣ. (न, य, श, ष).**

n is cerebralised (§ 7).

y becomes j (except in Mg.).

jadhā=*yathā* (Mg. yadhā). **jaï**=*yadi*, Śaur. also has **jadi** (Mg. yaï, yadi). **jogī**=*yogī*.

ś and ṣ become **s** (§ 8).

§ 2. The initial consonant of the second member of a compound is usually treated as if it was in the middle of a word. A verbal root however often retains its initial letter.

putta=*putra*, but *āryaputra* becomes **ajjaütta.**

M. paäsei=*prakāśayati*. Ś. **āadaṃ** or **āgadaṃ**=*āgatam*. (M. āaaṃ or āgaaṃ)

[1] See Love's Labour Lost, Act V. Holofornes the Schoolmaster.

§ 3. Enclitics are similarly treated. **kiṃ uṇa**=*kiṃ punar*. **vi**=*(a)pi*. **a**=*ca*.

In *tāvat* and *te* (2nd pers. pron.) Śaur. and Mg. change *t* to *d* as in the middle of a word. **mā dāva**=*mā tāvat*. **ṇa de**=*na te*. **piduṇo de**=*pitus te*. **tado de**=*tatas te*.

§ 4. In several dialects **bh** becomes **h** in the root **bhū** and its derivatives. M. **hoï**=*bhavati* (Saur. **bhodi**).

Ś. **havissadi** (Mg. haviśśadi)=*bhaviṣyati*.

Ś. Mg. **hodavva**=*bhavitavya*.

(5). **Ph** at the beginning of the second member of a compound is often retained as at the beginning of a word.

Ś. **cittaphalaa**=*citraphalaka*, **bahuphala**, **saphala**.

(6). *Aspiration*.

kh for **k**. **khujja**=kubja. **√kheḷ**=*√krīḍ*. [Skt. has *khel* 'shake, play' as early as the Rāmāyaṇa (J. Bloch), which may be Prakritic.]

ph for p. Ś. phaṇasa. M. paṇasa=*panasa* "bread-fruit tree." An aspirated sibilant becomes **ch**. AMg. chāva= Pāli chāpa=*śāba* or *śāva* "young animal." M. AMg cha=*ṣaṭ*, chaṭṭha=*ṣaṣṭha*.

(7). *Change of Place of Articulation*.

Examples. Palatal for Dental. M. **ciṭṭhaï**. S. **ciṭṭhadi**. Mg. ciṣṭhadi=*tiṣṭhati*.

Cerebral for Dental. M. ḍhaṅkha=*dhvāṅkṣa* "crow."

ṇ for **n**. **ṇūṇa**=*nūnam*, **ṇaaṇa**=*nayana*.

(8). The three sibilants **ś**, **ṣ**, **s** (श ष स) are reduced to one, the dental **s** (except in Māgadhî where we have the palatal **ś**).

§ 9. **B. Medial. Medial or intervocal k, g, c, j, t, d, are generally dropped.** (क, ग, च, ज, त, द).

M. **loa**=*loka*, **saala**=*sakala*, **aṇurāa**=*anurāga*, **juala**= *yugala*, **ṇaara**=*nagara*, **paüra**=*pracura*, **bhoaṇa**= *bhojana*, **rasāala**=*rasātala*, **hiaa**=*hṛdaya*.

Medial p, b, v, are sometimes dropped. (प, ब, व).

M. **rūa**=*rūpa*, viuha=*vibudha*, diaha=*divasa*.

Medial y is always dropped (य).

vioa=*viyoga*, **pia**=*priya*.

Note.—In place of the omitted consonant was pronounced a weakly articulated *ẏa* (*laghu-prayatnatara-ya-kāra*). This was weaker than the य of Sanskrit or Māgadhī, and was not expressed in writing, except in MSS. written by the Jains, e.g., hiẏaẏa=*hṛdaya*.

§ 10. This principle of omitting single consonants between vowels was carried to great lengths in the literary form of Mahārāṣṭrī used in Lyrics. It naturally leads to ambiguity. **Kaï** may represent *kati*, *kavi*, or *kapi*! A string of vowels like **uaa** (=*udaka*) has lost all the character of the original word. The fact that such changes were possible at all shows that the Indian consonants were, as now, weaker in articulation than the English consonants. The actual workaday dialects however were more conservative. In Apabhraṃśa, Hemacandra tells us, **k, t, p** between vowels were not dropped, but became **g, d, b**, respectively. ṇāagu=*nāyakaḥ*, āgado=*āgataḥ*, sabhalaū=*saphalakam*. Some of the literary Prākrits also have the same change. In the older stage, as in Pāli, k, t, p remain unchanged, or dialectically became sonants: Sāgala=*Sākala*.

§ 11. *Examples.*

Śaur: **adidhi**=*atithi*, **kadhedu**=*kathayatu*, **pāridosia**=*pāritoṣika*, **bhodi**=*bhavati*, **kadhido**=*kathitaḥ*, **Kirada**=*Kirāta*, **āṇedi**=*ānayati*, **tado**=*tataḥ*, **kida**=*kṛta*, **gada**=*gata*, **sakkada**=*saṃskṛta*, **Sarassadī**=*Sarasvatī* (M. Sarassaï).

Māgadhi: pālidośia=*pāritoṣika*, śāadaṃ=*svāgatam*, hage ("I") **ahakaḥ*, a derivative of *aham*.

Ardha-Māgadhī and Jain Māhārāṣṭrī: Asoga=*Aśoka*, loga =*loka*, āgāsa=*ākāśa*.

Pāli: loka, gacchati, rūpa.

§ 12. In this treatment of medial t we have one of the characteristic distinctions between the Śauraseni and Mahārāṣṭrī of the plays. Compare the following:—

Sauraseni.	*Māhārāṣṭrī.*	*Sanskrit.*
jāṇādi	jāṇāī	jānāti.
edi.	ei	eti.
hida	hia	hita.
pāuda	pāua	prākṛta.
maragada	maragaa	marakata.
ladā	laā	latā.
ṭhida	ṭhia	sthita.
pahudi	pahui	prabhṛti.
sada	saa	śata.
edaṃ	eaṃ	(etad).

§ 13. **The aspirates kh, gh, th, dh, ph, and bh between vowels are generally reduced to h. (ख, घ, थ, ध, फ, and भ become ह).**

muha=*mukha*, **sahī**=*sakhī*, **meha**=*megha*, **lahua**=*laghuka*, **jūha**=*yutha*, **ruhira**=*rudhira*, **vahū**=*vadhū* **sahara**=*śaphara*, **ahiṇava**=*abhinava*, **ṇaha**=*nabhas* or *nakha*.

§ 14. Here again Śauraseni, Māgadhī and some other dialects merely replace the surd **th** by the sonant **dh**.

Ś. **adidhi, kadhedu, tadhā, adha, jadhā**=*yathā*.

Mg. yadhā=*yathā*, tadhā. (Pāli retains the surd—atha, yathā, tathā.)

This forms another distinction between Śauraseni and Māhārāṣṭrī, e.g. :—

Śauraseni.	*Māhārāṣṭrī.*	*Sanskrit.*
adha	aha	atha.
maṇoradha	maṇoraha	manoratha.
kadhaṃ	kahaṃ	katham.
ṇādha	ṇāha	nātha.

§ 15. Sometimes instead of being dropped (§ 9) or reduced to h (§ 13) a consonant between vowels is **doubled.**

Ś. **ujju**=*ṛju*, M. ṇakkha=*nakha*, M. Ś. **ĕkka**=*eka.*

Note 1. Other consonants are similarly doubled, e.g. :—
jŏvvaṇa=*yauvana*, **tĕlla**=*taila*, **pĕmma**=*preman.*

Note 2. The vowel before the double consonant is always short. Here ए and ओ represent the short vowels ĕ, ŏ. (§ 68.)

Note 3. An aspirate is doubled by prefixing the corresponding non-aspirated sound: kkh, ggh, and so on.

Some MSS. literally double the aspirates, writing khkh, chch, and so on. This is merely an orthographical difference, the pronunciation was the same.

§ 16. *Cerebral surds* **ṭ ṭh** *between vowels become sonant* **ḍ ḍh** (ट, ठ become ड, ढ).

paḍa=*paṭa*, **paḍāa**=*paṭāka*, **kuḍila**=*kuṭila*, **kuḍumba** =*kuṭumba*, **vaḍa**=*vaṭa*, **paḍhaṇa**=*paṭhana.*

Some dialects had the further change of ḍ to ḷ. (§22) M. kakkoḷa=*karkoṭa.* Mg. śaaḷa=*śakaṭa* (Śaur. saaḍa). Mg. yūḷaka=*jūṭaka* (Śaur. *jūḍaa).

(17) **P** *if not omitted becomes* **V.** (प becomes व).

rūva=*rūpa*, **dīva**=*dīpa* (cf. Diwālī), **uvari**=*upari*, **uvaaraṇa**=*upakaraṇa*, **uvajjhāa**=*upādhyāya* (cf. Ojha). **avi**=*api*, **avara**=*apara* (Hindi aur), **tāva**=*tāpa.*

(18) **B** becomes **V.** (ब becomes व).

kavala=*kabala*, **savara**=*śabara.*

(19). **Aspiration.** Prakrit sometimes has kh instead of Sanskrit **k** (§ 6). This in the middle of a word generally becomes **h.**

M. ṇihasa=*nikaṣa*, M. Ś. phaḷiha=*sphaṭika.*

ṭa through ṭha becomes **ḍha.** AMg. vaḍha=*vaṭa*, ta becomes **tha,** then **ha.** M. bharaha=*bharata*, vasahi= *vasati* Rarer; **p** through ph becomes **bh.** AMg. kacchabha=*kacchapa.* **n, m, l** and the sibilants are sometimes aspirated. M. **ṇhāvia** (but Ś. Mg. **ṇāvia**)=*nāpita* i.e., **snāpita* from √*snā*.

AMg. lhasuṇa (also lasuṇa)=*laśuna*, cf. § 30.

Aspiration is sometimes shifted. M. dihi from **dithi*=*dhṛti*. M. **dhūā** Ś. Mg. **dhūdā**=*duhitā*, Ś. Mg. **bahiṇī**=*bhaginī*, M. ghĕttuṃ=*grahītum* (through **ghṛptum*). Aspiration is sometimes lost. Ś. saṅkalā=*śṛṅkhalā* but saṅkhalā and siṅkhalā are also found.

(20) *Change of place of articulation.*

Cerebral for Dental.

paḍi=*prati*, M. **paḍia** Ś. Mg. **paḍida**=*patita*, **paḍhama**=*prathama*. This cerebralising is much commoner in Ardhamāgadhī :

AMg. osaḍha=*auṣadha* (M. Ś. **osaha**).

In most dialects n regularly becomes ṇ (ण for न) **ṇūṇa**, **ṇaaṇa**.

(21) **Sibilants.** *The three sibilants of Sanskrit are represented by the dental* s (except in Māgadhī which has only the palatal **ś**), **asesa**=*aśeṣa*, etc.

Mg. **keśeśu**=*keśeṣu* (Śaur. etc. **kesesu**).

(22) **Ḍ often becomes ḷ.** (§ 16) (ड becomes ळ).

In North India books and MSS. use ल for ळ.

M. garuḷa (Ś. garuḍa ; Mg. galuḍa), M. Ś. **kīḷā**=*krīḍā*.

(23) **T** *and* **d** *sometimes become* ḷ *or* l. (त, द become ल or ळ).

Ś. **alasī**=*atasī*, M. Ś. **vijjuliā**=**vidyutikā* "lightning" (whence Hindi bijlī). M. Sālavāhaṇa=Sātavāhana. M. Ś. **dohaḷa**=*dohada*.

(24) **D** becomes r in adjectival and pronominal compounds with *-dṛś-dṛśa-dṛkṣa*.

erisa=*īdṛśa* (Ś. also īdisa) **kerisa**, **aṇṇārisa** **tumhārisa**, **sarisa**.

(25) In dialects **m** sometimes became **v**. (म become व).

So M. **vammaha** Śaur. **mammadha**=*manmatha*. M. oṇavia=*avanata* (from **avanamita*).

This change is more frequent in Apabhraṃśa which at the same time nasalises the preceding vowel and the semivowel, and then often omits either the semivowel or the nasal element. Thus Apa. kā̃vala=*kamala*, Jā̃ūṇā=Yamunā, ṇavahī=*namanti*. This nasalisation also appears in M., e.g. Cā̃uṇḍā=Śaur. Cāmuṇḍā.

This change accounts for forms like "Kanwar" from *Kumāra*, and gā̃v (गांव) with its many minute variations in the modern dialects. (Skt. *grāma*. Pāli and most Prākrits (g)gāma-). Cf. Beames, I, 254.

(26) In Māgadhi **r** always become **l**, in other dialects the change is exceptional. (र become ल).

M. Ś. **dalidda**=*daridra*, **muhala**=*mukhara*.

The change is more frequent in Ardha Māgadhī than in M. or Ś.

(27) Sometimes sibilants are replaced by **h**, either as a dialectic variation or in a particular group of words.

M. dhaṇuha=**dhanuṣa* for *dhanus*,

M. paccūha=*pratyūṣa* 'morning sun' but paccūsa 'dawn' (Pischel. Gr. § 263).

M. pāhāṇa=*pāṣāṇa*.

M. aṇudiahaṃ (Ś. aṇudiasaṃ)=*anudivasaṃ*.

Futures like M. ṇehii for *neṣyati*, AMg. gāhii for *gāsyati*, JM. pāhāmi for *pāsyāmi*, AMg. gamihii for *gamiṣyati*.

Genitives like Mg. kāmāha=*kāmasya*, Apa. kavvaha=*kāvyasya*.

Pronominal forms like Apa. eho=*eṣa*, Pkt. tumhe=**tuṣme*, M. tāha beside tāsa for tassa=*tasya*, tahiṃ for tassiṃ=*tasmin*.

This phenomenon is commoner in Apabhraṃśa and has been used to explain several features in the later system of declension and conjugation. The history of the change however is obscure and the extent of its influence has been questioned. (See Pischel Gr. § § 263, 422, 425, 520; J. Bloch Langue marathe, § 162; S. K. Chatterji, Bengali Language, pp. 549, 550, 555, 751, 963.)

28). Sometimes instead of **h** in Sanskrit we find an aspirate **dh** etc. in Prākrit, e.g. Ś. Mg. **idha**, M. **iha**, cf. Pāli idha. Here Śauraseni preserves the more original sound. H in Sanskrit often represents an original sonant aspirate. Cf. *hanti* and *aghnan*, *jaghāna*.

§ 29. C. *Final.* All final mutes are dropped.

Nasals become anusvāra. **aḥ** becomes **o**, otherwise visarga is dropped. Sometimes the final vowel is then nasalised.

For treatment of finals in compounds see Sandhi (Ch.VII).

CHAPTER V.

COMPOUND CONSONANTS.

§ 30. **At the beginning of a word only a single consonant can remain.**

Exceptions 1. **ṇh**, e.g., **ṇhāṇa**=*snāna*.

2. **mh** as in **mhi**=(*a*)*smi*, **mho mha**=*smaḥ* (enclitic).

3. At the beginning of the second member of a compound.

Note.—If ṇh and mh are regarded as aspirated ṇ and m rather than as conjuncts they are not exceptions.

The weakness of final consonants is a phenomenon observed in many languages. A final mute ceases to "explode" becoming merely "implosive." The vocal organs take up the right position but there is no sudden release of air, no "explosion," and no audible glide to another sound. There is only a moment of silence for a surd, a moment of vocal murmur for a sonant. The next stage is to omit the effort of taking up the position, then there is no on-glide and even the "implosive" has been lost.

The nasal resonance is more audible and survives.

§ 31. **In the middle of a word no group may exceed two consonants, and these must be only**

(1) **Doubled,** e.g, **kk** (or for aspirate **kkh**),

(2) **Mute after** nasal of the same class, e.g. **ṅk, ṇḍ,** *or*

(3) **Aspirated Nasal** (or **lh**).

§ 32. Consequently most compound consonants are either **assimilated** or separated by a **svarabhakti** vowel.

§ 33. **Assimilation.** The general rule is that **between equals the second prevails, between unequals the stronger prevails.**

The consonants can be arranged as follows in a scale of decreasing strength for this purpose.

(i) Mutes. (The five vargas less the nasals.)

(ii) Nasals.

(iii) l, s, v, y, r, in order.

h stands by itself (§§ 52–54).

§ 34. **Two mutes.** According to the rule given above, k+t becomes tt, g+dh becomes ddh, d+g becomes gg and so on.

Examples. **jutta**=*yukta*, **vappaïrāā**=*vākpatirājā*, **duddha**=*dugdha*, **chaccarṇa**=*ṣaṭ*+*caraṇa* (§ 6), **khagga** =*khaḍga*, **balakkāra**=*balātkāra*, **uppala**=*utpala*, **uggama**=*udgama*, **sabbhāva**=*sadbhāva*, **sutta**=*supta*, **khujja**=*kubja* (§ 6), **sadda**=*śabda*, **laddha**=*labdha*.

Thus of two mutes (nasals excluded) the assimilation is "progressive," *i.e.* the first is assimilated to the second.

This has been explained by the tendency of the first mute in a conjunct to be merely "implosive."

§ 35. A nasal before a mute of the same class remains, before a mute of another class it becomes anusvāra.

Saṅkhala=*śṛṅkhala*, **kŏñca**=*krauñca*, **kaṇṭha**, **manthara**, **jambū**, but **diṃmuha**=*diṅmukha*, **paṃti**=*paṅkti*, **viṃjha**=*vindhya* (§ 44).

§ 36. **A nasal following a mute is assimilated**

aggi=*agniḥ*, **viggha**=*vighna*, **savatti**=*sapatnī*, **jugga**=*yugma*.

Exceptions. (*a*) **jña** becomes **ṇṇa**. **āṇavedi**=*ājñāpayati*. **aṇahiṇṇa**=*anabhijña*. **jaṇṇa**=*yajña*.

Note 1. At the beginning of the second member of a compound *jña* can become *jja*, e.g. **maṇŏjja**=*manojña*.

Note 2. Māgadhī has *ñña* according to Hemachandra (4-293).

(*b*) *ātman* in M. nearly always, in Apa. always becomes **appa** (cf. Hindi āp). The other dialects vary between appa and atta.

(*c*) *dma* becomes *mma*, **pŏmma**=*padma* (also paüma, § 57).

§ 37. **L with a mute is assimilated.**

vakkala=*valkala*, **phagguṇa**=*phalguna*, **appa**=*alpa*., **kappa**=*kalpa*. [Exception √*jalp* becomes √jamp, but also japp]. **pavaṃga**=*plavaṃga*.

§ 38. **Mute and Sibilant.** The mute of course can only be a surd. **When the sibilant comes first, it is assimilated, and the mute is aspirated,** e.g. **sta** becomes **tth**. When however the sibilant stands at the end of the first member of compound, the following mute need not be aspirated, especially if the first member is a prefix like *dus*. **Śca** becomes **ccha**, **accharia**=*āścarya*, **pacchā**=*paścāt* but **ṇiccala**=*niścala*, **duccarida**=*duścarita*.

[In Māgadhī *śca* remains: niścala.]

Ṣka and **ṣkha** become **kkh**. Ś. **pŏkkhara**=*puṣkara*, **sukkha**=*śuṣka*. In this case however the aspiration is often omitted.

M. caükka. Ś. cadukka=*catuṣka*. M. Ś. **dukkara**=*duṣkara*. **ṇikkam**—for *niṣkram*—etc.

Ṣṭa and **ṣṭha** become **ṭṭh**. **diṭṭhi**=*dṛṣṭi*, **suṭṭhu**=*suṣṭhu*. Exception veḍha=*veṣṭa* (cf. Pāli veṭhati).

Ṣpa and **ṣpha** become **pph**. **puppha**=*puṣpa*, **ṇipphala**=*niṣphala*.

Sta and **stha** become **tth**. **thaṇa**=*stana*, **atthi**=*asti*, **hattha**=*hasta* (cf. Panjabi hatth), **avatthā**=*avasthā*, **kāatthaa**=*kāyasthaka*. Compound. duttara=*dustara*. Sometimes this **tth** is cerebralised. M. Ś. **aṭṭhi**=*asthi*. The √ *stha* especially varies between tth and ṭṭh. Śaur. thida or ṭhida=*sthita* (M. thia or ṭhia), M. Ś. ṭhāṇa =*sthāna* (M. also thāṇa). Ś. thidi or ṭhidi=*sthiti* (M. tshii or ṭhii.)

Spa and **spha** become **pph**. **phaṃsa**=*sparśa* (§ 49). **phaḷiha**=*sphaṭika*. A. Mg. phusaï=*spṛśati*.

§ 39. **When the sibilant follows the mute they become cch.** **acchi**=*akṣi*, **riccha**=*ṛkṣa*, M, chuhā=*kṣudhā*, **macchara**=*matsara*, **vaccha**=*vatsa* (also=*vṛkṣa*), **accharā**=*apsarā*, **jugucchā**=*jugupsā*.

§ 40. **Kṣa however more generally becomes kkh.** Śaur. **khattia**=*kṣatriya*, **khitta**=*kṣipta*, **akkhi**=*akṣi*, **ṇikkhividuṃ**=*nikṣeptum*, **sikkhida**=*śikṣita*, **dakkhiṇa**=*dakṣiṇa* ("Deccan").

Sometimes the dialects vary between **cch** and **kkh**. M. ucchu, Ś. ikkhu=*ikṣu*, M. kucchi, Ś. kukkhi=*kukṣi*, M. pĕcchaï, Ś. pĕkkhadi=*prekṣate*, M. Ś. sāriccha, Ś. sārikkha=**sādṛkṣa*.

Sometimes **kṣa** *becomes* **jjh.**

Ś. pajjharāvedi=**prakṣarāpayati*, M. Ś. jhīṇa=*kṣīṇa* (also khīṇa).

Note. Pischel distinguishes: (*a*) original kṣa (Avestan xša) becomes kkh, (*b*) kṣa from śṣa (Avestan ša) becomes ccha, (*c*) kṣa from źẓa becomes jjha. Śṣa and źẓa would seem rather difficult to pronounce. Presumably śṣa represents in origin a front palate stop plus the corresponding fricative, and źẓa the sonant equivalent, while the original kṣa is a back palate stop plus a fricative. The ष in क्ष can hardly have been originally identical with the Indian cerebral sibilant. The history of the different pronunciations of ष and क्ष, and the relation in Iranian languages of χ and š, need further investigation. Inscriptions and some other evidence suggest a dialectic division in India, **cch** in the West and North-West, **kkh** in the East. (J. Bloch. Langue marathe. § 104. cf. Pischel. Gr. §§ 318 to 321. Geiger. Pali Gr. § 56.)

§ 41. In compounds *–t+ś–* or *–t+s–* become *–ss–* or with lengthening of previous vowel simply *s* – **pajjussua** —*paryutsuka*, **ūsava**=*utsava*, Ś. **ussāsa**, M. **ūsāsa**= *ucchvāsa*.

§ 42. **V with a mute is assimilated.**

M. kaḍhia S. kaḍhida=*kvathita*, Ś. **pakka**–*pakva*, **ujjala** =*ujjvala*, **satta**=*sattva*, **dia**=*dvija*, but **uvvigga**= *udvigna*, and so always with the prefix **ud**.

§ 43. **Y with a mute is assimilated.**

Cāṇakka=*Cāṇakya*, **sŏkkha**=*saukhya*, **jŏgga**=*yogya*, **ṇaṭṭaa**=*nāṭyaka*, **abbhantara**=*abhyantara*.

§ 44. *A dental is first palatalised.*

Sacca=*satya*, **ṇevaccha**=*nepathya*, **accanta**=*atyanta*, **racchā**=*rathyā*, **ajja**=*adya*, **uvajjhāa**=*upādhyāya*, **saṃjhā**=*sandhyā*, **majjha**=*madhya*.

§ 45. **R with a mute is assimilated.**

takkemi=*tarkayāmi*, **cakka**=*cakra*, **magga**=*mārga*, **gāma**=*grāma*, **samucchida**=*samucchrita*, **ṇibbandha**

=*nirbandha*, **citta**=*citra*, **patta**=*pattra*, **attha**=*artha*, **bhadda**=*bhadra*, **samudda**=*samudra*, **addha**=*ardha*.

Exception—*atra* becomes **attha**, *tatra* becomes **tattha.**

[When R precedes a dental it sometimes cerebralises it first, especially in AMg. *vaṭṭadi*=*vartate*.]

§ 46. **Two Nasals.** ङ *ṅ* and ण *ṇ* before म *m* become anusvāra: न *n* is assimilated to following म *m* and म *m* to following न *n* (i.e., ण *ṇ*).

diṃmuha=*diṅmukha*. M. **chaṃmuha**=*ṣaṇmukha*. **ummuha**=*unmukha*, **ṇiṇṇa**=*nimna*, **Pajjuṇṇa**=Pradyumna.

§ 47. **Nasal with sibilant.** If the nasal precedes it becomes anusvāra. **When the sibilant precedes it becomes h and the order is reversed.**

Śna becomes ṇha. **paṇha**=*praśna*.

Śma becomes mha. Kamhīra=Kāśmīra.

Ṣṇa becomes ṇha. **uṇha**=*uṣṇa*, **Kaṇha**=Kṛṣṇa.

Ṣma becomes mha. **gimha**=*grīṣma*.

Sna becomes ṇha. **ṇhāṇa**=*snāna*.

Sma becomes mha. **amhe**=*asme*, **vimhaa**=*vismaya*.

Exceptions:

(1) *raśmi* always becomes **rassi,**

(2) Initial *śma becomes m*. **masāṇa**=*śmaśāna*.

(3) *Sneha*, *snigdha*, either ṇehā ṇiddha or siṇeha, siṇiddha.

(4) Loc. Singular Pronominal ending—*ṣmin* becomes *mmi*; —*smin* becomes either —*ssiṃ* or —*mmi*.

Ś. **edassiṃ**=*etasmin* M. eassiṃ or eammi. (AMg. *ṃsi* logaṃsi=*loke*).

§ 48. **Nasal with semivowel.** The semivowel is assimilated. **gumma**=*gulma*, **mĕccha**=*mleccha*, **aṇṇesaṇā**=*anveṣaṇā*, **puṇṇa**=*puṇya*, **aṇṇa**=*anya*, **sŏmma**=*saumya*, **dhamma**=*dharma*, **kaṇṇa**=*karṇa*.

Note. *my* after a long vowel become *m*. kāmāe=*kāmyāyā*.

§ 49. **Sibilant and semivowel.** The semivowel is assimilated. **sāhaṇīa**=*ślaghanīya*, **pāsa**=*pārśva*, M. āsa Ś. assa= *aśva*, **avassaṃ**=*avaśyam*, M. mīsa Ś. missa=*miśra*, **maṇussa**=*manuṣya*, Ś. parissaadi=*pariṣvajate*, **rahassa** =*rahasya*, **vaassa**=*vayasya*, **tassa**=*tasya*, **sahassa**= *sahasra*, **sahattha**=*svahasta*, Ś. Sarassadī=Sarasvatī, sāadaṃ=*svāgatam*.

Note 1. Sometimes this *ss* is reduced to *s* with (*a*) lengthening of the previous vowel (M. *mīsa*, *āsa* above) or (*b*) nasalisation of the previous vowel, which is more frequent from *śra* and general with *rśa*. **Aṃsu**=*aśru*, **phaṃsa**=*sparśa*, **daṃsaṇa**=*darśana* (§ 64.)

Note 2. A further dialectic change is *s* becomes *h*. So Māgadhi kāmāha, Apabhraṃśa kāmahŏ. Later on this had an important effect on inflections. (§ 27.)

§ 50. **Two semivowels.** The stronger prevails in the order **l, v, r, y.**

gallakka=*galvarka*, **mulla**=*mūlya*, **dullaha**=*durlabha*, **kavva**=*kāvya*, **parivvājaa**=*parivrājaka*, **savva**=*sarva*.

Exception. In **ry** *y* becomes *j*, hence it becomes **jj**, **ajja** =*ārya*, **kajja**=*kārya*. Sometimes *r* becomes *l*, hence ll, **pallattha**=*paryasta*.

Note. *yya* becomes *jja*, except in Māgadhī.

§ 51. **Visarga** *before* **k, kh, p, ph,** *is treated like a sibilant* **dukkha**=*duḥkha*, **antakkaraṇa**=*antaḥkaraṇa*; *so is visarga before a sibilant.* Ś. **cadussamudda**=*catuḥsamudra*, dussaha=*duḥsaha* (also M. Ś. dūsaha).

§ 52. *When* **h** *precedes a nasal or* **l**, *the group is inverted.* **avaraṇha**=*aparāhṇa*, **majjhaṇha**=*madhyāhna*, M. geṇhaï, Ś. geṇhadi=*gṛhṇāti*, **ciṇha**=*cihna* (M. also cindha), **bamhaṇa**=*brāhmaṇa*, **palhattha**=**prahlasta* (from √*hlas*=*hras*).

§ 53. *In* **hy** *the semivowel becomes j and then the group becomes* **jjh.** **Sajjha**=*sahya*, **aṇugejjhā**=*anugrāhyā*,

§ 54. *Hv* becomes either *bbh* (through *vh*) or *h*. vibbhala=*vihvala*, jīhā=*jihvā* (AMg. jibbhā). (For *hr*, *rh* see § 57.)

§ 55. **Cerebralisation.** Dental groups sometimes become cerebral. Ś. maṭṭiā=*mṛttikā*, Ś. M. vuḍḍha=*vṛddha*, gaṇṭhi=*granthi*.

In M. and Ś. this usually happens after an original **r** or **ṛ**; but in AMg. in other words also, especially after a sibilant. (Pischel. Gr. 289. cf. Geiger. Pali Gr. 64.)

§ 56. The same principles apply to groups of three consonants, e.g., *matsya* becomes maccha, *arghya* aggha, *astra* attha, and so on.

§ 57. **Svarabhakti.** *When one of two consonants is a nasal or a semivowel, the two may be separated by an inserted svarabhakti vowel.* The two consonants are then treated according to the rules for simple consonants. The vowel is generally *i*, or *u* with a labial, but sometimes *a*.

M. **raaṇa**, Ś. **radaṇa**, Mg. ladaṇa=*ratna*, M. Ś. salāhā=*ślāgha*, āmarisa=*āmarṣa*, **varisa**=*varṣa*, **harisa**=*harṣa*, **kilanta**=klānta, **kiliṇṇa**=*klinna*, **milāṇa**=*mlāna*, **tuvara**=*tvara*(*sva*), duvāra duāra=*dvāra*, **suvo**=*śvaḥ*, **ariha**=*arha*, **paüma**=*padma* (Pāli paduma) Ś. **sumaradi**=*smarati*.

§ 58. *If one of the consonants is y, this is then omitted.* **ācāria**=*ācārya*. (The actual difference of pronunciation here is slight) verulia=*vaiḍūrya*, coria=*caurya*, hio=*hyas*.

Sometimes ī appears. accharia *or* Ś. accharīa=*āścarya* (M. also acchera § 76). Ś. paḍhīadi=Pāli paṭhīyate =*paṭhyate*.

CHAPTER VI.

VOWELS.

§ 59. The sonants *ṛ* and *ḷ* (ऋ and ऌ) counted as vowels in Sanskrit Grammar disappear in Prākrit, as in Pāli. In the old Indian language ऋ was not pronounced *ri* (रि) as it is nowadays. It was not a consonant plus a vowel, but a "sonant" fricative used as a vowel. Its pronunciation may have been similar to the sonant *r* in some Slavonic languages, e.g. Srbi, the name of the Serbs in their own language. Languages not possessing this sound naturally represent it either with the neutral vowel *ə* or introduce a vowel sound before or after the consonant *r*. (Sometimes both before and after.) Hence it is more intelligible why (*a*) the guṇa of *ṛ* is *ar* (not *re*), (*b*) Vṛtrahan appears in Avestan as Vĕrĕth raghna, *ṛju* as ĕrĕzu, (*c*) Pāli has iritvija for *ṛtvij*, irubbeda for *ṛgveda*, and (*d*) Prākrits not possessing *e* (or a sign for it) replace *ṛ* by *a*, *i*, or *u* as well as by *ri*.

Still less does *lri* express the old pronunciation of ऌ. This was more like the final sound ('sonant' or syllabic *l*) in English "battle" where there is no vowel between the *t* and the *l*. Its guṇa is *al*. It is represented in Prākrits by *ili*, *li*, or *a*. Kilitta=*kḷpta*.

§ 60. **Substitutes for ṛ.**

ri. (for initial *ṛ*) [Māgadhī li.]

riddhi=*ṛddhi*, riccha=*ṛkṣa*, risi=*ṛṣi*.

a. M. kaa S. kada=*kṛta*, vasaha=*vṛṣabha*.

i. (commonest) **kiviṇa**=*kṛpaṇa*, giddha=*gṛdhra*, **diṭṭhi**=*dṛṣṭi*, siāla=*sṛgāla*, **hiaa**=*hṛdaya*.

u. (after labials or when another u follows).

M. ṇihua Ś. ṇihuda=*nibhṛta*, M. pucchai Ś. pucchadi=*pṛcchati*, muṇāla=*mṛṇāla*, vuttanta=*vṛttānta*.

Note 1. The vowel often varies even in the same dialect.

Ś. daḍha or diḍha=*dṛḍha*. M. ṇiatta or ṇivutta=*nivṛtta*.

Note 2. Nouns in *ṛ* generally have *u* for *ṛ* before the suffix *-ka*, and when they begin compounds. Ś. jāmādua=*jāmātṛka*, bhādusaa=*bhrātṛ-śata*. But *i* also occurs: Ś. bhaṭṭidāraa=*bhartṛdāraka*.

Note 3. *a, i, u,* also occur at the beginning of a word. AMg. aṇa=*ṛṇa*, Ś. isi=*ṛṣi*, ujju=*ṛju*.

(M. acchai, Pāli acchati derived by Pischel from *ṛcchati* is explained by others as an inchoative from *as* or *ās*. Pischel, Gr., § 480. Geiger, Pāli Gr., § 135. 2.)

Note 4. Long *ṝ* becomes *ī* or *ū*.

Note 5. For a dialectic division: S.W. *a,* E. Centre and N. *i* with *u* after labials, see J. Bloch, Langue marathe, § 31; S. K. Chatterjee, Bengali Language § 173; cf. Pischel, §§ 49-51; Geiger, Pāli Gr., § 12.

§ 61. *The Diphthongs* **ai, au** *are replaced by* **e, o**. Before double consonants *ĕ* and *ŏ* are short (§§ 15, 68).

Ś. edihāsia=*aitihāsika*, Erāvaṇa=*Airāvaṇa* **tĕlla**=*taila*, **vĕjja**=*vaidya*.

M. komuī, Ś. komudī=*kaumudī*, jŏvvaṇa=*yauvana*, sŏmma=*saumya*.

Note. Sometimes in M. and other dialects *ai* become *a—i*, and *au* becomes *aü*, e.g. vaïra=*vairin*, maüli=*mauli*. This is not correct for Śauraseni or Māgadhī.

§ 62. **Change of Quantity.** *A long vowel can be followed by only one consonant, and therefore every vowel before a double consonant is short.* This law obviously covers many cases where a long vowel in Sanskrit appears as a short vowel in Prākrit. There was also a tendency to shorten the consonant and lengthen the vowel in such cases. This is commoner in Māhārāṣṭrī (and especially in Ardha—Māgadhī and Jain-Māhārāṣṭrī) than it is in Śauraseni or Māgadhī. This principle has played a great part in the modern Indian languages (cf. Pr. aggi Panjabi agg, but Hindi āg).

§ 63. **Lengthening of short vowel.**

This occurs most frequently before *r*+consonant (especially a sibilant), and before sibilant+*ya*, *ra*, *va*, or sibilant. Ś. kādum̥=*kartum*, kādavva=*kartavya*. AMg. phāsa=*sparśa*, AMg. maṇūsa=*manuṣya* (Śauraseni maṇussa) M. āsa=*aśva* (Ś. assa). M. Ś. ūsava=*utsava*, dūsaha=*duḥsaha*.

§ 64. *Instead of being lengthened in such cases the vowel is often nasalised.* **daṃsaṇa**=*darśana*, **phaṃsa**=*sparśa* (§ 49) M. aṃsu=*aśru* (Ś. assu), AMg. aṃsi=*asmi* (Ś. mhi).

§ 65. Vice versa a vowel is sometimes lengthened instead of being nasalised before *r*, *s*, or *h*.

dāḍhā=*daṃṣṭrā*, M. pīsaī, Ś. pīsedi=**piṃsati* for *pinaṣṭi*, M. sīha=*siṃha* (also siṃgha, Ś. siṃha).

§ 66. There are a number of other cases where the vowel is lengthened: sometimes in the middle of a compound, before certain inflections, or by analogy with other words, e.g. M. Ś. sāriccha, Ś. sārikkha=**sādṛkṣa* for *sadṛkṣa* by analogy with *tādṛkṣa*, *yādṛkṣa*.

§ 67. **Shortening of vowels.** As stated above every vowel followed by a double consonant must be short, so must every vowel with anusvāra and a consonant.

A vowel is sometimes shortened when the previous vowel is accented: **alia**=*ắlīka*: or when the following vowel is accented: M. maṃjara=*mārjārá*, but also maṃjāra (Ś. majjāra).

Note. Māhārāṣṭrī follows rather the Vedic, and Śaurasenī the classical Sanskrit accent. The difference often accounts for divergences between Marathi and Hindi.

§ 68. A long vowel before a single consonant is often shortened, the consonant being doubled, if the word was originally accented on the last syllable.

ĕvvaṃ=*evám*. **Jŏvvaṇa**=*yauvaná*, **tĕlla**=*tailá*, **pĕmma** =*premán*.

Note 1. Final vowels are shortened before enclitics with double consonants, e.g. M. ṭhia mhi=*sthitâsmi*.

Note 2. Śaurasenī *jeva jĕvva*=*eva* becomes *jjeva jjĕvva* after a short vowel: e.g. ajjassa jjĕvva=*āryasyaiva*: or after a shortened ĕ ŏ: bhūmiĕ jjĕvva=*bhūmyāmeva*, idŏ jjĕvva=*ita eva*.

Note 3. Śrī becomes Siri.

Note 4. In M. the final *ā* of adverbs is very often shortened: jaha=*yathā*.

§ 69. **Vowel for vowel.** Examples.

a becomes i in syllables preceding the accent. (Commoner in M. than Ś. or Mg.) **pikka**=*pakvá* (Ś. also pakka).

M. majjhima but Ś. majjhama—*madhyama*,

M. kaïma but Ś. kadama—*katama*.

[*Note*. Hindi has pákkā, Marathi pikā̀.]

a becomes u (i) with labials: puloedi—*pralokayati* (commoner in M. AMg. than in Ś.)

(ii) stems in *a* especially- *jña*: **savvaṇṇu**—*sarvajña*.

ā becomes i (sometimes) after the accent: M. jampimo= *jálpāmaḥ*; before the accent: AMg. vihatthimitta= *vitastimātra*. In this case i generally becomes ĕ mĕtta- =*mātra*-.

§ 70. *i becomes u* if an *u* follows: M. ucchu=*ikṣu*, AMg. usu =*iṣu*. (But Ś. ikkhu.)

i becomes ĕ before a double consonant: **ĕttha**—*itthā*, **gĕjjha**—**gṛhya* (from* gijjha, from* *gṛhya* for *grāhya*).

ī becomes e in *īdṛśa* etc., *or* it remains: Ś. erisa, generally īdisa, so kerisa, kīdisa.

[*Note*. erisa is really from Vedic *ayā́*+*dṛś* Pischel § 121.]

§ 71. *u becomes a* in the first syllable when the second contains *u*. **garua**—*guruka*, **maüla**—*mukula*.

u becomes i. **purisa**—*puruṣa* (Mg. puliśa).

u becomes ŏ before a double consonant. Ś. pŏkkara=*puṣkara*, pŏtthaa=*pustaka* (cf. Hindi pōthī), mŏggara =*mudgara*, M. gŏccha=*guccha*.

ū becomes ŏ or o before double consonant, or where a compound consonant has been simplified. M. mŏlla=mūlya, thora from *thŏrra=*sthūra*, so **tambola**=*tāmbūla* [tāmbūla—*tambulla—*tambŏlla—tambola].

§ 72. *e becomes* **i** (i) in unaccented syllables: M. iṇá—*ená*, **viaṅā**=*vedanā*, diará=*devará*.

(ii) before double consonants: Ś. Mittea=Maitreya.

(iii) (dialect) after a long vowel: Ś. Mg. ediṇā=*etena* (also edeṇa).

§ 73. *o becomes u* (i) before double consonants: M. aṇṇuṇṇa for aṇṇŏṇṇa (§ 61)—*anyonya*.

(ii) In Apabhraṃśa where *o* comes from *aḥ*, as in the Nom. Sing. of nouns in *a*: e.g. loū=*lokaḥ*, sīhu =*siṃhaḥ*. [This survives in Sindhī, e.g. caṇḍu or caṇḍru=" moon."]

§ 74. **Omission of Vowels.** Examples.

AMg. posaha=*upavasathá*, Ś. vaṭṭhida=*avasthita*. M raṇṇa=*araṇya* ("Rann" of Kach).

api after anusvāra becomes **pi**, after vowels **vi**.

iti after anusvāra becomes **ti**, after vowels **tti**.

Ś. Mg. idānīṃ in its weaker sense "then" becomes **dāṇiṃ**.

M. piussiā=*pitṛṣvasṛkā* from *piusasiā.

M. Ś. pŏpphali=*pūgaphalī*—**khu**=*khalu*.

majjhaṇṇa=*madhyáṃdina*, Ś. Mg. **dhīdā**=*duhitā* (*du-*hītā*).

Note. Only unaccented vowels are omitted. Such omission therefore sometimes throws light on the accentuation of a word.

§ 75. **Saṃprasāraṇa.** The reduction of *ya* to *i* and of *va* to *u* is more frequent than in Sanskrit. *Aya* and *ava* become *e* and *o*. Ś. tiriccha=**tiryakṣa* from *tiryaka*, turida=*tvarita*, **kadhedu**=*kathayatu*, **odāra**—*avatāra* ṇomāliā=*navamālikā*, M. loṇa=*lavaṇa* Ś. bhodi= *bhavati*.

§ 76. **Epenthesis.** -*aria* from -*ārya* sometimes becomes -*era*, peranta=*paryanta*, M. acchera=*āścarya* (but also accharia as in Ś.), M. kera=*kārya*. Ś. tumhakera, amhakera.

[*Note.* From a derivative keraka was derived the Old Hindi and Old Gujarati kerō kerī used to form a genitive. Beames disputed the derivation of keraka from *kārya*, vide B. ii. 286. H. kā, kī, etc., Rājasthānī -ro -ri, etc., and Bengali -er have been derived from keraka, but see S. K. Chatterji. Bengali Language § 503.]

CHAPTER VII.

SANDHI.

A. Consonants.

§ 77. As Prākrit does not allow final consonants (§ 29) most of the complications of Sanskrit external sandhi disappear.

Sometimes however the final consonant, usually dropped has *survived* before a *vowel :*

AMg. jad atthi=*yad asti.* Mg. yad iścaśe=*yad icchase*, or before an *enclitic* : AMg. chacceva=*ṣaḍ eva* chap pi=*ṣaḍ api.* (These are common fixed phrases.)

R in *dur* and *nir* regularly remains.

Ś. durāgada=*durāgata*, ṇirantara.

m sometimes survives as in M. ĕkkam-ĕkkaṃ=*ekaikam.*

§ 78. This form is then declined, e.g. ĕkkam-ĕkke. Thus *m* comes to be used as a *sandhi consonant*, e.g. aniga-m-aṅgammi=*aṅge' ṅge*, AMg. goṇa-m-āī=*gavādayo*, esa-m- aggī=*eṣo'gniḥ*.

More rarely *ẏ* and *r* are used as sandhi consonants. AMg. dhi-r atthu=*dhig astu*.

§ 79. In *compounds* the final consonant of the first number is usually assimilated to the initial consonant of the second member: but sometimes the two are treated as separate words.

M. sarisaṃkula=*ṣaritsaṃkula*, dulaha=*durlabha* (usually dullaha), dusaha=*duḥsaha* (usually dussaha or dūsaha).

B. *Vowels.*

§ 80. Prākrit is tolerant of *hiatus*: but in *compounds* the final vowel of the first member is usually combined with the initial vowel of the second, as in Sanskrit.

Ś. kilesāṇala=*kleśānala*, jammantare=*janmāntare* (ă before two consonants) **rāesi**=rāa+isi=*rājârṣi*.

Sometimes however they are not combined. Ś. pūāariha =*pūjārha*, vasantussava-ūvāaṇa=*vasantôtsavôpāyana*.

§ 81. If the second member of a compound begins with *i* or *u* before a double consonant, or with *ī*, *ū*, the final *a* or *ā* of the first member is dropped.

M. gaïnda=*gajendra* Ś. ṇarinda=*narendra* manda-mārud'-uvvĕllida=*manda-mārutodvellita*, **maḥ'ūsava**=*mahotsava*, vasantūsava.

Exception. Sometimes when the second member begins with long *ī*, *ū* followed by a single consonant, the vowels are combined: Ś. mantharoru; so regularly with a prefix: Ś. pĕkkhadi, M. pĕcchaï, Mg. pĕskadi= *prekṣate*. Hiatus between ĭ or ŭ and a dissimilar vowel remains.

§ 82. *Hiatus caused by dropping intervocal consonants remains.*

Exceptions. (i) Similar vowels are sometimes contracted: pāikka for pāāikka=*pādātika* 'foot-soldier.'

(ii) *ă*, *ā* followed by *ĭ*, *ī* or *ŭ*, *ū*, **thera** for **thaïra**= *sthavira*.

M. pŏmma Ś. paüma=*padma*, **mora**=*mayūra* (also maūra), M. moha=*mayūkha* (also maūha).

(iii) In compounds. M. andhāria=*andhakārita*. D. cammāraa=*carmakāraka*. AMg. lohāra=*loha-kāra*. **deula**—*devakula*, Mg. lāūla=*rājakula*.

§ 83. *Between words in a sentence hiatus remains.*

Exceptions. (i) *Na* ("not") is often combined with an initial vowel. **ṇatthi**=*nāsti*, **ṇāhaṃ**=*na*+*aham*.

Ś. ṇādidūra=*nâtidūra*, nĕcchadi=*na*+*icchati*.

(ii) In Śaur. Mg. *nu*+*etad* make one word **ṇedam**.

(iii) Initial *a* after *e*, *o* is sometimes dropped, as in Sanskrit.

CHAPTER VIII.

DECLENSION.

§ 84. **Prākrit declensions differ from those of Sanskrit mainly through (*a*) the working of the phonetic rules given above and some others affecting particular inflections, (*b*) the simplification effected by transferring words from one declension to another, i.e. by *analogy*. There are a few cases where the Prākrits preserve old endings or methods not found in Sanskrit. There is little that is new. On the whole Prākrit Grammar represents the gradual wearing away of the old system rather than the building up of a new one.**

§ 85. **The Dual** has been lost. The **Dative** is almost entirely merged in the Genitive—(Dat. sing. of a-stems occurs in

M.). The general phonetic rules rule out the **consonantal** declension, though some traces of it remain.

The great majority of nouns are declined as :—

1. Masculine or Neuter stems in *a*.
2. Masculine or Neuter stems in *i* or *u*.
3. Feminine stems in *ā*, *i*, *ī*, *u*, *ū*.

§ 86. **Declension of A stems.** Normal.

Masc. : **putta**=*putra* "son."

		Śauraseni.	*Māhārāṣṭri.*
Singular :	Nom.	putto	putto
	Acc.	puttaṃ	puttaṃ
	Instr.	putteṇa	putteṇa(ṃ)
	Dat.	——	puttāa
	Abl.	**puttādo**	**puttāo**
	Gen.	puttassa	puttassa
	Loc.	putte	**puttammi** or putte.
Plural :	Nom.	puttā	puttā
	Acc.	**putte**	puttā or **putte**
	Instr.	**puttehiṃ**	puttehi(ṃ)
	Abl.	**(puttehiṃ-to)**	(various)
	Gen.	puttāṇaṃ	puttāṇa(ṃ)
	Loc.	puttesu(ṃ)	puttesu(ṃ).

Note. (i) puttādo puttāo, abl. sing.=**putratas*. Before this ablatival ending *-tas* a short vowel is lengthened, though when used adverbially it can keep the short vowel, e.g. aggado=*agrataḥ*, jammado=*janmataḥ*.

Probably puttādo has been influenced by *putrāt*.

(ii) putte acc. plur. by analogy with pronouns tumhe, ime, etc.

(iii) puttehiṃ instr. plur.=**putrebhiḥ* (as in the Ṛgveda) (§ 29).

(iv) abl. plur. is rarely found except in AMg. The form quoted=Instr. plur.+*tas*.

(v) puttammi=**putrasmin*. pronom. declension.

§ 87. Neut.: **phala**, "**fruit**."

This is declined like putta except:

Nom. Acc. Sing. phalaṃ. N. Acc. Plural **phalāiṃ**.

§ 88. **Declension of I stems, Normal.**

Masc.: **aggi**=*agni*, "fire."

Singular:	Nom.	aggī.
	Acc.	aggiṃ.
	Instr.	aggiṇā.
	Abl	Not common. Various forms.
	Gen.	**aggiṇo** or in M. **aggissa**.
	Loc.	**aggimmi**.
Plural:	Nom.	**aggīo** or **aggiṇo** (M. aggiṇo or **aggī**).
	Acc.	aggiṇo.
	Instr.	**aggīhiṃ** (M. aggīhi).
	Gen.	aggīṇaṃ (M. *or* aggīṇa).
	Loc.	aggīsu(ṃ).

Note. (i) Gen. Sing. aggiṇo like the Neuter in Sanskrit is borrowed from the declension of *in*-stems; aggissa by *analogy* with puttassa.

(ii) Loc. Sing. aggimmi compare puttammi.

(iii) Nom. Acc. Plural aggiṇo from *in*-stems aggīo compare the Feminines in *ī* plural-*īo*=*ī as*.

(iv) M. aggī by analogy with puttā from putta.

(v) aggīhiṃ Instr. Plur. The vowel is always lengthened before the endings *-hi hiṃ*, cf. puttehiṃ. The final anusvāra is optionally omitted in all these forms by M. and some other dialects.

§ 89. **Neut. dahī**=*dadhi*, "**curd.**"

This is declined like aggi except:

Nom. Acc. Sing. **dahiṃ** or dahi. Plur. **dahīiṃ**.

§ 90. *Closely parallel are the U stems.*

Thus **vāu**=*vāyu* (wind) has Sing. Nom. vāū, Acc. vauṃ, Instr. vāuṇā, Gen. vāuṇo (or in M. vāussa), Loc. vāummi.

Plur. Nom. vāuṇo (or in M. vāū), Acc. vāuṇo, Instr. vāūhi(ṃ), Gen. vāūṇa(ṃ) Loc. vāūsu(ṃ).

Neuter. **mahu**=*madhu*, 'honey,' has Nom. Acc. Sing. mahu(ṃ). Plur. mahūiṃ.

§ 91. **Feminine Declension.** The instrumental, genitive and locative singular have fallen together. Nouns in ā, ī, ū are exactly parallel.

Singular :	Nom.	mālā	devī	vahū, 'bride.'
	Acc.	mālaṃ	deviṃ	vahuṃ.
	Abl.	mālādo	devīdo	vahūdo.
		(M. mālāo)	(M. devīo)	(M. vahūo).
	I. G. Loc.	**mālāe**	**devīe**	**vahūe.**
	Voc.	māle	devi	vahu.
Plural :	Nom. Acc.	**mālāo** mālā	devīo	vahūo.
	Instr.	mālāhi(ṃ)	devīhi(ṃ)	vahūhi(ṃ).
	Abl.	(mālāhiṃto	devīhiṃto	vahūhiṃto).
	Gen.	mālāṇa(ṃ)	devīṇa(ṃ)	vahūṇa(ṃ).
	Loc.	mālāsu(ṃ)	devīsu(ṃ)	vahūsu(ṃ).

Note 1. Abl. Sing. **ādo-āo** from the masculine declension. Śauraseni also uses *āe*.

2. I. G. Loc. Sing. **-āe** from Skt *-āyai* used for Gen. Abl. in Yajur Veda and Brāhmaṇas.

3. Nom. Plural **-āo** by analogy with devīo, etc. (*-īo*=*ī*+*aḥ*).

§ 92. **Variants in the Normal Declensions.**

A stems. (i) Nom. Sing. in Mg. and AMg. ends in *e*: Mg. puliśe. AMg. purise=*puruṣaḥ*; in Apabhraṃśa Nom. Acc. Sing. in *u*.

(ii) AMg. has a Dat. Sing. in *āe* (from fem. decl.): devattāe=*devatvāya*.

(iii) Abl. Sing. *-āo* in M.AMg. becomes *āü* metri causa. raṇṇāu=*araṇyāt*.

M. AMg. have also a form in *ā* from *-āt*: vasā=*vaśāt*, gharā=*gṛhāt*.

Common in M. is Abl. Sing. in *hi*: mūlāhi, dūrāhi. Rarer is -hiṃto: hiaāhiṃ-to=*hṛdayāt*.

(iv) Gen. Sing. Mg. has *-śśa* or=*ha*. Cāludattaśśa or Cāludattāha.

(v) Loc. Sing. In M. forms in *-e -ammi* often stand together : gaammi paose=*gate pradoṣe*.

In AMg. the commonest form is in *ṃsi* (=*smin* §47). logaṃsi=*loke*.

Some dialects have Loc. in *-hiṃ*. Mg. davahaṇāhiṃ=*pravahaṇe*.

(vi) Neut. Plur. M. *āiṃ -aĩ -ai*. Forms in *āṇi* also occur in AMg. and Śauraseni.

Dialectic also *ā* (as in Veda) Ś. midhuṇā, jāṇavattā=*yānapātrāṇi*.

(vii) Acc. Plur. Masc. Dialectic *ā*=*ān* M. guṇā=*guṇān*, AMg. āsā=*aśvān* (common in Apabhraṃśa.)

§ 93. *I and U stems.*

(i) Abl. Sing. Examples. M. uahīu=*udadheḥ*, AMg. kucchīo=*kukṣeḥ*, JM. kammaggiṇo=*karmāgneḥ*.

(ii) Loc. Sing. In AMg. the commonest form is in *ṃsi* : kucchiṃsi=*kukṣau*; in Apabhramśa *hĩ* : āihĩ=*ādau*.

(iii) Nom. Plural. AMg. risāo=*ṛṣayaḥ*, sāhavo=*sādhavaḥ*, (Neuter) M. acchīiṃ=*akṣīṇi*, also acchīṇi, AMg. maṃsūiṃ or maṃsūṇi=*śmaśrūṇi*.

(vi) Masculines in *ī* and *ū* shorten these and are declined like nouns in *i* and *u*.

§ 94. *Feminine stems.* Ā stems.

(i) 1. G.L. Sing. *-āe* is shortened *metri causa* to *āĩ*.

(ii) A form in *-āa* is forbidden by some grammarians : but occurs as in M. jōṇhāa=*jyotsnayā*.

(iii) Abl. Sing. Commonest form is in M. -āo Ś. Mg. -ādo. Ś. Mg. also have *-āe*. imāe maa-taṇhiāe =*asyā mṛgatṛṣṇikāyaḥ*.

(iv) N. Acc. Plur. sometimes in *ā*: M. rehā=*rekhaḥ*.
Ś. pūijjantā devadā=*pūjyamānā devatāḥ*.

§ 95. I, Ū stems.

(i) For -*īe* M. often has *īa*.

(ii) Ś. diṭṭhiā=*diṣṭyā* preserves the older form of the Instr.

(iii) Nom. Acc. Plur. *īo ūo* become *īu ūu*, metri causa.

§ 96. **Stems derived from Skt. Ṛ stems.** The distinction between relations and agents is maintained. In the Nom. Acc. Sing. and Nom. Plural Prakrit follows the Sanskrit. Otherwise the stems become stems in *u* (or in *i*) or a new stem is made from the Accusative: piu-, pii-, or piara-=*pitṛ*-; bhattu, bhaṭṭi-, or bhattāra =*bhartṛ*.

§ 97. Agent. bhattu=*bhartṛ* Relation. piu.=*pitṛ*.

		Agent	Relation
Singular:	Nom.	bhattā	Ś. pidā, M. piā.
	Acc.	*bhattāraṃ*	*pidaraṃ, M. piaram.*
	Ins.	*bhattuṇā*	piduṇā, M. piuṇā.
	Gen.	bhattuṇo	piduṇo, M. piuṇo
	Loc.	*Ś. bhattāre*	
Plural:	Nom.	*bhattāro*	*Ś. pidaro, M. piaro.*
	Acc.		pidaro or pidare piaro or piuṇo.
	Ins.	*bhattārehiṃ*	piūhiṃ.
	Gen.	bhattārāṇa(ṃ)	piūnaṃ.
	Loc.	bhattāresu	piūsu(ṃ).

Note. 1. *bhartṛ*="lord" becomes an i-stem. Nom. bhaṭṭā. Acc. bhaṭṭāraṃ. Inst. bhaṭṭiṇā.

2. *mātṛ* Nom. M. māā. Ś. Mg. mādā.
Acc. M. māaraṃ. S. mādaraṃ.
Inst. māāe. Ś. mādāe.

Can be declined as māā—māī—**māū**—or māarā—

§ 98. *AN stems.* These are mostly reduced to A stems by omitting N (=middling base before *pada* endings and in compounds), or a new A stem is formed from the strong base.

So **pĕmma**=*preman* Nom. Acc. pĕmmaṃ; I. pĕmmeṇa; G. pĕmmassa: Loc. pĕmme (M pĕmmammi); Plur. Nom. Acc. pĕmmāiṃ; Gen. pĕmmāṇaṃ.

Muddhā or muddhāṇo=*mūrdhā*. AMg. Instr. muddheṇa or muddhāṇeṇaṃ (the Nom. Sing. in ā is often the only relic of the old declension). The old *-an* declension however is partially preserved, especially in the common words rājan and ātman.

§ 99. Declension of **rāa**=*rājan*.

Singular: Nom. rāā=*rājā*.
Acc. rāāṇaṃ=*rājānam*.
Ins. raṇṇā=*rājñā* (§ 36) or **rāiṇā** (with Svarabhakti vowel i).
Gen. raṇṇo=*rājñaḥ* or **rāiṇo**.
Loc. (rāimmi rāammi rāe).
Voc. rāaṃ=*rājan*.

Plural: Nom. (Acc). rāāṇo=*rājānaḥ*.
Ins. **rāīhiṃ** (as if from an I stem: from rāiṇā).
Gen. **rāīṇaṃ**.

Note. In Compounds *rāa* does not always follow the *A* declension. Ś mahārāo=*mahārājaḥ*, juarāo=*yuvarājaḥ*, Vaccharāo=*Vatsarājaḥ*, but AMg. devarāyā=*devarājaḥ*.

Ś. mahārāaṃ (acc.), mahārāeṇa (Ins.), mahārāassa (Gen.), but AMg. devarannā, devaraṇṇo.

§ 100. *Ātman* becomes **atta**-*or* **appa**- (§ 36*b*).

	M.	*Ś. Mg.*
Nom.	appā	attā.
Acc.	appāṇaṃ	**attāṇaaṃ**=**ātmānakaṃ*
Ins.	appaṇā	
Gen.	appaṇo *or* attaṇo	attaṇo (Mg. attāṇaaśśa).

AMg. also declines Nom. appo in the A declension.

New A stems are also formed; appāṇo, attāṇo, and in Compounds attaṇa-, appaṇa-.

§ 101. *-IN stems.* These partly retain the Sanskrit method, and partly become I stems. As the I stems in Prakrit have borrowed from the -IN declension the difference is apparent only in a few forms.

Nom. Sing. **hatthī**=*hastī*, but Acc. hatthiṃ=*hastinam* (occasionally Ś. has Acc. in *-iṇam*). Jain Prakrits often have Gen. in *-issa*, otherwise it is regularly *-iṇo*.

§ 102. *-AT stems.* Stems in *-at*, *-mat*, *-vat* form *A*-stems **anta, manta, vanta.**

Examples. Ś. **karĕnto**=*kurvan*, **puloanto**=*pralokayan*, karĕnteṇa-*kurvatā*, mahantassa=*mahataḥ*, gacchantehiṃ=*gacchadbhiḥ*.

§ 103. *Exceptions.* Ardha-Māgadhī often retains the old declension, *e.g.* kuvvaṃ=*kurvan*, mahao=*mahataḥ*. Other dialects do so in **bhavat** and **bhagavat.**

Nom.	bhavaṃ	bhaavaṃ
Acc.	bhavantaṃ	bhaavantaṃ
Ins. M. bhavaā.	Ś. bhavadā	M. bhaavaā. Ś. bhaavadā
Gen. „ bhavao.	Ś. bhavado	„ bhaavao. Ś. bhaavado.

§ 104. *Stems in -S.* Nouns in *-as -is -us* form stems in *-a -i -u*.

Examples. Ś. Purūravassa, dīhāuṃ=*dīrghāyuṣam*, AMg. sajoī=*sajyotiṣam*.

Exceptions. There are some traces of the old declension Ś. Purūravā (Nom.), Purūravasaṃ (Acc.), Purūravasi (Loc.) Old Instrumentals are common in AMg. JM. maṇasā, sahasā, tavasā=*tapasā*, teyasā=*tejasā*, cakkhusā=*cakṣuṣā*.

§ 105. Other exceptions or irregular forms consisting generally of the old forms subjected to phonetic changes, occur sporadically, and cannot be reduced to rules.

§ 106. **Pronouns.** A great variety of forms is found for the pronouns of the first and second persons.

The following table gives only the commonest :—

		1st Person.	*2nd Person.*
Singular :	Nom.	**aham** 'ham	**tumaṃ** (M. taṃ)
	Acc.	**maṃ** (M. mamaṃ)	**tumaṃ te**
	Ins	**mae**	**tae tue**
	Abl.	(mamão)	(tumāhiṃto) (a **plural** form)
	Gen:	**mama me maha**	**tuha te (AMg. tava)**
	Loc.	**mai**	**tai (M. tumammi)**
Plural :	Nom.	**amhe**	**tumhe**
	Acc.	**amhe, ṇo**	**tumhe, vo**
	Ins.	**amhehiṃ**	**tumhehiṃ**
	Abl.	**(amhehiṃto)**	**( )**
	Gen.	**amhāṇaṃ, ṇo**	**tumhāṇaṃ**
	Loc.	**amhesu.**	**(tumhesu).**

§ 107. *Personal Pronouns. Variants.*

1*st Person. Sing.* Nom. A group is derived from a form **ahakam* or *ahakaḥ*: M. ahaaṃ JM. ahayaṃ Mg. hage, Apa. haũ. Acc. M. Amg. JM. mamaṃ formed from Gen. mama. Ins. Apa. maĩ. also Acc. Loc. Mg. maï. Abl. is rare.

Gen. M. uses maha(ṃ) majjha(ṃ) (derived from *mahyam*) and me.

Plur. Nom. amhe=Vedic *asme*. AMg. also vayaṃ.

Acc. Ś. amhe, ṇo ; M. amhe amha ṇe ; Mg. aśme.

Gen. Mg. aśmāṇaṃ. M. AMg. JM. amhaṃ. Saur : very often ṇo.

2*nd Person Sing.* Nom. Commonest form is tumaṃ, taṃ is common in M. AMg. haṣ tume. Ṭakkī has tuhaṃ, Apa. tuhũ. Acc. mostly like the Nom. Apa. taĩ. te in AMg. and in Ś. Mg. where as enclitic it becomes de.

Ins. MSS. vary between tae tue. M. has also taï, tuï, tumāe, tumāi, tume. Abl. Ś. tatto=*tvattaḥ* also tuvatto. M. tumāhi, tumāhiṃto, tumāo.

Gen. Ś. tuha, te M. also tuhaṃ, tujjha(ṃ), tumhaṃ, tumma, tu.

Loc. Ś. taï, tui M. taï tuvi tumammi tume.

Plur. Nom. tumhe by analogy with amhe. AMg. has tubbhe.

Gen. M. also tumha. AMg. tubbhaṃ, M. Ś. also vo.

For the Abl. a great variety of forms is given by the Grammarians. Tumhatto, tubbhatto, tujjhatto, etc.

§ 108. *3rd Person.* sa- and ta-

		Masc.	*Neut.*	*Fem.*
Singular:	Nom.	so	taṃ	sā
	Acc.	taṃ		taṃ
	Ins.	teṇa(ṃ)		tāe *or* tīe
	Gen.	tassa		tāe *or* tīe
	Loc.	tassiṃ or tammi		tāe *or* tīe
Plural:	Nom. Acc.	te	tāiṃ (AMg. tāṇi)	tāo *or* tā
	Ins.	tehi(ṃ)		tāhi(ṃ)
	Gen.	tesiṃ *or* tāṇa(ṃ)		tāsiṃ *or* tāṇa(ṃ)
	Loc.	tesu		tāsu.

§ 109. *Variants.* From sa are found also: Nom. *Sing.* Mg. śe. Acc. AMg. se. Gen. M. AMg. Ś. se. Mg. śe (any gender). *Plur*. Nom. AMg. se. Mg. śe, also se for Acc. Gen.

From ta-, Abl. *Sing.* AMg. tāo. Ś. Mg. tado=*tatas*. M. tā=Vedic *tāt*.

Gen. Mg. taśśa. M. also tāsa. Fem. M. also tissā. AMg. tīse.

Loc. Ś. tassiṃ. Mg. taśśiṃ M. tammi. AMg. taṃsi.

Plur: Nom. te becomes de in Ś. Mg. after any other pronoun: ede de. Abl. AMg. tĕbbho tehiṃto.

§ 110. Similarly are declined :—

eso	esā	Ś. edaṃ	M. eaṃ	(= *etat*)
jo	ja		jaṃ	(= *yat*)
ko	kā		kiṃ	
imo	imā		imaṃ or iṇaṃ	(= *idam*)

The other stems used in Skt. with *idam* also occur :
Ś. aaṃ=*ayam*, AMg. ayaṃ is used for all three genders.
Ś. iaṃ=*iyam*. M. AMg. Ś. idaṃ (*only* Nom.).
M. assa=*asya*, eṇa=*anena*, AMg. Ś. aṇeṇa.
-iṇa becomes ṇa : ṇaṃ, ṇeṇa, ṇe.
AMg. has imeṇaṃ, imāo, imassa, imassiṃ.
Amū is declined like a Noun in u.

§ 111. *Pronominal adjectives* are similarly declined.

Examples. Ś. aṇṇassiṃ=*anyasmin*, kadarassiṃ=*katarasmin*, avarassiṃ=*aparasmin*, parassiṃ=*parasmin*-aṇṇe=*anyān*. Ś. savvāṇaṃ AMg. savvesiṃ=*sarve*, *ṣām*.

§ 112. *Declension of Numerals*.

1. ĕkka (AMg. ega) follows the pronominal declension. Loc. Sing. Ś. **ĕkkassiṃ** Mg. ĕkkaśśiṃ M. **ĕkkammi** AMg. egaṃsi or egammi. **Plur.** ĕkke AMg. ege.
2. do (=*dvau*) duve (from *dve* Neut. Dual.) also Neuter (by analogy with tiṇṇi (=*trīṇi*) dŏṇṇi dūnni. All are used without reference to gender. Ś. dŏṇṇi kumārīo=*dve kumāryau*. Ins. **dohi(ṃ)**, Gen. **doṇha(ṃ)**, Loc. **dosu**.
3. **tiṇṇi**=*trīṇi*, AMg. tao=*trayaḥ* (used without distinction of genders). Ins. **tīhiṃ**, Gen. **tiṇh(aṃ)**. Loc. **tīsu**.
4. **cattāri** is the commonest form. Cattāro from the Nom. Masc. and caūro from the Acc. occur and are used for either case. Ins. caūhi(ṃ), Gen. cauṇha(ṃ), Loc. caūsu.

5. **pañca** I. pañcahi(ṃ), G. pañcaṇha(ṃ), L. pañcasu.
6. **cha** I. chahiṃ, G chaṇha(ṃ), L. chasu, and so on up to 18.

19 to 58 are neuters in *-aṃ* or feminines in *-ā* in the Nom : other cases mostly like feminine singular, e.g. 20 Nom : vīsaṃ vīsā Acc. vīsaṃ I.G.L. vīsāe (also Nom. vīsaī and visaiṃ).

59–99 are neuters in *iṃ* or feminines in ī.

100. Ś. sada M. saa and 1000. sahassa are neuters and declined according to the A declension.

CHAPTER IX.

CONJUGATION.

§ 113. The Prākrit Verb has undergone greater changes than the Noun. The general phonetic laws have naturally disintegrated the consonantal conjugation, and by forbidding final consonants have tended to make the old forms ambiguous. There has been the same tendency, as in the case of declension, to reduce all verbs to one type. This process had not gone so far in the old Prākrits such as Pali, whereas by the Late Prākrit or Apabhraṃśa period only one conjugation remained, with a dwindling number of "irregularities," i.e. isolated survivals of the older system.

Moreover fewer forms were used. The **Dual** Number disappears : the **Ātmanepada** Voice has almost gone; apart from some scattered remnants all the wealth of **Perfects, Imperfects** and **Aorists** has been lost, and the past tense is expressed by a participle with, or without, an auxiliary verb. Thus of the old system there remain only : Present Indicative, Imperative, Optative, and Future : Active and Passive : Participles, Infinitive and Gerund.

In place of the old **Ten** classes of Verbs only two are normal :—

(i) the A-class including the great majority of verbs and the Passive.

(ii) the E-class (with *e* derived from *aya*) including all Causatives, most Denominatives and some simple verbs.

The inflections of the two classes are the same.

§ 114. Present Indicative. (*Normal Conjugation*)

A-Class.

Singular :	1.	**pucchāmi**=*pṛcchāmi*
	2.	**pucchasi**
	3.	**Ś. pucchadi M. pucchaï**
Plural :	1.	**pucchāmo**
	2.	**Ś. pucchadha M. pucchaha**
	3.	**pucchanti.**

E-Class.

		Ś.	M.
Singular :	1.	kadhemi	kahemi=*kathayāmi*
	2.	kadhesi	kahesi
	3.	kadhedi	kahei
Plural :	1.	kadhemo	kahemo
	2.	kadhedha	kaheha
	3.	kadhĕnti	kahĕnti.

Note 1. AMg. follows M. in pucchaï, pucchaha. Māgadhī has the same endings as Śaur. puścadi, puścadha, and of course puścaśi.

Note 2. Apabhraṃśa has travelled much further: Sing. 1. pucchaũ, 2. pucchasi or pucchahi, 3. pucchaï. Plur. 1. pucchahũ, 2. pucchahu, 3. pucchahĩ. From this stage it is not a long step to the modern forms, e.g. Hindi. Sing. 1. pucchū̃, 2-3. pucche. Plur. pucchẽ.

§ 115. *Ātmanepadam.*

In Śaurasenī this is rare, occurring occasionally in verse, and in stock expressions. It is somewhat commoner in M. AMg. JM. The endings are shown in: Sing. 1. jāṇe, 2. jāṇase, 3. jāṇae (Ś. would have jāṇade if it occurred) Plur. 3. jāṇante.

Examples. M. Ś. jāṇe, M. maṇṇe=*manye*, Ś. lahe =*labhe*, icche, M. jāṇase, Mg. iścaśe=*icchase*, M. pecchae=*prekṣate*, tīrae=*tīryate* (passive).

§ 116. **Imperative**.

Singular	1. (pucchāmu)	
	2. **puccha, kahehi**, pucchasu, kahesu.	
	3. **Ś. pucchadu**	**M. pucchaü.**
Plural	1. **pucchamha.**	**kahĕmha.**
	2. Ś. pucchadha	M. pucchaha (=Indic.)
	3. **pucchantu.**	**kahĕntu.**

Note 1. By rule hi is added to a long vowel in the 2nd Sing. AMg. generally, M. Mg. sometimes add it to a-stems lengthening the ă. AMg. gacchāhi (Ś. gaccha).

Note 2. The ending -su has been explained as a survival of the Skt. Ātmanepada ending *-sva.* Pischel (§ 467) explained it as a product of analogy: Indic. pucchadi, pucchanti: Imperat. pucchadu, pucchantu. ∴ Indic. pucchasi, Imperat. **pucchasu.** So also the 1st person Singular, Indic. pucchāmi: Imperat. *pucchāmu.* This *-āmu* however is found only in grammars. It is true that Śauraseni and Māgadhī often have the form in *-su* though otherwise they rarely use the Ātmanepadam. Ś. karesu=*kuru*, āṇesu=*ānaya*, kadhesu= *kathaya.* As however Pali derives *-ssu* from *sva*, and uses this also with Parasmaipada stems (E. Müller, Pali Grammar, p. 107), this is probably its origin, though analogy may have aided its adoption in the active voice.

Note 3. 1st Plur. -mha=*sma* is from the Aorist according to Pischel (§ 470), who compares Vedic *jeṣma deṣma* (Whitney 894 c.).

§ 117. **Optative.** This is common in AMg. JM., rarer in M. and exceptional in the other dialects.

There are two types—(i) the usual form in M. AMg. JM. derived from the Opt. of the 2nd conjugation. =*yām*, -*yāḥ*, -*yāt*, etc.

e.g., Singular 1. **vaṭṭĕjjā̆**, (vaṭṭejjāmi, analogy with Indic.)
2. **vaṭṭĕjjā̆si** (°ā̆hi) (°ā̆su).
3. **vaṭṭĕjjā̆**.
Plural 1. **vaṭṭĕjjāma**.
2. **vaṭṭĕjjā̆ha**
3. **vaṭṭĕjjā̆**=3rd Sing.

(ii) the only form in Śauraseni, also found in the others derived from the Opt. of the 1st conjugation, -*eyam*, -*eḥ* -*et*.

Singular 1. **vaṭṭeam** (vaṭṭe analogy with 2, 3, persons).
2. **vaṭṭe**.
3. **vaṭṭe** also used for 3rd Plural.

Note. The short ĕ in -*ĕjja* seems to be for ī̆ (§ 72). So *jāniyāt* becomes AMg. jāṇijjā, jāṇĕjjā, but doubtless its prevalence is partly due to the influence of the 1st conjugation.

§ 118. **Future.** (-*issa*- from -*iṣya*-)

Singular 1. **pucchissaṃ**, AMg. pucchissāmi.
2. **pucchissasi** (M. AMg. pucchihisi).
3. **pucchissadi**, M pucchissaï (or pucchihii).
Plural 1. **pucchissāmo**.
2. **pucchissadha**, M. pucchissaha.
3. **pucchissanti** (AMg. pucchihinti).

Note. The forms in *ihi* arose from forms in *hi* after diphthongs or long vowels. The 3rd Sing. pucchihii contracts to pucchihī as the metre requires. The grammarians give also 1st Singular in *ihāmi*, *ihimi*: (Apabhraṃśa has pĕkkhihimi=*prekṣiṣye*), 1st Plural -*ihimo*, 2nd Plural -*ihiha ihittha*.

§ 119. **Passive.** The Prakrit passive either (i) corresponds to the Sanskrit form in -*ya* (*y* being omitted in Ś Mg. and becoming -*jj*- in the others), or adds -*īa*- (S. Mg. *īa*, others -*ijja*) to (ii) the root, or more commonly to (iii) the present stem.

The endings are those of the (A-class) parasmaipada; but M. AMg. often have ātmanepada endings especially in the Present Participle.

Examples. (i) M. jujjaï. Ś. jujjadi=*yujyate*. M. gammaï, M. dijjaï, Ś. **dijjadi**=*dīyate*.

(ii) From √*gam* M. gamijjaï, Ś. **gamīadi**.

(iii) From gacch- Ś. **gacchīadi**.

		Śauraseni.	*Māhārāṣṭri.*
Singular	1.	**pucchīāmi**	pucchijjāmi,
	2.	**pucchīasi**	pucchijjasi,
	3.	**pucchīadi**	pucchijjaï,
		and so on.	and so on.

§ 120. **Causatives.** This is formed as in Skt. by the addition of *aya* (becomes **e**) to the *strong* form of the root. hāseï=*hāsayati*. After *ā* Skt. inserts *p*; -*paya* becomes Pkt. **ve**.

ṇivvāvedi=*nirvāpayati*. Prakrit extends this usage to many other stems, lengthening the *ă* of the present stem, e.g. **pucchāvedi**.

§ 121. **Participles.** The normal forms are shown in the following scheme:—

Active.

Present. **pucchanto**, F. pucchantā, N. pucchantaṃ, causal, pucchāvento..etc.

Future. **pucchissanto**, -tā, -taṃ.
Perfect. *nil.*

Middle (active meaning, common in AMg.)

Present. pucchamāṇo -ṇā (ṇī), -ṇaṃ.
Future. pucchissamāṇo etc.

Passive.

Present. Ś. **pucchīanto,** M. pucchijjanta, AMg. pucchijjamāṇo.

Future. ("Gerundive") **pucchidavvo** – M. pucchiavvo (pucchaṇīo). M. **pucchaṇijjo.** [kajjo=*kāryaḥ*] (§ 137).

Past. Ś. **pucchido,** M. **pucchio** (§§ 124-5).

§ 121*a*. **Infinitive.** Sanskrit -*tum* becomes Ś. Mg. -*duṃ*. M. -*uṃ*. The ending is added (*a*) to the root, (*b*) to the present stem (with i). Ś. **pucchiduṃ** M. **pucchiuṃ.**

Examples. gantuṃ, Ś. gacchiduṃ, gamiduṃ Ś. kāmeduṃ=*kāmayitum*, dhāriduṃ=*dhārayitum*, Ś. kāduṃ, and kariduṃ M. kāuṃ=*kartum*.

(For Inf. in -ttae see § 136.)

§ 122. **Gerund.**

Ś. **pucchia.** M. **pucchiūṇa.** AMg. pucchittā or pucchidūṇa. Ś. Mg. have **kadua**=*kṛtvā*, **gadua**=*gatvā*. Ś. has sometimes in *verse* the ending ūṇa-dūṇa, e.g. pekkhiūṇa, otherwise only **-ia** is correct.

Examples. Ś. **ṇaïa** (for *nītvā*)=**nayiya* but avaṇīa=*apanīya*, **odaria**=*avatīrya* (Mg. odalia), pĕkkhia, bhavia, pavisia.

In Māgadhī the form in -*ūṇa* is the commonest.

Examples. haūṇa, gantūṇa, hasiūṇa, kāūṇa.

AMg. prefers the form in *ttā* (*tā* after a nasal): bhavittā, gantā, hasittā, karittā, also *ttāṇaṃ*: bhavittāṇaṃ.

§ 123. **Irregular Verbs.**

The normal or regular conjugation being as given above, there are also numerous "*irregular*" forms. These are of two kinds : (*a*) those that agree with Sanskrit in their formation, only undergoing phonetic changes; (*b*) those that are irregular by both Sanskrit and Prakrit standards. These latter, which are not very numerous, may be due to analogy, or to the survival of forms used in the ancient spoken language, but not recognised by classical Sanskrit.

§ 124. A large number of "irregular" verbs in Prakrit differ from the normal conjugation only in the **Past Participle Passive.** It was natural that older forms should be preserved in the case of this participle. Some words like *gataḥ*, *kṛtaḥ* were in such constant use, that their phonetic equivalents, e.g. gado, gao, kido, kao, were likely to hold their own against new forms suggested by analogy such as *gacchido, karido. Moreover in many cases this participle has acquired a width of meaning as an adjective over and above its literal meaning as a participle. Words, e.g. like *snigdha*, *mugdha*, *Buddha* are not necessarily thought of as parts of verbs, though their derivation is clear. The degree to which normal analogous forms prevailed, or older forms survived (or were introduced from Sanskrit) varies with different dialects and different writers. It is not a matter of precise rule, nor would an extensive list of occasional exceptions be of much value. There are, however, a number of forms of more frequent occurrence, with which the student should be familiar from the outset (§ 125).

§ 125. **Past Participles Passive.**

Irregular Forms.

P. P. P.		Sanskrit.	Present Tense.
avaraddha	'offended'	*aparāddha*	M. avarajjhai.
āḍhatta	'applied'	(**āḍhatta*) *āhitā*	M. āḍhāi (or āḍhavai if Causal).

āṇatta	'ordered'	*ājñapta*	Ś. āṇavedi (§ 36).
āraddha	'begun'	*ārabdha*	Ś. ārambhadi.
ārūḍha	'mounted'	*ārūḍha*	M. āruhai.
āsaṇṇa	'sat down'	*āsanna*	Ś. āsīdadi.
utta	'spoken'	*ukta*	(AMg. vutta).
uttiṇṇa	'crossed'	*uttīrṇa*	M. uttaraï.
oiṇṇa Ś. odiṇṇa	'descended'	*avatīrṇa*	o-araï.
M. **kaa** AMg. kaẏa	'made'	*kṛta*	M. karei.
Ś. **kida** (§ 11) kada (§60)			Ś. karedi.
kiliṭṭha	'afflicted'	*kliṣṭa*	M. kilissai.
kuvida	'angered'	*kupita*	Ś. kuppadi.
—°kkanta	'gone'	*—°krānta*	Ś. kamadi.
M. **khaa**, (khāa), [Ś. khaṇida]	'dug'	*khāta*	(AMg. khaẏa, khatta), (khaṇṇa) M. khaṇaï.
M. **khaa**, Ś. khada	'hurt'	*kṣata*.	
khiṇṇa	'wasted'	*kṣīṇa*	M. khijjaï.
khitta	'thrown'	*kṣipta*	khivaï.
M. **gaa**, Ś. gada	'gone'	*gata*	Ś. gacchadi.
gaviṭṭha	'sought'	*gaveṣita*	M. gavesaï.
M. **gahia**, Ś. gahida	'seized'	*gṛhīta*	Ś. gĕṇhadi (§ 52).
gia	'sung'	*gīta*	M. gāaï.
gūḍha	'hidden'	*gūḍha*	Ś. gūhadi.
chiṇṇa	'cut'	*chinna*	M. chindaï, Ś. chindadi.
M. **jāa**, Ś. jāda	'become'	*jāta*	Ś. jāadi.
M. **jia**, Ś. jida	'conquered'	*jita*	Ś. jaadi, M. jiṇaï.
jutta	'yoked'	*yukta*	M. juñjaï, Ś. jujjadi (Pass. § 119).

catta	'abandoned'	*tyakta*	M. caaï.
M. ṭhia Ś. ṭhida (§ 12). thia thida (§ 38).	'stood'	*sthita*	Ś. ciṭṭhadi.
ṇada (M. ṇaa)	'bowed'	*nata*	ṇamadi.
ṇaṭṭha	'destroyed'	*naṣṭa*	ṇassadi.
M. ṇāa (Ś. ṇāda) [also jāṇi(d)a]	'known'	*jñāta.*	jāṇādi.
Ś. viṇṇāda	'discerned'	*vijñāta*	viṇṇavīadi (pass.).
paḍiṇṇāda	'promised'	*pratijñāta.*	
ṇīda (M. ṇīa)	'led'	*nīta*	ṇedi.

(Ś. avaṇīda=*apanīta*, paccāṇīda=*pratyānīta*, uvaṇīda=*upanīta*, pariṇīda=pariṇīta, duvviṇīda=*durvinīta*. āṇīda=ānīta.)

[M. also *ṇīa*. aïṇia=*atinīta*, āṇia=*ānīta*].

ṇhāa	'bathed'	*snāta*	ṇhāi (AMg. siṇāi).
tatta	'heated'	*tapta*	(also tavida).
tuṭṭa	'broken'	*truṭita* tuṭṭai	[cf. Hindi ṭūṭā].
tuṭṭha	'pleased'	*tuṣṭa*	tussadi.
ḍaṭṭha (ḍakka)	'bitten'	*daṣṭa*	ḍasai [Ś. daṃsadi daṃsida].
daḍḍha	'burnt'	*dagdha*	dahaï (Ś. ḍahadi) ḍahaï.
ditta	'lit'	*dīpta*	dippadi.
diṭṭha	'seen'	*dṛṣṭa*	dīsadi (pass.)
diṇṇa	'given'	*datta*	dedi.
paaṭṭa pavaṭṭa paatta pautta	'set out'	*pravṛtta*	pavaṭṭaï, etc.
pautta	'used'	*prayukta*	pauñjaï.
pauttha	'exiled'	**pravasta*,=*proṣita*	[pavasaï. (?)]
paiṇṇa	'scattered'	*prakīrṇa*	[païrījjai pakirīadi. (?)]

paḍivaṇṇa	'resorted to'	*pratipanna*	paḍivajjadi.
paṇṇatta	'declared'	*prajñapta*	paṇṇavei.
patta	'obtained'	*prāpta*	pāvaï, pāvedi.
{ M. palāia Ś. palāida M. palāa JM. palāṇa	'fled'	*palāyita* **palāta*	palāyaï.
paviṭṭha	'entered'	*praviṣṭa*	pavisadi.
pasattha	'praised'	*praśasta*	pasaṃsaï.
pīda	'drunk'	*pīta*	pivadi.
puṭṭha[1] [usually pucchida.]	'asked'	*pṛṣṭa.*	pucchadi.
baddha	'bound'	*baddha*	bandhaï.
buddha	'enlightened'	*buddha*	bujjhaï.
bhaṭṭha	'fallen'	*bhraṣṭa*	
bhiṇṇa	'split'	*bhinna*	bhindaï.
bhīa bhīda	'frightened'	*bhīta*	biheï (Ś. bhāadi).
Ś. bhūda	'become'	*bhūta*	bhodi.
bhutta	'enjoyed'	*bhukta*	bhuñjadi.
mukka	'released'	**mukna-mukta*	muñcadi.
muda (M. mua maa)	'dead'	*mṛta*	maradi.
mūḍha	'perplexed'	*mūḍha*	mujjhaï.
raa	'gratified'	*rata*	ramaï.
ratta	'reddened'	*rakta*	rajjadi.
ruia	'brightened'	*rucita*	ruccaï (Ś. ruccadi).
ruṭṭha	'vexed'	*ruṣṭa*	rusaï.
M. ruṇṇa (Ś. rudida)	'wept'	*rudita*	M. ruaï. Ś. rodadi roadi.
ruddha	'obstructed'	*ruddha*	rundhedi.
lagga	'fixed'	*lagna*	laggaï (Ś. laggadi).
laddha	'taken'	*labdha*	lahaï.

[1] Also 'touched' *spṛṣṭa*, (phusai).

lia, līṇa	'attached'	*līna*	lei.
līḍha	'licked'	*līḍha*	lihaï.
viṇṇatta	'reported'	*vijñapta*	viṇṇāveï.
vūḍha	'carried'	*ūḍha*	vahaï.
samāsattha	'consoled'	*samāśvasta*	samassasai. (?)
siṭṭha	'told'	*śiṣṭa* (√*śās*)	sāhaï.
sitta	'sprinkled'	*sikta*	siñcaï.
siddha	'accomplished'	*siddha*	sijjhaï.
sutta	'slept', 'asleep'	*supta*	suvaï.
suda (M. sua)	'heard'	*śruta*	suṇedi.
suddha	'purified'	*śuddha*	sujjhaï.
M. haa, Ś. **hada**	'killed'	*hata*	haṇaï.
haa	'seized'	*hṛta*	haradi.
M. hūa (Ś. bhūda)	'become'	*bhūta*	hoï.[1]

§ 126. **Irregularities in Present Indicative.**

Regular or Normal Indicatives are of the type **pucchadi** or **kadhedi** (§ 114) and are either (*a*) the phonetic equivalents of Sanskrit Indicatives of the 1st Conjugation, or (*b*) from roots in the 2nd Conjugation, equivalents of what Sanskrit would most naturally have had, if they had been included in the 1st Conjugation. Thus we may class as *regular* such forms as (*a*) gacchadi, icchadi, siñcadi, muñcadi, maradi, sumaradi pivadi, phusadi, kuppadi, ṇaccadi, kadhedi, takkedi, cintedi, (*b*) haṇadi (√*han*) sasadi (√*śvas*).

'*Irregular*' forms comprise (i) forms not of the normal type, e.g. ṭhāï; (ii) verbs attracted into the E class, e.g. karedi: (iii) forms diverging from Skt. types in (*a*); (iv) nasalised roots; (v) addition of *ṇ* original or by

---

[1] Hemacandra allows M. *hoï, huvaï, havaï, bhavaï*; Ś. *huvadi, bhavadi, havadi, bhodi, hodi.*

analogy; (vi) other survivals of Skt. conjugation; (vii) anomalies.

§ 127. (i) Type with 3rd Sing. in *āï* (S. ādi) arises (*a*) by *contraction*. Apa. khāï=khāaï=*khādati*; (*b*) *survival* of form in Skt. 2nd class. M. vāï=*vāti* but also vāaï (Ś. vāadi), M. paḍihāï=*pratibhāti* (Ś. paḍihāadi), Ś. bhādi=*bhāti*, vihādi=*vibhāti*; (*c*) by *analogy* M. ṭhāï=**sthāti* for *tiṣṭhati* (Ś. ciṭṭhadi) and so with all roots ending in ā. dhāi or dhāaï, gāi, jhāi (= Epic *dhyāti*).

Other *contracted* forms are *Ś*. *bhodi*=*bhavati*, **ṇedi**=*nayati*.

√dā to give has deṃi desi dedi—dĕnti.

dedi is from **dáyati*, cf. Ś. Fut. daïssaṃ. Absol. daïa.

§ 128. (ii) Many verbs are attracted to the E class (10th class in Skt.). *Examples*. **Karedi** (=*Karoti*) (distinguish from causal kāredi=*kārayati*), muñcedi (causal moāvedi), hasedi, sumaredi, ciṇedi, **suṇedī**, bhaṇedi, dhuvedi, etc.

§ 129. (iii) √ *ru* has ravaï (1st class), ruvai (6th) and **rovaï** Inf. rovium. (Ś. has forms from *rud*. rodiduṃ).

√ *dhau*. M. dhuvaï. AMg. dhovaï dhoveï Ś. dhoadi.

√ *bhū* has M. **hoi huvaï**. Ś. **homi hosi bhodi**. Opt. bhaveaṃ bhave. Infin bhaviduṃ.

ruccadi=**rucyate* (transferred to 4th class) (also roadi Mg. loadi)—similarly **laggadi**, vajjadi (√*vraj*), jujjadi =**yujyati* (Epic *yuñjati*).

§ 130. (iv) From *chid* come chindaï **chindadi**. This is natural as the root was nasalised in the Sanskrit Present. Similarly with other roots of the 7th class. Bhindai, bhañjai, bhuñjadi.

The nasal in rambhaï (√ *rabh*) is also familiar in Skt. derivatives. (Epic *rambhati*).

muñcadi (M. muñcaï) is regular, but M. has also muasi =*mucasi.

§ 131. (v) Ṇ. is preserved in ciṇai Ś. ciṇedi (*Skt. cinoti*), kuṇaï (Vedic *kṛṇoti*), suṇedi (M. suṇai), jāṇāï Ś. jāṇādi, na āṇādi, kiṇaï=*krīṇāti*, gĕṇhadi=*gṛhṇāti*, Ś. sakkaṇomi sakkuṇomi=*śaknomi*, dhuṇai (Ś. dhoadi, Pāli dhovati): by analogy in jiṇaï (Ś. jaadi), thuṇai (√ *stu*).

§ 132. (vi) √i "to go" has emi esi edi (M. ei)—ènti: √ *as* to be..mhi si atthi, mha (M. mho) ttha santi.

(*Note.*—Atthi the only common non-enclitic form is used with all numbers and persons).

√ *bhī*. M. bihei (Ś. bhāadi).

(vii) bhaṇādi as if from bha-ṇā-mi (9th class) also bhaṇedi. suṇādi=suṇedi as if in 9th class.

√ *svap* becomes suv, hence suaï and (by analogy with ruaï rovaï) sovaï Ś. sovadi.

§ 133. *Survivals of other conjugational forms.*

Imperfect. āsī=*āsīt* used for all persons of both numbers.

Optative. AMg. siyā=*syāt*, kujjā=*kuryāt*, būyā=*brūyāt*, sakkā=Vedic *śakyāt* (Pischel § 465).

Precative M. AMg. hojjā=*bhūyāt*. AMg. dĕjjā=*deyāt*.

Aorist. AMg. akāsī=*akārṣīḥ* or *akārṣīt*. Plural *-iṃsu* akariṃsu (cf. the Aorist in Pali).

Perfect. AMg. āhu=*āhuḥ*. Plural āhaṃsu.

§ 134. **Irregular Futures.**

Futures in *-issadi* (or M. *ihii*) are normally formed from the Present base: pucchissaṃ, kadhissaṃ, M. pucchihaṃ kaheham (§ 118). They are also formed from the root as in Sanskrit. M. ṇehii=*neṣyati*, but Ś. ṇaissadi, Ś. **gamissadi.**

From √ *bhū* various present bases are used to form the future. Ś. **bhavissaṃ,** huvissaṃ, Mg. huviśśaṃ M. *hohii* hossaṃ.

√ *Sthā* M. ṭhāhii (pres. ṭhāi). Ś. **ciṭṭhissadi** (pres. ciṭṭhadi). Other forms represent the Sanskrit—*syāmi* especially in M. AMg: so **daccham**=*drakṣyāmi*, (2. s. dacchisi, 3. s. dacchii, 3 pl. dacchinti), mŏccham (√*muc*) vĕccham (√ *vid*), rŏccham (√ *rud*) vŏccham (√ *vac*). daccham and the rest are not used in Ś. Mg.

Ś. **pĕkkhissaṃ** (M. pĕcchissaṃ) **rodissaṃ**, **vedissaṃ**.

Causatives and others in E-class form Futures (*a*) as in Sanskrit (omitting intervocal *y*). Ś. **kadhaissaṃ moāvaïssasi**=**mocāpayiṣyasi*. **ṇiaṭṭaissadi**=*nivartayiṣyati* (b) M. AMg. from the e-stem: vattehāmi=*vartayiṣyāmi* (c) omitting *aya*=e. M.**kahissaṃ**, Ś. **kadhissaṃ**, M. puloissaṃ=*pralokayiṣyāmi* Ś. takkissadi=*tarkayiṣyati*, sussūsaïssaṃ=*śuśrūṣayiṣyāmi* Mg. māliśśaśi=*mārayiṣyasi*.

√ *dā* has Ś. **daïssaṃ** M. dāhaṃ, √ kṛ has Ś. **karissaṃ** M. also kāhaṃ.

§ 135. **Irregular Passives.**

(*a*) Many passives that are often called irregular as not being formed with the commonest ending *-ijjaï Ś. īadi*, are regular equivalents of Sanskrit passives. (§ 119. (i)) e.g. **jujjadi**=*yujyate*, gammaï=*gamyate*. Other examples are:—Khippaï (*kṣip*), luppaï (*lup*), bhajjai (*bhaj*), bajjhai (*badh*: dhy becomes jjh § 44), rujjhai (*rudh*), ārabbhaï (*ā-rabh*), gijjaï (*gā*), khajjai (*khād*), labbhaï Ś. labbhadi (*labh*), chijjaï (*chid*), bhijjaï (*bhid*), bhujjai (*bhuj*), muccaï (*muc*), vuccai (*vac*), tīrai (*tṛ*) kīraï (*kṛ*).

(*b*) Others are similarly formed from obsolete roots or modified forms of roots, e.g. vubbhaï=*uhyate* (from **vubh*), dubbhai=*duhyate*, libbhaï=*lihyate*, rubbhai=*rudhyate*, ghĕppaï=*gṛhyate*; and with *uv* for ŭ ruvvaï=**ruvyate* (Ś. rodīadi), suvvaï (*śru*) (Ś. suṇīadi), thuvvaï (*stu*), dhuvvai (*dhū*) also dhuṇijjaï. Similar are civvaï (*cīv* for *ci*) also ciṇijjaï, Ś. cīadi, jivvaï (*jiv* for *ji*).[1]

(*c*) ādhappaï is a causative passive=*ādhāpyate*, so also vidhappaï.

(*d*) jammaï, "is born," is derived from *janman* Pkt. jamma; similar is the case with hammaï (√*han*) khammaï (√*khan*).

Anomalous summai (*śru*), cimmai (√*ci*).

Note.—Śaurasenī and Māgadhī often prefer the form from the present base. M. labbhaï, Ś. labbhadi, but also *lambhīadi*; M. muccaï, Ś. *muñcīadi*; M. suvvaï, Ś. *suṇīadi*, Mg. śuṇīadi; M. ruvvai, Ś. *rodīadi*; M. bhujjai, Ś. *bhuñjīadi*; M. kīraï, Ś. *karīadi* (AMg. kajjaï=**karyate*); M. ṇajjaï, Ś. *jāṇīadi*; M. bhaṇṇaï, Ś. *bhaṇīadi*.

§ 136. **Infinitives** (Variations).

The commonest form especially in Śaurasenī is that derived from *itum* (M. *iuṃ*, Ś. *iduṃ*) added to the present base, *i.e.* gacchiduṃ, aṇucitṭhiduṃ (*sthā*), geṇhiduṃ (*grah*), jāṇiduṃ (*jñā*), dahiduṃ (*dah*), khividuṃ (*kṣip*), hariduṃ (*hṛ*). Causatives, kāreduṃ, dhāreduṃ, daṃseduṃ=*darśayitum* (sometimes uncontracted Ś. ṇiattāiduṃ=*nivartayitum*), or by analogy with A-stems: dhāriduṃ, māriduṃ, kadhiduṃ.

Equivalents of Sanskrit forms in *-tum* are also found in Śaur.: but are commoner in M.

Ś. ṭhāduṃ (*sthā*), pāduṃ (to drink), kāduṃ, M. kāuṃ (*kr*), gantuṃ (*gam*). M. bhöttuṃ=*bhoktum*, daṭṭhuṃ=*draṣṭum*, dāuṃ (*dā*), ṇeuṃ (*nī*), pāuṃ (*pā*), Ś. pāduṃ, JM. piviuṃ, souṃ (*śrotum*), jeuṃ (*ji*) (AMg. jiṇiuṃ),

---

[1] The two passives civvai jivvai are assigned to *ci* and *ji* by the Grammarians. They have been explained as analogous to the forms from roots in u or ū. Pischel held that civvai was a regular passive from *cīv* **given in the Dhātupāṭha** (=' take' or ' cover') and jivvai probably from *jiv* (=' please'). Vide Pischel, § 537.

laddhuṃ (*labh*), voḍhuṃ (*vah*), chĕttuṃ (*chid*), bhettuṃ (*bhid*), mŏttuṃ (*muc*), ṇāuṃ (*jñā*). Similarly formed are ghĕttuṃ (§ 19) (=**ghṛp-tum* for *grahītum*)[1] sŏttum(=*sov-tum for *svaptum* cf. rŏttuṃ=*rotum*). √*vac* has M. vŏttuṃ Ś. vattuṃ.

Ardha-Māgadhī often uses the *-tum* form as a gerund, so that kāuṃ means *kṛtvā*. For the Infinitive this dialect prefers a form in *ttae* or *ittae*, ciṭṭhittae (*sthā*), gacchittae (*gam*). This is derived from a Dative Infinitive as found in Vedic.

§ 137. **Gerundives** (Varieties). (cf. § 121.)

(*a*) From *-tavya*, either (i) with the present stem, or (ii) with the root (strong form).

(i) pucchidavva, gacchidavva, hodavva (§ 4) or bhavidavva, aṇuciṭṭhidavva, dādavva, suṇidavva, jāṇidavva, gĕṇhidavva.

(ii) sodavva M. soavva (*śru*), ghĕttavva, kādavva (§ 63), M. kāavva (*kṛ*).

(*b*) From *-nīya*. M.AMg. *-aṇijja*, Ś. Mg. *-aṇīa*: karaṇīa, daṃsaṇīa, (from Present stem pucchaṇīa), M. karaṇijja, daṃsaṇijja.

(*c*) From *-ya*. **kajja** (§ 50)=*kārya*. AMg. vŏjjha=*vāhya*; from Present stems: gĕjjha (§ 70)=**gṛhya* from present stem **gṛha*.[2]

---

1 Also M. gahiuṃ, AMg. giṇhiuṃ, JM. gĕṇhium, Ś. gĕṇhiduṃ.

2 This is Pischel's derivation. However *grāhya* would become * gajjha, and association with the group gĕṇhadi ghĕttuṃ, etc., might account for the change of vowel *a* to *ĕ*.

CHAPTER X.

CLASSIFICATION OF PRAKRITS.

The rules and examples given in the last six chapters deal mainly with Māhārāṣṭrī and Śaurasenī, other languages being mentioned incidentally.

The principal peculiarities of some of these may now be brought together.

Māgadhī. It is a matter for regret that the sources of information about this language are not more abundant, as it is in some ways the most interesting of the Prakrits. We have here striking variations in phonetics that are not easily accounted for.

Ś for S (श for स) is an equation that is reflected in the modern languages of the East of India, where people speak, and even write of the "Shām Ved" and "Sheeta." As other Prakrits use only स *s* this law should cause the student no difficulty: **bhaviśśadi** is easily recognised as the equivalent of Ś. *bhavissadi*, **taśśiṃ** of *tassiṃ*, **śā of** *sā*, **puttaśśa** of *puttassa*, and so on.

L for R (ल for र) is more striking, especially at the beginning of a word. **lāāṇo**="kings."

puliśe=Ś. *puriso*, **galuḍa**=Ś. *garuḍa*, Cāludatta, ovālidaśalīla=*apavāritaśarīra*, śamale=*samare*, ṇagalantala=*nagarāntara*.

This change *l* for *r* is found occasionally in other Prakrits (§ 26) and in Pali (taluṇo=*taruṇo*); it is found also in the Vedic language, where *alam* √ *kr* replaces *aram*-(*kṛṇoti*), and √ *luc* replaces *ruc*. There are many instances in other languages, and it is often difficult to determine which was the original sound.

It is, however, remarkable to find an Aryan dialect without an R sound at all. The modern dialects of Bihar and Bengal have not replaced every *r* with an *l*. Perhaps this rule for dramatic Māgadhī is a conventional exaggeration of a marked tendency of the Eastern dialects. Possibly as Māgadhī is put in the mouths of only low-class people, it represents only the habit of a non-āryan stratum of society, which like the Chinese coolies of to-day may have had no R's.

On the other hand if we go back to Aśoka's time (3rd cent. B.C.) we find the same change in the Eastern dialect of the Inscriptions which seems to have been the language of the Court at Patna and which was used on the Pillars now at Allahabad and Delhi and with slight variations in the Rock Inscription at Kalsi.

Y remains and replaces J (य for ज).

yadhā=Ś. jadhā (§ 1), **yāṇadi**=*jānāti*.
yāṇidavvaṃ=Ś. jāṇidavvaṃ, yaṇavada=*janapada*.
yāyade=*jāyate*. (jh becomes yh. Yhatti=*jhaṭiti*.)

Dy. rj. ry. all become yy. So that where Śaurasenī has jj, Māgadhī has yy. (य्य for ज्ज).
ayya=*adya* or *ārya* (Ś. ajja).
avayya=*avadya*, mayya=*madya*.
(dhy becomes yyh: mayyhaṇṇa=majjhaṇṇa § 74).
ayyuṇa=*arjuna*, kayya=*kārya* (kajja § 50).
duyyaṇa=*durjana*.

From these examples it is clear that य in Māgadhī represents a front palate fricative different from the semi-vowel sound in English "yes." The equivalent of य was used in the North-west to express a foreign sound written Z in Greek. So on coins of King Azes we find the genitive Ayasa. Words spelt in Bengali with the equivalent of ज, are pronounced in some dialects with a sound resembling Z in 'zeal' or zh in 'azure.' A similar sound is commonly given to य in many words, e.g. ৻য=ये pronounced zhe.

Ñy, ny, jñ, ñj become ññ.

puñña=*puṇya* (Ś. puṇṇa § 48). **añña**=*anya* (Ś. aṇṇa).
kaññakā=*kanyakā*. **lañño**=*rājñaḥ* (Ś. raṇṇo § 99).
aññali=*añjali* (Ś. keeps ñj).

Medial cch becomes śc. (च्छ becomes श्च.)[1]

gaśca=*gaccha*, **iścīadi**=*icchati* (**icchyate*), uścaladi=*uccha-lati*, puścadi=*pṛcchati*.

tiliści peskadi=M. tiricchi pĕcchai=*tiryak prekṣate*.

A sibilant is retained at the beginning of a group of consonants. Grammarians differ as to which sibilant should be written. MSS. vary too much to give much help in the matter.

Ṣka. ष्क becomes स्क according to Hemacandra, otherwise we find शुश्के śuśke=*śuṣkaḥ*, Tuluśka=Turuṣka.

Ṣṭa ṣṭh become sṭa (or śṭa): कष्ट becomes कस्ट or कश्ट *suṣṭhu* becomes śusṭu or śuśṭu.

Ṣpa, ṣpha become spa, spha, ṇisphala=*niṣphala* (M.Ś. ṇipphala, § 38).

Ska, skha. paskhaladi=*praskhalati*.

Sta. stha become sta (or śta) **haśte** or **haste**=*hastaḥ* (M.Ś. hattho § 38), uvastida=*upasthita*.

Spa. Buhaspadi=Bṛhaspati (or Bihaśpadi).

Kṣa becomes ska. **peskadi**=prekṣate (or it is written śka. paśka=*pakṣa*. Hemacandra says paẖka, i.e. with visarga jihvāmūlīya).

The real Māgadhī sound may have been neither the स nor the श of the Midland Sanskrit. These groups being difficult, it is not surprising to find that MSS. generally write the assimilated forms *tth*, etc.

---

[1] As verbal forms in *ccha* go back to I.E. forms in *-SKA* the Māgadhī *śc* might be regarded as more archaic than the Vedic *cch* (however pronounced): cf. Slavonic, but this is considered inadmissible as Māgadhī has śc also for secondary cch as in uścaladi, maścalī (=Fish. *matsya-lī*-Pr. maccha), cf. Hindī machlī. On the other hand if originally correct for icchadi, etc., the same group would be readily introduced in other cases where Śaurasenī, etc., had *cch*.

rth becomes st. (or śt) so tista=*tīrtha*. aste=*arthaḥ*. This may be merely conventional analogy,[1] e.g. Śaurasenī hattho : Māgadhī haste ∴ Ś. attho : Mg. aste. In **grammar** the two characteristic points are Nom. Sing. in -e. śe haste=so hattho and hage="I" (§ 107). Otherwise the grammar closely follows Śaurasenī.

Some *Dialects of Māgadhī* appear in the plays.

Śākāri is spoken by the King's brother-in-law in the Little Clay Cart.

Peculiarities.—A weak y before palatals. Yciṣṭha=*tiṣṭha*.[2] *ḍa* in Past Participles especially from roots in *ṛ*. kaḍa=*kṛta* (the same feature is found in AMg.). Gen. Sing. in *āha* as well as *aśśa* Cāludattāha. Loc. Sing. āhiṃ. pavahaṇāhiṃ=*pravahaṇe* Voc. Plur-āho. (Vedic-*āsaḥ*). These last three points resemble Apabhraṃśa.

Cāṇḍālī and **Śābarī** appear to be dialects of Māgadhī.

Māthura and the two gamblers in the Mṛcchakaṭikā speak a dialect called **Ḍhakkī** by Pischel, who supposed it to be a dialect of Māgadhī. Sir George Grierson has shown that the form Ṭākkī has better authority and ascribes it to the country of the Ṭakkas round about Sialkot.[3]

Ardha-Māgadhī. Jacobi called this Jaina Prākrit and regarded it as an older, more archaic Māhārāṣṭrī. The Indian grammarians called the language of the old Jain Sūtras

[1] On the other hand the change *rt* becomes *ś* is found in Iranian. Avestan mašyo=*martyaḥ*. G.I.P., I, § 289.

[2] Mārkaṇḍeya gives this for Māgadhī and Vrācaḍa Apabhraṃśa, Ycilaṃ=*ciraṃ*. The pronunciation is not clear (*vide* Selections, Māgadhī).

[3] If Ṭākkī was a Panjab dialect it is strange that Mārkaṇḍeya should identify this with the Drāviḍī Vibhāṣā. (See Grierson, J.R.A.S., 1913. p. 882; 1918, p. 513.) Ṭākkī according to Mārkaṇḍeya is a "mutual mixture of Sanskrit and Śaurasenī" employed by "professional gamblers and by merchants of lowly position." The vowel *u* often appears at the end of a word, but not always. It has both *sa* and *śa, la* and *ra*. In the Panjab Hills there is a common script called Ṭakrī or Ṭākrī generally derived from the same name of a people, Ṭakka.

"Ārṣam" from Ṛṣi. Hemacandra explains that all his rules have exceptions in "Ārṣa." Trivikrama, another grammarian, excluded "Ārṣa" from his treatise, because its meanings were *rūḍha*, or conventional, not strictly in accordance with etymology, i.e. not based on Sanskrit.

Namisādhu commenting on Rudraṭa's Kāvyālaṃkāra (2-12), derives the word Prākrit from *prakṛti* in the sense of natural speech free from the rules of grammarians, or from *prāk kṛta*, 'created of old!' because, says he, the Prakrit of the Ārṣa canon, Ardha-māgadhī is the language of the gods. *Ārisa-vayaṇe siddhaṃ devāṇaṃ Addhamāgahā vāṇī.* Obviously Namisādhu was a Jain. The Jains indeed supposed that Ardha-Māgadhī, the language in which Mahāvīra preached, was the original language from which all others were derived.[1]

There is some difference between the prose and verse portions of the Canon. Verses often have Nom. Sing. in *-o* instead of the characteristic *-e* (like Mg.), gerunds in *tūṇa ūṇa* (like M.) while prose prefers *ttā* or *ttāṇaṃ* (§ 122).

Other points are: Verse mĕccha, prose milakkhu. Verse kuṇai, prose kuvvaī (=**kurvati*). The verse dialect is thus somewhat nearer to M. than the prose.

Ardha-Māgadhī agrees with Māgadhī in the Nom. Sing. in *-e*, the use of Gen. Sing. *tava*; past participles in *ḍa* for *ta* after roots in *ṛ* (but not always); in *ka* becomes *ga* "Asoga" (but this is rare in Mg.); and in Pluti of *-a* in Voc. Sing. (common in Apabhraṃśa).

It differs markedly in the retention of *ra* and *sa*. In general AMg. (like Pali) retains more archaic features than the dramatic Prakrits. AMg. is assigned by the Bhāratīya-nāṭya-śāstra (followed by Sāhityadarpaṇa) to servants, Rajputs, and the heads of guilds. The Jain monks in the plays who might be expected to speak AMg. appear to speak ordinary Māgadhī.[2]

---

1 *Vide* Pischel, § 16.

2 One of the dialects in the fragments of Buddhist dramas found in Central Asia is classed by Lüders as Old Ardha-Māgadhī.

AMg. differs in many respects from Māhārāṣṭrī.[1]

Phonetics.—am becomes ām before eva and avi (=*api*).

iti becomes i after pluti vowel or in *iti vā*.

prati drops i: paḍuppanna=*pratyutpanna* (rare in other dialects).

dentals for palatals. teicchā=*cikitsā*.

ahā=yathā.

use of sandhi consonants (§ 78).

Noun: dative in -ttāe (§ 92),

instrumental in sā (§ 104),

locative in -ṃsi (§ 92 v.).

Verbs: √khyā āïkkhaï (Pāli ācikkhati) M. akkhāï,

kuvvai (in prose, see above).

Relics of Aorists, e.g., 3 plur. pucchiṃsu.

Infinitives in ṭṭu -ittu used as gerunds, e.g., kaṭṭu (means *kṛtvā*), avahaṭṭu (means *apahṛtya*) suṇittu, jāṇittu.

Infinitives in -ttae, -ittae (§ 136).

Gerunds in -ttā, -ttāṇaṃ, -ccā, -ccāṇa(ṃ), -yāṇa(ṃ).

Moreover, where they agree what is common in AMg. is often rare in M. Cerebralisation is much commoner in AMg. and so is the change *la* for *ra*.

The vocabulary is also often quite distinct.

It will be obvious that AMg. differs still more from Śaurasenī.

The later Jain writings belong to times when the sect had spread more widely and were influenced by other dialects. Owing possibly to the popularity of this religion among the rich mercantile communities on the West coast, the non-canonical writings of the Śvetāmbara Jains are in a language which may be regarded as a form of Māhārāṣṭrī, although it

---

[1] Jacobi considered the language of the Jain Canon to be an older form of Māhārāṣṭrī. Kalpa Sūtra, S.B.E., XXII. Pischel showed this view to be untenable. Pr. Gr., § 18.

retains a number of the peculiarities of AMg., e.g., infinitive in *-ittu,* gerund in *-ittā* and *ga* for *ka*. This is the main dialect of Jacobi's Selected Narratives in Māhārāṣṭrī, and is generally known as **Jain Māhārāṣṭrī.**

The language of the Digambara canon has Nom. Sing. in *o*: t, th become d, dh. Hence it has been called **Jain Śaurasenī.** It has however much that is foreign to Śaurasenī, but found in either M. or AMg. In the direction of Gujarat were many strongholds of Jainism, and here the Śaurasenī type of dialect would meet Māhārāṣṭrī. That JŚ. preserves rather more of the peculiarities of AMg. than JM. does, is probably due to the fact that it is somewhat older.

The resemblances and differences of the principal Prakrits given above would not necessarily lead to a closer classification. We have an **Eastern** Prakrit (Māgadhī), a Southern Prakrit (Māhārāṣṭrī), and a Central Prakrit (Śaurasenī). Ardhamāgadhī appears to resemble the Southern more than the Central Prakrit. **Hoernle,**[1] on the basis of a comparative study of some of the modern Indo-Aryan languages, supposed that the whole of Aryan-speaking India was at one time divided between two languages, a "*Śaurasenī tongue*" and a "*Māgadhī tongue.*" Māhārāṣṭrī he regarded as an artificial literary language, without any direct relation to the spoken language of Mahārāṣṭram. Further study of the Prakrits and of the modern dialects has shown that this view is untenable.

Māhārāṣṭrī (and Jain Māhārāṣṭrī) has peculiarities which can be traced in modern Marāṭhī, and there can be no doubt that this Prakrit was based on the language of the Marāṭha country.[2]

Grierson[3] with more abundant material has developed the

---

1 Grammar of the Gauḍian Languages, 1880. Introd., p. xxx.

2 See Introduction to volume on Marāṭhī in the Linguistic Survey of India.

3 See Article on Prakrit in Encyclop. Britannica, 11th edition, and chapter on Language in Imperial Gazetteer of India.

idea of the geographical classification of the Prakrits on the basis of a comparison with modern dialects. His classification is—

Central Prakrit ..	.. Śaurasenī.
Outer Prakrits ..	.. E. Māgadhī.
	S. Māhārāṣṭrī.
Intermediate ..	.. Ardha-Māgadhī.

This is a convenient classification inasmuch as Śaurasenī is the most Sanskritic, and the representative of the Madhyadeśa, which was the centre of Hindu culture after the early Rigvedic times: while literary centres at a distance from this middle point naturally show more independence from Sanskrit. This classification is indeed connected with a theory relating to the immigration of the Aryan-speaking tribes into the Peninsula. The speakers of the dialects out of which classical Sanskrit was created, and on which later on Śaurasenī was based, are supposed to have forced their way into the Madhyadeśa some time after a previous Aryan invasion. The descendants of those first-comers produced the "Outer Band" of languages.

Much may be said both for and against this particular theory as an explanation of certain linguistic facts. It is however possible to accept a classification based on such facts, without necessarily accepting this particular explanation.

A weak point in the classification might appear to be the position of Ardha-Māgadhī. If this was centred in Oude, one would expect the language to be roughly speaking half Māgadhī and *half Śaurasenī*. Now Māgadhī, as far as we know it, hardly differs from Śaurasenī except in striking phonetic variations. If we allowed Ardha-Māgadhī a Nom. Sing. in e, a certain amount of l for r, and ś for s with perhaps some traces of the other phonetic peculiarities of Māgadhī, we could invent a Prakrit that would fit in with the scheme, but it would be quite different to the real Ardha-Māgadhī of the old Jain Canon. Eastern Hindi does indeed lie between Western Hindi and the dialects of Bihar, and combines some of the peculiarities of the languages on either side; but the Prakrit Ardha-Māgadhī does not look as if it occupied the same position or was the ancestor of Eastern Hindi.

It must, however, be remembered that this classification deals primarily with the spoken languages on which the literary languages were based. The literary Prakrits were not all crystallised at the same time, and so do not represent strictly contemporary dialects. Ardha-Māgadhī is obviously more archaic than Śaurasenī. It has indeed been suggested that the Eastern dialect of Aśoka's inscriptions should be regarded as an older form of Ardha-Māgadhī. Lūders calls it Old Ardha-Māgadhī. This, it is presumed, was the current language of the Mauryan court. Very similar, it is thought, was the language in which the teachings of Gautama Buddha were first recorded, before either the Pali Canon or the Sanskrit Canon was established.

A language widely used in the Ganges valley would be quite likely to be neither pure Māgadhī nor pure Śaurasenī. Without necessarily being exactly the dialect of Kāśī either, it might very well be based on the speech of the country lying intermediate between the two ends of the valley. Later on when the centre of Jainism had travelled further to the West, Later Ardha-Māgadhī would have taken on the Māhārāṣṭrī colouring which we find in the Jain Canon. Other circumstances had in the meantime led to the conversion of the Buddhist scriptures into Pāli. (See S. Lévi: Journal Asiatique, 1912, p. 495.)

Paiśācī Prākrit.—Paiśācī lies outside the circle of languages dealt with so far. The term seems to have been used (*a*) of the language of demons "Bhūtabhāṣā," (*b*) of a number of uncivilized languages, including some Apabhraṃśas, (*c*) the Paiśācī dialect of the grammarians (especially Hemacandra) with a subdialect Cūḷikā Paiśicī (C.P.). This Paiśācī dialect is archaic in character. Its chief peculiarity is the substitution of surd mutes for sonants. Tāmotara=*Dāmodara*. C.P. nakara =*nagara*, rācā=*rājā*, khamma=*gharma*, kantappa=*kandarpa*.

ṇa ण becomes *na* न, ल *la* becomes ळ *ḷa* : य *ya* remains. Intervocal consonants are not dropped. Aspirates are not reduced to *h*; *jñ*, *ny* become *ññ* (as in Mg. and probably every other dialect at a sufficiently early stage).

Who were the speakers of this dialect? The Shāhbāzgarhī Edict agrees with this dialect in a number of particulars. The Bṛhatkathā of Guṇāḍhya was composed, according to the story, in Paiśācī. This work was popular in Kashmir in the 11th century. Somadeva produced one version in the Kathāsaritsāgara, and Kṣemendra a shorter one in the Bṛhatkathāmañjarī. Some scholars have concluded that Cūlikā Paiśācī was a dialect of the North-West of India. Sir George Grierson connects it with the Dard and Kāfir languages of the Hindu Kush, including Shiṇā and the under-layer of Kashmīrī.[1]

On the other hand it is admitted that Guṇāḍhya was a South-Indian. The Bṛhatkathā was composed many centuries before that late literary development in Kashmir which produced Kṣemendra, Bilhaṇa, Somadeva and Kalhaṇa. ण ṇa becomes न *na*, and ल becomes ळ ḷ are suggestive of Dravidian influence. Other features, such as the retention of medial *t*, and of *y*, are merely archaic. Surd for sonant can be paralleled in the South as well as in the North. It is a common corruption when a language is adopted by an alien race.[2] The student will remember the Welsh parson, Sir Hugh Evans, in the Merry Wives of Windsor. Speakers of Gaelic have the same tendency. Any such corrupt dialect on the fringes of Aryan speech would

---

1 *Vide* the Piśāca Languages of North-Western India. R. As. Soc. Mon. Vol. VIII, 1906. The author's theory that these, mostly mixed, dialects should be provided with a separate compartment between the Iranian and Indian subdivisions of Aryan, because they combine Indian and Iranian peculiarities, is not convincing. Nor is the connection with C. Paiśācī obvious, as the main peculiarity of C.P. (surd for sonant) is *exceptional* in this area.

2 It is quite probable that the same change in Armenian (tasn = 'ten') and Teutonic (Gothic taihun) is due to the same cause.

necessarily disappear with the continued extension of Aryan speech. So that it seems quite as possible that the original Cockscomb[1] Demons belonged to the Vindhyas as that they were Cannibals of Kashmir.[2]

Old Prākrit. The oldest Prākrit recorded is found in the **Inscriptions of Aśoka.** The Kharoṣṭhī script was used in the North-West (Śāhbāzgarhī and Mānsehrā) but all the other inscriptions, whether on rocks or on pillars, are in the oldest form of Brāhmī writing. The language used is not so uniform. There is a marked contrast between the Eastern dialect and the Western.

The Eastern dialect is found with only minor variations on the pillars in the Ganges-Jumna basin and in the rock edicts of Kālsī and Orissa.

In this dialect *ra* is represented by *la* and the Nom. sing. of masculine and neuter nouns of the -*a* declension ends in -*e* as in Māgadhī. On the other hand we have *sa* and not the palatal *śa* (but also *ṣa* at Kālsī.) This language has been called Māgadhī but Lüders claims that it is really Ardha-Māgadhī. Whatever be the best name for it, this seems to have been the language used by Aśoka and his Court. The influence of this official language shows itself in the other inscriptions of the West and North, which are evidently not in pure local dialects. Forms due to this influence are generally called *Magadhisms.*

The West is represented by the Rock Edict of **Girnār.** The language here has Nom. sing. in -*o* and neuter -*aṃ*, with *ra* and *sa*. (Magadhisms are *priye*, *jane* for *priyo*, *jano*, and *mūle* for *mūlaṃ*, etc.) In a number of particulars it reminds us of Pali, but it is not identical with that language.

---

1 If that is the meaning of *cūlikā*, *cūḷikā*.

2 References: Grierson's Monograph, pp. 1 and 2. Sten Konow: Home of Paiśācī Z.D.M.G. lxiv, pp. 95 ff. Grierson. Z.D.M.G.lxvi, pp. 393–421.

See also Dardic Languages in the Linguistic Survey of India and Morgenstierne: Report on a Linguistic Mission to Afghanistan.

One may suppose that this Western dialect represents more or less closely the current language of Ujjain, which was the capital of an important province in the Mauryan Empire.

Inscriptions found in the South of India resemble the Western rather than the Eastern edicts, but have their own peculiarities.

The **North-Western** edicts differ from both East and West, Mānsehrā has more Magadhisms than Śāhbāzgarhī. Both have *ra*, *sa* and *śa*. Śāhb. prefers Nom. sing. *-o* neut. *-aṃ* while Mān. prefers the *-e* of (Ardha)Māgadhī. Both preserve many conjuncts with *r*, often with metathesis: *Priyadrasi* instead of *Piyadasi*; *bhutapruva*=Girnār *bhūtapurvaṃ*=Dhauli *hūtapulavā*; Śāhb. *trayo*=Girnār *tri*; Śāhb. *mrugo*, Mān. *mrige*= =Girnār *mago*=Eastern *mige*.

This last example illustrates another difference between East and West. (Cf. § 60.)

Śāhbāzgarhī retains *kṣ* as in *kṣamitaviya* but at Girnār we find *chamitave* and in the East *khamitave*. (Cf. § 40.)

Conjuncts such as *pr* in *priya* which are found both in the West and the North-West, were regarded at one time as *Sanskritisms*. They are rather survivals of the old phonetics. In the modern dialects of the North-West such conjuncts still exist *e.g.*, Lahndā *tre* 'three', cf. Sindhi *ṭrạṇ*.

When comparing the North-West forms with others it should be borne in mind that Kharoṣṭhī does not distinguish long vowels from short.

It should also be remembered that neither the Kharoṣṭhī nor the Brāhmī of Aśoka's inscriptions writes doubled consonants. Thus we have *cakavāke* not *cakkavāke*, *cakhudāne* not *cakkhudāne*.

The Bairāt-Bhābrā inscription now at Calcutta mentions some of Aśoka's favourite passages of Scripture. The language of this inscription has been much discussed. The forms *Lāghula* which appears as Rāhula in Pāli, and *adhigicya* (=*adhikṛtya*) cannot be paralleled in the edicts. They seem to indicate an earlier language of the Buddhist scriptures. (See above p. 64.) The forms *Priyadasi*, *sarve*, *prāsāde*, and *abhipretaṃ* which Hultzsch reads on this rock appear strange in a dialect which has *la* for all the single *ras*. It must be admitted that all these conjunct *ras* depend on the perception of a small dash, which is in no case very clear and is perhaps in every case nothing but a slight unevenness in the stone.

It will be seen that the division of the Aśokan dialects does not coincide with that of later Prākrits. This is not surprising. Unless several centres of literary culture maintain a continuous tradition the distribution of languages used for general purposes is likely to be different after the lapse of several centuries. Among the Prākrits used in the Drama there is nothing to represent the language of the Panjab and North-West. We have noted the claim put forward on behalf of Paiśācī Prakrit. There is evidence of another Prākrit being used by the Buddhists of the North. The fragments of a Kharoṣṭhī manuscript of the Dhammapada found near Khotan, which is known as the Dutreuil de Rhins manuscript, show certain peculiarities that are found in modern dialects of the North-West. Journal Asiatique (Senart.), 1898, p. 193. (J. Bloch.), 1912. p. 331.

Pāli. *Pāli* originally meaning a "boundary, limit, or line" was applied to the *Canon* of the Hīnayāna Buddhists. Thence it is used of the *language* of that Canon, found also in some non-canonical books: all being preserved in what were originally the missionary Churches of Ceylon, Burma and Siam. Thence again 'Pali' is sometimes applied to (*a*) the inscriptions of Aśoka, although these comprise three or four distinct dialects; (*b*) the official court language of Aśoka's Empire, a form of Middle Indian widely understood,[1] and (*c*) 'monumental Prakrit' including all the inscriptions down to the time when Sanskrit ousted Prakrit (or "Pali").[2] The Pali language of

---

[1] See Rhys Davids, Buddhist India.

[2] This wide use of "Pali" is made by Dr. Otto Franke, Pāli und Sanskrit.

the Buddhist books forming a separate academic subject (a classical language appropriate to Buddhists of Burma), has not been much studied in India. Nevertheless it is important for the study of (*a*) the history of Indian speech, and (*b*) the Old Prakrit inscriptions.

For the study of classical Pali numerous grammars, readers, texts and translations are available.[1] Only a very general description need be given here.

Characteristics of Pali. Pali retains more of the old grammatical system than AMg. The ātmanepada is commoner; Aorists, especially the S-Aorists, abound. (The Aorist and Imperfect have fused together). The reduplicated Perfect is rare, but occurs. There are more survivals of the old conjugational classes, e.g., suṇoti=Ś. suṇādi; karoti (Ātm. kubbate)=Ś. karedi; dadāti (also deti)=Ś. dedi.

In Phonetics the striking points are :—the sibilant is dental स, *y* remains, *r* sometimes becomes *l*, but not always as in Mg., *n* is sometimes cerebralised but not always. Intervocal consonants generally remain, and surds are only exceptionally replaced by sonants. Hence we have bhavati, or hoti, katheti, pucchati, gacchati, etc.: mato=*mṛtaḥ*, kato=*kṛtaḥ*.

In some words conjuncts like dr-, br- remain.

Svarabhakti is common. Ārya becomes ayya or ariya.

From these examples it will be seen that Pali is more archaic than the Prakrits described above, with the exception of the Aśokan dialects.

The geographical basis of Pali has been disputed. The Buddha was supposed by tradition to have preached in Māgadhī. The Scriptures were naturally supposed by Southern Buddhists to be in the language of the Buddha. Therefore Pali should be Māgadhī. As a matter of fact it is not. The Nom. Sing. in -o, the presence of sa, ra, ja show this clearly. Some regard it as the language of Ujjain, whence Mahinda,

---

1 See Bibliography.

the son of Aśoka, took the sacred Canon to Ceylon, others as the Aryan language of the Kaliṅga country.

Another view, finding some points of resemblance with Paiśācī (unvoicing of sonant stops), prefers some point near the Vindhyas, while others again would bring Pali to Taxila to get this colouring. Geiger returning to the tradition of Māgadhī thinks Pali may have developed from some kind of Ardha-Māgadhī, though it is not the unmixed language of any area.

If however the Pali Canon is not the oldest literary version, the argument based on tradition vanishes. Buddha's preaching and the earliest records thereof were doubtless in an Eastern speech. Afterwards they were rendered in other dialects and one of these new versions became the Pali Canon. Dr. S. K. Chatterji says that this Pali is shown by its phonology and morphology to be a Western dialect of the Midland (an old form of Śaurasenī) but retaining many relics of the original dialect. When the domination of the Mauryas declined the wide use of the Eastern official language (Ardha-Māgadhī) came to an end. It was succeeded, it would appear, in many districts by a Western *lingua franca* akin to Pali, which appears in the inscription of Khāravela.

Whatever may be the exact truth of the matter, it is clear that Pali contains several different strands in its composition and that it varies also according to its age. The oldest type is seen in the Gāthās, then come the prose portions of the Canon followed by non-canonical literature and finally still later layers. The development of Pali has been influenced by Sanskrit.

Of the **Prakrit Inscriptions** later than Aśoka many are too brief for their dialect to be classified with certainty. Khāravela's inscription at the entrance to the Hāthīgumphā Cave, usually assigned to the second century B.C., resembles the Western or Southern dialects of Aśoka's inscriptions rather than the Eastern. In many respects it resembles Pali but in others it differs from that language.

An inscription in the Jogīmārā Cave on Rāmgarh Hill appears to be in an old form of Māgadhī.

Aśvaghosha. Some fragments of palm-leaf manuscripts found in Central Asia[1] and pieced together by Prof. Lüders. reveal portions of two Buddhist dramas. In one of these only Sanskrit is used, at any rate in the surviving portions. In the other play, which is ascribed to Aśvaghosha the famous Buddhist writer of Kanishka's time, more than one Prakrit has been used. The Rascal speaks a form of Māgadhī: *s* > *ś*, *r* > *l*, nom. sing. *e* for *o*. In some respects the Prakrit is more archaic than the Māgadhī of the Grammarians and the Dramas: *ahakaṃ* "I" for *hage*, *kiśśa* for *kīśa*. Lüders classes this as Old Māgadhī. The speech of another character, which closely resembles the dialect of the Pillar Inscriptions is thought to represent an old stage of Ardha-Māgadhī. The dialect of the Courtesan and the Jester appears to be Old Śaurasenī. It retains intervocal consonants, *n* is not cerebralised and *y* does not become *j*.

An intermediate form of Prakrit representing a stage of development roughly half-way between Aśvaghosha and Kālidāsa, Bhavabhūti, etc. has been recognised by some scholars in the Trivandrum plays ascribed by their discoverer to **Bhāsa.** At first sight no doubt the Prakrit in these plays appears to be later than that used by Aśvaghosha and more archaic than that of the Gupta poets. If we date Bhāsa in the second or third century A.D. and if we can accept these plays as the work of Bhāsa, several points fit in quite well.[2]

Unfortunately we do not know that the plays were written by Bhāsa. We know them only from South Indian MSS. and South Indian MSS. of plays written in the seventh century and even later preserve similar features.

---

1 They were found by Dr. von Le Coq in one of the Cave Temples of Ming Öi to the West of Kucha. They have been reproduced in facsimile and edited with a translation and notes by Prof. Lüders. *Bruchstücke Buddhistischer Dramen.* Berlin, 1911.

2 See V. Lesný. Z.D.M.G. 1918, 203–208, and Wilhelm Printz. Bhāsa's Prakrit. Frankfurt, 1921.

The South Indian traditional spelling of Prakrit was evidently more archaic than that of the North. In the South, where the ordinary speech was Dravidian, the pronunciation of Prakrit would be less liable to change than in the North.

The archaic forms found in the Southern MSS. are of interest for the history of Prakrit, but there is no conclusive evidence so far to connect them with Bhāsa in particular or with the second century, though doubtless they have come down from a time previous to our MSS. of Kālidāsa, etc. and to the Prakrit Grammarians.

In the Trivandrum plays we find Śaurasenī and Māgadhī. Indra in the Karṇabhāra and the two warriors speak a dialect which resembles Ardha-Māgadhī.

In the Śaurasenī the chief peculiarities are: *l* > *ḷ*, *jñ* > *ññ* as well as *ṇṇ* but *ny* > *ṇṇ*.

	Trivandrum		Ordinary Prakrit.
	udy > *uyy*	as in Pali.	*ujj-*
	ry *yy*	,, ,, ,, . (Aśv.)	*jj*
Acc. pl. m.	*-āṇi*	cf. Old Ardha-Māgadhī.	*-e*
N. Acc. pl. neut.	*-āṇi*	(Pali-āni)	*-āiṃ*
Loc. s. fem.	*-āaṃ*	cf. Pali-āya (ṃ)	*-āe*
	tava	(Aśv.)	*tuha*
	kissa	Pāli kissa (Aśv. Mg. kiśśa)	*kīsa*
	gaṇhadi	cf. Pali ganhāti	*geṇhadi.*
Pres. Part. Pass.	*-iamāṇa*	cf. Pali iyamāna only once	*-ianta.*
	kattuṃ, *kattava*	also	*kāduṃ*; *kādavva.*
Gerund.	*karia*		*kadua.*
	gacchia		*gadua.*

Late Prakrit. Apabhraṃśa. (See Ch. II, p. 6.)

For the student of philology it will be of interest to notice some of the main features of the Apabhraṃśa stage. Whereas in Old Prakrit the typical phonetic and grammatical changes are not carried so far as in Dramatic Prakrits, so naturally in this Late Prakrit such changes are carried further. When more archaic forms occur in an Apabhraṃśa text, these may be ordinary Prakrit words used by the author for literary purposes, or occasionally they may retain ancient features that had survived in local dialects outside the main current of linguistic development. Some dialects of the "Outer Band" preserve quite ancient features to the present day.

The following tables of typical declension and conjugation (based on Hemacandra's account) gives only forms peculiar to Apabhraṃśa, not those shared with the Prakrits.

Declension.

Sing.	Nom.	Acc. puttu
	(Neut.	phalu)
	Ins.	puttẽ
	Abl.	puttahẽ puttahu
	Gen.	puttassu puttahŏ puttaha
	Loc.	putti puttahĩ.
Plur	Nom.	Acc. putta (Neut. phalaĩ)
	Ins.	puttahi (ṃ)
	Abl.	puttahũ
	Gen.	puttahã
	Loc.	puttahĩ

If the oblique forms be compared it is apparent that it needed only the blurring of the final vowels to reduce these to one form for the singular and a nasalised form for the plural. (See Beames, II. § 42.) The Apabhraṃśa Nom. Sing. in *u* is seen in the Sindhi forms with a very short *u*.[1]

In the Gen. Sing. an *s* form survives in Apabhraṃśa. This *s* appears in the pronominal declension of Hindi tis-kā kis kā.[2] It occurs in the "Romani" of Gypsies in Europe, cores-kero—

[1] Nom. Sing. in *o* (***Rājasthānī*** and Western Hindi dialects) or *ā* (Standard Hindi and Panjabi) is derived directly or by analogy from forms in *-aka-*. *K* was dropped, hence from **-ako* we get **-a-o*, Apa. *-a-u* which becomes either *o* or *ā*.

[2] These forms have fused with the old feminine *tissā*, etc.

'of a thief.' Kashmiri has an oblique form in *-s*, tsuras nish— 'near a thief,' guras nish— 'near a horse,' which is used as a dative. Marāṭhī also preserves the form in the dative.

Conjugation.

Sing. 1.	**pucchaū̃**	Plur. 1.	pucchahū̃
2.	pucchasi or -hi		**pucchahu**
3.	**pucchaï**		**pucchahī̃.**

This is very close to Old Hindi and not far from the modern forms pucchū̃, pucche, puccho, pucchẽ.

Among the more striking of the phonetic innovations of Apabhraṃśa may be mentioned the following :—

Loss of *v* before *u* : āhau for *āhava* ; sahāu for *svabhāva* ;

Loss of *m* before *u* and also before *a* : Jauṇā for *Jamunā*, bhauhā for bhamuhā meaning *bhrū* ; duggau for *durgama* (also duggamu).

Nasalisation of final *i* and *u* : 3. sing. suṇaī̃, bhaṇaī̃ ; 2. sing. ramahī̃ ; nom. sing. bhaṇiū̃, bhamiū̃.

Intervocalic *m* becomes ṽ or *v* (written also *ṃv*): kuṽara for *kumara* ; bhaṃvaṇa=*bhramaṇa* ; savaṇa=*śramaṇa* ; paṽāṇa= *pramāṇa*.

Shortening of vowels : vaṇijja=*vāṇijya* ; karaṇa=*kāraṇa* ; niya=*nīta* ; piya=*pīta*.

Contraction : andhāra=*andhakāra* ; bhaṇḍāra=*bhāṇḍāgāra* ; uṇhāla=*uṣṇakāla* ; piyāra=*piyayara=*priyatara*.

Shortening double consonants (and lengthening vowels) : sahāsa for sahassa=*sahasra* ; bhavīsa for bhavissa=*bhaviṣya*.

Noun stems are frequently extended by adding *-a*, *-(a)ḍa*, *ulla*. These suffixes are found in earlier Prakrit but not so frequently. Thus we have in Prakrit *-āla*, *-ālu*, *-illa*, *-ulla*, in the sense of *-mat*, *-vat* or of place 'belonging to.'

Examples. *-āla* : M. sihāla for *śikhāvat* ; AMg. saddāla for *śabdavat* ; dhaṇāla for *dhanavat*. *-āla+ka* : AMg. mahālaya for *mahat*.

-ālu : ṇiddālu=*nidrālu*. (This suffix appears in Sanskrit.)

-illa (common in M. JM. AMg.) M. kesarilla, kandalilla, tūlilla,

ṇeurilla. AMg. niyaḍilla=*nikṛtimat*; māilla=*māyāvin*; bhāillaga =*bhāgin*; goilla=*gomat*; kaṇailla 'parrot' from *deśī* kaṇa; bāhirilla 'external'; M. AMg. gāmilla 'peasant'; AMg. JM. puvvilla 'previous.'

-ulla is rarer in Prakrit: dappulla= *-darpin*.

Other adjectival suffixes are *-alla* (for *-ala*) and *-ira*. M. AMg. mahalla=*mahat*; navalla=*nava*; bhamira 'wandering'; lambira 'hanging'; hasira 'laughing.'

Without change of meaning *-ka* and *-ḍa* (Sanskrit *-ṭa*.) desaḍaa=*deśa*; dosaḍa=*doṣa*; raṇṇaḍaa=*araṇya*.

These two become very common in Apabhraṃśa.

In general it may be said that the Apabhraṃśa forms, whenever these can be ascertained, should be taken as the starting point for the derivation of words in the modern languages and the comparative study of their phonology.[1] Thus to derive Hindi *pahlā* "first" we should start from an Apabhraṃśa form *pahilaü* rather than from *prathamaḥ* or paḍhamo.[2]

According to the older grammarians the three varieties of Apabhraṃśa, that is literary Apabhraṃśa, were Vrācaṭa, Nāgara and Upanāgara. Jacobi has shown[3] that **Vrācaṭa** or **Vrācaḍa** is the oldest of the three. Grammarians of the 17th century say it belongs to Sindh. It appears to be the same as *Ābhīrī bhāṣā*, the language of the Ābhīras (modern Ahīrs). The name Vrācaṭa Jacobi derives from *vraja* 'herdsmen's station' and compares the similar name of a Hindi literary language Braj Bhākhā. The chief peculiarity of this Apabhraṃśa was the maintenance or addition of *r* after consonants and the maintenance of *ṛ*.

Nāgara ('urban') Apabhraṃśa seems to have been a more polished and sophisticated medium, distinguished from the

---

1 See Grierson's Phonology of the Indo-Aryan Vernaculars.

2 Grierson derives from an Apabhraṃśa *paḍhavillaü* apparently deduced from AMg. *paḍhamilla* with the suffix -illa so frequent in M.; cf. Pischel §449 who assumes Old Indian **prathila*

3 Introd. to Bhavisattakaha.

rougher herdsmen's dialect and from the less cultivated Upanāgara and Grāmya. This is the Apabhraṃśa which Hemacandra describes and illustrates. Two varieties of it differing somewhat from Hemacandra's Nāgara are described by Jacobi. One of these is represented by the Nemināhacariu of Haribhadra written 1159, A.D. at Aṇahilla-Pāṭaka, the Gurjara capital. The language may be called "Gurjara Apabhraṃśa" and seems to have been preferred by the Śvetāmbara Jains. The Bhavisattakaha of Dhaṇavāla, which may be older and is written in a more popular style with less Prakrit and less ornament, is in another form of Nāgara Apabhraṃśa, which Jacobi calls "Northern." It may have been preferred by the Digambara Jains. The differences in the grammar lie mainly in the vowels used in the declension of the noun.

The term Apabhraṃśa as used by the older grammarians and poets seems to have connoted literary dialects like Nāgara, which may have arisen in a particular centre, but which came to be used over a much wider area. Apabhraṃśa in this sense belonged to the West of India, the region now occupied by Gujarātī, Sindhī and Mārwāṛī, but might be imitated elsewhere. The term was also used, at any rate later, for various local speeches, or *deśa-bhāṣā*. In this sense there were various forms of Śaurasenī Apabhraṃśa actually spoken in the districts round Muttra when Śaurasenī Prakrit had become a literary language. Similarly in the Māgadhī and Māhārāṣṭrī areas there should have been Māgadhī and Māhārāṣṭrī Apabhraṃśas. Unless, however, the differences were clearly marked they would hardly be noticed and ordinarily nothing would be recorded of a dialect that had produced no literature.

A number of *vibhāṣās* are mentioned by Bharata as suitable for certain characters in plays, including Śākārī (based on Māgadhī), Cāṇḍālī, Śābarī, Ābhīrī and Ṭākkī.[1]

Mārkaṇḍeya gives some details about these and mentions a list of twenty-seven including Drāviḍa. Drāviḍa here seems to

[1] Grierson. J.R.A.S. 1918. p. 489ff.

mean not a Dravidian language such as Tamil, but the corrupt form of late Indo-Aryan spoken in the Tamil country.[1] Rāmatarkavāgīśa gives some notes on these *vibhāṣās* such as Pāñcālī, Mālavī, Madhyadeśīyā, etc. These all seem to have been local variations of the Apabhraṃśa in general use, that is of the literary Apabhraṃśa of the West rather than independent local dialects. In the development of Marāthī and of Bengali from the Māhārāṣṭrī and Māgadhī Prakrits no Apabhraṃśa stage has been recorded. The older *vibhāṣās* would have been local (or tribal) variants of a recognised Prakrit rather than the records of a mediaeval Linguistic Survey. Consequently though we may attempt to classify elements in them we cannot locate these varieties in a family tree of the Indo-Aryan languages.

CHAPTER XI.

PRAKRIT LITERATURE.

The earliest recorded Prakrit is in **Aśoka's Inscriptions** of the third century B.C. There were Buddhist scriptures before that. As we have seen, Aśoka quotes a few titles of his favourite passages. The form in which he quotes them indicate that those scriptures were not yet in the Pali of the Canon, as known to the Church of the Little Vehicle in Burma and Ceylon. We cannot date any Pali text as certainly older than Aśoka.

Inscriptions do not usually figure in an account of literature. If, however, Aśoka's edicts had been preserved in a manuscript copy they would obviously be taken into account as the earliest dated documents of Prakrit literature. Of the dialects used and their variations something has already been said. The style is

---

[1] Grierson. J.R.A.S., 1913, p. 875. For Jacobi's views on the difference between Apabhraṃśa and Deśa-bhāṣā see the Introduction to his Edition of the Bhavisattakaha. (German.)

of interest for the history of prose. Free of all ornament they express the sincerity and earnestness of the Emperor. It is reasonable to suppose that they were drafted by the royal hand for there is no trace of the habitual flattery of the courtier or scribe.

The style has been compared with that of the famous Rock Inscription of Darius the Great. It is quite possible that the idea of engraving the deeds of the Great King on solid rock had come from Persia. That the Old Persian language was well enough known in the court at Pāṭaliputra to influence the phrasing of Aśoka's edicts is an interesting suggestion, that is far from being proved. In any case there is a vast difference in the outlook of the two series. Darius rejoices in the defeat of his opponents by the aid of Ahuramazda and in the establishment of his wide Empire. Aśoka almost repents of his conquest of Kaliṅga. His main purpose is to promote Dhamma, the moral law or "law of piety," far and wide. He recounts the measures he has taken and issues orders in that behalf. Incidentally some light is thrown on the organisation of the Mauryan Empire and the nature of the public works carried out by a benevolent ruler of that period.

Some of Aśoka's measures however must be regarded as peculiar to himself. In their simplicity the Edicts possess a dignity of their own, which is missing in the flowery panegyrics of later times.

Taking Prakrit literature in the wide sense, we must assign the most important place to **Pali**. Its claim to this place is due not only to its antiquity, but also to the inherent worth and historical interest of the early Buddhist literature. Of all the Indian religions, Buddhism has had the profoundest effect on Asia as a whole. The Pali **Tipiṭaka** or "Triple Casket" contains the oldest surviving scriptures of that religion. Moreover from the Pali books we get incidentally a view of Indian life, that serves to supplement the more pedantic outlook of the orthodox priesthood and the romances of the bards.

Every student of Indian History should at least read some of the **Jātakas** or Birth Stories of the Buddha.[1] Representations of these stories and scenes from the life of the Buddha occur continually on the sculptured panels of Buddhist *stūpas* and *vihāras*. Indeed without a knowledge of the outlines of the Buddhist doctrine, and some comprehension of the lives of Buddhists, lay and cleric, as revealed by these old scriptures, the student cannot really grasp what was one of the dominant factors in Indian History for more than a thousand years after the Founder's death. The student of Indian Philosophy will find that acute reasoning and bold speculation were not confined to the orthodox schools of thought, but also found among the Bauddhas.

History is represented by the versified monkish chronicles contained in the **Mahāvaṃsa** dealing with the early history of Ceylon.

The term Prakrit Literature however does not ordinarily include Pali Literature. If Pali works be excluded, then the greater part of the whole of Prakrit Literature is made up of **Jain Literature.** This, as we have seen, is found in three distinct Prakrits.

Ardha-Māgadhī is the language of the oldest Jain books, which form the Canon of the **Śvetâmbara** sect. This canon comprises 45 *āgamas* including eleven *aṅgas* and twelve *upâṅgas*. These are sometimes spoken of under their Prakrit names and sometimes under the Sanskrit equivalents, e.g.,

1st Aṅga. Āyāraṅga-suttaṃ = *Ācārâṅga-sūtram*.
2nd ,, Sūya-gaḍaṅgaṃ = *Sūtrakṛtâṅgam*.
7th ,, Uvāsaga-dasāo = *Upāsaka-daśāḥ*.[2]
1st Upâṅga. Ovavāīya-suttaṃ = *Aupapātika-sūtram*.

This great collection of writings was arranged by Devaḍḍhi Gaṇin in the 5th century A.D. The date of the completion of

---

[1] See Bibliography.

[2] Edited and translated by Hoernle in the Bibliotheca Indica.

the work is given as 980 years after the entrance to *nirvāṇa* of the Founder of Jainism, i.e., A.D. 454 (or possibly A.D. 514).

The older books, called *Pūrvas*, on which this redaction was based, have completely disappeared. Thus the collection contains materials of different centuries mixed together, so that it is difficult to distinguish them. Some portions are ascribed to Bhadrabāhu (about 300 B.C.). One such work is the **Kappa-suttaṃ**[1] (*Kalpa-sūtram*) which contains a life of Mahāvīra. This apparently is not really older than the 5th century A.D.

The style of the oldest prose books is diffuse, delighting in elaborate descriptions and endless repetitions. Their chief interest to the general student lies in their incidental references to facts and circumstances of the ordinary everyday life in India.

The oldest *Kāvya* work in Jain literature is the Paümacariÿa, which gives a version of the Rāmāyaṇa. It dates perhaps from the 3rd century A.D.[2]

In **Jain Māhārāṣṭrī** there are non-canonical books of the Śvetâmbaras, consisting mainly of collections of stories: stories from the lives of famous saints, and narratives of the conversion of various people to the Jain religion. The Śvetâmbara literature has as yet been only partially explored by modern scholars, and much material both for philology and for history awaits scientific treatment. Even less known are the works of the **Digambara** sect in **Jain Śaurasenī**. Bhandarkar has published extracts from the Pavaÿaṇa-sāra of Kundakund-âcārya and the Kattigeÿâṇupĕkkhā of Kārttikeyasvāmin, both of which are in verse.

Jain literature is neither so famous, nor so widely studied as the Pali Buddhist literature. Much of it is still in manuscript, or in uncritical editions. Much of it again is difficult without (and even with) a commentary.

---

[1] Edited by Jacobi, and translated in Sacred Books of the East Series. See Bibliography.

[2] It contains a number of vulgarisms, which foreshadow the Apabhraṃśa stage.

Apart from the Jain Canon the early literary development of Ardhamāgadhī has been deduced from its occurrence in certain inscriptions, and in fragments of plays[1] ascribed to Aśvaghoṣa or his contemporaries. Jain Māhārāṣṭrī is found in the Kakkuka inscription.

For the purposes of **Kāvya** however the most important Prakrit was from an early date **Māhārāṣṭrī**.[2] This was the language of the Prakrit Epics and Lyrics, and formed the starting point for Prakrit Grammarians.

Most famous of the Epics is the **Setubandha**, a work of such excellent technique, that it has often been ascribed to Kālidāsa. The poem, which is called in Prakrit *Rāvaṇavaho* or *Dahamuhavaho*, relates the story of Rāma, but is supposed to commemorate the building of a bridge of boats in Srinagar by Pravarasena, king of Kashmir.[3]

The **Gaüḍavaho** celebrates the conquest of Bengal by Yaśovarman of Kanauj about the end of the seventh century A.D. Its author's name was **Bappaïrāa** (= *Vākpatirāja*) possibly a *nom de plume*. The same author composed another Epic *Mahumahaviaa* of which only one or two verses have been preserved.

The Rāvaṇavaho and the Gaüḍavaho have both been much influenced by Sanskrit models, and delight in long compounds.

The last eight cantos of Hemacandra's *Dvyāśraya-Mahākāvyam* form a small Prakrit Epic entitled *Kumārapālacarita* describing

---

1 See p. 74.

2 Jacobi (Selected Narratives, Introd., 1886) suggested the 4th century A.D. as about the time when M. attained this position. Early inscriptions of M. country are of the Pali type: the latest of these (showing some instances of elision of single intervocal consonants) date from 150 and 200 A.D. The Jain Canon according to tradition was written down in 454 A.D. Its language [AMg.] was influenced by M. [Pischel denies this]. Daṇḍin praises the Setubandha.

3 Macdonell. Sanskrit Literature, p. 331. For Pravarasena II see Rājataraṅgiṇī, *Stein's trans.*: Bk. III, V. 354. For an attempted identification of Kālidāsa with Mātṛgupta, see Stein's note on verse 129.

the deeds of Kumārapāla of Aṇhilvāḍa in Gujarat. The object of these cantos, as of the whole work, is to illustrate the rules of the author's compendious Sanskrit and Prakrit grammar called Siddha-Hemacandra.

The most important work for the study of Māhārāṣṭrī is the **Sattasaī** (*Saptaśatakam*) of **Hāla**. This is an anthology comprising verses by many poets. One commentary gives 112 names, another, that of Bhuvanapāla, gives 384. The various recensions differ very much in the distribution of the verses, and probably few can now be definitely assigned to their authors. The collection is evidence of the immense amount of Māhārāṣṭrī poetry that must have been composed, but not preserved. Besides *Hāla* who is identified with *Sātavāhana* (spelled variously Śālivāhana, etc.) there are a few names known from other sources. *Hariuddha*, *Ṇandiuddha* and *Poṭṭisa* are mentioned in Rājaśekhara's Karpūramañjarī, Act I, p. 19,2. The Vidūṣaka says, "tā ujjuaṃ jeva kiṃ ṇa bhaṇīadi : amhāṇaṃ ceḍiā Hariuḍḍha-Ṇandiuḍḍha-Poṭṭisa-Hāla-ppahudīṇaṃ pi purado sukaï tti."[1]

The date of this anthology has not been determined. Weber put it in the 3rd century at earliest, but earlier than the 7th century. Macdonell says, the poet Hāla probably lived before 1000 A.D. Some confusion has been caused by the identification of this Hāla-Sātavāhana with the 17th king of the Andhra dynasty (68 A.D.).[2] Jacobi on the other hand identified him with the Sātavāhana, king of Pratiṣṭhāna, who induced the Jains to change their Church Calendar in 467 A.D.

There can be no doubt that this anthology, including lyric poets well known in the time of Rājaśekhara, was not put

---

1 In Lanman's racy translation this runs: "Then why don't you say it straight out: Our little pussy's a first-rate poet, ahead even of Harivṛddha, Nandivṛddha, Poṭṭisa and the rest." (Sukaï=*Sukavi.*)

2 See Vincent Smith, Early History of India, 2nd edition, p. 196, whence it has been copied by school histories of India.

together in the 1st century A.D.[1] when we should rather expect early Prakrit of the Pali stage. The introductory verses of the Sattasaī rather suggest that these love lyrics of the South were not so universally on the lips of men as they had formerly been.

Another anthology of similar material is the **Jaavallahaṃ** or Vajjālagga of Jayavallabha a Śvetâmbara Jain. It contains some 700 verses. Some of these are common to Hāla's collection.

Dramatic Prakrits. The ordinary use of three Prakrits (M. Ś. Mg.) in Sanskrit plays is familiar to every student of Sanskrit. The authorities however differ as to the precise allotment of the Prakrits among the rôles. The Mṛcchakaṭikam is one of the richest in its variety of Prakrit dialects.

The Hero of course, and male characters of similar standing, except the Vidūṣaka, speak and sing in Sanskrit. It is exceptional for a woman to speak Sanskrit, but the Nun in Mālatīmādhavam does so. A purely Prakrit play in which even the Hero speaks Prakrit is also exceptional. A well-known instance is the Camphor-cluster.

The author however thinks it well to explain why no Sanskrit has been used. In the Prologue the Stagemanager reflects, "Then why has the poet abandoned the Sanskrit language and undertaken a composition in Prakrit?" His assistant replies in Māhārāṣṭrī—

"parusā Sakkaabandhā Pāüa-bandho vi hoī suumāro |
"purisa-mahilāṇaṃ jettiam ihantaraṃ tettiam imāṇaṃ ||

"Sanskrit poems are harsh: but a Prakrit poem is very smooth: the difference between them in this respect is as great as that between man and woman."

Śaurasenī is the ordinary prose language of ladies and of the

1 Vincent Smith has evidently given too much weight to his "latest leading authority, on the relations between the vernacular language and the 'classical' or 'secondary' Sanskrit," i.e., Professor O. Franke's "Pali and Sanskrit," 1902. This is a book of some ingenuity, but little historical judgment.

jester. Māhārāṣṭrī is the corresponding verse dialect. Māgadhī is used by menials, dwarfs, foreigners and the like, e.g., the two policemen and the fisherman in Śakuntalā. It is also spoken by Jain monks and small boys.[1] MSS. and texts often assign the dialects contrary to the rules of Poetics and the statements of commentators. They also confuse the dialects, so that Māgadhī appears almost the same as Śaurasenī.

This mixture of languages in the Indian Drama has been much discussed, and various explanations suggested.

There is no exact parallel to the Indian usage. Comedy has always made fun of the speech of foreigners. Aristophanes brings in the Thracian barbarian Triballos, who speaks a jargon with a vague resemblance to Greek. The Phoenician tongue was parodied in Latin comedy, though the readings are too corrupt for much to be made of it now. Shakespeare's Welshmen and Frenchmen are familiar. Again the vulgar speech of common people, as opposed to the language of the educated, has always found its way on to the comic stage. Dialect also, in a more or less conventional form, has appeared even in serious plays from Shakespeare's time onwards. Moreover in Greek Tragedy we have the chorus singing in a dialect different to the general language of the play. The Doric chorus

---

[1] The following note of characters supposed to speak Māgadhī as recorded by Pischel (§23) may be useful to students of the Drama.

Mṛcchakaṭikam: Śakāra, his servant Sthāvaraka, the shampooer-Kumbhīlaka, Vardhamānaka, the two Cāṇḍālas and Rohasena. *Śakuntalā*: Fisherman and two policemen; Sarvadamana, Śákuntalā's young son. *Prabodhacandrodaya*: the Cārvāka's pupil and the messenger from Orissa. *Mudrārākṣasa*; servant, Jain monk, messenger, Siddhārthaka and Samiddhārthaka while they appear as Cāṇḍālas. *Lalita-vigraharāja*: the bards and the spy (who also speaks Ś.). [Otherwise Turuṣka captives and spy. The Indian spy speakes Ś.]. *Veṇīsaṃhāra*: the Rākṣasa and his wife. *Mallikāmārutam*: elephant-keepers. *Nāgānanda*: servants. *Caitanyacandrodaya*: servants. *Caṇḍakauśikam*: Cāṇḍālas and Rascal. *Dhūrtasamāgama*: barber. *Hāsyārṇava*: Sādhuhiṃsaka. *Laṭakamelaka*: Digambara Jain. *Kaṃsavadha*: the Hunchback. *Amṛtodaya*: Jain monk.

in the Attic play, like other lyric poetry, is in a *conventional* dialect, a literary poetic language based on the Doric dialects,[1] in fact what in India would be called a (literary) Prakit.

The Indian usage however differs from all these partial parallels. In the first place we may find four, and regularly three, different dialects used in the same household, nay by members of the same family; secondly, one of these is a learned ('dead') language belonging to a previous stage of linguistic development; thirdly, dialects purporting to represent widely distant areas are combined in a single play, and assigned to particular characters without any obvious reason; and finally, the practice has been reduced to definite rules.

The systematisation of the Dramatic Prakrits is not surprising. Everything else about the Drama has been classified and codified, from the virtues of the various sorts of Hero to the 'faults' in the endless kinds of poetic ornament. The making of minute rules seems to have characteristic of the Brahman in all ages.

Explanations of this Sanskrit-Prakrit Drama may follow two or three different lines. One line is the **Realistic**: namely that the conversations in the plays represent the actual conditions of Indian life in say the Gupta period. Grierson writes: "In India there is nothing extraordinary in such a polyglot medley. It is paralleled by the conditions of any large house in Bengal at the present day, in which there are people from every part of India each of whom speaks his own language and is understood by the others, though none of them attempts to speak what is not his mother tongue."[2] Beames suggested a similar explanation.[3] Of course it is admitted that the dialects are conventional in form, not faithful copies of spoken vernacular,

---

[1] See Giles, Manual of Comparative Philology. §§ 614–6. Almost every word of these three sections dealing with Greek dialects can be applied to Indian dialects.

[2] Encyclopaedia Britannica, 11th ed., Vol. 22, p. 254.

[3] Grammar, Vol. I, p. 7.

also that the assignment of a particular dialect to a particular sort of menial may have been more or *less* true to fact. Again, granted that educated men could speak Sanskrit and that ladies generally could not, it is not to be supposed that the men could speak nothing but Sanskrit, and habitually addressed not only their wives but even their grooms in that language.

The well-educated man was able to speak Sanskrit. The hero therefore spoke Sanskrit, and by a stage convention spoke it always, just as stage kings almost always, and real kings rarely, wear a crown.

Of course this explanation implies that the form of the classic drama was fixed in the Śaurasenī country. Another line must be adopted to explain the use of Māhārāṣṭrī in verse. This is clearly a case of Literary convention. A school of lyric poetry developed in the South and became famous far beyond the borders of the Great Kingdom. Māhārāṣṭrī verses were doubtless sung throughout India as Persian verses still are. It was natural to regard this dialect as the only appropriate one for Prakrit songs.

It is more difficult to account for the use for the other dialects along this line.[1] The solution of the problem is obviously bound up with the history of the origin and development of the Indian drama. Of this we have little direct knowledge. Opinions have differed as to whether richness in Prakrit, as in the case of the Mṛcchakaṭikam, is a sign of early or of late date. Again some authorities believe in an original Prakrit drama to which Sanskrit was added later.

A Prakrit origin has been proposed not only for the Drama, but also for the Epic and Purāṇas,[2] that the Bṛhatkathā was

---

[1] Sylvain Lévi—Le Théatre Indien (1890), p. 331, suggested that the use of Śaurasenī was connected with the development of the Krishṇa cult at Mathurā, the capital of the Śūrasena country. The use of Māgadhī he would regard as a legacy from the ancient *Māgadhas,* the bards of Magadha.

[2] Pargiter. Dynasties of the Kali Age. Grierson. Enc. Brit. Prakrit, p. 253. Compare also the theories of the origin of the Pañcatantra

composed in Paiśācī Prākriṭ is recorded by literary tradition (*vide* p. 79 above). The evidence for Prakrit originals of the Mahābhārata and Purāṇas consists in small points of grammar and metre considered to point to *translation* from Prakrit. The question cannot be discussed here. It should be remembered however that all poetry and verse, that has had a *popular* origin, must have existed (in some form however indefinite and fluctuating) in the popular speech before it was crystallised in Sanskrit. If the poem be old enough, the original must have been current in Primary Prakrit, not in Middle Indian. Primary Prakrit would not be identical with the "Sanskrit" of Pāṇini but it would bear a strong family resemblance thereto. Progressive Sanskritising at a later period, acting unevenly on various portions of the work, would produce much the sort of phenomenon we actually find in the Epic Dialect. Such a Sanskritisation of Primary Prakrit is very different in its significance from translation out of a Middle Indian Prakrit into the Classical Sanskrit.

A special section of Prakrit Literature is formed by the **Prakrit Grammars.**

The oldest authority is the *Bhāratīyanāṭyaśāstra* which gives only a short description of Prakrit grammar in verses 6–23 of Chapter 17. Chapter 32 contains examples in Prakrit. Unfortunately the text of this work is so corrupt, that little use can be made of it.

There seems to be no good authority for ascribing to Pāṇini a grammar called *Prākṛtalakṣaṇa*. The oldest Prakrit grammar extant is the **Prākṛtaprakāśa** of **Vararuci Kātyāyana,** who has been identified with the author of the *Vārttikas* on Pāṇini.[1] The oldest commentary on the *Prākṛta-prakāśa* is the Manoramā of Bhāmaha. With this commentary the work has been edited

(Hertel). Jayadeva's Gītagovinda is supposed to be based on an Apabhraṃśa original. (Pischel.)

[1] For the authorities see Pischel Gr. § 32.

and translated by Cowell. (See Bibliography.) In Chapter X on Paiśācī Bhāmaha gives two short quotations which may be from the lost Bṛhatkathā.[1]

Caṇḍa in his **Prākṛtalakṣaṇa** deals with M. and the Jain Prākrits (AMg. JM. JŚ.) together. The arrangement of the work shows it is comparatively ancient.

The most important of the Prakrit grammars is that of **Hemacandra** of Gujarat (1088–1172 A.D.).

This forms the eighth chapter of his Siddha-Hemacandra, the first seven chapters of which deal with Sanskrit grammar. The same author compiled a Deśīnāmamālā.

Other grammars are :—The last chapter of the *Saṃkṣiptasāra* of *Kramadīśvara* ; this follows Vararuci and is of little value. *Prākṛtavyākaraṇa* of *Trivikramadeva* (about 13th century) follows Hemacandra.

Prākṛtasarvasvam of *Mārkaṇḍeya Kavīndra* who lived in Orissa in the reign of a Mukundadeva (perhaps 17th century).

Prākṛtakalpataru of Rāmatarkavāgīśa and many others of less importance.

Isolated verses in **Apabhraṃśa** occur in Jain works, in treatises on poetics and in late collections of stories like the Seventy Tales of a Parrot and the Twenty-five Tales of the Vampire. More remarkable is the inclusion by many MSS. of Apabhraṃśa verses in the 4th Act of the Vikramôrvaśīyam to be recited by King Purūravas.[2] Another source of Late Prakrit or Apabhraṃśa verses is the Prākṛta-Paiṅgalam, a work on metre of the fourteenth century or later.[3] The language is so late that Jacobi questions its right to be called Apabhraṃśa.

---

1 Under Sūtra 4. *ivasya pivaḥ* || Kamalaṃ piva mukhaṃ. Sūtra 14. *hṛdayasya hitaakaṃ* || Hitaakaṃ harasi me taluni.

2 S.P. Pandit (Bombay Sanskrit Series) omits them as spurious. His reasons for doing so have been disputed, but they are now generally regarded as later additions.

3 Edited by C. M. Ghosh in the Bibliotheca Indica, with commentaries, various readings and glossary.

It is almost to be classed with the old forms of the modern vernaculars.

The most important Apabhraṃśa work now available is the **Bhavisattakaha** of **Dhaṇavāla.**[1] This describes the adventures of a merchant's son Bhaviṣyadatta, his travels abroad and the part he took in the war between Kurujāṅgala and Potana, which last Jacobi thinks may be Taxila. Then comes the history of the chief characters in former and later births.

[1] Edited with introduction and vocabulary by H. Jacobi. Munich, 1918. (German.)

PART II.

Śauraseni. **Extract No. 1.**

Interlude preceding the 2nd Act of the **Ratnāvalī**. A dialogue between the heroine's two girl-friends Susaṅgadā and Ṇiuṇiā.

Susaṅgadā enters with a *maina* in a cage.

Susaṅ: Haddhī haddhī[1] | Adha kahiṃ dāṇiṃ mama hatthe imaṃ sāriaṃ ṇikkhivia[2] gadā me piasahī Sāariā bhavissadi? (*Looking another way*) Esā khu[3] Ṇiuṇiā, idŏ jjĕvva āacchadi.

[*Enter Nipuṇikā*].

Nipu: Uvaladdho[4] khu mae bhaṭṭiṇo vuttanto: tā jāva gadua bhaṭṭiṇīe ṇivedemi. (*Steps round*).

Susaṅ: Halā Ṇiuṇie! Kahiṃ dāṇiṃ vimhaâkhittahiaā[5] via idha-ṭṭhidaṃ maṃ avadhīria ido adikkamasi?

Nipu: Kadhaṃ Susaṅgadā? Halā Susaṅgade! suṭṭhu tae jāṇidaṃ.[6] Edaṃ[7] khu mama vimhaassa kāraṇaṃ.

---

1 Haddhī=*hā dhik*. Adha § 14. Kahiṃ in form a loc. sing.=*kasmin* also used for "where?" and "whither?" dāṇiṃ § 74.

2 ṇikkhivia gerund of ṇikkhivadi (*ni+kṣip*). In the previous Act the Heroine Sāgarikā mentioned giving her *maina* into Susaṅgadā's charge, "Sāriā mae Susaṅgadāe hatthe samappidā" (=*samarpitā*) before going with Queen Vāsavadattā to the Love God's grove, where indeed she saw not the God but the King. gadā § 125. piasahī §§ 9, 45, 13.

3 Capoller has Esă kkhu for esā khu (=*khalu* § 74) but only e and o should be so shortened in Ś. (Pischel, § 94). idŏ jjĕvva § 68 (2).

4 uvaladdho §§ 17, 125. mae § 106. bhaṭṭiṇo § 96. tā from vedic *tāt* "so." jāva §§ 1,29. gadua, gerund § 122. "So I will go and tell my mistress."

5 vimhaa § 47. ākhitta (*ā√kṣip*) § 125. hiaa §§ 9, 60. via=*iva* (from (*v*)*iva*). (ṭ)ṭhida (*√sthā*) § 125. adikkamasi (*ati√kram*).

6 suṭṭhu § 38. jāṇidam § 125 (*√jñā*) "you are quite right."

7 edaṃ § 12.

Ajja[1] kila bhaṭṭā Siri-pavvadādo āadassa Siri-Khaṇḍa-Dāsaṇāmadheassa dhammiassa saāsādo aāla-kusuma-sañjaṇaṇa-dohalaṃ sikkhia, attaṇo[2] parigahidaṃ ṇomāliaṃ kusuma-samiddhi-sohidaṃ[3] karissadi tti edaṃ vuttantaṃ devīe ṇivedidum pesida mhi. Tumaṃ uṇa[4] kahiṃ paṭṭhidā ?

Susaṅ: Piasahiṃ Sāariaṃ aṇṇesiduṃ.[5]

Nipu: Diṭṭhā[6] mae Sāariā gahida-samuggaa-citta-phalaa-vattiā kaalīharaṃ pavisantī. Tā gaccha piasahiṃ. Ahaṃ pi Devīsaāsaṃ[7] gamissaṃ.

[*Exeunt*].

Translation.

Susaṅ: Oh dear, oh dear! Now wherever has Sāariā got to after thrusting this mainā into my hand? (*Looking another way*) Why, here is Ṇiuṇiā coming this way.

[*Enter Nipuṇikā*].

Nipu: Well I have received this news from the master, so I will just go and tell my mistress. (*Steps round.*)

Susaṅ: Hullo Ṇiuṇiā! why, how is this? you seem altogether perplexed, and go walking off without noticing me standing here.

Nipu: What Susaṅgadā? Hullo Susaṅgadā! You are quite right. This is the cause of my perplexity. To-day the

---

[1] ajja § 44. Siri § 68. pavvadādo "from the mountain." § 50, § 86. āada § 2. dhammia 'righteous' here="juggler," dhammiassa saāsādo "from a juggler" (*sakāśāt*). aāla=*akāla*.

[2] attaṇo § 100. gahida (√*grah*) § 125. ṇomāliā § 75.

[3] "bright with an abundance of flowers." tti § 74. pesidā mhi § 68(1) (*pra+iṣ*).

[4] uṇa "but" (*punar* in this meaning is treated as an enclitic § 3: meaning "again" it becomes puṇo). paṭṭhidā (*pra*+√*sthā*).

[5] aṇṇesidum Inf. fr. aṇṇesadi (*anu*+√*iṣ*).

[6] diṭṭha (*dṛś*) § 125. samuggaa "box" (*samudga+ka*). citta-phalaa "painting tablet," vattiā "paint brush" (*vartikā* also means "wick," cf. H. battī). kaalīharaṃ for kaalīgharaṃ.

[7] saāsaṃ "to," pi § 74.

master learned from a juggler named Siri Khaṇḍa Dāsa, returned from the mountain of Śrī, about the longing to see flowers produced out of season, and I have been sent to inform the Queen, that he will make a jasmine bright with an abundance of flowers if she will embrace it. But where are you off to ?

Susaṅ : To hunt for our Sāariā.

Nipu : I saw Sāariā with her paint-box, tablet and brush going into the plantain-house. So go to your friend. I will go to the Queen.

Śaurasenī. Extract No. 2.

Ratnāvalī, Act II. Soliloquy of Sāgarikā and conversation with Susaṅgatā.

[*Enter Sāgarikā with a painting tablet, and evidently in love*].

Sā : Hiaa, pasīda pasīda.[1] Kiṃ imiṇā[2] āāsa-mettaphalaeṇa dullahajaṇa-ppatthaṇâṇubandheṇa ? Aṇṇaṃ ca. Jeṇa jĕvva diṭṭhamĕtteṇa īdiso[3] saṃtāvo vaṭṭadi puṇo vi taṃ jĕvva pekkhiduṃ ahilasasi tti aho de[4] mūḍhadā ! Adiṇisaṃsa[5] hiaa. Jammado[6] pahudi saha saṃvaḍḍhidaṃ imaṃ jaṇaṃ pariccaia khaṇa-mĕtta-daṃsaṇaparicidaṃ[7] jaṇam aṇugacchanto ṇa lajjasi ? adha vā ko tuha doso ? Aṇaṅga-sarapaḍaṇabhīdeṇa[8] tae evvaṃ ajjhavasidaṃ. Bhodu ! Aṇaṅgaṃ dāva uvālahissaṃ.[9] (*Tearfully*) Bhaavaṃ Ku-

---

[1] Pasīda (*pra*+√*sad*).

[2] imiṇā=aṇeṇa. -mĕtta § 69. dullaha 'hard to attain', ppatthaṇā 'desire' (*prārthanā*). aṇṇaṃ § 48.

[3] īdiso § 70. saṃtāvo 'anguish' (*tap*). vaṭṭadi § 45. ahilasasi (*abhi*+*laṣ*).

[4] de § 3.

[5] *ati-nṛśaṃsa* 'very cruel.'

[6] Jammado 'from birth' pahudi § 12. vaḍḍhida past. part. (*vṛdh*). pariccaia cf. sacca § 44. (*pari*+*tyaj*).

[7] daṃsaṇa §§ 49, 64.

[8] paḍaṇa § 20 (cf. H. पड़ना). ajjhavasidaṃ cf. § 44. (*adhi*+*ava*+*so*) bhodu cf. § 75.

[9] uvālahissaṃ 'I will reproach' (*upa*+*ā*+*labh*).

sumâuha ṇijjida-surâsuro [1] bhavia, itthījaṇaṃ paharanto ṇa lajjasi? savvadhā mama mandabhāiṇīe imiṇā duṇṇimitteṇa [2] avassaṃ maraṇaṃ uvaṭṭhidaṃ. (*Looks at her tablet*) Tā jāva ṇa ko vi idha āacchadi tāva ālĕkkha-samappidaṃ [3] taṃ ahimadaṃ jaṇaṃ pekkhia [4] jadhāsamīhidaṃ karissaṃ. (*Takes the tablet and resolutely fixes her attention, then sighs*) Jaï vi adi-saddhaseṇa [5] vevadi aaṃ adimĕttaṃ me aggahattho, tadhā vi tassa jaṇassa aṇṇo daṃsaṇôvāo [6] ṇatthi tti jadhā tadhā ālihia pekkhissaṃ. [*Enter Susaṅgatā*].

Susaṅ: Edaṃ khu kaalīharaṃ tā jāva pavisāmi. (*Enters and looks surprised*) Kiṃ uṇa esā garuâṇurāâkhitta-hiaā [7] ālihantī ṇa maṃ pekkhadi. Tā jāva diṭṭhivadhaṃ se [8] parihaṛia ṇirūvaïssaṃ. (*Goes softly behind her, and looks over her shoulder. Delightedly*) Kadhaṃ? Bhaṭṭā ālihido! sāhu Sāarie sāhu! Adha vā ṇa kamalâaraṃ [9] vajjia rāahaṃsī aṇṇassiṃ ahiramadi.

Sā: (*Tearfully*) Ālihido mae eso. Kiṃ uṇa ṇivaḍantabāhasalilā [10] me diṭṭhī pekkhiduṃ ṇa pabhavadi. (*Looking up and forcing a smile*) Kadhaṃ Susaṅgadā? Sahi Susaṅgade ido uvavisa. [11]

---

1 ṇijjida (*nir+ji*). bhavia § 122 itthī (=*strī*) held to indicate old form *istrī. paharanto pres. part. (*pra+hṛ*).

2 duṇ-ṇimittaṃ 'omen.' uvaṭṭhidaṃ (*upa+sthā*).

3 =*ālekhya-samarpitam*.

4 pekkhia § 122.

5 saddhasa=*sādhvasa*.

6 uvāo. 'means' § 17. ṇatthi "isn't" § 83.

7 garua "heavy" § 71.

8 diṭṭhivadha=dṛṣṭipatha se 'her' § 109. parihaṛia. gerund (*pari+hṛ*). ṇirūvaissaṃ 'I will investigate' § 17.

9 kamalâaraṃ 'mass of lotuses,' a lotus pool. vajjia gerund of vajjadi (*vṛj*) "excepting."

10 ṇivaḍanta § 17. -bāha- (*bāṣpa*) against § 38. For "tear," apparently bappha becomes *bāpha—bāha (§§ 63. 13). In the meaning 'steam," etc., it remains bappha (cf. H. बाफ, भाप) (Pisch. § 305).

11 uvavisa (*upa+viś*).

Susaṅ : (*Approaching and looking at the tablet*) Sahi, ko eso tae ālihido ?

Sā : Sahi ṇaṃ paütta-mahûsavo[1] Bhaavaṃ Aṇaṅgo.

Susaṅ : (*Smiling*) Aho de ṇiuṇattaṇaṃ ! Kiṃ uṇa suṇṇaṃ via cittaṃ paḍibhādi ! tā ahaṃ pi ālihia Radi-saṇādhaṃ karissaṃ. (*Takes the brush and paints.*)

Sā : (*Indignantly on recognising the drawing*) Kīsa[2] tae ahaṃ ettha ālihidā ?

Susaṅ : Sahi kiṃ aāreṇa kuppasi[3]? Jādiso tae Kāmadevo ālihido, tādisī mae Radī ālihidā tā aṇṇadhā-saṃbhāviṇi kiṃ tuha ediṇā[4] ālavideṇa ? Kadhehi savvaṃ vuttantaṃ.

Sā : (*In confusion aside*) Ṇaṃ[5] jāṇida mhi piasahīe. (*Aloud*) Piasahi, mahadī khu me lajjā. Tā tadhā karesu[6] jadhā ṇa edaṃ vuttantaṃ avaro ko'vi jāṇissadi.

Susaṅ : Sahi, mā lajja, mā lajja.

Translation.

Sā : Be quiet, my heart, be quiet. What is the use of keeping on wanting a person that is unattainable ! It only results in trouble. Another thing—What folly is this, that though the mere sight of him results in such anguish, thou desirest to see him again ! Cruel, cruel heart ! art not thou ashamed to desert this person that has grown up with you from birth, and go after one known only from a moment's glance ? Nay what fault is it of thine ? Thou didst so determine when frightened by the falling of the Love-God's arrows. Be it so, then I will chide the God of Love. Revered Lord of the Flower Bow, after vanquishing Gods and Demons art not ashamed to harry womenfolk ?

---

1 paütta § 125 (*pra+vṛt*).

2 Kīsa "why ?" ettha "here" § 70.

3 kuppasi "art angry."

4 ediṇā=edeṇa. ālavida (ā+*lap*). savva § 45. (H. sab).

5 ṇaṃ=*nūnám*.

6 karesu § 116. avaro § 17. (H. aur).

Utterly ill-fated that I am, this omen inevitably means my death is imminent.

So while no one is coming, I will just gaze at this beloved one in picture limned, and gaze to my heart's content. Although perturbation makes my finger shake so violently, yet I have no other means of seeing him, so I shall see him just as I draw him.

Susaṅ : This must be the plantain house. So I will go in. Why her heart is so beset with deep attachment that she does not see me as she draws. I will avoid her line of vision and find out what she is up to. What ? drawn the master, Bravo, Sāariā bravo ! Of course a swan does not delight in ought but a lotus-pool.

Sā : I have drawn him, but my sight is drowned in falling tears and cannot see him. What Susaṅgadā ? Sit down here my dear Susaṅgadā.

Susaṅ : Who is this you have painted ?

Sā : The Revered Lord of Love, whose great Festival it is.

Susaṅ : Ah, how clever you are ! But the picture seems rather empty. So I will paint in Rati at his side.

Sā : Why have you drawn *me* there ?

Susaṅ : My dear, why are you angry without any reason ? I have drawn a Rati to match your God of Love ! So, dissembler, away with circumlocution, and tell me all about it.

Sā : So she has found me out—the dear !

My dear, I am much ashamed. So do take care that nobody else comes to know of it.

Susaṅ : My dear, there's nothing to be ashamed of.

Śauraseni. **Extract No. 3.**

This extract is taken from the Bengal recension edited by Pischel (1877) p. 29. (Act II, beginning.) A comparison with usual or "Devanāgarī" version will show that considerable liberties must have been taken with the original text. Here the king carries a bow in his hand and wears a garland of forest flowers, in the other version he is attended by **Javaṇīhiṃ** 'with Yavana women' who carry the bows and wear the flowers. There the king passes a sleepless night thinking of his beloved, here it is the Vidūṣaka who cannot sleep though worrying about his return—to luxury!

The Vidūṣaka in the second act of Śakuntalā describes his troubles as companion to a sportive monarch.

Hī māṇahe,[1] hado mhi, edassa miaā-sīlassa[2] raṇṇo vaassabhāveṇa ṇivviṇṇo. 'Aaṃ mao,[3] aaṃ varāho' tti majjhandiṇe vi gimhe virala-pādava-cchāāsu vaṇa-rāīsuṃ[4] āhiṇḍia, patta-saṃkara-kasāa-virasāiṃ[5] uṇha-kaḍuāiṃ pijjanti giri-ṇaī-salilāiṃ. Aṇiada-velaṃ[6] ca uṇhuṇhaṃ maṃsaṃ bhuñjīadi. Turaa-gaāṇaṃ ca saddeṇa rattiṃ[7] pi ṇatthi pakāma-suidavvaṃ. Mahantě jjeva paccūse[8] dāsīe puttehiṃ sāuṇia-luddhehiṃ kaṇṇôvaghādiṇā[9] vaṇagamaṇa-kolāhaleṇa pabodhīāmi.[10] ettikeṇâvi[11] dāva pīḍā ṇa vuttā jado gaṇḍassa uvari vipphoḍao

---

[1] Hī māṇahe, an exclamation assigned by high authority to Vidūṣakas, expressing weariness. Another reading is Hī hī bhō. This however is said to express astonishment.

[2] miaā 'hunting.' raṇṇo § 99. ṇivviṇṇo 'disgusted' (*nir+vid*).

[3] mao "deer." majjhaṃdiṇe cf. § 69. gimhe 'in summer' § 47. pādava 'tree' § 17.

[4] vaṇa-rāīsu 'in forest tracks.' āhiṇḍia 'wandering' hiṇḍ a Prākritic, possibly non-āryan root, "to wander" cf. āhiṇḍaa=traveller (Mṛcch.)

[5] patta 'leaf' § 45. saṃkara "mixture." uṇha 'hot' § 47. kaḍua 'bitter.' pijjanti Passive 'are drunk.'

[6] aṇiada 'uncertain' (√*yam*). bhuñjīadi Passive 'is eaten.'

[7] rattiṃ pi, acc. of duration, 'Through the night': the other version has rattimmi vi 'even at night.' suidavvaṃ=suvidavvaṃ from suvadi 'sleeps.'

[8] paccūse 'at dawn' cf. § 44. sāuṇia (=*śākunika*) -luddha (=*lubdha*, commoner *lubdhaka*) 'hunter, 'fowler.'

[9] 'ear-splitting.' kaṇṇa cf. Panjabi kann, H. kān. vaṇa-gamaṇa 'forest-going,' i.e. of foresters not of ascetics. The other version has -ggahaṇa 'forest-taking' explained by commentary as a "drive." This makes better sense.

[10] pabodhīāmi 'am awakened' passive.

[11] Ś. ěttika (M. ěttia) *etāvat*. vuttā 'finished' (*vṛt*). vipphoḍao 'a pimple on top of a boil' (*vi+sphuṭ*).

saṃvutto. Jeṇa[1] kila amhesuṃ avahīṇesuṃ tattha-bhavadā maâṇusāriṇā assama-padaṃ paviṭṭheṇa[2] mama adhaṇṇadāe Saüntalā ṇāma kā vi tāvasa-kaṇṇaā diṭṭhā. Taṃ pekkhia sampadaṃ ṇaara-gamaṇassa kadhaṃ[3] pi ṇa karedi. Edaṃ jjeva cintaantassa mama pahādā[4] acchīsuṃ raaṇī. Tā kā gadī? Jāva ṇaṃ kidâāraparikammaṃ[5] pia-vaassaṃ pekkhāmi. Eso bāṇâsaṇa-hattho hiaa-ṇihida-pia-aṇo vaṇa-puppha-mālā-dhārī ido jjeva āacchadi piavaasso. Bhodu aṅga-madda-vialo[6] bhavia ciṭṭhissaṃ, evaṃ pi ṇāma vissāmaṃ[7] laheaṃ.

Translation.

Heigho! I am weary to death of being companion to this king with his hunting habits. After wandering along tracks in the jungle with hardly a tree to give shade, in the middle of a summer day, mind you, with cries of 'Here's a deer' or 'Here's a boar'; then the water we drink is from mountain streams warm, bitter, and with a nasty astringent flavour from being mixed with leaves. Meals at ungodly hours, and nothing to eat but meat, burning hot! Even during the night it is impossible to get proper sleep for the noise the horses and elephants make. At earliest dawn the rascally[8] fowlers wake me with the earsplitting din of a forest drive.[9] And with all this my troubles are not ended, for now there's a pimple on top of the boil. For (yesterday) after leaving us behind, His

1 The other version has hio 'yesterday' § 58. amhesuṃ loc. plur. § 106. The anusvāra is optional.

2 paviṭṭha (*pra+viś*) adhaṇṇadā 'misfortune,' § 48. Saüntalā, this is correct not Saündalā.

3 kadhaṃ 'mention' § 13. (*kathām*).

4 pahādā (*pra+bhā*). acchīsuṃ loc. plur. § 39.

5 kida § 125, āāra (*ācāra*), parikammo "toilet."

6 madda 'crushing,' 'bruising' (*mṛd*); the other version has bhaṅga. vialo (=*vikalo*) 'lame.'

7 vissāmaṃ 'rest' (*vi-śram*). laheaṃ opt § 117, (ii) (*labh*).

8 Literally 'sons of a slave (girl),' mere abuse like the mediaeval "whoreson" so frequent in Shakespearian comedy.

9 Reading -ggahaṇa.

Highness in pursuit of a deer entered a hermitage and to my misfortune, caught sight of some hermit girl called Saüntalā. From the moment he saw her, not a word does he say about returning to town. I was thinking of this when night dawned on my eyes. Well, what's to be done ? I will go and see my good friend when he has finished his usual toilet. (*Steps round and looks up*). Here he comes with bow in hand, his beloved fixed in his heart, and a garland of forest flowers round his neck. Good, I will pretend my limbs are so knocked about I can't stand up straight. So perhaps I may get a rest. (*Stands leaning on his staff*.

Śaurasenī. Extract No. 4.

Śakuntalā before the King, who has forgotten her (Act 5).[1] (*Aside*) Imaṃ avatthantaraṃ [2] gade tādise aṇurāe kiṃ vā sumarāvideṇa.[3] Adha vā attā dāṇiṃ me sodhaṇīo.[4] Bhodu, vavasissaṃ.[5] (*Aloud*) Ajjaütta, (*Breaks off*) Adha vā saṃsaido[6] dāṇiṃ eso samudāāro.[7] Porava! juttaṃ[8] ṇāma tuha purā assamapade sabbhāv-uttāṇa-hiaaṃ[9] imaṃ jaṇaṃ tadhā samaa-puvvaṃ[10] saṃbhāvia saṃpadaṃ īdisehiṃ akkharehiṃ paccācakkhiduṃ.[11]

---

1 Pischel's Edition, p. 104. cf. Monier Williams, p. 203.

2 'Changed condition.'

3 Past part. caus. of sumaredi.

4 sodhaṇīo caus. gerundive (*śudh*). The other version has soaṇīo 'to be sorrowed for.'

5 vavasissaṃ fut. (*vi+ava+so*) 'I will decide.' Comm. supplies 'to tell a secret.' Perhaps "will make an effort." Ajjaütta § 2.

6 "questionable" (*sam+śī*).

7 =*samudācāro* "address." i.e. the word 'Ajjaütta." In the drama this is the regular form of address for a wife to her husband, but it is not limited to this relation.

8 juttaṃ ṇāma 'It is fitting forsooth' § 34. Other version has ṇa juttaṃ ṇāma.

9 "Open-hearted through good nature."

10 With (preceded by) a contract (*samaya*). saṃbhāvia. The other version has patāria 'having seduced' or 'misled,' akkhara 'syllable,' 'word.'

11 'To repulse' (*prati+ā+cakṣ*).

The King is shocked and indignant.[1]

Śakuntalā continues :—

Bhodu. Paramatthado[2] jaï para-pariggaha-saṅkiṇā tae edaṃ paüttaṃ, tā ahiṇṇāṇeṇa[3] keṇa vi tuha[4] saṃdehaṃ avaṇa-issaṃ.[5]

[The King mutters a legal phrase about the 'Primary Rule'].

Haddhī haddhī! aṅgulīaa-suṇṇā[6] me aṅgulī. (*Turns in distress to Gautamī*).

Gautamī: Jāda[7] ṇaṃ de Sakkâvadāre Sacītitthe[8] udaaṃ vandamāṇāe pabbhaṭṭhaṃ aṇgulīaaṃ.

[The King smiles and reflects on female cunning].

Śak: Ettha[9] dāva vihiṇā daṃsidaṃ pahuttaṇaṃ,[10] Avaraṃ de kadhaissaṃ.[11]

[The King is still willing to listen].

Ṇaṃ ekkadiasaṃ vedasa-ladā-maṇḍavae ṇaliṇī-vatta-bhāaṇa-gadaṃ[12] udaaṃ tuha hatthe saṃṇihidaṃ āsī.[13]

[The King still listens].

Takkhaṇaṃ[14] so mama putta-kidao maa-sāvao uvatthido. Tado tae aaṃ dāva paḍhamaṃ[15] pivadu tti aṇukampiṇā uva-

---

1 Sanskrit coming between the Śaurasenī speeches has been omitted.

2 =*paramārthato* 'really.' jaï **Ś.** has also jadi § 1. pariggaha 'wife.' pauttaṃ § 125 (*yuj*).

3 'token.' The name of the play in Śaurasenī would be Ahiṇṇāṇa-Saüntalaṃ.

4 Pischel read tava. In 1900 he would have preferred the other reading tuha. cf. Grammar § 421.

5 (*apa+nī*).

6 'devoid of its ring.'

7 Jāda "my son"

8 Śakrāvatāre Śacītīrthe. pabbhaṭṭhaṃ 'slipped off' (*pra+bhraṃś*).

9 ettha 'here.' § 70.

10 =(*prabhu-tvam*) -ttaṇaṃ goes back to= -*tvanam*.

11 kadhaissaṃ § 134.

12 'lying in a lotus-leaf cup.'

13 āsī § 133.

14 =*tat kṣaṇam*. puttakidao 'foster-child.' The compound is inverted. maa-sāvao 'fawn' (-*śābaka*).

15 paḍhamaṃ § 20. uvacchandido 'coaxed' (*upa+chand*).

cchandido. Ṇa uṇa de avaricidassa[1] hatthādo udaaṃ avagado pādum. Pacchā tassiṃ jjevva udae mae gahide[2] kado teṇa paṇao.[3] Etthantare vihasia bhaṇidaṃ tae. "Saccaṃ savvo sagandhe vīsasadi,[4] jado duve vi tumhe āraṇṇakāo" tti.

[The King is touched, but thinks that these are "false honied words," and to Gautamī's protest replies with a verse on the guile of female cuckoos—much more the guile of women!]

Śakuntalā is indignant.

Aṇajja! attaṇo hiaâṇumāṇeṇa kila savvaṃ edaṃ pekkhasi. Ko ṇāma aṇṇo dhamma-kañcua-vavadesiṇo[5] taṇa-chaṇṇa-kūvôvamassa tuha aṇukārī bhavissadi.

[Duṣyanta's acts are well known—says the King. This is nonsense].

Sutthu. Dāṇiṃ attacchandâṇuāriṇī saṃvutta mhi jā imassa Puru-vaṃsassa paccaeṇa[6] muha-mahuṇo hiaa-pattharassa hattha-bbhāsaṃ uvagadā.

(*Hides her face in the end of her sārī and weeps*).

Translation.

Śak: (*Aside*) When such love has so changed, what use is there in bringing it to mind? Yet it is for me to clear myself. Well, I will try. (*Aloud*) My sweet lord! (*Breaks off*) Nay this address may now be questioned. Scion of the Purus! It is meet forsooth for thee after union with me at that time in the hermitage, after a solemn pledge to me, that am open-hearted through good nature, now to repulse me with such words as those.

So be it. If in real truth you think I am another's wife and

---

1 avaricida 'stranger' (*a+pari+ci*).

2 gahida § 125.

3 paṇao 'confidence' (*pra+nī*).

4 vīsasadi=vissasadi (*vi+śvas*) cf. § 63. dhamma § 48.

5 vavadesi 'pretending' (*vi+apa+diś*). chaṇṇa "hidden."

6 paccaa (=*pratyaya*). patthara (cf. H. patthar) (*pra+stṛ*). abbhāsaṃ (=*abhyāśam*) sometimes written (*abhyāsam*) 'proximity,' etc.

hence your attitude, then I will remove your doubts with a token—alas! there is no ring on my finger.

Gautamī: Why, your ring must have slipped off when you were worshipping the water at Śacī's tīrtha in Śakrâvatāra.

Sak: In this indeed Fate shows its power! I will tell you another thing.—One day then in the Cane Bower some water lying in a lotus-leaf cup was resting in your hand—at that moment my fosterling, the fawn came up. Then you coaxed it gently that it should drink first. But it would not come to drink the water from your hand, as you were a stranger. Afterwards when I took that very water it gained confidence. Then you laughed and said—"Truly, everything trusts its kin, and both of you are forest-born."

Caitiff! You look at all this in the light of your own conscience. What other could resemble you airing the garb of virtue, but all the while like a hidden well in the grass?

Very well! Now am I become a wanton, who through trust in this race of Puru sought refuge with a man of honey-lips and a heart of stone.

Śauraseni. **Extract No. 5.**

Karpūra-mañjarī. Act. IV.[1]

The Heroine "Camphor Blossom" has been shut up in a room in the Queen's section of the palace, but there is a subterranean passage from this room to the palace-garden. The Queen has had the garden end of this passage closed up.

Sāraṅgikā enters to the King and Jester with a message from the Queen.

---

1 Harvard Oriental Series, No 4. An excellent edition of this play by Dr. Sten Konow with Vocabulary, and also a racy translation by Prof. Lanman, with some touches of Western *apabhraṃśa*! Text pp. 102-110. Trans. pp. 281–285.

Sāraṅgikā: (*Looking before her*) Eso mahārāo maragada-puñjādo[1] Kaalīgharaṃ aṇuppaviṭṭho. Tā gadua devīe viṇṇāvidaṃ[2] ṇivedemi. (*Approaches*) Jaadu jaadu bhaṭṭā. Devī viṇṇavedi jadhā sāaṃsamae[3] tumhe mae pariṇāi-davva[4] tti

Jester: Bhodi kiṃ edaṃ akaṇḍa-kumbhaṇḍa-paḍaṇaṃ ?[5]

King: Sāraṅgie savvaṃ vitthareṇa kadhesu.

Sāra: Edaṃ viṇṇavīadi.[6] Aṇantarādikkanta-caduddasī-divase[7] Devīe pömma-rāa-maī Gorī Bheravāṇandeṇa kadua paḍiṭṭhāvidā.[8] Aaṃ ca dikkhā-vihi-ppaviṭṭhāe[9] Devīe viṇṇatto[10] joīsaro guru-dakkhiṇā-ṇimittaṃ. Bhaṇidaṃ ca teṇa "Jaï avassaṃ dakkhiṇā dādavvā, tā esā dīadu."[11] Tado Devīe viṇṇattaṃ. "Jaṃ ādisadi Bhaavaṃ" ti. Puṇo vi ullavidaṃ[12] teṇa. "Atthi ettha Lāḍadese Caṇḍaseṇo ṇāma rāā. Tassa duhidā Ghaṇa-sāra-mañjari tti. Sā devva-ṇṇaehiṃ[13] ṇidiṭṭhā jadhā esā Cakkavaṭṭi-ghariṇī bhavissadi tti. Tado sā mahārāeṇa pariṇedavvā,[14]

---

1 maragada § 12. "emerald-heap" apparently the name of a seat or an arbour, whence the king watched 'Camphor-cluster' on the swing. aṇuppaviṭṭho (*anu+pra+viś*).

2 Past part, caus. (*vi+jñā*).

3 sāaṃsamae "in the evening."

4 Gerundive of causal (*pari+nī*), lit. "you are to be made to marry by me."

5 akaṇḍa 'unexpected' kumbhaṇḍa 'white gourd.' § 62. Lanman renders "shower of water-melons from a clear sky."

6 Causal Passive.

7 'On the fourteenth day just past'. pömma § 36 'made of rubies.'

8 Caus. p. part. (*prati+sthā*).

9 dikkhā 'consecration' vihi 'observances' -ppaviṭṭha (*pra+viś*) 'begun.'

10 viṇṇatto 'consulted' (=*vijñapto*), joīsaro 'sorcerer'—lord of *yoga*. dakkhiṇā 'present,' 'fee.'

11 dīadu Pass. Imperative 'let it be given.'

12 (*ut+lap*).

13 devvaṇṇaa 'soothsayer' (*daiva-jña+ka*), ṇidiṭṭhā (*ni+diś*). ghariṇī 'wife,' of a Cakkavaṭṭi 'Emperor.'

14 'Must be married.'

jeṇa gurussa[1] vi dakkhiṇā diṇṇā bhodi; bhaṭṭā vi Cakkavaṭṭī kido bhodi. Tado devīe vihasia bhaṇidaṃ "Jaṃ ādisadi Bhaavaṃ" ti. Ahaṃ ca viṇṇavedum pesidā. Guru-dakkhiṇā vi diṇṇā.

Jester: (*Laughing*) Edaṃ taṃ sīse sappo, desantare vejjo ?[2] Idha ajja vivāho, Lāḍadese Ghaṇasāramañjarī!

King: Kiṃ de Bheravāṇandassa pahāvo parŏkkho ?[3]

Sāra: Devīe kāridaṃ pamad-ujjāṇassa[4] majjha-ṭṭhida-vaḍa-tarumūle Cāmuṇḍâadaṇaṃ.[5] Bheravāṇando vi Devīe samaṃ tahiṃ āgamissadi. Tag-gade[6] a tak-khaṇa-vihide kodua-ghare vivāho bhavissadi—(*Steps about and exit*).

King: Vaassa! savvaṃ edaṃ Bheravāṇandassa viambhidaṃ[7] ti takkemi.

Jester: Evaṃ ṇedaṃ.[8] Ṇa hu maa-lañchaṇaṃ[9] antareṇa aṇṇo miaṅka-maṇi-puttaliaṃ[10] pajjharāvedi sehāliā-kusum-ukkaraṃ vā karedi.

[*Enters the magician Bhairavānanda*].

Bhaira: Iaṃ sā vaḍa-tarumūle ṇibbhiṇṇassa[11] suraṅgā-duvā-rassa pidhāṇaṃ Cāmuṇḍā. (*Stretches out his hand to her in worship and recites a verse in Māhārāṣṭrī*)—"Victorious is Kālī," etc. (*Enters and sits down*) Ajja vi ṇa ṇiggacchadi suraṅgā-duvāreṇa Kappūra-mañjarī.

---

1 gurussa § 90. diṇṇa § 125. viṇṇavedum "to inform."

2 Proverb. "Snake on the head, and doctor abroad," vejjo=*vaidyo* § 61.

3 pahāvo, "power" (*pra+bhū*), parokkha *paro'kṣa*.

4 'Pleasure-garden' (*pra+mad*), majjha § 44, -ṭṭhida §§ 38, 125.

5 āadaṇaṃ 'sanctuary' (*āyatanam*), tahiṃ § 27.

6 tag-gade=Skt. *tad-gate*, kodua=*kautuka*.

7 viambhidaṃ 'exploit, machination' (*vi+jṛmbh*). takkemi § 45.

8 ṇu+idaṃ.

9 'moon' (*mṛga-lāñchana*).

10 miaṅkamaṇi 'moon-gem,' puttaliā 'statue,' pajjharāvedi 'causes to ooze' caus. (*pra+kṣar*) § 40. sehāliā (=*śephālikā*), ukkara 'multitude.'

11 ṇibbhiṇṇa (*nir+bhid*), duvāra 'door' § 57.

[*Enters Karpūra-mañjarī making an opening in the mouth of the passage*].

Karpū : Bhaavaṃ paṇamāmi[1]!

Bhaira : Uidaṃ[2] varaṃ lahasu. Idha jjevva uvavisa.

[*Karpūra-mañjarī sits down*].

Bhaira : (*Aside*) Ajja vi ṇa edi Devī.

[*Enter the Queen*].

Queen : [*Stepping about and looking in front of her*]. Iaṃ Bhaavadī Cāmuṇḍā [*Bows. Then looking round*]. Iaṃ Kappūra-mañjarī. Tā kiṃ ṇedaṃ? (*To Bhairavānanda*) Idaṃ viṇṇavīadi,[3] ṇia-bhavaṇe vivāha-sāmaggiṃ kadua āada mhi. Tā geṇhia[4] āgamissaṃ.

Bhaira : Vacche evaṃ karīadu.

[*The Queen steps round as if departing*].

Bhaira : (*Laughing to himself*) Iaṃ Kappūra-mañjarī-ṭhāṇaṃ aṇṇesiduṃ[5] gadā.

(*Aloud*) Putti Kappūra-mañjari suraṅgā-duvāreṇa jjeva turida-padaṃ[6] gadua sa-ṭṭhāṇe ciṭṭha. Devīe āgamaṇe puṇo āgantavvaṃ.

[*Karpūra-mañjarī does so*].

Queen : Idaṃ rakkhā-gharaṃ.[7] (*Enters, looks around—aside*). Ae, iaṃ Kappūra-mañjarī! Sā kā vi sārikkhā[8] diṭṭhā. (*Aloud*) Vacche Kappūra-mañjari kīdisaṃ[9] de sarīraṃ?

---

1 (*pra+nam*).

2 =*ucitam*. lahasu § 116, note ii (*labh*). uvavisa (*upa+viś*).

3 viṇṇavīadi Caus. Pass. (*vi+jñā*). ṇiabhavaṇe 'in (my) own house.

4 geṇhia Gerund of geṇhadi (*grah*), vacchā 'girl' (=*vatsā*).

5 'to search.'

6 'at a quick pace' § 75. gadua § 122. sa-ṭṭhāṇe 'in your own room cf. § 20.

7 =*rakṣā-gṛham*.

8 sārikkhā 'like' §§ 66, 40.

9 kīdisaṃ § 70.

(*In the air*) Kiṃ bhaṇāsi maha siro-veaṇā [1] samuppaṇṇa tti. (*To herself*) Tā puṇo tahiṃ gamissaṃ. (*Enters and looks to every side*) Halā sahīo vivāhôvaaraṇāiṃ [2] lahuṃ geṇhia āacchadha. (*Steps about*).

[*Karpūra-mañjarī enters and sits down just as before*].

Queen: (*Looking before her*) Iaṃ Kappūra-mañjarī!

Bhaira: Vacche Vibbhamalehe āṇīdāiṃ [3] vivāhôvaaraṇāiṃ?

Queen: Adha iṃ! Kiṃ uṇa Ghaṇa-sāra-mañjarī-samuidāiṃ āharaṇāiṃ [4] visumaridāiṃ. Tā puṇo gamissaṃ.

Bhaira: Evaṃ bhodu.

[*Queen acts in pantomime as if making an exit*].

Bhaira: Putti Kappūra-mañjari taṃ jeva karīadu.[5]

[*Exit Karpūra-mañjarī*]

Queen: (*Pretends to enter the prison-room—seeing Karpūra-mañjarī*) Ae! Sārikkhadāe viṇaḍida [6] mhi. (*Aside*) Jhāṇavimāṇeṇa ṇivvigghaṃ parisappiṇā taṃ āṇedi joīsaro. (*Aloud*) Sahīo jaṃ jaṃ ṇivedidaṃ taṃ geṇhia āachadha. (*Pretends to return to Cāmuṇḍā's shrine and sees Karpūra-mañjarī*) Aho sārikkhadā!

Bhaira: Devi uvavisa. Mahārāo vi āado jjeva vaṭṭadi.

Śaurasenī. **Extract No. 6.**

Karpūra-mañjarī. Act II. (pp. 40, 41 and 245-6).

Specimen of decadent punning style—The Vidūṣaka describes his master's love-fever.

---

1 siro-veaṇā 'headache.'

2 uvaaraṇa=*upakaraṇa* § 17. lahuṃ 'quickly' (=*laghu*).

3 (ā+*nī*).

4 āharaṇa 'ornament,' visumarida 'forgotten,' cf. sumaradi § 57.

5 Imperat. Pass.

6 viṇaḍidā "puzzled" (ṇaḍ a Pkt. root). jhāṇa 'meditation, magic' § 44. ṇiv-vigghaṃ 'without hindrance' § 36. vaṭṭadi § 45. In such more or less redundant verbs "to be" we have the beginnings of the later system of auxiliary verbs. āado vaṭṭadi cf. ā gayā hai, diṇṇā bhodi cf. diyā hai, kido bhodi cf. kiyā hai.

Eso piavaasso haṃso via mukkamāṇaso,[1] karī via maakkhāmo,[2] muṇāladaṇḍo[3] via ghaṇaghammamilāṇo,[4] diṇadiṇṇadīvo[5] via vialidacchāo,[6] pabhāda-puṇṇimā-cando via paṇḍuraparikkhīṇo ciṭṭhadi.

Śaurasenī. Extract No. 7.

Little Clay Cart. Act 6. [Edition Hiranand and Parab. Bombay 1902]. Vasantasenā and a maid.

Maid : Kadhaṃ ajja vi ajjaā[7] ṇa vivujjhadi. Bhodu. Pavisia paḍibodhaissaṃ. (*Steps around.*)

[*Enter Vasantasenā wrapped up and sleepy.*]

Maid : Utthedu[8] utthedu Ajjaā! Pabhādaṃ saṃvuttaṃ.

Vasa : (*Waking*) Kadhaṃ ratti[9] jjeva pabhādaṃ saṃvuttaṃ?

Maid : Amhāṇaṃ eso pabhādo. Ajjaāe uṇa ratti jjeva.

Vasa : Hañje,[10] kahiṃ uṇa tumhāṇaṃ jūdiaro?

Maid : Ajjae, Vaḍḍhamāṇaaṃ samādisia pupphakaraṇḍaaṃ[11] jiṇṇujjāṇaṃ gado ajja Cārudatto.

Vasa : Kiṃ samādisia?

Maid : Joehi[12] rattīe pavahaṇaṃ, Vasantaseṇā gacchadu tti.

---

1 (*a*) 'out of spirits,' (*b*) 'having left (Lake) Mānasa.'

2 (*a*) 'thin with love-fever' (*kṣāma*), (b) 'thin as an elephant with rut.'

3 muṇāla § 60.

4 (*a*) 'languishing from violent ardour,' (*b*) 'wilted in the intense heat,' milāṇa § 57.

5 'a lamp given in day-time.' Note the alliteration "like a lamp that is lit in daylight."

6 vialida 'vanished' (*vi+gal*). chāā (*a*) colour, (*b*) light.

7 Ajjaā 'my Lady.' vivujjhadi 'awakes' (*vi+budh*).

8 utthedu 'let her get up' (*ut+sthā*). pabhādaṃ 'morning.'

9 'What, it's night, how is it morning?' saṃvuttaṃ is neuter. In the next sentence pabhādo is masculine.

10 Hañje regular form of address by a lady to her maid. Jūdiaro 'gambler' (*dyūtakaro*).

11 puppha § 38. karaṇḍaa 'basket,' jiṇṇa 'old' (*jṝ*), ujjāṇa 'garden.'

12 joehi 'harness' imperat. caus. (*yuj*). rāttīe as in the edition quoted is impossible. Bombay edn. rādīe.

Vasa: Hañje, kahiṃ mae gantavvaṃ?

Maid: Ajjae, jahiṃ Cārudatto.

Vasa: (*Embracing the maid*) Suṭṭhu ṇa ṇijjhāido[1] rattie. Tā ajja paccakkhaṃ[2] pekkhissaṃ. Hañje, kiṃ paviṭṭhā ahaṃ iha abbhantara-cadus-sālaaṃ?

Maid: Ṇa kevalaṃ abbhantara-cadus-sālaaṃ. Savvajaṇassa vi hiaaṃ paviṭṭhā.

Vasa: Avi saṃtappadi[3] Cārudattassa pariaṇo.

Maid: Saṃtappissadi.

Vasa: Kadā?

Maid: Jado ajjaā gamissadi.

Vasa: Tado mae paḍhamaṃ saṃtappidavvaṃ. (*Persuasively*) Hañje, geṇha edaṃ raaṇâvaliṃ.[4] Mama bahiṇiāe[5] ajjā-Dhūdāe gadua samappehi! Bhaṇidavvaṃ ca 'Ahaṃ Siri-Cārudattassa guṇaṇijjidā dāsī, tadā tumhāṇaṃ pi. Tā esā tuha jjeva kaṇṭhâharaṇaṃ hodu raaṇâvalī.'

Maid: Ajjae, kuppissadi[6] Cārudatto ajjāe dāva.

Vasa: Gaccha. Ṇa kuppissadi.

Maid: (*Taking the necklace*) Jaṃ āṇavedi. (*Exit and re-enter*) Ajjae, bhaṇādi ajjā Dhūdā—'ajjaüttena tumhāṇaṃ pasādīkidā.[7] Ṇa juttaṃ mama edaṃ geṇhiduṃ. Ajjautto jjeva mama āharaṇa-viseso tti jāṇādu bhodī.'

[*Enter* **Radanikā** *with a child.*]

Rada: Ehi vaccha, saaḍiāe[8] kīlamha.

---

1 =*nidhyāto*.

2 *pratyakṣam*. cadus-sālaaṃ 'having four halls.'

3 'Is in distress.'

4 raaṇa 'jewel' § 51. Śaur. has also radaṇa.

5 bahiṇiā 'sister.' **baghinī*=*bhaginī*, cf. H. bahin, Pañj. bhaiṇ). samappehi imperat. caus. (*sam*+*ṛ*).

6 kuppissadi 'will be angry.'

7 'presented it to you,' i.e. the necklace.

8 saaḍiā 'toycart' (*śakaṭikā*); kīlamha 'let us play' § 22, § 110.

Child: (*Mournfully*) Radaṇie! Kiṃ mama edāe maṭṭiāe[1] saaḍiāe? Taṃ jjeva sovaṇṇa-saaḍiaṃ dehi.

Rada: (*Sighing despondently*) Jāda, kudo amhāṇaṃ suvaṇṇavavahāro. Tādassa puṇo vi riddhīe[2] suvaṇṇa-saaḍiāe kīlissasi. Tā jāva viṇodemi[3] ṇaṃ. Ajjaā-Vasantaseṇāe samīvaṃ uvasappissaṃ.[4] (*Approaches*) Ajjae paṇamāmi.

Vasa: Radaṇie, sāadaṃ de. Kassa uṇa aaṃ dārao?[5] Aṇalaṃkida-sarīro vi candamuho āṇandedi mama hiaaṃ.

Rada: Eso kkhu ajja-Cārudattassa putto Rohaseṇo ṇāma.

Vasa: (*Stretching out her arms*) Ehi me puttaa āliṅga. (*Sets him on her lap*) Aṇukidaṃ aṇeṇa piduṇo[6] rūvaṃ.

Rada: Ṇa kevalaṃ rūvaṃ, sīlaṃ pi takkemi. Ediṇā ajja-Cārudatto attāṇaaṃ viṇodedi.

Vasa: Adha kiṃ-ṇimittaṃ eso roadi.[7]

Rada: Ediṇā paḍivesia-gahavaī-dāraa-keriāe[8] suvaṇṇa-saaḍiāe kīlidaṃ. Teṇa a sā ṇīdā. Tado uṇa taṃ maggantassa[9] mae iaṃ maṭṭiāsaaḍiā kadua diṇṇā. Tado bhaṇādi "Radaṇie, kiṃ mama edāe maṭṭiā-saaḍiāe. Taṃ jjeva sovaṇṇasaaḍiaṃ dehi" tti.

Vasa: Haddhī haddhī. Aaṃ pi ṇāma para-saṃpattīe saṃtappadi. Bhaavaṃ Kaanta[10] pokkhara-vatta-paḍida jala-

---

1 maṭṭiā 'earth' § 55 (cf. H. miṭṭī, māṭī). Rohasena the son of Cārudatta is supposed to speak Māgadhī: but the text here gives him ordinary Śaurasenī.

2 riddhī=*ṛddhi* § 60.

3 Caus. imperat. (*vi+nud*).

4 (*upa+sṛp*). H. P. read—seṇāāe.

5 'boy.'

6 piduṇo § 97.

7 roadi 'weeps,' cf. roda, rodasi further down, and rodissaṃ.

8 paḍivesia 'neighbour,' gahavai (=*gṛhapati*), keriā, 'belonging to' fem. of keraa, hence the Genitive in kerau (in Chand Bardai's Old Hindi).

9 magganta Pres. Part. of maggadi 'demands,' Skt. *mārgati* (H. māgnā).

10 Kaanta 'Fate.' pokkhara § 38, § 71, 'vatta' leaf.

bindu-sarisehiṃ kīlasi tumaṃ purisa-bhāadheehiṃ. (*Tearfully*) Jāda, mā roda ![1] sovaṇṇa-saaḍiāe kīlissasi.

Child : Radaṇie, kā esā ?

Vasa : Piduṇo de guṇa-ṇijjidā dāsī.

Rada : Jāda, ajjaā de jaṇaṇī bhodi.

Child : Radaṇie, aliaṃ[2] tumaṃ bhaṇāsi. Jaï amhāṇaṃ ajjaā jaṇaṇī, tā kīsa alaṃkidā ?

Vasa : Jāda, muddheṇa muheṇa adikaruṇaṃ mantesi. (*Putting off her jewels—and weeping*) Esā dāṇiṃ de jaṇaṇī saṃvuttā. Tā geṇha edaṃ alaṃkāraaṃ. Sovaṇṇa-saaḍiaṃ ghaḍāvehi.[3]

Child : Avehi. Ṇa geṇhissaṃ. Rodasi[1] tumaṃ.

Vasa : (*Wiping away her tears*) Jāda, ṇa rodissaṃ. Gaccha kīla. (*Fills the clay-cart with jewelry*) Jāda, kārehi sovaṇṇasaaḍiaṃ.

[*Exit Radanikā with the child*].

There is an excellent translation of this play in the Harvard Oriental Series, Vol. 9, Dr. A. W. Ryder.

Śaurasenī **Extract No. 8.**

Two of the Jester's speeches in the **Little Clay Cart** to illustrate the use of long compounds. (Act 4, p. 114).

A maid says to the Jester: Pekkhadu ajjo. amha-keraaṃ geha-duāraṃ.

The Jester looks and says with admiration: Aho salila-sitta-majjida-kida-haridôvalevaṇassa[4] viviha-suandhi-kusumôvahāra-citta-lihida-bhūmi-bhāassa[5] gaaṇa-talâaloaṇa-kodūhala-dūr-

---

[1] roadi 'weeps,' cf. rodasi further down, and rodissaṃ.

[2] aliaṃ § 67.

[3] Caus. from √*ghaṭ* fashion, make (cf. H. gharnā gharānā).

[4] sitta 'sprinkled' (*sic*), majjida 'swept' (*mṛj*), harida 'green,' uvalevaṇa 'smearing' (with cowdung) (*upa+lip*).

[5] suandhi 'fragrant,' uvahāra 'oblation-scattering,' citta-lihida lit., 'picture painted.' bhāa= *bhāga*.

uṇṇāmida-sīsassa[1] dolāamāṇâvalambid-Erāvaṇa-hattha-bbhamāida-malliā-dāma-guṇâlaṃkidassa[2] samucchida-danti-danta-toraṇâvabhāsidassa[3] mahā-raaṇôvarāôvasohiṇā pavaṇa-bal-andolaṇā-lalanta-cañcal'-aggahatthena 'ido ehi' tti vāharan-teṇa via maṃ sohagga-paḍāā-nivaheṇôvasohidassa[4] toraṇa-dharaṇa-tthambha-vediā-ṇikkhitta-samullasanta-harida-cūda-pallava-lalāma-phaṭiha-maṅgala-kalasâbhirāmôhaa-pāsassa[5] mahāsura-vakkha-tthala-dubbhejja-vajja-ṇirantara-paḍibaddha-kaṇaa-kavāḍassa[6] duggada-jaṇa-maṇorahâāsa-karassa[7] Vasantaseṇā-bhavaṇa-duārassa sassirīadā[8]! Jaṃ saccaṃ majjhatthassa vi jaṇassa balādiṭṭhiṃ āāredi.[9]

---

1 gaaṇa='sky,' tala+a(v)aloaṇa, uṇṇāmida 'raised high,' sīsa 'head, top.'

2 avalambida 'hanging'-bbhamāida. Comm. gives = *bhramāgata* This should be Ś. -bbhamāada. Rather it is -bbhamā(v)ida 'agitated,' cf. rodāvida, 'made to weep' in this play. malliā-dāma-guṇa 'festoons of jasmine.'

3 'Shining with an elevated portal of ivory.'

4 uvasohida 'made brilliant' ṇivaheṇa 'by a multitude' of sohagga 'auspicious' paḍāā 'flags,' vāharanteṇa, 'calling' [Pres. part. from vāharadi—(*vi+ā+hṛ*)], uvasohiṇā 'brilliant' with uvarāa 'colouring' of mahā-raaṇa 'precious jewels' or (=*mahārajana*) 'safflower,' agga-hatthena 'with finger' cañcala 'quivering' lalanta, 'waving to and fro' with the andolaṇā 'swing,' from the bala 'force' of the pavaṇa 'wind.'

5 'Having both (uhaa) its sides (pāsa, § 44) charming (abhirāma) with auspicious pitchers (maṅgala-kalasa) made of crystal (phaṭiha § 19, phaḍiha or phaḷiha would be better *vide* Pischel, § 206) placed (ṇik-khitta) on the 'altar' or balcony' (vediā) of the columns (-tthambha) supporting (dharaṇa) the gateway (toraṇa), and brilliant (samullasanta) with head-ornaments (lalāma) of green mango shoots (harida-cūda pallava).' [pāsaa is impossible.]

6 'With golden door-panels (kaṇaa-kavāḍa) studded (paḍibaddha) closely (ṇirantara) with impervious (dubbhejja) [*dur+bhid*] adamant (vajja) like the breast-expanse (vakkha-tthala) of a mighty demon (mahâsura).'

7 'Which causes (kara) trouble (āāsa) to poor people (dug-gada=*durgata*).'

8 sassirīadā=*saśrīkatā* 'beauty' loveliness,' -ss- as if the *svarabhakti* vowel had not been used. cf. sakkuṇodi=*śaknoti*.

9 Edition has 'balāddiṭṭhiṃ' which is impossible. balā is found in M., perhaps balādo is better Śaur. āāredi causal (*ā+kṛ*), majjhattha, 'in-different.'

The maid says: Edu edu. Imaṃ paḍhamaṃ paoṭṭhaṃ [1] pavisadu ajjo.

The Jester enters and looks about: Hī hī bho! Idho vi paḍhame paoṭṭhe sasi-saṅkha-muṇāla-sacchāhāo [2] viṇihida-cuṇṇa-muṭṭhi-paṇḍurāo [3] viviha-raaṇa-paḍibaddha-kañcaṇa-sovāṇa[4]-sohidāo pāsāda-pantīo [5] olambida-muttā-dāmehiṃ phaṭiha-vādâaṇa[6]-muhacandehiṃ ṇijjhāanti [7] via Ujjaïṇiṃ. Sottio [8] via suhôvaviṭṭho ṇiddāadi dovārio. Sadahiṇā [9] kalamôdaṇeṇa palohidā ṇa bhakkhanti vāasā baliṃ sudhā-savaṇṇadāe. Ādisadu bhodī.

A sentence of such enormous length as this "Aho——Vasantaseṇā-bhavaṇa-duārassa sassirīadā" is difficult to translate into English. Dr. Ryder breaks it up into nine separate sentences, of which the eighth is—"Yes Vasantasenā's house-door is a beautiful thing." (H. O. S., vol. 9, p. 67.)

Extract No. 9.

Māhārāṣṭrī. Hāla's Sattasaī.

Verse 2. Amiaṃ pāüa-kavvaṃ
padhiuṃ souṃ a je ṇa āṇanti,
Kāmassa tatta-tantiṃ
kuṇanti, te kaha ṇa lajjanti ?

---

[1] paoṭṭhaṃ 'courtyard' (=*prakoṣṭham*).

[2] 'Having the same hue as' (sa-cchāhāo cf. M. chāhā 'shadow,' but M. Ś. chāā, 'beauty.' Pischel (§ 255) derives chāhā from **chākhā* from **chāyākhā* from **chāyākā*). 'moon, conch, or lotus-stalks.'

[3] muṭṭhi 'handful,' cuṇṇa 'lime.' (Apa. cuṇṇaü, H. cūnā.)

[4] sovāṇa 'stairs,' § 17.

[5] 'rows of palaces,' § 35.

[6] 'window' "where the wind comes in" (*vātâyana*). [The English word means "wind-eye"]

[7] ṇijjhāanti 'look at' (*nir+dhyai*).

[8] sottio=*śrotriyo,* niddāadi "slumbers" (H. nīd), dovārio door-keeper.'

[9] sadahiṇā instr. 'with sour milk' (*dadhi* cf. H. dahī), kalama 'autumn rice,' palohida (*pra-lubh*), bhakkhanti 'eat' (*bhakṣ*), vāasā 'crows,' [Edn. has *vāyasā* which is Sanskrit not Śaurasenī].

Amia=*amṛta*. pāūa, Śaur. pāūda, § 12. kavvaṃ § 50. paḍhiuṃ, 'to read,' H. paṛh. souṃ "to hear." āṇanti, 'know' § 131. tatta-tantiṃ. This is the reading in the Kāvyamālā, which represents it by *tattva-cintām* in the Sanskrit version, in accordance with Gaṅgādhara Bhaṭṭa's commentary, which adds, however, *tantravārtāṃ vā*. Weber (1870) finding the reading taṃttataṃttiṃ conjectured *tantratantrīm*. In his edition (1881) he read on the authority of other MSS. tattatattiṃ (=-*taptiṃ*). We may translate it either—'practise the mysteries of love;' or 'take thought on the principles of love,' i.e. on the principles laid down in the Kāmaśāstra. kaha=kahaṃ, 'how.'

Verse 3. Satta saāiṃ[1] kaï-vacchaleṇa koḍia majjhaārammi ।
Hāleṇa viraïāiṃ sâlaṅkārāṇa gāhāṇaṃ ॥

"The Seven Centuries of embellished verses were arranged from among a *crore* by Hāla devoted to the poets."

Kaï=*kavi*, vacchala, § 39. 'devoted to poets.' koḍia, 'of a crore,' § 95,i. majjhaāra JM. majjhaẏāra *deśī* word for *madhya*.

Verse 4. ua ṇiccala-ṇipphandā[2]
bhisiṇī-vattammi[3] rehaï balāā[4] ।
ṇimmala-maragaa-bhāaṇa-
-pariṭṭhiā[5] saṅkhasutti vva ॥

ua 'Lo!' Weber explained as a shortened form from the vedic √*ūh*, 'mark, observe.' Pischel conjectured a *√*up* whence oppaṃ, 'seen' in Trivikrama. bhisiṇī=*bisinī*, S. bisiṇī. Pali and AMg. have bhisa for bisa. Aspiration of a sonant is rare, of a surd commoner, § 6. vattammi=*patre*, rehaï, 'shines' cf. Vedic *rebhati*, 'crackles,' etc., *rebhāyati*, 'shines.' bhāaṇa, 'platter.' saṅkhasutti, 'mother of pearl.' This verse is

---

1 KM. satāiṃ, *wrong*.

2 KM. ṇippandā. pph is commoner.

3 pattammi.

4 W. valāā following majority of MSS.

5 Km. -ṭṭhidā, *wrong*.

quoted by the Kāvyaprakāśa and other works on poetics to illustrate *vyaṅgya*—the suggestive.

"Lo there gleams a crane quite motionless on a lotus leaf, like mother of pearl at the edge of a platter of pure emerald."

Verse 8. attā! taha ramaṇijjaṃ
amhaṃ[1] gāmassa maṇḍaṇī-hūaṃ ।
lua-tila-vāḍi-saricchaṃ
sisireṇa kaaṃ bhisiṇī-saṇḍaṃ ॥

attā cf. attiā in Mṛcch. (p. 110). Commentators "mother-in-law." Apparently used to any elder lady in the household, mother, elder-sister, etc. lua, 'cut' (=**luta* for *lūna*). vāḍi, 'garden' (=*vāṭī*). cf. H. bāṛā (*vāṭa+ka-*).

"Oh mother! so the mass of lotuses that was so delightful and the ornament of our village, the cold has made like a garden of cut sesamum."

Thus the lady gives a hint to a lover. As to her precise meaning the paṇḍits differed. Some said the lotus-tank was to replace the sesamum garden as a meeting place, as people would be going and coming to harvest the sesamum. The frost-bitten lotuses would be deserted. Another view was, that neither place was suitable.

Verse 13. randhaṇa-kamma-ṇiuṇie!
mā jhūrasu, ratta-pāḍala-suandhaṃ ।
muha-māruaṃ pianto
dhūmāi sihī, ṇa pajjalai ॥

"Skilled in the work of destruction," i.e. in love's magic. jhūrasu, 'be angry,' √*jvar* or *jūr*, 'get hot' (because the fire does not burn). dhūmāi=*dhūmāyate*. The denominative *-āya-* becomes -āa-, so Mg. cilāadi=*cirāyati*, Ś. sīdalāadi=*śītalāyati*; this -āa- often contracts to -ā- in M., etc. pajjalaï 'blazes' (*pra+jval*). While the fire can drink in the breath of thy mouth, fragrant as red pāṭalas he will only smoke and not burst into flame, for then thou wouldst blow no more.

---

[1] KM. ahmaṃ, *wrong*.

Verse 16. amaa-maa gaaṇa-sehara
raaṇī-muha-tilaa canda de chivasu ।
chitto jehi piaamo
mamaṃ pi tehiṃ cia karehiṃ ॥

Addressed to the moon. amaa-maa consisting of *amṛta*. de said to=*he*. chivasu imperat. of chivaī, 'touch' (√*kṣip*), chitto p.p.p. of the same. cia (KM. reads via) a restrictive particle 'with these very hands.'

Verse 42. ārambhantassa dhuaṃ
Lacchī Maraṇaṃ va hoi purisassa ।
taṃ Maraṇaṃ aṇārambhe
vi hoi, Lacchī uṇa ṇa hoi ॥

dhuaṃ, 'certainly' (*dhruvam*). Lacchī=*Lakṣmī*.

Verse 49. thoaṃ pi ṇa ṇīsareï[1]
majjhaṇhe ua sarīra-tala-lukkā ।
āava-bhaeṇa chāhī
vi, tā pahia kiṃ ṇa vīsamasi ॥

thoaṃ, 'a little' (*stokam*). ṇīsarei for ṇīsarai (=*niḥsarati*); majjhaṇha, 'mid-day,' § 52. ua see v, 4.

-lukkā 'sticking to,' as explained in Skt. by *līna* : 'torn loose or torn out' =**lukna* connected with √*luñc* (Pischel, § 466). Cf. Panj. luknā 'to be hidden.' āava 'heat' (*ātapa*). chāhī 'shadow,' not derived directly from *chāyā*, but from **chāyākī* >*chāyākhī (aspiration, § 19)>*chāāhī contracts to chāhī. (Pischel, § 255). pahia 'traveller.' vīsamasi (*vi*+*śram*). For short vowel cf. forms from √*kram* ṇikkamaī, Ś. adikkamasi, etc., so from *śram* M. JM. vīsamaī, etc., Ś. vīsama, pass. vīsamīadu.

At midday the shadow does not move out, even a little way from the body—*or* but clings to the body—from fear of the heat—so traveller stay by me.

---

[1] KM. ṇīsarai. Weber rejected this as against the metre Later he adopted ṇīti.imā.

Verse 76. ṇa vi taha viesa-vāso
doggaccaṃ maha jaṇei santāvaṃ ।
āsaṃsiattha-vimuho
jaha paṇaïaṇo ṇiattanto ॥

viesa 'abroad' (*videśa*). doggaccaṃ 'poverty' (*daurgatyam*). vimuho 'indifferent to, without a thought of.' āsaṃsia 'desired' (*ā+śaṃs*). paṇaï 'beloved' (*praṇayi*), -aṇo= jaṇo. ṇiattanto 'returning' (*ni+vṛt*).

Verse 81. addaṃsaṇeṇa pemmaṃ
avei, aïdaṃsaṇeṇa vi avei ।
pisuṇa-jaṇa-jampieṇa vi
avei, emea vi avei ॥

'Out of sight, out of mind' and 'familiarity breeds contempt.' avei=*apeti*. emea=*evameva* (Pischel, § 149).

Verse 94. suaṇo jaṃ desam alaṃ-
-karei, taṃ cia karei pavasanto ।
gāmâsaṇṇ'ummūlia-
-mahā-vaḍa-ṭṭhāṇa-sāricchaṃ ॥

pavasanto (*pra+vas*). vaḍa 'fig-tree' (*vaṭa*). ummūlia 'rooted up.' The *rendezvous* is cancelled.

Verse 107. Goḷā-aḍa-ṭṭhiaṃ pecchiūṇa
(=KM. ii. 7). gaha-vaï-suaṃ halia-soṇhā ।
āḍhattā uttariuṃ
dukkh'uttārāĕ paavīe ॥

Goḷā=Godāvarī, -aḍa 'bank' (*taṭa*). -suaṃ 'the son' of gahavaï (=*gṛhapati*). sŏṇhā 'daughter-in-law,' for commoner suṇhā contracted from *suṇuhā, cf. Paiśācī sunusā=*snuṣā*. āḍhattā 'she began' (*ā+dhā*. caus. āḍhavaï with pass. āḍhappai p.p. āḍhatta). halia 'ploughman.' paavīe 'by a path.'

She wishes to see if he will help her.

Verse 115. savvattha disā-muha-pasariehi
(=KM. ii. 15). aṇṇoṇṇa-kaḍaa-laggehiṃ ।
challiṃ va muaï Viṃjho
mehehi visaṃghaḍantehiṃ ॥

challiṃ 'mantle, skin.' muai (√*muc*). meha 'cloud.' kaḍaa 'slope,' etc. (*kaṭaka*). *vi*+*saṃ*+*ghaṭ* 'dispersing.'

The end of the rains.

Verse 128. mahu-māsa-māruâhaa-
(=KM. ii. 28). -mahuara-jhaṃkāra-ṇibbhare raṇṇe
gāï virah'akkharâvaddha-
-pahia-maṇa-mohaṇaṃ govī ||

In a forest full of the buzzing of bees carried by the vernal zephyr there sings of love in absence maddening to the traveller's heart, the maiden with the kine.

Verse 171. Goḷā-ṇaïe kacche
(=KM. ii. 71). cakkhanto rāïāï pattāiṃ |
upphaḍaï makkaḍo khokkhei
a poṭṭhaṃ a piṭṭeï ||

'On the bank of the Goḷā river,' cf. 107 above. cakkhanto pres. p. cakkhai =*jakṣati* 'devours,' cf. Marathi, H. √ cākh. rāïā. 'mustard,' *rājikā* H. rāī. makkaḍo 'ape' (*markaṭo*). upphaḍai KM. gives -*utpatati* which should=uppaḍai. Weber suggests √sphaṭ related to *sphuṭ*, cf. phuḍai phiḍai. khokkhei 'snarls' *deśī* word. poṭṭhaṃ 'belly'? -*proṣṭham* 'bench or stool.' piṭṭei 'crams' *deśī*. Weber suggests a connection with √*piṇḍ*.

"On the bank of the Goḷā river, devouring the leaves of black mustard, there leaps the monkey, snarls and stuffs his belly."

Māhārāṣṭrī. Extract No. 10.

Verses from Śakuntalā.

(*a*) Spring song in Prologue.

Īsīsi-cumbiāiṃ [1] bhamarehiṃ suumāra-kesara-sihāiṃ
odaṃsaanti [2] daamāṇā pamadāo sirīsakusumāiṃ ||

---

[1] īsīsi=*īṣadīṣat*. [2] (*ava*+*taṃs*).

(*b*) Grief at Śakuntalā's departure.

Ullalia-dabbhakavalā [1]maī pariccatta-ṇaccaṇā [2] morā ।
osaria-paṇḍu-vattā [3] muanti aṃsūiṃ va [4] laāo ॥

(*c*) Act III, Śakuntalā reads the verse she has composed at her friend's bidding.

Tujjha ṇa āṇe hiaaṃ, mama uṇa maaṇo divā a rattiṃ ca ।
ṇikkiva dābaï baliaṃ tuha hutta-maṇorahāi aṅgāiṃ ॥

ṇa āṇe 'I do not know,' cf. No. 9, verse 1. maaṇo Monier-Williams reads kāmo. ṇikkiva 'cruel' *niṣkṛpa*. dābaï comm. gives *tāpayati*. Pischel (p. 154) says, not exactly *tāpayati* but Marathi dābṇẽ, Gujarāti dābavũ, Urdu dābnā 'to press, compress' (M.W. tabei, i.e. tavei=*tapayati*). baliaṃ (*balīyaḥ*). hutta 'facing' Comm. '*abhimukha*.' Derivation uncertain. With numerals M. huttaṃ AMg. khutta=*kṛtvaḥ*. M.W. reads vutta=*vṛtta*. -āi gen. sing. divā a=*divā ca*.

"Thy heart I know not, cruel one, but day and night does Love grievously afflict my limbs, whose desires are fixed on thee."

(*d*) Act V. Haṃsapadikā is overheard singing.

Ahiṇava-mahu-loluvo tumaṃ
taha paricumbia cūa-mañjariṃ
kamala-vasaï-metta-ṇivvuo
mahuara vīsario 'si ṇaṃ kahaṃ ?

loluvo 'greedy,' Bengal version has loha-bhāvio. cūa 'mango.' metta § 69. ṇivvuo (*nir+vṛt*), M.W. reads ṇivvudo

---

1 Ullalia, *deśī* word (cf. H. ulṭnā, ulālnā). *udgalita* is an explanation, hence the Pkt. reading uggalia. (Pischel's edn., p. 191.) -kavala 'mouthful.' maī 'doe' as in Pischel's edn. Devanāgarī MSS. have miīo. Boehtlingk conjectured miā 'deer.'

2 -ccatta=*tyakta*. ṇaccaṇā, cf. H. nācnā. morā 'peacocks,' Pischel morī 'a peahen.'

3 osaria (*ava+sṛ*). vatta 'leaf.' muanti (*muc*).

4 Pischel, Bengali version reads aṅgāiṃ va. Devanāgarī MSS. have assūṇi via. Boehtlingk conjectured aṃsū-. 'assūṇi (for assūiṃ) via ladāo' is Śaur. not Māhā. The reading above aṃsūiṃ va laāo suits dialect, metre and meaning. aṃsu, §§ 49, 64. laā, § 12.

which is Śaur. mahuara 'bee.' vīsario 'forgotten.' M.W. has vimharido. He supports this by Vararuci iii. 32, by which vimhaa, etc., cf. § 47. But -ido is not M. M. has vīsaria, visaria. Ś. visumarida (JŚ. vīsarida, JM. vissariya, dialectic vimharia), cf. Hindī bisarnā. The past part. is active in meaning.

(e) Act VI. (MW. p. 230, Pisch. p. 120).

Arihasi me cūaṅkura diṇṇo Kāmassa gahia-cāvassa
saccavia-juai-lakkho pañcabbhahio saro houṃ.

gahia=Śaur.gahida, cāva 'bow.' saccavia, past part. of saccavai=*satyāpayati* 'make true, verify, contract.' juai=*yuvati*. pañca+*abhy-adhika*. houṃ 'to be.' M.W. differs, for arihasi houṃ he has hohi 'be,' and begins with tuṃ si mae "Thou art offered by me to"; for saccavia the easier pahiajaṇa, cf. Megh. 8. *pathika-vanitāḥ*.

"Oh mango-sprout, given by me to Kāma grasping his bow, do thou become the best arrow of his five, with contracted maidens as thy mark."

Māhārāṣṭrī. Extract No. 11.

Mṛcchakaṭikam.

(a) (Verse 19).

Vicalaï ṇeurajualaṃ, chijjanti a mehalā maṇi-kkhaiā
valaā a sundaraarā raaṇaṅkura-jāla-paḍibaddhā.

ṇeura, regular Pkt. for Skt. *nūpura*; from a form **nepūra* cf. *keyūra*, Pkt. keūra. (P. § 126). chijjanti, pass. (*chid*). khaia (*khac*). sundaraara=Śaur. sundaradara. raaṇa § 51.

(b) Act II. Karṇapūraka (verse 20).

Āhaṇiūṇa sarosaṃ taṃ hatthiṃ Viñjha-sela-siharâbhaṃ
moāvio mae so dantantara-saṃṭhio parivvājao.

āhaṇiūṇa gerund (*ā+han*). Viñjha, § 35. sela=*śaila* [H.P. edition reads "saila" which is not Prakrit. *vide* Pischel, gr. § 60]. moāvio past part. causal (*muc*). ṭhio § 38. parivvājao 'mendicant.'

(*c*) Act IV (verse 30). The Vidūṣaka mocks at Vasantasenā's mother.

sīhu-surâsava-mattiā
eâvattham̱ gaā hi attiā,
jai marai ettha attiā,
hoi siāla-sahassa-pajjattiā.

sīhu 'rum' (*sīdhu*). surā 'wine, etc.' āsava 'intoxicating drink made from uncooked vegetables and water,' 'toddy.' eâvattham̱=*etad*+*avasthām*. attiā 'mother,' *vide* M.W. Dic. *sub* attā, apparently a non-aryan word. pajjattiā 'sufficiency' (*paryāptikā*). "She would make a good meal for a thousand jackals." Texts read gadā and bhodi, these are Śaur. forms.

Māhārāṣṭrī. Extract No. 12.

Karpūramañjarī.

(*a*) Act II. Verse 10.

ṇīsāsā hāra-laṭṭhī-sarisa-pasaraṇā candaṇ-uccoḍakārī,
caṇḍo dehassa dāho, sumaraṇa-saraṇā hāsa-sohā muhammi,
aṅgāṇam̱ paṇḍu-bhāvo diaha-sasi-kalā-komalo; kim̱ ca tīe
ṇiccam̱ bāha-ppavāhā tuha, suhaa, kae hŏnti kullāhi tullā.

ṇīsāsa 'sigh.' laṭṭhī 'a lāṭhī,' also 'a necklace string' ["escape like pearls from off their string" Lanman.] uccoḍa 'withering,' *cuṭ* meaning not certain; *cuṭ* is said to mean 'split off' or 'grow small.' Perhaps the sandal 'throws out' fragrance owing to the moist heat of the sighs. caṇḍo 'fierce.' sumaraṇa-saraṇā "has memory as its refuge." tuha kae 'for thee.' suhaa=*subhaga*. kullā 'river-canal.' tulla 'equal to.' bāha (*vide* p. 84).

(*b*) The Jester's rejoinder. (Verse 11.)

Param̱ jŏṇhā uṇhā, garala-sariso candaṇa-raso,
khaa-kkhāro hāro, raaṇi-pavaṇā deha-tavaṇā,
muṇālī bāṇâlī, jalaï a jala-ddā taṇu-laā
variṭṭhā jam̱ diṭṭhā kamala-vaaṇā sā su-ṇaaṇā.

joṇhā 'moonlight.' uṇha § 47. garala 'poison.' khaa 'a wound.' khāra 'alkali,' *kṣāra*. -tavaṇā (*tap*). jalai 'blazes.'

jala-dda, 'running with water.' taṇu-laā 'body-creeper,' § 12. variṭṭhā 'the choicest maid.'

Note the internal rhymes.

(*c*) Verse 25.

Ṇisagga-caṅgassa vi māṇusassa sohā samummīlaï bhūsaṇehiṃ
maṇīṇa jaccāṇa vi hīraehiṃ vihūsaṇe laggaï kā vi lacchī.

ṇisagga 'nature' (*ni*+*sṛj*). caṅga "handsome," cf. Panjābi caṅgā 'good.' maṇīṇa for maṇīṇaṃ, gen. plur. jaccāṇa, gen. plur. 'genuine' (*jātya*). lacchī=*lakṣmī*.

(*d*) Describes the swinging of the Heroine. (Verse 32.)

Raṇanta-maṇi-ṇeuraṃ jhaṇa-jhaṇanta-hāra-cchaḍaṃ
kaṇakkaṇia-kiṅkiṇī-muhalā-mehalā-ḍambaraṃ
vilola-valaâvalī-jaṇia-mañju-siñjā-ravaṃ
ṇa kassa maṇa-mohaṇaṃ sasi-muhīa hindolaṇaṃ.

raṇ 'to tinkle.' jhaṇajhaṇ 'to jingle.' chaḍā 'mass-lustre.' kaṇa-kkaṇ 'to ring' (*kvaṇ*). kiṅkiṇī 'bell.' muhala 'noisy' § 26 *mukhara*. ḍambara 'mass-noise' siñjā 'jingle.' sasi-muhī 'moon-faced maiden.' Lanman describes this stanza as "a '*tour de force*' in the use of imitative words," p. 255.

(*e*) Even the Jester waxes eloquent, and describes the swinging in eight verses concluding: (Verse 40).

Ia eāi vilās-ujjalāiṃ dolā-pavañca-cariāiṃ
kassa ṇa lihaï va citte ṇiuṇo kandappa-cittaaro?

ia 'thus' related to iti. eāi=Śaur. edāiṃ. pavañca 'display,' *prapañca*. citta 'heart.' citta-aro 'picture-maker.'

(*f*) Act III, Verse 2.

Maragaa-maṇi-gutthā hāra-laṭṭhi vva tārā
bhamara-kavaliantā mālaï-mālia vva |
rahasa-valia-kaṇṭhaṃ tīa diṭṭhī variṭṭhī
savaṇa-paha-ṇiviṭṭhā māṇasaṃ me paviṭṭhā ||

guttha 'strung' (*gumph*). tārā 'bright.' kavalia 'eaten, sucked.' anta 'end.' rahasa 'impetuously.' valia 'turned round.' savaṇa 'ear' (*śru*). paha=*patha*.

(*g*) Verse 31. The Heroine's composition.

Maṇḍale sasaharassa gorīe danta-pañjara-vilāsa-corae
bhāi lañchaṇa-mao phurantao keli-koïla-tulaṃ dharantao.

sasa-hara 'hare-bearer=moon.' danta 'ivory.' bhāi 'is bright' ["appears in all its beauty"]. -mao 'antelope.' phurantao 'manifest' (*sphur.*) -tulaṃ 'likeness.'

(*h*) Act IV, Conclusion. "*Bharata-vākyam.*"

Aṇudiahaṃ viphuranto maṇīsi-jaṇa-saala-guṇa-viṇāsa-aro
rittattaṇa-dāvaggī viramaü kamalā-kaḍakkha-varisena.

maṇīsi 'clever, learned.' rittattaṇa 'emptiness—Poverty.' dāvaggī 'forest-fire.' Kamalā=Lakṣmī. kaḍakkha 'side-long glances.' varisa 'rain' § 57.

Māhārāṣṭrī. Extract No. 13.

Ratnāvalī.

(*a*) Act I. Madanikā sings.

Kusumâuha-piya-dūao maülāia-bahu-cūao
siḍhilia-māṇa-ggahaṇao vāaï dāhiṇa-pavaṇao.
viraha-vivaḍḍhia-soao kaṅkhia-pia-aṇa-melao
paḍivālaṇâsamatthao tammaï juvaī-satthao.
iha paḍhamaṃ mahumāso jaṇassa hiaāiṃ kuṇaï maüāiṃ
pacchā vijjhaï kāmo laddha-ppasarehiṃ kusuma-bāṇehiṃ.

vāaï 'blows.' dāhiṇa 'south,' dakkhiṇa becomes *dākhiṇa by lengthening the vowel, hence dāhiṇa by § 13. Cf. 'Deccan' and H. dāhinā 'right.' kaṅkhia 'longed for.' pia-aṇa 'lovers,' vālaṇa (*pāl*). asamatthao 'unable.' satthao 'troop.' kuṇaï 'makes.' maüa 'tender' (*mṛduka*). pacchā § 38. vijjhai (*vidhyati*) § 35. laddha-ppasara 'unimpeded.'

"The south wind blows, sweet messenger of Love, making many a mango blossom, and dissolving fits of sulky temper. With pangs increased by separation, longing for union with their lovers, a troop of ladies is faint with love, incapable of defence. First comes the month of sweetness and softens mortals' hearts, then Love wounds them with his flowery arrows unimpeded."

(*b*) Act IV. The Magician.

Paṇamaha calaṇe indassa indaālammi laddhaṇāmassa,
taha ajja-Sambarassa vi māā-supaḍiṭṭhia-jasassa.
kiṃ dharaṇīe miaṅko āāse mahiharo jale jalaṇo,
majjhaṇhammi paoso, dāvijjaü dehi āṇattiṃ.

paṇamaha, imperat. (*pra+nam*). calaṇe, masc. acc. plur. for Skt. neut. indaāla (*indrajāla*) 'illusion.' paḍiṭṭhia (*prati+sthā*). jasa 'renown.' āāsa 'sky.' jalaṇo (*jval*). majjhaṇha § 52. dāvijjaü, imperat. pass. caus. (*dā*) 'let it be caused to be given-demanded.' āṇattiṃ (*ā+jñā*).

"Revere the deeds of Indra, who takes his name from sorcery, so also those of worthy Śambara whose renown is well established by his magic. What shall it be? moon on the ground, earth in the sky, or flames in water? or dusk at noon? give your commands."

(*c*) Kiṃ jappieṇa bahuṇā, jaṃ jaṃ hiaeṇa mahasi sandaṭṭhuṃ,
taṃ taṃ daṃsemi ahaṃ guruṇo manta-ppahāveṇa.

mahasi 'desirest.'

(*d*) Hari-Hara-Bamha-ppamuhe deve daṃsemi devarāaṃ ca,
gaaṇammi Siddha-Vijjāhara-vahu-satthaṃ ca ṇaccantaṃ.

Bamha, cf. § 52. deve. acc. plur.

[There is very little Māhārāṣṭrī in this play. Note its simplicity, and the great contrast with the decadent Camphor Cluster which uses the same motif of the magician producing a vision of the Heroine, by bringing on the lady herself.]

Māhārāṣṭrī. Extract No. 14.

Setubandha or **Rāvaṇavaho.**

Bk. I. Verse 57. How the monkeys crossed the mountain streams.

Bolanti a pecchantā paḍimā-saṃkanta-dhavala-ghaṇa-saṃghāe |
phuḍa-phaḍiha-silā-saṃkula-khaliôvari-patthie via ṇai-ppavahe ||

√bol 'pass, cross,' cf. boleï 'passes (the time).' M. pecchaï =Ś. pekkhadi § 40. pecchantā, nom. plur. pres. part. paḍimā-saṃkanta- 'reflected.' saṃghāe, acc. plur. § 86. khalia= Ś. khalida. patthia=Ś. patthida (*pra-sthā*). -ppavahe=*pravāhān*.

"And they cross the streams of rivers that they see reflecting masses of white clouds, as if trickling through and running over a welter of clear crystal rocks."

Bk. VII. Verse 56. The waves splash on high as the monkeys drop in the mountains.

Utthaṅghia-duma-ṇivahā giri-ghā'-uvvatta-mucchia-
mahā-macchā,
velā-sela-kkhaliā uddhaṃ bhijjanti uahi-jala-kallolā.

utthaṅghia. Comm.=*uttambhita* (*ut+stambh*). This is regularly in M. uttambhia, Ś. uttambhida. uvvatta (*ud+vṛt*). mucchia 'stunned,' maccha § 56. -kkhalia (*skhal*). bhijjanti pass. of *bhid*. uahi 'ocean.'

"Supporting a multitude of trees, with mighty fish turned over stunned by the impact of the mountains, the ocean billows break on high checked by the rocks of the shore."

Bk. VIII. Verse 3. The sea subsides.

Giri-saṃkhoha-vimukkā jhīṇā appatta-paḍhama-gamaṇ-oāsā,
mand-andolaṇa-maüā gaägaa ccia samudda-salila-uppīḍā.

saṃkhoha=*saṃkṣobha*. vimukka (*vi+muc*). jhīṇa § 40. appatta (*a+pra+āp*) paḍhama § 20. oāsa=*avakāśa*. maüa= *mṛduka*. ccia 'like.' uppīḍā 'bursts, jets.'

"The jets of sea-water when freed from the shock of the mountains do not mount so high as before, but subside, and oscillate in a slow and gentle swing."

Verse 6. Mingled spoil of land and sea.

Mottā-ghaḍanta-kusumaṃ sama-maragaa-vatta-bhaṅga-
bhariâvattaṃ,
vidduma-milia-kisalaaṃ sa-saṅkha-dhavala-kamalaṃ pasam-
maī salilaṃ.

mottā 'pearl.' ghaḍanta, pres. part. (*ghaṭ*) 'being joined with.' maragaa 'emerald' § 12. vatta 'leaf.' āvattaṃ (*ā+vṛt*). vidduma 'coral.' pasammaī (*pra+śam*).

"Quiet grows the water, blossoms united with pearls, the whirlpool filled with fragments of leaves and emeralds, buds mingled with coral, white lotuses with the Triton's shells."

Verse 14. Weariness of the workers—(Sugrīva speaks to Nala).

Khavio vāṇaraloo dūraṭṭhia-virala-pavvaaṃ mahi-veḍhaṃ,
ṇa a dīsaï seu-vaho, mā hu ṇamejja guruaṃ puṇo Rāma-dhaṇuṃ.

Khavio 'exhausted' (*kṣap* caus. of *kṣi*). pavvaa 'mountain.' mahi 'earth.' veḍha=*veṣṭa* 'enclosure' § 38, cf. M. veḍhia, Śaur. veḍhida, Comm. gives the meaning as *mahī-pṛṣṭham*. dīsaï= *dṛśyate*. -vaho= *-patho*. ṇamejja, opt. 3rd person sing. or plur. The Comm. is uncertain whether -dhaṇuṃ is nom. or acc.

(*a*) Nom. then neuter, 'may Rāma's bow not bend,'

(*b*) Acc. 'let not him (i.e. Rama) bend Rāma's bow.' Comm. suggests *namayata* but ṇamejja is not 2nd person plural.

"The monkey-people are exhausted, the surface of the earth has mountains left, but few and far between, yet the mole of the Bridge is not in sight, so let not Rāma's bow bend[1] heavily again.

Verse 20. Nala's reply.

Khavio pavvaa-ṇivaho daliaṃ va rasā-alaṃ dhuŏ vva sa-muddo,
jīaṃ va pariccattaṃ ajja va saṃbhāvaṇā tuhaṃ ṇiv-vūḍhā.

pariccattaṃ (*pari+tyaj*). Comm. *vā* is affirmative. After ajja one Comm. would prefer to read vi.

"A multitude of mountains has been exhausted, the surface of the earth may be torn up, the sea may be agitated, and life despaired of, but now must your design be carried out."

---

[1] Comm. says samudra-tāḍanāya, 'to chastise the sea.'

The Rākṣasas show Sitā a vision of Rāma's severed head.—Bk. XI. Verse 61, p. 345.

Pecchaï a sarahas-ôharia-maṇḍalaggâhighāa-visama-cchiṇṇaṃ,
dūra-dhaṇu-saṃghiañcia-sara-puṅkhâliddha-sāmaliaāvaṅgaṃ,

oharia, past part. (*ava* + *hṛ*) *maṇḍalâgra* 'scimitar.' ahighāa (*abhi* + *han*). saṃghiañcia = *saṃhita* + *añcita* § 65. sara-puṅkha 'shaft of arrow.' āliddha (*ā* + *lih*) = **āligdha*. avaṅga 'eye-corner' § 17. The object of pecchai comes in verse 69. —"Rāma-siraṃ."

"And Sita saw (a human head) rudely lopped, hacked off with a scimitar's stroke, the corners of the eyes darkened by the shaft of the arrow set to the bow and drawn far back."

Verse 62. ṇivvūḍha-ruhira-paṇḍura-maülanta-cchea-
māsa-pellia-vivaraṃ,
bhajjanta-paḍia-paharaṇa-kaṇṭha-cchea-
dara-lagga-dhārā-cuṇṇaṃ,

ṇiv-vūḍha = (*nirvyūḍha*). maülanta lit. 'budding' (*mukula*) § 71. chea 'the cut.' pellia through *pelia *peria = *prerita*. Comm. gives the meaning as *mudritam*, 'sealed up.' bhajjanta part. from bhajjaï 'is broken.' dara 'a little.'

"The dust of the sword-edge clung to the cleft hewn in its neck where the weapon fell breaking in pieces, while the pale bloodless flesh at the wound had shrivelled and sealed the hollow thereof—"

Verse 63. ṇiddaa-saṃdaṭṭhâhara-mūl-ukkhitta-dara-
diṭṭha-dāḍhā-hīraṃ,
saṃkhāa-soṇia-paṅka-paḍala-pūrenta-
kasaṇa-kaṇṭha-ccheaṃ,

ṇiddaa 'ruthless.' saṃdaṭṭha (*saṃ* + *daṃś*). ahara = *adhara*. ukkhitta (*ut* + *kṣip*). dāḍhā 'tusk,' § 65. saṃkhāa Comm. = *saṃstyāna* 'coagulated' from the rare root *styai*. Rather from a past part. *saṃ-styāta* through **saṃskyāta*. kasaṇa = *kṛṣṇa*.

"A tooth of adamant is slightly visible at the raised base of the lower lip, ruthlessly bitten through, and the dark neck-wound is filled with a muddy film of blood congealed."

Verse 64. ṇisiara-kaa-ggahâṇia-ṇilāḍa-aḍa-ṇaṭṭha-
bhiuḍi-bhumaā-bhaṅgaṃ,
galia-ruhir-addha-lahuaṃ aṇahia-ummil-
latāraaṃ Rāmasiraṃ!

ṇisi-ara=*niśicara. kaa-ggaha 'hair-seizing' (kaca-). āṇia=āṇīa. ṇilāḍa 'forehead' also ṇalāḍa, Pāli nalāṭa or lalāṭa and with metathesis M. ṇaḍāla or M. Ś. ṇiḍāla. Apa. ṇiḍalā (Pischel § 260). -aḍa=*taṭa*, bhiuḍi Comm.=*bhrukuṭi* really=*bhṛ-kuṭi*, which occurs. AMg. bhiguḍi. The forms bhuuḍi huuḍi Pischel says are incorrect. (P. § 124). bhumaā 'brow.' aṇahiaa means *ahṛdaya* cf. aṇamilia=*amilita*, aṇadīhara=*adīrgha*. ummilla=**unmīlna*=*unmīlita*.

"The frown that furrowed its brows had faded from its broad forehead, for the demons brought it with a grip of the hair—lighter by half with the blood poured forth, with its orbs open but devoid of soul—the head of Rāma."

Sītā's Lament.

Verse 75 (p. 350).

Āvāa-bhaa-araṃ cia ṇa hoi dukkhassa dāruṇaṃ ṇivvahaṇaṃ,
jaṃ mahilā-vīhatthaṃ diṭṭhaṃ sahiaṃ ca tuha mae avasāṇaṃ.

Āvāa=*āpāta*. cia (AMg. ciya), ccia after vowels, means *eva*: also cea. (*caiva* cf. ṇeya=*naiva*). vīhatthaṃ=*bībhatsam*. sahiaṃ 'endured.'

'Though frightful in its onset the end of sorrow is not so terrible, if I can view a sight loathsome to women and endure thy death.'

Sītā not knowing that the vision is unreal, marvels that she should continue to exist. The commentary takes mahilā-vīhatthaṃ to mean 'a cause of reproach among women.'

Verse 76. vāh-uṇhaṃ tujjha ure jaṃ mocchihimi tti
saṃṭhiaṃ maha hiae,
ghara-ṇiggamaṇa-paattaṃ sāhasu taṃ
kammi ṇivvavijjaü dukkhaṃ?

vāha or bāha "tear." uṇhaṃ 'hot.' Text has uhṇaṃ, incorrect. tujjha this oblique base of tuaṃ survives in H. tujh ko; it comes from **tuhyam* analogous to *mahyam*. ure loc. of uro 'breast.' 'mocchihimi. Fut. of *muc*, also moccham. ṭhia § 12. paattaṃ=*pravṛttam*. sāhasu 'tell' imperat. *śās*. kammi loc.=Śaur. kassiṃ. ṇiv-vavijjaü (*nir*+*vap*) pass. imperat. 'let it be poured out.'

"It was fixed in my heart from the moment of leaving home, that I would dissolve my sorrow with hot tears on thy breast. Now tell me, where shall my grief be out-poured?"

Verse 77. virahammi tujjha dhariaṃ dacchāmi
tumaṃ ti jīviaṃ kaha vi mae,
taṃ esa mae diṭṭho phaliā vi maṇorahā
ṇa pūrenti mahaṃ.

dacchāmi 'I shall see,' also dacchimi and dacchaṃ; Śaur. uses pekkhissaṃ. kaha vi=*katham api*, kahaṃ is commoner. Final anusvāra in pronouns and adverbs tends to be optional. So mahaṃ=maha. esa=eso. esa is used freely, according to Hemacandra, for all genders. sa on the other hand is rare.

"In separation from thee my life was barely stayed by the thought of seeing thee. Now I see thee thus, my desires though bearing fruit bring no satisfaction."

Verse 78. Puhavīa hohii paī bahu-purisa-visesa-cañcalā Rāasirī,
kaha tā mahaṃ cia imaṃ ṇīsāmaṇṇaṃ uatthiaṃ
vehavvaṃ.

Puhavī 'Earth,' Śaur. Puḍhavī, oblique forms in -īa are common in M. paī=*patiḥ*. hohii "will be." 'tā=Vedic *tāt*. ṇīsāmaṇṇaṃ=*niḥsāmānyam*. uatthia (*upa*+*sthā*). vehavvaṃ 'widowhood.'

"Of the Earth there will be a Lord. Royal Fortune is fickle with many distinguished men, so why falls absolute widowhood on me alone?"

[Earth and Royal Fortune are regarded as the other wives of Rāma. 'Absolute,' lit. having nothing in common (with those other two.)]

Verse 79. Kiṃ ea tti palattaṃ visa-ummillehi loaṇehi a
diṭṭhaṃ,
vialia-lajjāe mae phuḍaṃ Ṇāha tuha muhaṃ ti
parunnaṃ.

eaṃ ti (Śaur. edaṃ ti) is more usual. palattaṃ=**pralaptam.* visa meaning *viṣama*; reading should apparently be visam-ummill°. vialia (*vi+gal*). phuḍa § 38. paruṇṇaṃ (*pra+rud*) past. part. by analogy with *bhid, bhinna; chid, chinna,* etc., Śaur. rudida.

"'What is this?' I cried, and looked with obliquely opened eyes, then casting modesty aside I shrieked. 'Clearly it is thy face, my lord.'"

Verse 80. Sahio tujjha vioo raaṇi-arīhi samaaṃ sahīhi va vuṭṭhaṃ,
datṭhuṃ tumaṃ ti hottaṃ jai ettāhe vi jīviaṃ vialantaṃ.

vioo 'separation' § 9. vuṭṭhaṃ=**vyuṣṭam* 'dawned.' Pischel § 303,**vastam* with a>u. daṭṭhuṃ=*draṣṭum.* hottaṃ= hontaṃ pres. part. of hoï. ettāhe (Comm.=*idānīm*) cf. ettio 'so much'? *ettādṛśe *ettāise *ettāhe cf. Apa. taisa for tārisa and M. divaha for divasa. Hottaṃ and vialantaṃ are used in the sense of the conditional, cf. the Hindi usage, agar hotā.

"Separation from thee I endured with female demons as friends—it dawned with the stars as companions—were it only to see thee, then would my life melt away."

Verse 81. Jāe paraloa-gae tumammi vavasāa-matta-suha-daṭṭhavve
harisa-chāṇe vi mahaṃ ḍajjhaï adiṭṭha-Dahamuha-vahaṃ hiaaṃ.

matta=*mātra* commonly mĕtta § 69. daṭṭhavva=*draṣṭa-vya.* -chāṇe Comm.=*sthāne*; this should be (t)thāṇe, or perhaps we should read harisa-cchaṇe. chaṇa=*kṣaṇa,* but this generally means 'festival,' 'moment' being khaṇa (Pischel, § 322).

"Now that thou hast gone to the other world, and I may see thee with joy though only through tribulation, in place of that joy my heart burns, not to have seen the slaying of the Ten-Headed demon."

Verse 82. Vāhaṃ ṇa dhareï muhaṃ āsābandho vi me ṇa rumbhaï hiaaṃ,
ṇavari a cintijjante ṇa viṇajjai keṇa jīviaṃ samruddhaṃ.

rumbhai means *ruṇaddhi* (*rudh* forms rundhaï); this is from a root **rubh*, analogous to libbhaï=*lihyate* from a root **libh* (Pischel §§ 266, 507). ṇavari "thereupon," some say from *na pare*, Pischel disputes this (§ 184): cf. ṇavaraṃ "only." cintijjante pres. part. pass. vi-ṇajjai pass. (*vi+jñā*).

"My face bears no tear, even the bond of hope does not stay my heart, and when it is considered, it is not seen by what my life is restrained."

Verse 83. Bolīṇo maara-haro majjha kaeṇa maraṇaṃ pi de paḍivaṇṇaṃ,
ṇivvūḍhaṃ Ṇāha tume ajja vi dharai akaaṇṇuaṃ maha hiaaṃ.

Bolīṇo 'passed.' Form appears to be pres. part., cf. melīṇa from melai (*mil*). maara-hara 'home of sea-monsters.' paḍivaṇṇaṃ (*prati+pad*). akaaṇṇua cf. savvaṇṇu § 69.

"For my sake thou didst cross the ocean and incur thy death. Thou hast gone my lord, and yet my ungrateful heart survives."

Verse 84. Uggāhihi Rāma tumaṃ guṇe gaṇeūṇa purisa-maio tti jaṇo,
galia-mahilā-sahāvaṃ saṃbhariūṇa a mamaṃ ṇiattihii kahaṃ.

uggāhihi 'will sing.' gaṇeūṇa 'counting.' gerund. ṇiattihii. Fut. caus. (*ni+vṛt*). bhariūṇa 'remembering' gerund from bharaī; *mbharai *mharai=*smarati* Śaur. sumaredi, sumaria. kahaṃ 'story.'

"Folk will sing of thee, Rāma, counting thy virtues as of one made of valour, and remembering me that missed a woman's nature they will change the story."

Verse 85. Tuha bāṇukkhaa-ṇihaaṃ dacchimmi Daha-kaṇṭha-
muha-ṇihāaṃ ti kaā,
maha bhāadhea-valiā vivarā-huttā maṇorahā pal-
hatthā.

ukkhaa for ukkhāa 'destroyed.' ṇihaa (*ni*+*han*). dacchimi or dacchāmi have better authority (see v. 77 above). ṇihāa =*nighāta*. vivarā=*vi*+*parāṅ*-huttā, Comm.=*mukhā*, this has the same meaning, but the form is like AMg. khutta for *kṛtvaḥ* as with numerals (Pischel § 206) cf. AMg. aṇanta-khutta 'endless times, endless-ly'; *k* becomes *kh* becomes *h*, cf. ṇihasa § 19. palhattha, Comm.=*paryasta* 'upset,' but that would be pallattha (*r* assimilates *y* and becomes *l*). palhattha=**prahlasta* from root *hlas*=*hras* to diminish.

"Those wishes of mine, that I might see Ten-necks with his faces smashed, destroyed and struck down by thy arrow, have gone awry reversed by destiny and come to nought."

Verse 86. Jaṃ taṇuammi vi virahe pemā-bandheṇa saṅkaī
jaṇassa jaṇo,
taṃ jāaṃ ṇavara imaṃ pecchantīe a tārisaṃ maj-
jha phalaṃ.

taṇua 'short.' pemā- =*premā-*, pemma is commoner § 68. ṇavara, Comm.=*kevalam*, means "only," cf. ṇavari v. 82 above, Pischel's objection (§ 184) to the derivation from *na param* 'no more,' i.e. that the anusvāra appears to be secondary, is not conclusive.

"What a body dreads through love of another, even in a tiny separation, such a dread result has come to pass for to me only gazing at this sight."

Bk. XV. Verse 94. Happy return to Ayodhyā.

Ghettūṇa Jaṇaa-taṇaaṃ kañcaṇa-laṭṭhiṃ va hua-vahammi
visuddhaṃ,
patto puriṃ Raghuvaī kāuṃ Bharahassa sapphalam aṇu-
rāaṃ.

Ghettūṇa 'taking' cf. ghettuṃ § 136. laṭṭhi (Hindi lāṭhī) the equation with *yaṣṭi* is curious. kāuṃ=Ś. Mg. kāduṃ Śaur.

also has karidum. sapphalam, Comm.=*saphalam*, but this would be saphalam (§ 5), rather=*sat-phalam*.

"Taking Janaka's daughter, purified in the fire like a staff of gold, Raghupati arrived at the city, to give good fruits to Bharata's loving kindness."

Jain Māhārāṣṭrī.] Extract No. 15.

Maṇḍiya.

[Jocobi's Selected Stories, No. IX.]

Veṇṇāyaḍe ṇayare[1] Maṇḍio ṇāma tuṇṇāo[2] para-davva-haraṇa-pasatto āsī. so ya duṭṭha-gaṇḍo mi tti jaṇe pagāsento jāṇu-deseṇa niccam eva addâvaleva-litteṇa baddha-vaṇa-paṭṭo[3] rāya-magge tuṇṇāga-sippam uvajīvai. cakkamanto vi ya daṇḍa-dharieṇam pāeṇam kilimmanto kahaṃci cakkamai.[4] rattiṃ ca khattaṃ khaṇiūṇa davvajāyaṃ ghettūṇa—nagara-saṇṇihie ujjāṇ'ega-dese bhūmi-gharaṃ, tattha nikkhivai.[5] tat-

---

1 Veṇṇāyaḍa or Beṇṇāyaḍa (*Bernātaḍa*) a town in Western India. The letter *y* in this section represents the *laghuprayatnayakāra* ẏ not the strong य (*vide* p. 9). ṇaẏara, hence in many modern names= -nair, -ner.

Jacobi reads with his MSS. uvajīvati cakkamati, etc. The more regular forms uvajīvai. cakkamai, etc., have been inserted for the benefit of the student.

In AMg. JM. JŚ. single *n* can remain at the beginning of a word and double *nn* in the middle. The MSS. vary.

2 tuṇṇāo or tuṇṇāgo appears to mean a 'beggar' with an implication of rascality. Exact derivation uncertain, but evidently connected with *tūrṇa* as in *tūrṇa-ga* a 'swift goer.' pagāsento pres. part. of pagāseī "shows" (*pra+kāś*). For k > g compare AMg. Asoga (§ 11).

3 duṭṭha=*duṣṭa*. gaṇḍo has a variety of meanings in Sanskrit including "cheek," "pimple," "rhinoceros"; for Prakrit Hemacandra gives *vanaṃ* ('abundance' ?) [*dāṇḍa-pāśiko* M.W. 'policeman,' Jacobi (for this passage) 'nightwatchman,' 'beggar', (Probably slang), *laghu-mṛgo* (?) and *nāpitaḥ* 'barber.' adda 'damp' (*ārdra*). avaleva 'ointment, (*ava+lip*). litta 'smeared.' vaṇa 'wound' (*vraṇa*). -paṭṭa 'bandage' whence *paṭṭikā* modern paṭṭī. This context suggests that duṭṭhagaṇḍo is bahuvrīhi and means 'one with a bad boil.' The trick is still familiar enough.

4 cakkamai 'goes in circles,' 'wanders.' pāeṇa 'with his foot.' Kilimmanto pres. part. kilimmai 'gets weary' (*klam*).

5 khattaṃ 'hole.' -jāya (*jāta*) "quantity." -saṇṇihie 'in the vicinity' (*saṃ+nidhā*). egadesa "portion," cf. § 11.

tha ya se bhaginī kaṇṇagā ciṭṭhai. tassa bhūmi-gharassa majjhe kūvo. jaṃ ca so coro davveṇa palobheuṃ[1] sahāyaṃ davva-voḍhāraṃ āṇei, taṃ sā se bhaginī agaḍa-samīve puvva-natthâsaṇe ṇivesiuṃ pāya-soya-lakkheṇa pāe geṇhiūṇa taṃmi kūvae pakkhivai.[2] tao so vivajjai.[3] evaṃ kālo vaccai[4] ṇayaraṃ musantassa. cora-ggāhā taṃ ṇa sakkenti geṇhiuṃ. tao ṇayare bahu-ravo jāo.[5] tattha ya Mūladevo rāyā puvva-bhaṇiya-vihāṇeṇa jāo.[6] kahio ya tassa paūrehiṃ takkara-vaïyaro, jahā: ettha ṇayare pabhūya-kālo musantassa vaṭṭai kassai takkarassa, ṇa ya tīrai keṇai geṇhiuṃ.[7] tā kareu kiṃpi uvāyaṃ. tāhe so annaṃ nagarârakkhiyaṃ ṭhavei, so vi ṇa sakkai coraṃ geṇhiuṃ. tāhe Mūladevo sayaṃ nīla-paḍaṃ pāuṇiūṇa rattiṃ ṇiggato.[8] Mūladevo aṇajjanto egāe sabhāe ṇivaṇṇo acchai jāva, so Maṇḍiya-coro āgantuṃ bhaṇai: ko ettha acchai?[9] Mūladeveṇa bhaṇiyaṃ: ahaṃ kappaḍio. teṇa bhaṇṇai: ehi, maṇūsaṃ karemi.[10] Mūladevo uṭṭhio. egaṃmi īsara-ghare khattaṃ khayaṃ.[11] su-vahuṃ davva-jāyaṃ ṇīṇeūṇa Mūladevassa uvariṃ caḍāviyaṃ.[12] payaṭṭā ṇayara-

---

[1] palobheuṃ from palobhei "entices, allures" causal (*pra+lubh*); form infin. used as gerund.

[2] agaḍa Pkt. word "well," "spring." nattha 'placed' (*nyasta*). ṇivesiuṃ gerund of causal (*ni+viś*). soya 'washing' (*śauca*).

[3] vivajjaï "perishes" (*vi+pad*).

[4] vaccaï "goes, passes," generally referred to *vraj* (a case of c for j), but Pischel thinks possibly from *vrātya* so="tramps"; **vṛtyate* would be a simpler explanation. (cf. Pischel, Gr. § 202) H. bacnā.

[5] sakkenti. From *śak* either sakkei or sakkai.

[6] vihāṇa 'manner' (*vi+dhā*).

[7] vaïyaro 'story' (*vyatikara*). kassai (*kasya+api*). tīrai pass. from $\sqrt{t\bar{r}}$ 'is accomplished.'

[8] pāuṇiūṇa 'putting on' (*prā+vṝ*) pāuṇomi, p.p p. pāuṇia.

[9] aṇajjanto 'unknown' pres. part. of ṇajjai 'is known' pass. (*jñā*). ṇivaṇṇo (*ni+pad*). acchai 'stays' § 60. Pischel refers to *ṛcchati* (Gr. § 480. He quotes the other theories). āgantuṃ gerund.

[10] kappaḍio 'pilgrim,' *kārpaṭika*. bhaṇṇai pass. of bhaṇai.

[11] īsara 'rich man.'

[12] caḍāvia past part. caus. from caḍai which Hemacandra represents by *ā+ruh*. (cf. H. caṛh-nā). suvahuṃ=*subahum*.

vāhiriyaṃ.[1] Mūladevo purao, coro asiṇā kaḍḍhieṇa[2] piṭṭhao ei. saṃpattā bhūmi-gharaṃ. coro taṃ davvaṃ ṇihaṇium[3] āraddho. bhaṇiyā ya ṇeṇa bhagiṇī: eyassa pāhuṇayassa[4] pāya-soyaṃ dehi! tāe kūva-taḍa-[5]sanniviṭṭhe āsaṇe ṇivesio. tāe pāya-soya-lakkheṇa pāo gahio, kūve chuhāmi-tti.[6] jāva atīva-sukumārā pāyā, tāe ṇāyaṃ, jah': esa koi aṇubhūya-puvva-rajjo vihaliy'aṅgo.[7] tīe aṇukampā jāyā. tao tāe pāya-tale saṇṇio: ṇassa tti mā mārijjihisi tti. pacchā so palāo. tāe volo kao:[8] ṇaṭṭho ṇaṭṭho tti. so-y-asiṃ kaḍḍhiūṇa magge olaggo.[9] Mūladevo rāya-pahe aïsannikiṭṭhaṃ ṇāūṇa caccara-siv'antario ṭhio.[10] coro taṃ siva-liṅgaṃ, esa puriso tti kāuṃ kaṅkamaeṇa asiṇā duhā-kāuṃ[11] paḍiniyatto gao bhūmi-gharaṃ. tattha vasiūṇa pahāyāe rayaṇīe tao niggantūṇa gao bāhiṃ. antar'āvaṇe tuṇṇāgattaṃ karei. rāiṇā purisehiṃ saddāvio.[12] teṇa cintiyaṃ, jahā: so puriso ṇūṇaṃ ṇa mārio, avassaṃ ca esa rāyā bhavissai tti. tehiṃ purisehim āṇio. rāiṇā abbhuṭṭhāṇeṇa pūio āsaṇe ṇivesāvio,[13] su-vahuṃ ca

---

1 payaṭṭā=*pravṛttāḥ*. vāhiriya=bāhiriya "outside."

2 kaḍḍhia 'drawn' from kaḍḍhai (H. 4. 187=*kṛṣ*); *kṛṣṭa* could give *kaṭṭha thence *kaḍḍha.

3 ṇihaṇiuṃ 'to bury' (*ni+khan*).

4 pāhuṇaya 'guest' (*prāghūrṇaka*).

5 taḍa 'edge.'

6 chuhai or chubhai "throws." Hemacandra=*kṣip*: rather from *kṣubh* cognate with English "shove."

7 vihaliya (*vihvalita*) 'trembling.'

8 saṇṇio (*saṃjñitaḥ*) 'made a sign.' mārijjai pass. of mārei "kills." palāo 'fled' past part. of palāyai 'flees.' volo=bolo 'a cry' in M. bolo='speech' cf. modern bolnā.

9 so-y-asiṃ 'and he' (drawing his) 'sword' *or y* is merely a sandhi consonant. olaggo 'followed' means *anulagna*, but the form is *ava* or *apa* +*lagna*.

10 aï-sannikiṭṭhaṃ=*ati-saṃ-nikṛṣṭam*. caccara 'square' (*catvara*) Pischel. § 299. antario 'hidden.'

11 kaṅkamaa 'shaped like a heron's beak.' duhā kāuṃ 'having split' (*dvidhā kṛtvā*).

12 āvaṇa 'market.' saddāvio (*śabdāpitaḥ*).

13 ṇivesāvio past part. of ṇivesāvei fuller form of ṇivesei.

piyaṃ ābhāsio saṃlatto: mama bhagiṇiṃ dehi tti. teṇa diṇṇā, vivāhiyā rāiṇā. bhogā ya se saṃpadattā.[1] kaisuvi[2] diṇesu gaesu rāiṇā Maṇḍio bhaṇio: davveṇa kajjaṃ ti. teṇa su-vahuṃ davva-jāyaṃ diṇṇaṃ. rāiṇā saṃpūjio. aṇṇayā puṇo maggio; puṇo vi diṇṇaṃ. tassa ya corassa atīva sakkāra-sammāṇaṃ pauñjai.[3] eeṇa pagāreṇa savvaṃ davvaṃ davāvio.[4] bhagiṇiṃ se pucchai; tīe bhaṇṇati: ettiyaṃ ceva vittaṃ. tao puvvâveiya-lekkhâṇusāreṇa[5] savvaṃ davvaṃ davāveūṇa Maṇḍio sūlāe ārovio.

Maṇḍio.

In the town Bernātaḍa there lived a beggar named Maṇḍio addicted to taking other people's property. He used to practise the beggar's art on the high-road, tied up in bandages, with a smear of grease, kept always wet, about his knee, to show that he suffered from a virulent sore. Mouching wearily around with his foot supported on a crutch he wandered at random. And at night he would dig a hole (in a wall) and taking a lot of property—to a cellar[6] in a corner of a garden near the town—would bury it there. And there lived his unmarried sister. In the middle of that cellar, there was a well. Anybody the thief brought with him to carry his loot, having allured him therewith, the sister would have sit down on a seat previously arranged at the edge of the spring, and then, taking hold of his feet on the pretence of washing them, she would tip him into the well. And so he perished. Thus time went on while he robbed the town. The thief-catchers were unable to catch him, and a great noise about it arose in the town.

Now Mūladeva had become king there in the manner related above. The citizens told him about the thief; that a

---

1 saṃpadattā (*sam+pra+dā*). se 'on her.'
2 kaisuvi (*katiṣu+api*).
3 sakkāra 'favour.' pauñjai 'employs' (*pra+yuj*).
4 pagāra 'manner' (*prakāra*). davāvio past. part. caus. (*dā*).
5 āveia past part. of āveei causal (*ā+vid*) lekkha 'list.'
6 An underground room or *tahkhāna* built for coolness in the hot season.

certain thief had been for some time robbing the town, and that nobody had succeeded in catching him—so he should devise some remedy. Thereupon he appoints another superintendent of the town police. He also is unable to catch the thief. Then Mūladeva himself put on a dark cloak and went out one night. Mūladeva goes and lies down *incognito* in a certain hall and stays there. The thief Maṇḍio comes and says, 'Who is it stopping here?' Mūladeva said, 'I am a pilgrim.' The other said, 'Come I will make a man of you.' Mūladeva got up. A hole was cut in a certain rich man's house. He took out a great quantity of plunder and piled it up on Mūladeva. They set out for the outskirts of the town. Mūladeva goes in front, the thief comes up behind with a drawn sword. They came to the cellar. The thief set to work to bury the loot, and he said to his sister, 'Wash the feet of this guest'; she set him on the seat placed on the edge of the well, and took hold of one of his feet as if to wash it, meaning to shove him into the well. As his feet were very delicate she perceived that this was some one who had enjoyed royalty and had sensitive limbs. She took pity on him, and made a sign on the surface of his foot. "Flee, lest you be slain." After that he made his escape. She raised a cry—"He's fled, he's fled," and the other drew his sword and pursued him down the road. Mūladeva finding he was very close to him on the highway, stood hidden behind a *liṅgam* in a square. The thief mistook this Śiva's *liṅgam* for a man, split it in two with his heron-bill sword, and went back to his cellar. He stayed there till the night grew light; and then he came out and went abroad. He plays the beggar in the market-place. The king sent men to summon him. He thought to himself, "so that fellow was not killed, and no doubt he will turn out to be the king."

The king rose to greet him, and made him take a seat. After several friendly remarks the king said to him, 'Give me your sister.' He gave her, and the king married her. Wealth was bestowed upon her.

When a few days had passed, the king said to Maṇḍio, 'I need some treasure.' So he gave him a good quantity. The king honoured him. Then again he asked, and again it was given. He lavishes the greatest favour and consideration on the thief. In this way he made him give all his wealth. He asks his sister. She said, he had just so much property. Then he caused all this wealth to be given away according to a list previously announced, and Maṇḍio he had impaled.

Jain Māhārāṣṭrī.] **Extract No. 16.**

Domuha.

[Jacobi's No. V.]

Sampai Dummuha-cariyaṃ.[1] atthi ih' eva Bhārahe vāse Kampillaṃ nāma puraṃ. tattha Hari-kula-vaṃsa-saṃbhavo Jao nāma rāyā. tassa Guṇamālā nāma bhāriyā. so ya rāyā tīe saha rajja-sirim aṇuhavanto gamei kālaṃ. annayā atthāṇa-maṇḍava-ṭṭhieṇa pucchio dūo:[2] kiṃ n'atthi mama, jaṃ anna-rāīṇaṃ atthi? dūeṇa bhaṇiyaṃ: deva, citta-sabhā tumha n'atthi. tao rāiṇā āṇattā thavaiṇo,[3] jahā: lahuṃ citta-sabhaṃ kareha! āesaṇâṇantaraṃ samāḍhattā.[4] tattha dharaṇīe khan-namāṇīe kammagarehiṃ[5] pañcama-diṇe savva-rayaṇâmao jal-aṇo-vva teyasā jalanto diṭṭho mahā-maūḍo, sa-harisehiṃ siṭṭho[6] Jaya-rāiṇo. teṇa vi parituṭṭha-maṇeṇaṃ nandī-rava-puvvayam uttārio bhūmi-vivarāo. pūiyā thavai-m-āiṇo[7] jahā'riha-vattha-m-āihiṃ. theva-kāleṇa[8] vi nimmāyā uttuṅga-

---

1 sampai "now" (*samprati*). Dummuha=Do-muha 'two-faces.'

2 atthāṇa 'audience hall' (ā+*sthā*). dūo 'envoy.'

3 āṇattā 'commanded' (*ā+jñā*) § 125. thavai 'architect' (*sthapati*).

4 samāḍhattā 'begun' past pass. part. (*sam+ā+dhā*) for dha becomes ḍha, compare § 7. The derivation from ārabdha is quite impossible.

5 dharaṇīe khannamāṇīe 'during the excavations.' kammagara 'workman,' cf. Asoga.

6 siṭṭho 'told' p.p.p. of sāhai (*śiṣṭa: *śāsati*) § 125.

7 thavai-m-āiṇo 'the architects, etc.' -m- is a sandhi consonant.

8 theva 'little' (Pali theva) √*stip* 'drop.'

siharā citta-sabhā. sohaṇa-diṇe kao citta-sabhāe paveso. ārovio maṅgala-tūra-saddeṇa[1] appaṇo uttim'aṅge maüḍo. tap-pabhāveṇa do-vayaṇo so rāyā jāo. loeṇa[2] tassa Domuho tti nāmaṃ kayaṃ.

aikkanto koi kālo. tassa ya rāiṇo satta taṇayā jāyā. duhiyā me n'atthi tti Guṇamālā addhiiṃ[3] karei. Mayaṇâbhihāṇassa jakkhassa icchai uvāiyaṃ.[4] annayā ya pāriyāya-mañjarī-uvalambha-suviṇa-sūiyā tīse duhiyā jāyā. kayaṃ ca vaddhā-vaṇayaṃ.[5] dinnaṃ jakkhassa uvāiyaṃ. kayaṃ ca tīe nāmaṃ Mayaṇamañjarī kameṇa ya jāyā jovvaṇatthā.

io ya Ujjeṇīe Caṇḍapajjoya-rāyā. tassa dūeṇa sāhiyaṃ, jahā: rāyā domuho jāo. Pajjoeṇa bhaṇiyaṃ: kahaṃ? dūeṇa bhaṇiyaṃ: tassa eriso maüḍo atthi; tammi ārovie do muhāṇi havanti. mauḍass' uvariṃ Pajjoyassa lobho jāo. dūyaṃ Domuha-rāiṇo pesei:[6] eyaṃ maüḍa-rayaṇaṃ mama pesehi! aha na pesesi, jujjha-sajjo[7] hohi! Domuha-rāiṇā dūo bhaṇio Pajjoya-santio: jai mama jaṃ maggiyaṃ deha, to aham avi maüḍaṃ demi. dūeṇa bhaṇiyaṃ: kiṃ maggaha? rāiṇā bhaṇiyaṃ:

deha: Nalagirī hatthī Aggībhīrū tahā raha-varo ya |
Jāyā ya Sivā devī lehâriya Lohajaṅgho ya ||

eyaṃ Pajjoyassa rajja-sāraṃ. paḍigao dūo Ujjeṇiṃ. sāhiyaṃ Pajjoyassa Domuha-santiyaṃ paḍivayaṇaṃ. kuddho[8] aīva Pajjoo, calio caüraṅga-baleṇa: donni lakkhā mayaga-lāṇaṃ,[9] donni sahassā rahāṇaṃ, pañca ajuyāṇi hayāṇaṃ,

---

[1] tūra 'musical instrument.'

[2] loeṇā 'by the people' § 9.

[3] addhii "care, anxiety." (*adhṛti.*)

[4] jakkhassa 'to a demon.' icchai 'promises.' uvāiyaṃ 'offering' (*upa+ā+kṛ*).

[5] sūiya 'revealed' (*sūc*). Śaur. sūida. suviṇa 'dream.' pāriyāya= *pārijāta* "coral tree." vaddhāvaṇayaṃ 'birth ceremony' *vardhāpana.*

[6] pesei 'he sends.'

[7] jujjha-sajjo 'ready for battle.'

[8] kuddho "wroth."

[9] mayagala 'elephant' (*madakala*).

satta koḍīo payāi-jaṇāṇaṃ.[1] aṇavaraya-payāṇachiṃ[2] patto Pañcāla-jaṇavaya-sandhiṃ. iyaro vi Domuha-rāyā caüraṅga-bala-samaggo[3] nīhario nayarāo. gao paḍisaṃmuhaṃ Pajjoyassa. Pañcāla-visaya-sandhīe raio garuḍa-vūho[4] Pajjoeṇa, sāgara-vūho Domuheṇa. tao saṃpalaggaṃ doṇha vi balāṇa jujjhaṃ. so maüḍa-rayaṇa-pahāveṇa ajeo[5] Domuharāyā. bhaggaṃ[6] Pajjoyassa balaṃ. bandhiūṇa Pajjoo pavesio nayaraṃ. dinnaṃ calaṇe kaḍayaṃ.[7] suheṇa tattha Pajjoya-rāiṇo vaccai kālo.

annayā diṭṭhā teṇa Mayaṇamañjarī. jāo gāḍhâṇurāo. tao kāmâggiṇā ḍajjhamāṇassa cintā-saṃtāva-gayassa voliyā[8] kahavi rāī. paccūse ya gao atthāṇaṃ. diṭṭho parimilāṇa-muha-sarīro Domuha-rāiṇā; pucchio sarīra-paüttiṃ, na dei paḍivayaṇaṃ. sâsaṅkeṇa ya gāḍhayaraṃ puṭṭho. tao dīhaṃ nīsasiūṇa jaṃpiyaṃ[9] Pajjoeṇa:

Mayaṇa-vasagassa, nara-vara vāhi-vighatthassa[10] taha ya mattassa ı
kuviyassa marantassa ya lajjā dūrujjhiyā hoi ‖[11] [eyaṃ ı
tā jai icchasi kusalaṃ payaccha to Mayaṇamañjariṃ
niya-dhūyaṃ[12] me nara-vara na desi pavisāmi jalaṇammi ‖

tao Domuheṇa nicchayaṃ nāūṇa dinnā. sohaṇa-diṇa-muhutte kayaṃ pāṇiggahaṇaṃ. kaivaya-diṇehiṃ dhario,[13] pūiūṇa visajjio, gao Ujjeṇiṃ Pajjoo.

---

1 payāi 'footsoldier' (*padāti*).

2 aṇavaraya 'incessant.'

3 samaggo 'complete.'

4 raio=*racito*. vūha 'order of battle' (*vyūha*).

5 ajeo 'invincible.'

6 bhaggaṃ 'broken.'

7 kaḍaya 'fetter' (*kaṭaka*).

8 ḍajjhamāṇa 'being consumed.' voliyā 'passed,' cf. bolei.

9 nīsasiūṇa 'sighing.' jampiyaṃ (*jalpitam*) § 37.

10 vāhi 'illness' (*vyādhi*). vighattha 'consumed' (*vi+ghas*).

11 kuvia 'angry.' dūr-ujjhiya 'left far behind.'

12 dhūyaṃ 'daughter,' dhūyā=M. dhūā Ś.Mg. dhūdā —*dhūtā from *dhuktā (Pischel, § 65).

13 dhario 'waited' (*dhṛ*).

annayā āgao Inda-mahūsavo. Domuha-rāiṇā āiṭṭhā[1] naya ra-jaṇā: ubbheha indakeuṃ[2]! tao maṅgala-nandī-mahāraveṇa dhavala-dhaya-vaḍāho ḍoya-khiṅkhiṇī-jālâlaṃkio[3] avalambiya-vara-malla-dāmo maṇi-rayaṇa-mālā-bhūsio ṇāṇāviha-palambamāṇa-phala-nivaha-ciñcaio[4] ubbhio indakeū. tao naccanti naṭṭiyāo, gijjanti[5] sukai-raiyā kavva-bandhā, naccanti nara-saṃghāyā, dīsanti diṭṭhi-mohaṇāiṃ indayālāiṃ, indayāliṇo[6] ya dijjanti tambolâiṃ; khippanti kappūra-kuṅkuma-jala-chaḍā, dijjanti mahā-dāṇāiṃ, vajjanti muiṅgâiāojjāiṃ.[7] evaṃ mahā-moeṇa gayā satta vāsarā. āgayā puṇṇimā. pūio mahā-vicchaḍḍeṇa[8] kusuma-vatthâīhiṃ Domuha-rāiṇā indakeū. mahā-tūra-raveṇa annaṃmi diṇe paḍio meiṇīe. diṭṭho rāiṇā amejjha-mutta-duggandhe nivaḍio jaṇeṇa pariluppamāṇo ya.[9] daṭṭhūṇa cintiyaṃ: dhir-atthu vijju-[10]reha-vva cañcalāṇaṃ pariṇāma-virasāṇaṃ riddhīṇaṃ. eyaṃ cintayanto saṃbuddho, patteyabuddho[11] jāo. pañca-muṭṭhiyaṃ loyaṃ kāūṇa pavvaio.[12] *uktaṃ ca:*

---

1 āiṭṭhā 'commanded' (*ā+diś*).

2 ubbheha 'erect' imperat. from ubbhei 'erects' from ubbha= *ūrdhva* (also uddha uḍḍha). For dhv becomes bbh compare dv becomes bb. bārasa 'twelve'=(*dvādaśa*). -keu 'banner.'

3 dhaya=*dhvaja*. vaḍāho (*-patāko*). ḍoya "*dāruhasta*"? 'clapper.' cf. Panj. ḍoī 'wooden ladle.'

4 ciñcaio 'adorned,' Pkt. root.

5 gijjanti 'are sung' § 135.

6 indayāliṇo 'magicians.'

7 khippanti pass. of khivai 'throws' § 135. chaḍā 'abundance (*chaṭā*). vajjanti "are sounded" (*vādyante*). muiṅga 'drum.' āojja "musical instrument" (*ātodya*).

8 vicchaḍḍa 'liberality' (*vi+chṛd*).

9 amejjha 'impurity' (*amedhya*), mutta=*mūtra*, pariluppamāṇa 'being destroyed.'

10 vijju "lightning."

11 patteya-buddho=*pratyeka-buddho* 'one who obtains enlightenment all alone.' By analogy with paccūsa, etc., one might expect *pacceya (cf. Pali pacceko). Pischel (Gr. § 281) explains patteya in this phrase, patteyaṃ (=*pratyekam*) and patti in M. pattiai, JM. AMg. pattiyai, Ś. Mg. pattiāadi=*pratiyāti* as being derived not from *prati* but from **parati *parti*, and compares Greek *porti* beside the ordinary *proti*.

12 muṭṭhiya 'handful.' loya explained as *luñcana* 'plucking out (hair)' pavvaio 'he entered the Order' (*pra+vraj*).

jo indakeū suyalaṃkiyaṃ taṃ daṭṭhuṃ paḍantaṃ pavi-
luppamāṇaṃ |
riddhiṃ ariddhiṃ samupehiyāṇaṃ Pañcāla-rāyā vi samik-
kha[1] dhammaṃ |

Domuha.

Now comes the story of Double-face :—

In this land of Bhārata there is a town called Kampilla. There was a raja named Jaya born of the lineage of Hari. His wife was Guṇamālā. And he passed the time together with her enjoying his royal fortune. One day in the pavilion of the audience hall he asked an envoy, "What do I lack, that other kings have?" The envoy said, "Your Highness has no picture-gallery." Then the raja commanded his architects, saying, 'Quickly build a picture-gallery.' They started work immediately on the command. While the excavations for this work were going on, the workmen found on the fifth day a great diadem of all sorts of gems flashing with brilliance like fire, and in great glee reported this to Raja Jaya. He was very pleased, and had it taken out of the hole in the ground, after the recitation of a blessing. The architects and the rest were honoured with appropriate robes and the like. In a very short time a picture gallery with lofty pinnacles was completed. On an auspicious day came the opening ceremony. To the sound of happy music the raja placed the diadem on his head, and so shone with the light of a double countenance. So the people dubbed him "Double-face."

Some time passed, and there were born to the raja seven sons. Guṇamālā grieved that she had no daughter, and promised an offering to a demon named Mayaṇa. And then was born a daughter revealed to her in a dream in which she received a cluster of the Coral Tree. The birth ceremony was performed, and the offering given to the demon. They named

---

1 samupehiyāṇaṃ gerund (*sam+ut+prekṣ*) shortened for samuppe° to scan. This verse is in AMg. quoted from āvaśyaka-niryukti 17. 44. samikkha "*samīkṣate,*" i.e. for samikkhai which is regularly contracted in AMg. verse to samikkhe, but this would not scan here.

the baby Maẏaṇa-mañjarī, and in course of time she grew to maid's estate.

Now king Candra-Pradyota of Ujjain was told by an envoy that the raja had become double-faced. "How?" asked Pradyota. The envoy said, "He has such a diadem, on putting it on he has two faces." Pradyota was filled with desire for that diadem. He sent a messenger to King Domuha, "Send me that jewel of a diadem! If you don't send it, prepare for battle." King Domuha said to Pradyota's messenger, "If you give me what I ask, I will give the diadem." The messenger said, "What are you asking?" The raja said, "Give me—there's the elephant Nalagiri, and the excellent chariot Agnibhīru, and the consort Queen Śivā, and the writer Lohajaṅgha."

This was the cream of Pradyota's kingdom. The messenger returned to Ujjain, and told Pradyota Domuha's answer. Pradyota was exceedingly angry and set out with an army of the four arms: two lakhs of elephants, two thousand chariots, fifty thousand horse, and seven crores of footsoldiers. He reached the frontier of the Pañcāla country by forced marches. King Domuha on the other side came out of the city with all his army, and went to meet Pradyota. On the Pañcāla frontier Pradyota took up the "Garuḍa" formation, and Doubleface the "Ocean" order. Then both forces joined issue. Through the puissance of that jewel of a diadem Doubleface was invincible. Pradyota's force was broken. Pradyota was bound and brought into the city. A ring was fixed on his foot. And there king Pradyota quietly passed his days.

One day he saw Maẏaṇa-mañjarī. He became deeply enamoured. Then consumed with the fire of love, and fallen into a fever of thought he passed the night as best he could. At dawn he went to the audience-hall. King Domuha noticed his pale face and emaciated form, and asked what ailed him. He gave no answer. He was anxiously questioned more closely. Then with a deep sigh Pradyota quoted—

"The man in the power of Love, good sir, the man that is drunk or consumed by disease, he that's wroth, and he that is on the point of death—has left modesty far behind. So if you wish my welfare, vouchsafe me this Mayaṇamañjarī: if you give me not your own daughter, good sir, I shall enter the fire."

So Domuha, perceiving his determination, gave her to him. The wedding was celebrated on an auspicious day and hour. After staying some days Pradyota, having paid his respects and taken his departure, went to Ujjain.

One day there came the Great Indra Festival. Domuha instructed the citizens to raise an Indra Banner. Then the Banner was erected with a great roar of auspicious blessings, with white pennons and flags, adorned with a chain of bells and their clappers, hung with fine festoons, decorated with strings of jewels and gems, and laden with an abundant variety of pendent fruits. Then the dancers dance; poems composed by good poets are sung, crowds of people dance, dazzling illusions are shown, and the magicians are given betel and the like. Quantities of camphor, saffron and water are thrown in the air, masses of alms are given away, the bands crash with drums and the rest. Thus in great delight pass seven days. The full-moon came. King Domuha honoured the Indra-Banner with great liberality, with flowers, robes and the like. On another day with a great roar of music down it fell on the ground. The king saw it fallen in a place foul with dung and dirty water, and plundered by the people. Seeing this he reflected—"Out on the pomps of this world fleeting as a flash of lightning, ending in disgust!" As he thought thus he was enlightened, and became a Pratyeka-Buddha. Plucking out his hair in five handfuls he entered the Order. 'Tis said:

'What was an Indra-Banner, that he saw adorned, but fallen and plundered.

"And perceiving the pomp that was no pomp, Pañcāla's king discovered the Law."

Jain Māhārāṣṭrī.] **Extract No. 17.**

From an inscription found near Ghaṭayāla, a village situated about twenty miles north of the city of Jodhpur. Text and translation published in the Journal of the Royal Asiatic Society 1895, Vol. 27, p. 513. The inscription is dated Saṃvat 918. This probably refers to the Vikrama era, and is equivalent to about 861 A.D. It records that a chief named **Kakkuka** founded a Jain temple, established a market, and erected two pillars.

Oṃ. Saggâpavagga-maggaṃ paḍhamaṃ saẏalāṇa kāraṇaṃ devaṃ ।
ṇīsesa-duria-dalaṇaṃ parama-guruṃ ṇamaha Jiṇa-ṇāhaṃ ॥ 1.
Rahu-tilao paḍihāro āsī Siri-Lakkhaṇo tti Rāmassa ।
teṇa Paḍihāra-vanso samuṇṇaiṃ ettha sampatto ॥ 2.
vippo **Hariando** bhajjā āsi tti khattiā **Bhaddā** ।
tāṇa suo uppaṇṇo vīro Siri-**Rajjilo** ettha ॥ 3.
assa vi **Ṇarahaḍa** ṇāmo jāo Siri-**Ṇāhaḍo** tti eassa ।
assa vi taṇao **Tāo**, tassa vi **Jasa-vaddhaṇo** jāo. ॥ 4.
assa vi **Candua**-ṇāmō uppaṇṇo **Silluo** vi eassa ।
Jhoṭo tti tassa taṇuo, assa vi Siri-**Bhilluo** cāī ॥ 5.
Siri-**Bhilluassa** taṇuo Siri-**Kakko** guru-guṇehi gāravio ।
assa vi **Kakkua**-ṇāmo **Dullahadevīe** uppaṇṇo ॥ 6.
Īsiviāsaṃ hasiaṃ, mahuraṃ bhaṇiaṃ, paloiaṃ sommaṃ ।
ṇamaẏaṃ jassa ṇa dīṇaṃ ro [so] theo, thirā mettī ॥ 7.
ṇo jampiaṃ, ṇa hasiaṃ, ṇa kaẏaṃ ṇa paloiaṃ, ṇa sambhariaṃ ।
ṇa thiaṃ, ṇa paribbhamiaṃ, jeṇa jaṇe kajja-parihīṇaṃ ॥ 8.
sutthā dutthā vi paẏā ahamā taha uttimā vi sokkheṇa ।
jaṇaṇi vva jeṇa dhariā ṇiccaṃ ṇiya-maṇḍale savvā ॥ 9.
uaroha-rāa-macchara-lohehim i ṇāẏa-vajjiaṃ jeṇa ।
ṇa kao doṇha viseso vavahāre kavi[1] maṇaẏaṃ pi ॥ 10.
diavara-diṇṇāṇujjaṃ jeṇa jaṇaṃ rañjiūṇa saẏalaṃ pi ।
ṇimmacchareṇa jaṇiaṃ duṭṭhāṇa vi daṇḍa-ṇiṭṭhavaṇaṃ ॥ 11.

[1] Read *kovi* or *kahavi*.

dhaṇa-riddha-samiddhāṇa vi paūrāṇaṃ ṇiakarassa abbhahiaṃ ।
lakkhaṃ saẏañca sarisantaṇañca taha jeṇa diṭṭhāiṃ ॥ 12.
ṇava-jovvaṇa-rūa-pasāhieṇa siṅgāra-guṇa-garukkeṇa ।
jaṇavaẏa-ṇijjam alajjaṃ jeṇa jaṇe ṇeẏa sañcariaṃ ॥ 13.
bālāṇa gurū taruṇāṇa taha sahī gaẏavaẏāṇa taṇao vva ।
iẏa-sucariehi ṇiccaṃ jeṇa jaṇo pālio savvo ॥ 14.
jeṇa ṇamanteṇa saẏā sammāṇaṃ guṇathuiṃ kuṇanteṇa ।
jampanteṇa ẏa laliaṃ diṇṇaṃ paṇaīṇa dhaṇa-ṇivahaṃ ॥ 15.
Marumāḍa-Valla-Tamaṇī-*pariaṅkā-ajja*-**Gujjarattāsu** ।
jaṇio jeṇa jaṇāṇaṃ saccaria-guṇehim aṇurāo ॥ 16.
gahiūṇa gohaṇāiṃ, girimmi jālāu[lā]o pallīo ।
jaṇiāo jeṇa visame **Vaḍaṇāṇaẏa**-maṇḍale paẏaḍaṃ ॥ 17.
ṇīluppala-dala-gandhā rammā māẏanda-mahua-vindehiṃ ।
vara-icchu-paṇṇa-cchaṇṇā esā bhūmī kaẏā jeṇa ॥ 18.
varisa-saesu a ṇavasuṃ aṭṭhārasam'aggalesu Cettammi ।
ṇakkhatte vihu-hatthe Buhavāre dhavala-bīāe ॥ 19.
siri-**Kakkueṇa** haṭṭaṃ mahājaṇaṃ vippa-paẏaī-vaṇi-bahulaṃ ।
Rohinsakūa-gāme ṇivesiaṃ kitti-viddhīe ॥ 20.
Maḍḍoarammi ekko, bīo **Rohinsakūa**-gāmammi ।
jeṇa jasassa va puñjā ee tthambhā samutthaviā ॥ 21.
teṇa siri-**Kakkueṇaṃ** Jiṇassa devassa duria-ṇiddalaṇaṃ ।
kāraviaṃ acalam imaṃ bhavaṇaṃ bhattīe suha-jaṇaẏaṃ ॥ 22.
appiam eaṃ bhavaṇaṃ siddhassa **Dhaṇêsarassa** gacchammi ।
taha santa-Jamba-Ambaẏa-vaṇi-Bhāuḍa-pamuha-goṭṭhīe ॥ 23.

Notes.—Verse 1. Apavagga 'final beatitude' (*apa* + *vṛj*). ṇīsesa 'all' (*niḥśeṣa*) § 63. duria 'sin' (*durita*).

V. 2. -paḍihāro 'door-keeper,' or name of clan. vanso, better spelling vaṃso.

V. 3. bhajjā 'wife' § 50.

V. 5. Inscription has -nāmā a mistake for -ṇāmo as in the next verse. cāī 'generous' (=*tyāgī*) cf. AMg. catta=*tyakta*. § 44. § 119. gāravio means *gauravitaḥ* 'highly esteemed' cf. M. AMg. JM. gārava for M. Ś. gorava (=*gaurava*); Pali garu; Skt. *garīyas*.

V. 7. ṇamaẏaṃ perhaps corrected to ṇamiyaṃ 'meekness.' theo=thevo 'little.'

V. 9. paẏā=*prajāḥ*, ṇiya=*nija*.

V.10. uaroha 'favour' or 'ill-will, obstructiveness' (*upa* + *rudh*). macchara 'envy' cf. vaccha § 39. i=*iti*. In AMg. ti after a long vowel becomes i (Pischel § 93). In JM. maṇiyaṃ pi is more usual.

V.11. dia 'twice-born.' § 42. ṇiṭṭhavaṇaṃ 'infliction' (*niḥ*+*sthāpanam*) for short vowel cf. ṭhavei=*sthāpayati*. § 67.

V.12. paūra=Ś. pora (=*paura*) § 61. abbhahiaṃ=*abhyadhikam*. Kielhorn suggested sarisattaṇañca. =**sadṛśatvanaṃ ca*; -ttaṇa=vedic-*tvana* is common instead of -*tva*. (His translation of this verse is tentative and he notes that the wording of the original may be wrong.)

V.13. garukka 'heavy with,' 'full of'=**garukya* cf. Pali garu; Skt. *guruka* (Pischel § 299). jaṇavaẏa=*janapada*. ṇijja=*nedya* 'to be blamed.' ṇeẏa=*naiva*.

V.14. gaẏa-vaẏa 'aged' (=*gata-vayas*); iẏa, JM. AMg. =*iti*.

V.15. saẏā=*sadā*. paṇai=*praṇayin*.

V.16. Marumāḍa prob.=Mārwāṛ. Gujjara=*Gurjara* 'Gūjar.' Here we have an older form of the modern 'Gujarāt.' -pariaṅkā ajja has not been explained.

V.17. gohaṇa 'herd,' (*go-dhana*). pallī 'hamlet.' jālâula=*jvālâkula*, paẏaḍaṃ=*prakaṭam*, M. paaḍa AMg. pagaḍa.

V.18. māẏanda 'mango tree' (*mākanda*).

V.19. aggala (=*argala*) used technically in dates, see *Indian Antiquary*, vol. xix, p. 61, note 52. vihu 'moon.' hattha=Hasta the constellation. bīa 'second,' AMg. JM. bīya biiya.

V.20. mahājaṇaṃ as an adjective 'for merchants.' payaï 'foot soldier,' also payāi (*padāti*).

V.23. appiaṃ (*arpita*). gaccha 'series,' 'lineage,' i.e. 'school.' goṭṭhī 'society.'

Translation.[1]—Om! Bow to the lord of the Jinas, who is the

1 Follows what is apparently Kielhorn's. J.R.A.S. quoted above.

path to heaven and beatitude, the god who is the first cause of all things, the destroyer of every sin, the supreme preceptor.

V. 2. The glorious Lakṣmaṇa, the ornament of the Raghus, was Rāma's doorkeeper; hence the *Pratihāra* clan has attained here to eminence.

V. 3. There was a Brāhman named *Haricandra;* his wife was *Bhadrā* of the Kshatriya caste. To them a valiant son was born, named Rajjila.

V. 4. To him, again, *Narabhaṭa* was born, and to him Nāhaḍa (=*Nāgabhaṭa*); his son was *Tāta,* and his son, *Yaśovardhana.*

V. 5. To him *Canduka* was born, and to him *Śilluka;* his son was Jhoṭo, and his, the generous *Bhilluka.*

V. 6. *Bhilluka's* son was Kakko highly esteemed for his noble qualities; and to him was born from *Durlabhadevī*, **Kakkuka.**

V. 7. His smile is [like a] slightly opening [flower-bud], his speech sweet, his glance benign, his meekness not timid, his anger slight, his friendship firm.

V. 8. He never has spoken, or smiled, or acted, or looked, or remembered a thing, without benefiting mankind.

V. 9. Like a mother he constantly has kept in comfort all the people in his dominion, the poor and the prosperous, the lowest as well as the highest.

V.10. And never has he, departing from what was right, through favour, affection, envy, or greed, made the slightest difference between the parties in a suit.[1]

V.11. Following the advice given by the best of the twice-born, he has pleased everybody, and free from passion has also caused punishment to be inflicted on the wicked.

V.12. Even to citizens possessed of abundance of wealth he has assigned more than his revenue (?), a lakh and a hundred and the like(?)[2]

---

[1] K. "transaction." [2] "As much as was suitable (?)"

V.13. Though adorned with the freshness of youth and beauty, and full of the sentiment of love, he never has behaved to people so as to incur men's reproaches, or without modesty.

V.14. To children like a *guru*, to young men like a friend and to the aged like a son, by such good conduct has he constantly cherished everyone.

V.15. Always showing respect with politeness, praising virtues, and speaking pleasantly he has given an abundance of wealth to those attached to him.

V.16. By his good behaviour and virtues he has won the affection of the people in Marumāḍa, Valla, Tamaṇī, ...and Gujarāt.

V.17. He has taken away the herds of cattle and has made a conspicuous illumination[1] of the villages on the mountain in the rugged *Vaṭanānaka* district.

V.18. This land he has made fragrant with the leaves of blue lotuses, and pleasant with groups of mango and *madhuka* trees and has covered it with the leaves of excellent sugar-cane.

Vv.19 and 20. And when nine hundred years were increased by the eighteenth, in Caitra, when the moon's nakshatra was Hasta, on Wednesday, the second lunar day of the bright half, the illustrious Kakkuka, for the increase of his fame, founded a market, fit for traders, crowded with Brāhmans, soldiers, and merchants at the village of *Rohinsakūpa*.

V.21. He has erected like heaps of his renown these two pillars, one at Maḍḍoara, and another at the village of *Rohinsakūpa*.

V.22. This illustrious **Kakkuka** piously has caused to be built this imperishable temple of the god Jina, which destroys sin and creates happiness.

---

1 K. "has boldly destroyed by fire."

V.23. And he has entrusted this temple to the community presided over by the ascetics Jamba and Ambaya (?) and the merchant Bhākuṭa (?) in the *gaccha* of the holy *Dhaneśvara*.

Jain Māhārāṣṭrī.] Extract No. 18.

From story of **Kālakâcārya.** Jacobi Z.D.M.G. Vol. 34 (1880), p. 262.

Failing to influence Gardabhilla the wicked King of Ujjain, who had the nun Sarasvatī conveyed into his harem, and then refused to give her up, Kālakâcārya, the saintly brother of the nun, went abroad to contrive Gardabhilla's overthrow.

taṃ ca kuo vi nāūṇa niggao nayarīo sūrī, aṇavarayaṃ ca gacchanto patto **Saga-kūlaṃ** ṇāma kūlaṃ.[1] tattha je sāmantā, te **Sāhiṇo** bhaṇṇanti; jo sāmantâhivaī sayala-narinda-vanda-cūḍāmaṇī so **Sāhāṇusāhī** bhaṇṇai.[2] tao Kālaga-sūrī ṭhio egassa Sāhiṇo samīve, āvajjio[3] ya so manta-tantâīhiṃ. io ya aṇṇayā kayāi[4] tassa Sāhiṇo sūri-samanniyassa harisa-bhara-nibbharassa nāṇāviha-viṇoehiṃ ceṭṭhamāṇassa[5] samāgao paḍihāro, vinnattaṃ ca teṇa, jahā: "sāmi! Sāhāṇusāhi-dūo duvāre ciṭṭhai." Sāhiṇā bhaṇiyaṃ: "lahuṃ pavesehi." pavesio ya vayaṇeṇa antaraṃ eva nisanno ya diṇṇâsaṇe. tao dūeṇa samappiyaṃ uvāyaṇaṃ[6] taṃ ca daṭṭhūṇa nava-pāusa[7]-kāla-nahayalaṃ va andhāriyaṃ vayaṇaṃ Sāhiṇo. tao

---

[1] kuo vi=*kuto'pi.* nāūṇa √*jñā*, JM. usually does not cerebralise initial *n*. Saga-kūla 'the shore (land) of the Śakas'; for the form cf. Asoga.

[2] ahivai "overlord' Sāhi=*ṣāhi*, i.e. Pers. *šāh* or *šāhi*. This word, and also *ṣāhānuṣāhi*=Pers. *šāhanšāh* 'King of Kings,' occur in the Allahabad *praśasti*. (Fleet, Gupta Inscriptions, No. 1, Samudra.). The context there indicates the use of these two terms in the West of India in connection with the Śakas.

[3] āvajjio (*ā+vṛj*).

[4] *itaś ca-anyadā kadācit.*

[5] 'busying himself' (*ceṣṭ*).

[6] 'gift.'

[7] pāusa 'rains' (*prāvṛṣa*).

cintiyaṃ: "hanti, kāmaṃ apuvva-karaṇaṃ uvalakkhijjai,[1] jao sāmi-pasāyaṃ āgayaṃ daṭṭhūṇa jalaya-daṃsaṇeṇaṃ va sihiṇo harisa-bhara-nibbharā jāyanti sevayā, so sāma-vayaṇo dīsai. tā pucchāmi kāraṇaṃ" ti. etth' antarammi Sāhi-purisa-daṃsiya-viḍahare[2] gao dūo. tao pucchiyaṃ sūriṇā: "hanta, sāmi-pasāe samāgae kiṃ uvviggo viva lakkhīyasi?" teṇa bhaṇiyaṃ: "bhayavaṃ, na pasāo, kiṃ tu kovo samāgao: jao amha pahū jassa rūsai, tassa nām'aṅkiyaṃ muddiyaṃ churiyaṃ paṭṭhavei.[3] tao keṇai kāraṇeṇa amho' variṃ[4] rūsiūṇa pesiyā esā churiyā. eīe ya appā amhehiṃ ghāiyavvo:[5] ugga-daṇḍo tti kāūṇa na tav-vayaṇe viyāraṇā kāyavvā." sūriṇā bhaṇiyaṃ: "kiṃ tujjha ceva ruṭṭho, uyāhu[6] annassa vi kassa vi?" Sāhiṇā bhaṇiyaṃ: "mama vajjiyāṇaṃ aṇṇesiṃ pi pañcāṇaui-rāīṇaṃ, jao dīsai chan-ṇauimī imīe satthiyāe aṅko tti.[7]" sūriṇā jampiyaṃ: "jai evaṃ, tā mā appāṇaṃ viṇāsehi." teṇa bhaṇiyaṃ: "na pahuṇā ruṭṭheṇa kula-kkhayaṃ antareṇa chuṭṭijjai[8]; mae puṇa maeṇa sesakulassa khemaṃ bhavai." sūriṇa bhaṇiyaṃ: "jai vi evaṃ, tahā vi vāharesu[9] niya-dūya-pesaṇeṇa pañcāṇauiṃ pi rāyāṇo: jeṇa **Hinduga**-desaṃ vaccāmo."[10] tao teṇa pucchio dūo, jahā: "bhaddā! ke te anne pañcāṇauī rāyāṇo, jesiṃ kuvio devo?" teṇa vi savve niveiyā. tao dūyaṃ visajjiūṇa savvesiṃ pi pesiyā patteyaṃ[11] niya-dūyā, jahā: "samāgacchaha mama samīve, mā niya-jīviyāiṃ pariccayaha, ahaṃ savvattha bhali-

---

1 hanti=hanta. uvalakkhijjai pass. of uvalakkhei (*upa+lakṣ*).

2 -viḍahara apparently "rogues' hall" (**viṭa-ghara*).

3 paṭṭhavei 'sends' caus. (*pra+sthā*).

4 uvariṃ=uvari.

5 eīe ins. fem. 'with this.' ghāiyavva fut. part. from caus. of *han*.

6 uyāhu 'or' (*utāho*).

7 chan-ṇauimī 96th. satthiā 'weapon' (*śastrikā*), 'for the number of his weapon appears as 96th.'

8 chuṭṭijjai pass. √*chuṭ* 'cut off, leave off' cf. H. chūṭnā, chuṭṭī.

9 vāharesu 'summon' (*vi+ā+hṛ*).

10 Hinduga=Pers. Hinduk. vaccāmo "we are going."

11 patteyaṃ 'severally' *pratyekam*.

ssāmi."[1] tao te duparicoayaṇīyattaṇāo[2] pāṇāṇaṃ savvasāmaggiṃ kāūṇa āgayā jhaḍa tti[3] tassa samīvaṃ, te ya samāgae daṭṭhūṇa teṇāvi pucchiyā sūriṇo: "bhayavaṃ kiṃ amhehiṃ sampayaṃ kāyavvaṃ?" sūrīhiṃ bhaṇiyaṃ: "sabala-vāhaṇā uttariūṇa **Sindhuṃ** vaccaha **Hinduga**-desaṃ. tao samāruhiūṇa jāṇavattesu[4] samāgayā **Suraṭṭha**-visae. etth' antarammi ya samāgao pāusa-samao; tao duggamā magga tti kāuṃ Suraṭṭha-visao chaṇṇaui-vibhāgehiṃ vibhañjiūṇa ṭhiyā tatth' eva.

[Then came the Autumn—elaborately described.]

evaṃvihaṃ ca saraya-kāla-sirim[5] avaloiūṇa niya-samīhiya-siddhi-kāmeṇa bhaṇiyā te **Kālaya**-sūriṇā, jahā: "bho, kim evaṃ nirujjamā ciṭṭhaha?" tehiṃ bhaṇiyaṃ: "āisaha kiṃ puṇo karemo." sūriṇā bhaṇiyaṃ: "giṇhaha **Ujjeṇiṃ**, jao tīe paḍibaddho pabhūo **Mālava**-deso: tattha pajjattīe tumhāṇaṃ nivvāho[6] bhavissai." tehiṃ bhaṇiyaṃ: "evaṃ karemo: paraṃ n'atthi sambalayaṃ, jamhā[7] eyammi dese amhāṇaṃ bhoyaṇa-mettaṃ ceva jāyaṃ." tao sūriṇā joga-cuṇṇa-cahuṇṭiyā-metta-pakkheveṇa suvaṇṇī-kāūṇa savvaṃ kumbhakārâvaṇaṃ bhaṇiyā:[8] "eyaṃ sambalaṃ giṇhaha." tao te taṃ vibhañjiūṇa savva-sāmaggīe patthiyā **Ujjeṇiṃ** pai.[9] antare ya je ke vi **Lāḍaya-visaya-rāyāṇo**, te sāhettā[10] pattā **Ujjeṇi**-visayasandhiṃ. tao **Gaddabhillo** parabalaṃ āgacchantaṃ

---

[1] bhalissāmi fut. of bhalai=bharai., either from =*bhṛ* 'take care of' or from *smṛ* through *mharai.

[2] =*duḥparityajanīyatvāt*. [3] *jhaṭ iti*.

[4] jāṇavatta 'vessel' (*yānapātra*), § 92.

[5] saraya 'autumn' (*śarad*).

[6] nivvāho 'abundance, livelihood' (*nirvāha*). pajjatti 'sufficiency' (*paryāpti*).

[7] sambalayaṃ 'stores, supplies' (*śambalam*). jamhā abl. sing. (*yasmāt*) used adverbially 'since.'

[8] cuṇṇa 'powder' H. cūn. cahuṇṭiyā 'a pinch.' cf. H. cyõṭī, Panj. cūṇḍhī.

[9] pai=*prati*.

[10] sāhettā gerund of sāhei=sāhai (*śasti*) 'telling, summoning.' Lāḍaya, *i.e.* Lāṭa=S. Gujarāt.

soūṇa mahābala-sāmaggīe niggao patto ya visaya-sandhiṃ.
tao doṇhaṃ pi dapp'-uddhara-sennāṇaṃ laggaṃ āohaṇaṃ.[1]

Translation.

When the sage by some channel came to know of this, he departed from the city, and travelling without stopping he came to the land called the Land of the Śakas. Those who are chiefs there, are called Shāhīs, and he that is overlord of the chiefs, the crest-jewel of the whole bevy of princes, is styled Shāhānushāhī. Then the Kālaka sage abode with one of the Shāhīs, and won his favour by charm and spell. Now once upon a time when this Shāhī was with the sage and full of great delight was passing the time with various amusements, the porter entered and made this announcement, "My lord, a messenger from the Shāhānushāhī is standing at the door." The Shāhī said: "Bring him in at once." At the word he entered and sat down on the seat given him. Then the messenger handed over a present. At the sight of this the Shāhī's face grew black as the sky at the beginning of the rains. Then thought (the sage), "Well, surely this seems an extraordinary thing; for servants when they see a mark of favour sent by their master become filled with great joy like peacocks at the sight of clouds—but his face is black. I will ask him the reason." Meanwhile the messenger went to the quarters (?) shown him by the Shāhī's people. Then the sage asked: "Come now, why do you seem distressed at the coming of a favour from your lord?" He replied: "Your Reverence, this is no favour, but a mark of his anger that has come. For with whomever our king is wroth, to him he sends a dagger marked with his name, so for some reason or other being wroth with us, he has sent this dagger; and with this same must I slay myself. His word may not be gainsaid under pain of dreadful punishment." The sage said: "Is he wroth with you only, or with some other also?" The Shāhī said: "With ninety-five other kings besides myself for the weapon is marked with the number 96."

---

1 uddhara=*uddhura*. āohaṇa 'battle' (ā + *yudh*).

Quoth the sage: "If that is so, do not do away with yourself." The other said: "When the king is enraged, he does not stop short of destroying a family, but when I am dead, the rest of my family will be left in peace." The sage said: "If that is so, send the word to all the ninety-five kings by your own messenger, that you are going to the Hinduk country." Then he questioned the messenger thus, "Good sir, who are the other five and ninety kings with whom His Majesty is angry?" He gave all their names. Then dispatching a messenger he sent his own message to them all severally, saying, "Come to me, do not abandon your lives, I will take thought for everything." Then they came to him straightway with all their gear, for it is hard for a man to abandon his life, and seeing they had arrived, he asked the sage: "Your Reverence, what are we to do now?" The sage replied: "Cross the Indus with troops and transport and go to the Hinduk country." Then they embarked on vessels and reached the district of Surat, and in the meanwhile the rainy season arrived. Then finding the roads were difficult, they divided the district of Surat into ninety-six parts and stayed there.

Observing the glory of the autumn season as described above, the Kālaka sage, with the desire of fulfilling his own wish, said to them: "Ho, why are you idling here?" Said they: "Direct us what we should do."

The sage said: "Capture Ujjain, for that is the key to the Mālava country; there you will find subsistence in abundance." They said: "We will do so; but we have no supplies, for in this country we have obtained barely enough to eat."

Then the sage turned all the potters' stuff into gold by simply sprinkling it with a mere pinch of magic powder and said to them: "Take this as supplies."

So they divided it and with all their gear set out for Ujjain. And meantime all the kings of the Lāṭa region, these they summoned and arrived at the frontier of the Ujjain country.

Then Gardabhilla, hearing of the approach of a hostile army, went out with a great army all complete and reached the frontier. Then began a battle between the two armies swelling with pride.

Ardha-Māgadhī.] **Extract No. 19.**

Udāyaṇa.

[Jacobi No. III, Portions.]

(p. 28) teṇaṃ kāleṇaṃ teṇaṃ samaeṇaṃ Sindhu-Sovīresu jaṇavaesu Vīyabhae nāmaṃ nayare hotthā; [1] Udāyaṇe nāmaṃ rāyā, Pabhāvaī devī. tīse jeṭṭhe putte Abhiī nāmaṃ juvva-rāyā hotthā; niyae bhāiṇejje [2] Kesī nāmaṃ hotthā. se naṃ Udāyaṇe rāyā Sindhu-Sovīra-pāmokkhāṇaṃ [3] solasaṇhaṃ jaṇavayāṇaṃ Vīyabhaya-pāmokkhāṇaṃ tiṇhaṃ tevaṭṭhīṇaṃ nayara-sayāṇaṃ[4] Mahaseṇa-pāmokkhāṇaṃ dasaṇhaṃ rāyāṇaṃ baddha-mauḍāṇaṃ viiṇṇa-seya-cāmara-vāya-vīyaṇāṇaṃ annesiṃ ca rāīsara-talavara-pabhiīṇaṃ āhevaccaṃ kuṇamāṇe viharai.[5] evaṃ ca tāva eyaṃ.

* * * * *

The tale then switches into Jain Māhārāṣṭrī and tells of Kumāranandī the uxorious ('itthilolo') goldsmith who collected 500 wives at 500 of gold apiece, and was chosen as their lord by the demi-goddesses of Five-Rock Island. Eventually the story comes round to Udāyaṇa, and we are told in Ardha-Māgadhī (i.e., scripture language), of his conversion.

(p. 32.) tae naṃ se Udāyaṇe rāyā annayā kayāi posaha-sālāe posahie ege abīe pakkhiyaṃ posahaṃ sammaṃ paḍijā-

---

1 Vīyabhae=*Vītabhayo*, nom. sing. in *e* being a characteristic of this Prakrit. hotthā 3rd sing. aor. ātm. of ho=*bhava-*, used also of other persons and numbers.

2 bhāiṇejja 'sister's son' (*bhāgineya*). niyaya=niya 'own' (*nija*).

3 pāmokkha (*pramukha*).

4 tevaṭṭhi 'sixty-three' (also tesaṭṭhi). saya 'hundred' (*śata*) § 112. Apparently means "of 363 towns."

5 viiṇṇa 'bestowed' (*vi+tṛ*). seya 'white' (*śveta*). vīyaṇa 'fanning' (*vīj*). annesiṃ gen. pl. 'of others' (M. has aṇṇāṇaṃ). rāīsara 'princes' (*rājeśvara*). talavara 'chief.' talāro in Deśī-nāma-mālā='*nagarārakṣa-ka*.' āhevaccaṃ 'overlordship' (*ādhipatyam*). kuṇamāṇe ātm. pres. part. of kuṇai.

garamāṇe viharai.[1] tao tassa puvvarattâvaratta-kāla-samayaṃsi jāgariyaṃ karemāṇassa eyārūve ajjhatthie samuppajjitthā:[2] dhannā ṇaṃ te gāma-nagarā, jattha ṇaṃ samaṇe Vīre viharai, dhammaṃ kahei; dhannā ṇaṃ te rāīsara-pabhiïo, je samaṇassa Mahāvīrassa antie kevali-pannattaṃ dhammaṃ nisāmenti,[3] evaṃ pañcâṇuvvayaṃ sattasikkhāvaiyaṃ sāvaga-dhammaṃ duvālasa-vihaṃ[4] paḍivajjanti, evaṃ muṇḍā bhavittā āgārāo aṇagāriyaṃ pavvayanti.[5] taṃ jai ṇaṃ samaṇe bhagavaṃ Mahāvīre puvvâṇupuvviṃ dūijjamāṇe ih' eva Vīyabhae āgacchejjā,[6] tā ṇaṃ aham avi bhagavao antie muṇḍe bhavittā jāva pavvaejjā. tae ṇaṃ bhagavaṃ Udāyaṇassa eyārūvaṃ ajjhatthiyaṃ jāṇittā Campāo paḍinikkhamittā, jeṇ' eva Vīyabhae nayare, jeṇ' eva Miyavaṇe ujjāṇe, teṇ' eva viharai. tao parisā[7] niggayā Udāyaṇe ya. tae ṇaṃ Udāyaṇe Mahāvīrassa antie dhammaṃ soccā haṭṭha-tuṭṭhe evaṃ vayāsī:[8] jaṃ navaraṃ jeṭṭha-puttaṃ rajje ahisiñcāmi, tao ṇaṃ tubbhaṃ antie pavvayāmi. sāmī bhaṇai: ahāsuhaṃ, mā paḍibandhaṃ karehi! tao ṇaṃ Udāyaṇe ābhiogiyaṃ hatthi-rayaṇaṃ duruhittā[9] sae gihe āgae. tao Udāyaṇassa eyārūve ajjhatthie

---

1 kayāi=*kadācit.* posaha 'fast' (*upavasatha*) § 74. a-bīe 'without a second.' pakkhiyaṃ 'fortnightly.' sammaṃ (*samyak*). paḍijāgaramāṇa 'keeping vigil,' 'performing religious duty.'

2 puvvaratta 'first part of the night,' avaratta 'second half of the night.' karemāṇa atm. pres. part. from karei. eyārūva 'of this form.' ajjhatthiya 'thought' (*ādhyātmika*). samuppajjitthā, aorist (*sam+ud pad*) cf. hotthā 'was.'

3 kevali 'possessing supreme or absolute knowledge.' -pannattaṃ (*prajñaptam*). nisāmenti 'hear' (*ni+śam*).

4 aṇuvvayaṃ 'ordinance' (*anuvrata*): 5 commands for laymen, Jain technicality. sikkhāvaiya 'precept' (**śikṣāpadika*). duvālasa 'twelve.'

5 bhavittā gerund § 112. āgāra 'house.'

6 puvvâṇupuvviṃ 'in succession.' dūijjamāṇa 'wandering' (*du*) āgacchejjā, opt.

7 parisā 'community' (*pariṣad*).

8 soccā 'having heard' (*śrutvā*). cf. caccara=*catvara*. JM. haṭṭha=*hṛṣṭa*. vayāsī 'spoke.' aorist (*vad*).

9 ābhiogiya (*ābhiyogika*) sometimes a kind of deity 'belonging to the heavenly service.' Here Jacobi suggests a *state* elephant. duruhittā 'having mounted' (*uduruh for *ud+ruh*).

jāe: jai ṇaṃ Abhiiṃ kumāraṃ rajje ṭhavittā pavvayāmi, to Abhiī rajje ya raṭṭhe ya jāva jaṇavae ya māṇussaesu ya kāma-bhogesu mucchie aṇāiyaṃ aṇavayaggaṃ saṃsāra-kantāraṃ aṇupariyaṭṭissai.[1] taṃ seyaṃ khalu me niyagaṃ bhāiṇejjaṃ Kesiṃ kumāraṃ rajje ṭhavittā pavvaittae.[2] evaṃ sampehettā[3] sobhaṇe tihi-karaṇa-muhutte koḍumbiya-purise ya saddāvettā[4] evaṃ vayāsi: khippām eva Kesissa kumārassa rāyâbhiseyaṃ uvaṭṭhaveha![5] tao mahiḍḍhīe[6] abhisitte Kesī kumāre rāyā jāe jāva pasāsemāṇe viharai. tao Udāyaṇe rāyā Kesiṃ rāyaṃ āpucchai: ahaṇ-ṇaṃ, devâṇuppiyā,[7] saṃsāra-bha'uvviggo pavvayāmi. tao Kesī rāyā koḍumbiya-purise saddāvettā evaṃ vayāsī: khippām eva Udāyaṇassa ranno mah'atthaṃ mah'arihaṃ nikkhamaṇâbhiseyaṃ uvaṭṭhaveha! tao mahayā vibhūīe abhisitte siviyârūḍhe[8] bhagavao samīve gantūṇa pavvaie jāva bahūṇi cauttha-chaṭṭh'-aṭṭhama-dasa-ma-duvālasa-mās'aḍḍhamāsâīṇi tavo-kammāṇi kuvvamāṇe[9] viharai.

(p. 34) tao se Udāyaṇe aṇagāre bahūṇi vāsāṇi sāmaṇṇa-pariyāgaṃ pāuṇittā saṭṭhiṃ bhattāiṃ aṇasaṇāe cheettā[10] jass'

---

1 mucchiya 'greedy' (*mūrch*). aṇāiya 'without beginning.' aṇavayagga 'without end,' lit. 'having the point not bent' (*anamadagra*=Pali anamatagga Pisch. §251). aṇupariyaṭṭissai 'will wander through' (*anu+pari+vṛt*).

2 seyaṃ 'better' (*śreyas*). pavvaittae, infin.

3 sampehettā 'having pondered over' (*sam+pra+ikṣ*). This treatment of *kṣ* especially in the root *īkṣ* is common in AMg. JM. aṇujāhanti=*anuprekṣante*. dāhiṇa=*dakṣiṇa* occurs also in M. and Śaur.

4 koḍumbiya 'belonging to the family.' saddāvettā, gerund of saddāvei caus. of saddei nominal from sadda (*śabda*).

5 khippām eva (*kṣipram eva*) AMg. regularly lengthens *a* of final *-am* before enclitic *eva*: juttām eva=*yuktam eva* (Pischel § 28). uvaṭṭhaveha caus. (*upa+sthā*)

6 iḍḍhi=*ṛddhi*.

7 devāṇuppiyā, voc. sing. deva+aṇuppiya.

8 siviyā 'pālkī' (*śibikā*).

9 kuvvamāṇe cf. karemāṇassa and kuṇamāṇe above.

10 sāmaṇṇa abstract of samaṇa (*śramaṇa*). pariyāga 'wandering' means *paryāya*; another form is pariyāya. Pischel doubts derivation from *paryāyaka*, suggests **pariyāva* with ga for va (cf. AMg. juvala=*yugala*), so also AMg. JM. pajjava=*paryāyá*; JŚ. pajjaya. pāuṇittā 'having ful

aṭṭhāe[1] kīrai nagga-bhāve muṇḍabhāve, taṃ aṭṭhaṃ patte jāva dukkha-pahīṇe tti.

*   *   *   *   *

tae ṇaṃ Abhii-kumārassa puvvarattâvaratta-kāla-samayaṃsi evaṃ ajjhatthie jāe: ahaṃ Udāyaṇassa jeṭṭhaputte Pabhāvaīe attae; maṃ rajje aṭṭhāvettā Kesiṃ rajje ṭhāvettā[2] pavvaie. imeṇaṃ māṇuseṇaṃ dukkheṇaṃ abhibhūe samāṇe[3] Vīyabhayāo niggacchittā Campāe Koṇiyaṃ uvasaṃpajjittāṇaṃ viula-bhoga-samannāgae yāvi hotthā.[4] se ṇaṃ Abhiī kumāre samaṇôvāsae[5] abhigaya-jīvâjīve Udāyaṇeṇaṃ raṇṇā samaṇu-baddha-vere yāvi hotthā. tao Abhiī kumāre bahūiṃ vāsāiṃ samaṇôvāsaga-pariyāgaṃ pāuṇittā addhamāsiyāe saṃlehaṇāe tīsaṃ[6] bhattāiṃ cheettā tassa ṭhāṇassa aṇāloiya-paḍikkante kālaṃ kiccā[7] Asurakumārattāe uvavanno. egaṃ paliovamaṃ ṭhiī[8] tassa; Mahāvidehe sijjhihi tti.[9]

Translation.

Udāyaṇa.

At that period and at that very time there was a city Vītabhaya by name in the countries of Sindh and Sauvīra. Udāyaṇa was the king thereof, and Prabhāvatī his queen whose eldest son was crown prince, Abhijit by name. He had a nephew named Keśin. Now that Udāyaṇa the king was wielding the overlordship of sixteen countries whereof Sindh and

---

filled' (*pra*+*āp*). aṇasaṇa 'fasting.' cheettā 'having cut' cf. *chettuṃ* M. JM. chĕttūṇa (*chĕttettā chetettā).

1 aṭṭhāe 'on account of.'

2 attae 'son' (*ātmajaḥ*). ṭhāvetta, gerund caus. (*sthā*).

3 samāṇa 'being.'

4 uvasaṃpajjittāṇaṃ gerund (*upa*+*sam*+*pad*). samannāgaya 'provided with' (*sam*+*anu*+*ā*+*gam*). yāvi (*ca*+*api*).

5 samaṇovāsaya 'lay believer.'

6 saṃlehaṇā 'final mortification' (before death) (*saṃlekhanā*). tīsaṃ 'thirty.'

7 aṇāloiya-paḍikkanta 'unrepented and unconfessed' (*anālocita-pratikrānta*). kiccā gerund (*kṛ*).

8 paliovama=*palyopama*, a very high number. ṭhii 'durance' § 12.

9 sijjhihī 'will be fulfilled,' fut. of sijjhai, i.e. 'will attain perfection.'

Sauvīra were the chief, of three hundreds of townships and sixty-three, with Vītabhaya as the chief, of ten crowned rajas of whom Mahāsena was the chief, granted the right of fanning with white *chauris*, and of other princes, chiefs, and the like. And even so it was.

Now once upon a time that king Udāyaṇa fasted in the hall of fasting, all alone, the fortnightly fast, duly performing his sacred duty. Now while he was keeping vigil in the middle of the night there came to him such a thought as this: rich are those villages and towns, wherein the ascetic Vīra dwells, and declares the law; rich are those princes, and the like, who in the presence of the ascetic Mahāvīra hear the law perceived by absolute knowledge, who accept the twelvefold Disciples' Law, consisting of the Five Ordinances and the Seven Precepts, and stripped of all leave their homes, and homeless enter into the Order. If now the holy ascetic Mahāvīra wandering from place to place should come here to Vītabhaya, then would I before the holy one strip me and enter the Order. Now the holy one knowing this thought of Udāyaṇa's departed from Campā and took up his abode near that very town of Vītabhaya, where the Deer-park was, and the community came out, and also Udāyaṇa. Then Udāyaṇa having heard the law in the presence of Mahāvīra was pleased and delighted and spake as follows: "I will even now consecrate my eldest son in the kingship, and then will I enter the Order before thee." The master said: "Please make no obstacle!" Then Udāyaṇa mounted a splendid state elephant and went within his house. Then there came to Udāyaṇa such a thought as this: "If now I put Prince Abhijit on the throne, and enter the Order, then Abhijit on the throne, in the kingdom and the country, lusting among the human joys of passion will wander along through the wilderness of rebirth without beginning, without end, so is it better to place my nephew Prince Keśin on the throne before I enter the Order." Having pondered this over, on an auspicious lunar day, half-day and moment, he summoned the men of his household and spake thus: "Quickly prepare the coronation of Prince Keśin." Then with great pomp Prince Keśin became king, and continued reigning. Then King Udāyaṇa took leave of King Keśin: "I now, Oh beloved of the gods, disquieted by the fear of rebirth, will enter the Order." Then King Keśin summoned the men of his household and said: "Quickly prepare a rich and sumptuous ceremony of initiation for King Udāyaṇa."

Then was he consecrated with great *éclat*, and getting into a palanquin went into the presence of the holy one and entered the Order, and continued to perform many an act of penance, fasts of the fourth, sixth, eighth, tenth and twelfth,[1] those of the half-months, months and the like.

Then that Udāyaṇa having for many years fulfilled the ascetic's vow of homeless wandering, and in his fasting having cut off sixty meals, he attained that end, for the sake of which a man becomes naked and shorn—release from pain.

Now in the middle of the night a thought occurred to Abhijit as follows: "I am the eldest son of Udāyaṇa, the son of Prabhāvatī. Setting me aside, he has set Keśin on the throne, and entered the Order." Overwhelmed by this human trouble, he left Vītabhaya and found his way to Koṇiya in Campā where he was provided with plentiful enjoyments. Now that Prince Abhijit was a lay believer with a knowledge of the living and the dead, and he retained an enmity against the King Udāyaṇa. Then Prince Abhijit having for many years fulfilled the wandering of a lay adherent, having cut off thirty meals in the half-monthly final mortification, and having his deeds of that stage unconfessed and unrepented met his fate to become a Demon prince. The duration thereof is one myriad; he will attain perfection in great Videha.

Ardha-Māgadhī.] Extract No. 20.

From the Seventh Lecture of the **Uvāsagadasāo.**

(180). Polāsapure nāmaṃ nayare, Sahassambavaṇe ujjāṇe. Jiya-sattū rāyā.

---

[1] To last 1, 2, 3, 4 and 5 days.

(181). Tattha ṇaṃ Polāsapure nayare Saddāla-putte nāmaṃ kumbhakāre Ājīviôvāsae[1] parivasai. Ajīviya-samayaṃsi[2] laddh'aṭṭhe gahiy'aṭṭhe pucchiy'aṭṭhe viṇicchiy'aṭṭhe abhigay'aṭṭhe aṭṭhi-miṃja-pemâṇurāga-ratte[3] ya "ayam āuso,[4] Ājīvia-samae aṭṭhe ayaṃ param'aṭṭhe, sese aṇaṭṭhe" tti Ājīviya-samaeṇaṃ appāṇaṃ bhāvemāṇe viharaï.

(182). Tassa ṇaṃ Saddālaputtassa Ājīviôvāsagassa ekkā hiraṇṇa-koḍī nihāṇa-pauttā, ekkā vaḍḍhi-pauttā, ekkā pavitthara-pauttā, ekke vae dasa-go-sāhassieṇaṃ vaeṇaṃ.[5]

(183). Tassa ṇaṃ Saddālaputtassa Ājīviôvāsagassa Aggimittā nāmaṃ bhāriyā hotthā.

(184). Tassa ṇaṃ Saddālaputtassa Ājīviôvāsagassa Polāsapurassa nayarassa bahiyā pañca kumbhakārâvaṇasayā hotthā. Tattha ṇaṃ bahave purisā diṇṇabhaï-bhatta-veyaṇā kallākalliṃ[6] bahave karae ya vārae ya pihaḍae ya ghaḍae ya addha-ghaḍae ya

---

1 Ājīviovāsae, 'an adherent, follower (*upāsaka*) of the Ājīvikas.' The Ājīvika sect was founded by Gosāla, the son of Maṅkhali, a contemporary of Mahāvīra. Gosāla's doctrine was "that there is no such thing as exertion or labour or power or vigour or manly strength, but all things are unalterably fixed." Uvāsaga-d,° VI, 166. (*Vide* Hoernle's note, 253.)

2 "in the doctrine," loc. sing. § 92. v.

3 miṃja, 'marrow': Panjabi miñjh, mijjh: Sindhī miju: Guj. mīj. H. mīgī (Skt. *majjā*). Hoernle translates "being filled with a passionate love towards them as for the most excellent thing," i.e. as in his note "as for the marrow of bones." The marrow is rather the physical basis of passion, not its object.

4 āuso 'longlived' voc. (Skt. base *āyuṣmat*) used as a title of respect. Hoernle, following the commentary on another passage, takes ayamāuso together, this being the form of address used by a teacher to his pupil.

5 vae 'herd' (*vrajaḥ*).

6 bhai 'hire' (*bhṛti*), veyaṇa 'wages, salary' (*vetana*). Hoernle takes it "received food in lieu of wages." Compare however *bhṛtyannam* 'board and wages.' It would appear that their salary comprised food *and* wages. Kallākalliṃ (Skt. *kalyaṃ kalyam*) 'every morning.' For ending, compare puvviṃ (=*pūrvim*).

kalasae ya aliñjarae ya jambūlae ya uṭṭiyāo ya karenti,[1] anne ya se bahave purisā diṇṇa-bhai-bhatta-veyaṇā kallākalliṃ tehiṃ bahūhiṃ karaehiṃ ya *jāva* uṭṭiyāhi ya rāya-maggaṃsi vittiṃ kappemāṇā viharanti.

(185). Tae ṇaṃ se Saddālaputte Ājīviôvāsae annayā kayāi puvvâvar'aṇha-kāla-samayaṃsi jeṇeva Asoga-vaṇiyā teṇeva uvāgacchai, *-ttā*[2] gosālassa Maṅkhaliputtassa antiyaṃ dhamma-paṇṇattiṃ uvasaṃpajjittāṇaṃ[3] viharai.

(186). Tae ṇaṃ tassa Saddālaputtassa Ājīviôvāsagassa ege deve antiyaṃ pāubbhavitthā.[4]

(187). Tae ṇaṃ se deve antalikkha-paḍivaṇṇe sakhiṅkhiṇiyāiṃ *jāva* parihie Saddālaputtaṃ Ājīviôvāsayaṃ evaṃ vayāsī. "Ehii ṇaṃ, devâṇuppiyā, kallaṃ ihaṃ mahā-māhaṇe uppanna-ṇāṇa-daṃsaṇa-dhare 'tīya-paccuppanna-m-aṇāgaya-jāṇae[5] Arahā Jiṇe Kevalī savvaṇṇū savva-darisī te-lokka-vahiya-mahiya-pūie, sa-deva-maṇuyâsurassa logassa accaṇijje vandaṇijje sakkāraṇijje sammāṇaṇijje kallāṇaṃ maṅgalaṃ devayaṃ ceiyaṃ[6] *jāva* pajjuvāsaṇijje,[7] tacca-[8]

---

1 *karaka* "water-vessel, esp. one used by students or ascetics." M.W. *vāraka* 'kind of vessel,' *piṭharaka* 'pot, pan,' *ghaṭaka* H. ghaṛā, *kalaśa* 'pitcher' aliñjara ("small earthen water jar" M.W.), jambūlaya and uṭṭiyā 'three very large kinds of jars.' Hoernle.

2 -ttā after a verb stands for the corresponding gerund. gacchai, ttā= gacchai, gacchittā 'he goes, and having gone.'

3 Gerund from uvasaṃpajjai (*upa+sam+pad*).

4 ātm. aor. of pāubbhavai (*prādur+bhū*) 'appeared.'

5 'tīya- 'past' (*atīta*), paccuppanna 'present' (*prati+ud+pad*), -m- sandhi consonant, aṇāgaya 'future.' Text has paḍupanna for paḍuppanna, i.e. paḍi+uppanna.

6 ceiya 'sacred' lit.=*caitya* 'sacred shrine.' vahiya 'rapturously gazed at' (Dési).

7 'Worshipful' (*pari+upa+ās*).

8 tacca 'meritorious.' Comm. says=*tathya*, so also Hemacandra II, 21; but Pali has taccha. Otherwise from *tattva*. Pischel (§ 281) says rather **tattva* through **tāttya*. Cf. Romani tatcho='true.'

kamma-sampaya-sampautte taṃ ṇaṃ tumaṃ vandejjāhi *jāva* pajjuvāsejjāhi, pāḍihārieṇaṃ[1] pīḍha-phalaga-sijjā-saṃthāraeṇaṃ uvanimantejjāhi." Doccaṃ pi taccaṃ pi evaṃ vayai, *-ttā* jām eva disaṃ pāubbhūe tām eva disaṃ paḍigae.

Hearing of the arrival of Mahāvīra—

(190). Tae naṃ se Saddālaputte Ājīviôvāsae imīse[2] kahāe laddhaṭṭhe samāṇe "evaṃ khalu samaṇe bhagavaṃ Mahāvīre *jāva* viharai, taṃ gacchāmi ṇaṃ samaṇaṃ bhagavaṃ Mahāvīraṃ vandāmi *jāva* pajjuvāsāmi," evaṃ saṃpehei;[3] *-ttā* ṇhāe *jāva* pāyacchitte[4] suddhappāvesāiṃ[5] *jāva* appa-mahagghâbharaṇâlaṃkiya-sarīre maṇussa-vaggurā[6]-parigae sāo[7] gihāo paḍi-ṇikkhamaī, *-ttā* Polāsapuraṃ nayaraṃ majjhaṃ majjheṇaṃ niggacchai, *-ttā* jeṇeva Sahassambavaṇe ujjāṇe jeṇeva samaṇe bhagavaṃ Mahāvīre teṇeva uvāgacchai, *-ttā* tikkhutto[8] āyāhiṇaṃ payāhiṇaṃ[9] karei *ttā* vandai namaṃsai *-ttā jāva* pajjuvāsai.

Mahāvīra addressed the company and accepted Saddālaputta's hospitality.

(195). Tae ṇaṃ se Saddāla-putte Ājīviôvāsae annayā kayāi

---

1 ***prātihārika*** "a Jain technical term, meaning 'what is always kept ready for the use of some one.'" Hoernle.

2 imīse=M. imīe, imīa JM. imīe, imāe Ś. imāe.

3 saṃpehei 'reflects' (*sam+pra+īkṣ*). kkh > kh > h. This change occurs in both AMg. and JM.

4 Comm.=*prāyaścitta* 'expiation,' i.e. precautionary rites. Another interpretation is 'touched by the feet,' chitta from chivai 'touch' (*kṣip*).

5 Comm. *śuddhâtmā-vaiṣikāṇi* '(clothes) fit to adorn a purified person,' or *śuddha-prāveśyāni* 'clean and fit for entering a king's court.'

6 vaggurā 'crowd' (*vāgurā* "toils").

7 sāo 'from his own' (*sva*), giha 'house' (so also JM. commoner geha).

8 tikkhutto 'thrice' (**triṣkṛtvaḥ* or *trikṛtvaḥ*). Cf. AMg. dukhutto, dukkhutto 'twice.'

9 āyāhiṇaṃ payāhiṇaṃ=*ā-dákṣiṇa-pradakṣiṇam.*

vāyāhayayaṃ kolāla-bhaṇḍaṃ anto sālāhiṃto bahiyā ṇiṇei, -ttā āyavaṃsi dalayai.[1]

(196). Tae ṇaṃ samaṇe bhagavaṃ Mahāvīre Saddālaputtaṃ Ājīviôvāsayaṃ evaṃ vayāsī. "Saddālaputtā, esa ṇaṃ kolāla-bhaṇḍe kao ?"[2]

(197). Tae ṇaṃ se Saddālaputte Ājīviôvāsae samaṇaṃ bhagavaṃ Mahāvīrāṃ evaṃ vayāsī. "Esa ṇaṃ bhante puvviṃ maṭṭiyā āsī, tao pacchā udaeṇaṃ nimijjai; -ttā chāreṇa ya karīseṇa ya egayao mīsijjai;-ttā cakke ārohijjai; tao bahave karagā ya *jāva* uṭṭiyāo ya kajjanti."

(198). Tae ṇaṃ samaṇe bhagavaṃ Mahāvīre Saddālaputtaṃ Ājīviôvāsayaṃ evaṃ vayāsī. "Saddālaputtā, esa ṇaṃ kolālabhaṇḍe kiṃ uṭṭhāṇeṇaṃ *jāva* purisakkāraparakkameṇaṃ kajjanti, udāhu aṇuṭṭhāṇeṇaṃ *jāva* apurisakkāra-[3]parakkameṇaṃ kajjanti ?"

Saddālaputta maintains that they are made without effort, *etc.* because effort does not exist, but he is refuted and convinced.

Translation.

(180). *There was* a town called Polāsapura. *Near it there was* the garden Sahassambavaṇa. Jiya-sattū *was* king.

(181). There in the town of Polāsapura lived a potter named Saddālaputta, a follower of the Ājīviyas. Having heard of, and acquired a knowledge of the tenets of the Ājīviyas, and having questioned, determined and mastered the meaning thereof, he became enamoured of these with a passionate love suffusing the very marrow of his bones and continued to

---

1 āyavaṃsi 'in the heat of the sun' (*ātape*). dalayai comm.=*dadāti*, also dalai (dalāmi) usual form in AMg. for 'gives.'

2 kao 'from what' (*kutaḥ*, i.e. **ka-taḥ*), Ś. kado.

3 purisakkāra=*puruṣātkāra* 'as can be made by a man.' cf. balakkāra =*balāt-kāra*. Ordinary Skt. word *puruṣa-kāra*, Pali purisa-kāra.

conduct himself in accordance with the doctrine of the Ājīviyas, considering this to be the truth, the highest truth, and all the rest to be false.

(182). That Saddālaputta, the follower of the Ājīviyas, had one crore of gold placed in deposit, one crore put out at interest, one crore invested in estate, and one herd with ten thousand head of cattle.

(183). That Saddālaputta, the follower of the Ājīviyas, had a wife named Aggimittā.

(184). That Saddālaputta, the follower of the Ājīviyas, had five hundred potter-shops outside the town of Polāsapura. Therein a large number of men receiving wages in the form of food and goods, used to make from day to day numerous bowls, pots, pans, pitchers of three sizes and three sizes of water-jars; and another large number of men, receiving wages in the form of food and goods, used to carry on a trade on the king's highway with those numerous bowls, pots, pans, pitchers of three sizes and three sizes of water-jars.

(185). Then that Saddālaputta, the follower of the Ājīviyas, at one time or another at the time of the midday hour used to betake himself where there was a little grove of *aśoka* trees; this he did and he was living in conformity with the law which he had received in the presence of Gosāla Maṅkhaliputta.

(186). Then in the presence of Saddālaputta, the follower of the Ājīviyas, there appeared a certain deva.

(187). Then that deva standing in mid-air and decked out (*as described above, down to* "with small bells") spoke thus to Saddālaputta, the follower of the Ājīviyas: "There will come here to-morrow, O beloved of the devas, a great Māhaṇa, who possesses fully formed knowledge and insight, who knows the past, present, and future, who is an Arhat, and Jina, a Kevalin, who knows all and sees all, who is rapturously gazed at, adored and worshipped by the *dwellers in* the three worlds, who for the world with devas, men and asuras is an object of worship, praise, honour, respect and service as something excellent, auspicious, divine and sacred (*and so on*), who is furnished with an abundance of meritorious works, him shouldst thou praise (and *as above, down to* 'wait upon') and hospitably invite to a standing provision of stool, plank and bedding." A second and a third time he said this, and having done so he returned in that direction whence he had appeared.

* * * * *

(190). Then that Saddālaputta, the follower of the Ājīviyas, being informed of this news thinks to himself: "So then the Ascetic, the blessed Mahāvīra (*and so on, down to*) is paying a visit here; I will go and praise the Ascetic, the blessed Māhavīra, and I will (*so on, down to*) wait upon him." Thinking thus he bathed and (*as before*) *performed* precautionary rites, *put on* clean robes, adorned his person with a few costly jewels, and surrounded by a crowd of men-servants came out of his house. Having come out, he passed right through the midst of the town of Polāsapura. Having passed through he approached the place, where there was the Sahassambavaṇa Garden, where the blessed Mahāvīra was, and having approached, he circumambulated him three times from left to right. Having done so he praises him, and worships him and (having praised him, and worshipped him, *and so on, down to*) he stands in waiting upon him.

(195). Then that Saddālaputta, the follower of the Ājīviyas, at some time or other brought out his air-dried potter's ware from within his workshops: and having done so placed it in the heat of the sun.

(196). Then the Ascetic, the blessed Mahāvīra, spoke thus unto Saddālaputta, the follower of the Ājīviyas, "Saddālaputta, what is this potter's ware made of?"

(197). Then that Saddālaputta, the follower of the Ājīviyas, spake unto the Ascetic, the blessed Mahāvīra, as follows: "This ware was at first clay, and after that it is kneaded with water; and then it is thoroughly mixed with potash and dung; and then it is placed upon the wheel and thence are made many bowls (*and the rest as before*)."

(198). Then the Ascetic, the blessed Mahāvīra, spake thus unto Saddālaputta, the follower of the Ājīviyas: "Saddālaputta, is this potter's ware made with exertion and (*so on, down to*) manly strength, or is it made without exertion and (*so on, down to*) manly strength?"

Ardha-Māgadhī.] **Extract No. 21.**

Jinacaritra.

Being part of the **Kalpasūtra** ascribed to Bhadrabāhu. Edited by Jacobi.

(56). Tae[1] ṇaṃ Siddhatthe khattie paccūsa-kāla-samayaṃsi koḍumbiya-purise saddāvei, *-ttā* evaṃ vayāsī:

(57). "khippām[2] eva, bho Devâṇuppiyā! ajja savisesaṃ bāhiriyaṃ uvaṭṭhāṇa-sālaṃ[3] gandhôdaya-sittaṃ suiya-saṃmajjiôvalittaṃ[4] sugandha-vara-pañca-vanna-pupphôvayāra[5]-kaliyaṃ kālāguru-pavara-kundurukka-turukka-ḍajjhanta-dhūva-maghamaghanta-gandh-ud-

---

[1] J. reads tate in this and some other places. Other MSS. have tae.

[2] *Vide* page 63.

[3] 'assembly-room, pavilion.'

[4] 'cleaned' (*śuc*) 'swept' (*sam+mrj*) and 'smeared' (*upa+lip*).

[5] uvayāra 'decorations, festoons' (*upa+kṛ*).

dhuyâbhirāmaṃ[1] sugandha-vara-gandhiyaṃ gandha-vaṭṭi[2]-bhūyaṃ kareha kāraveha, karittā ya kāravittā ya sīhāsaṇaṃ rayāveha,[3] -*ttā* maṃ eyam āṇattiyaṃ khippām eva paccappiṇaha.[4]"

(58). Tae ṇaṃ te koḍumbiya-purisā Siddhatthenaṃ rannā evaṃ vuttā samāṇā, haṭṭha-tuṭṭha-*jāva* -haya-hiyayā, karayala- *jāva* kaṭṭu:[5] "evaṃ sāmi!" tti āṇāe viṇaeṇaṃ vayaṇaṃ paḍisuṇanti, -*ttā* Siddhatthassa khattiyassa antiyāo paḍinikkhamanti, -*ttā* jeṇ'eva bāhiriyā uvaṭṭhāṇa-sālā, teṇ'eva uvāgacchanti, -*ttā* khippām eva savisesaṃ bāhiriyaṃ uvaṭṭhāṇa-sālaṃ gandhôdaya-sittaṃ suia-*jāva* sīhāsaṇaṃ rayāvinti, -*ttā* jeṇ'eva Siddhatthe khattie, teṇ'eva uvāgacchanti, -*ttā* karayala-pariggahiyaṃ dasa-nahaṃ sirasā vattaṃ añjaliṃ kaṭṭu Siddhatthassa khattiyassa taṃ āṇattiyaṃ paccappiṇanti.

(59). Tae ṇaṃ Siddhatthe khattie kallaṃ pāu-ppabhāyāe rayaṇīe, phull'uppala - kamala - komal'ummilliyammi aha-paṇḍure pabhāe, rattâsoga-ppagāsa-kiṃsuya-suya-muha - guñj'addha - rāga-sarise[6] (bandhujīvaga - pārāvaṇa-calaṇa-nayaṇa - parahuya-suratta-loyaṇa-jāsuyaṇa-kusuma-rāsi - hiṃgulaya - niyarâireya - rehanta-sarise)[7]

---

[1] aguru 'aloe.' kundurukka 'olibanum.' turukka 'incense.' maghamaghanta cf. Panj. maghṇā 'burn,' H. maghan 'redolent.' uddhuya= *uddhūta*. dhūva 'incense.'

[2] vaṭṭi (*varti*).

[3] rayāveha 'have prepared' caus. (*rao*).

[4] 2nd plur. imperat. of paccappiṇai 'returns' denom. from *pratyarpaṇa*.

[5] kaṭṭu (*kartu*° originally infin. used as gerund *kṛtvā*).

[6] -ppagāsa (*prakāśa*). kiṃsua "*Butea frondosa*" (*kiṃśuka*). suya "parrot" (*śuka*). guñjaddha. The construction is Siddhatthe....sayaṇijjāo abbhuṭṭhei; with locative absolute rayaṇīe, pabhāe, sūre diṇayare, andhayāre, jīvaloe.

[7] *bandhujīvaka* "Pentapetes Phœnicia." pārāvaṇa 'pigeon' (*pārāvata*). parahuya 'cuckoo' (*parabhṛta*). jāsuyaṇa 'Chinese rose.' hiṅgulaa 'cinnabar.' *nikara* 'mass.' *atireka* 'excess.' rehanta 'shining.'

kamalâyara-saṇḍa-bohae[1] uṭṭhiyammi sūre, sahassa-rassimmi diṇayare teyasā jalante, (ahakkameṇa uie divāyare, tassa ya kara-paharâparaddhammi andhayā-re, bālâyava-kuṅkumeṇaṃ khacie vva jīva-loe)[2] sayaṇijjāo abbhuṭṭhei.

(60). -ttā pāya-pīḍhāo paccoruhai,[3] -ttā jeṇ' eva aṭṭaṇa-sālā,[4] teṇ'eva uvāgacchai, -ttā aṭṭaṇa-sālaṃ aṇupavisai, -ttā aṇega-vāyāma-jogga-vaggaṇa-vāmaddaṇa-malla-juddha-karaṇehiṃ,[5] sante parissante saya-pāga-sa-hassa-pāgehiṃ[6] sugandha-tilla-m-āiehiṃ pīṇaṇijje-hiṃ dīvaṇijjehiṃ mayaṇijjehiṃ viṃhaṇijjehiṃ dappa-ṇijjehiṃ savv'indiya-gāya-palhāyaṇijjehiṃ abbhaṅ-gie,[7] tilla-cammaṃsi ṇiuṇehiṃ paḍipunna-pāṇi-pāya-sukumāla-komala-talehiṃ purisehiṃ abbhaṅgaṇa-pari-maddaṇ-uvvalaṇa-karaṇaguṇa-nimmāehiṃ[8] cheehiṃ dakkhehiṃ paṭṭhehiṃ kusalehiṃ mehāvīhiṃ[9] jiya-parissamehiṃ aṭṭhi-suhāe maṃsa-suhāe tayā-suhāe[10] roma-suhāe cauvvihāe suha-parikammaṇāe saṃvā-haṇāe saṃvāhie samāṇe avagaya-parissame aṭṭaṇa-sālāo paḍiṇikkhamai.

(61). -ttā jeṇ'eva majjaṇa-ghare, teṇ 'eva uvāgacchai, -ttā

---

1 bohae 'awakening' (*bodhakaḥ*).

2 aha-kkameṇa 'in due time' (*yathā-krameṇa*). pahara 'blows' (*prahāra*). aparaddha 'driven away' (*apa+rādh*). bālāyava 'young sun.' khacie, text has khaciya.

3 descends (*prati+ava+ruh*).

4 aṭṭaṇa-sālā 'gymnasium' meaning shown by context. Kādambarī has *vyāyāma-śālā*.

5 vaggaṇa 'jumping.' vāmaddaṇa (*vi+ā+mardana*). mallajuddha, 'wrestling.'

6 saya-pāga- 'refined a hundred times' (*śata-pāka-*).

7 abbhaṅgie 'anointed' Mg. abbhaṅgide JM. abbhaṅgio retain the old *g*. (Skt. *abhyakta* √*añj*). *prīṇanīya* 'soothing.' *madanīya* 'invigorating.' *bṛṃhaṇīya* 'nourishing.' -*prahlādanīya* 'refreshing.'

8 *nirmāta* 'experienced.' *udvalana* 'stretching.'

9 *cheka* 'clever.' *prasṭha* 'pre-eminent.' *medhāvin* 'intelligent.'

10 tayā 'skin' (**tvacā=tvak*).

majjaṇa-gharaṃ aṇupavisai, -ttā sa-mutta-jālâkulâbhirāme[1] vicitta-maṇi-rayaṇa-koṭṭima-tale[2] ramaṇijje nhāṇa-maṇḍavaṃsi, nāṇā-maṇi-rayaṇa-bhatti-cittaṃsi[3] nhāṇa-pīḍhaṃsi suha-nisanne pupphôdaehi ya gandhôdaehi ya usiṇôdaehi ya suddhôdaehi ya kallāṇa-karaṇa-pavara-majjaṇa-vihīe majjie, tattha kouya-saehiṃ[4] bahu-vihehiṃ kallāṇaga-pavara-majjaṇâvasāṇe pamhala-sukumāla-gandha-kāsāiya-lūhiy'-aṅge[5] ahaya-sumah'aggha-dūsa-rayaṇa-susaṃvuḍe[6] sarasa-surabhi-gosīsa-candaṇâṇulitta-gatte[7] sui-mālā-vannaga-vilevaṇe[8] āviddha-maṇi-suvaṇṇe kappiya-hār'-addhahāra[9]-tisaraya-pālamba-palambamāṇe kaḍi-suttaya-kaya-sobhe[10] piṇiddha-gevijje[11] aṅgulijjaga-laliya-kayâbharaṇae[12] vara-kaḍaga-tuḍiya-thambhiya-bhue[13] ahiya-rūva-sassirīe kuṇḍala-ujjoviyâṇaṇe[14] mauḍa-ditta sirae hār'otthaya-sukaya-raiya-vacche[15] muddiyā-piṅgal'-aṅgulīe pālamba-palambamāṇa-sukaya-paḍa-uttarijjenāṇā-maṇi-kaṇaga-rayaṇa-vimala-mah'ariha-niuṇôviya-misimisinta - viraiya-susiliṭṭha-visiṭṭha-naddhâviddha-vīra-valae;[16] kiṃ bahuṇā: kappa-

1 jāla; 'lattice windows of stone work.'

2 koṭṭima 'mosaic pavement' (*kuṭṭima*).

3 bhatti (*bhakti*), 'variegated decoration, arabesques.'

4 kouya 'pleasure' (*kautuka*).

5 pamhala 'long-haired, downy' (*pakṣmala*). kāsāiya 'dyed red.' lūhiya 'dried' (*lūṣita ?*).

6 ahaya 'new' (*ahata*). dūsa 'robe' (cf. *dūṣya* 'tent, cotton').

7 gosīsa 'cow's-head—a rich sandal'

8 vannaga 'sandal' (*varṇaka*).

9 hāra 'necklace of eighteen strings.' tisaraya 'of three strings.'

10 kaḍi 'hip' (*kaṭi*). suttaya, 'belt' (*sūtraka*).

11 piṇiddha 'put on' (*pinaddha*). *graiveya* 'collar.'

12 kaya 'hair' (*kaca*).

13 kaḍaga 'bracelet' (*kaṭaka*). tuḍiya 'bangle' ? (*truṭika*), cf. Panj. ṭōṛā.

14 ujjoviya 'lighted up' (*ud+dyut* but Pischel § 243 refers to √*dyu*).

15 otthaya 'covered with' (*ava+stṛ*), cf. M. otthaia (*ava+sthag*).

16 oviya 'decorated.' misimisinta 'shining brightly,' onomatopœic denominative, taken into Sanskrit as *miṣamiṣāyate*. Pischel § 558.

rukkhae ceva alaṃkiya-vibhūsie nar'inde sa-koriṇṭa-malla-dāmeṇaṃ chatteṇaṃ dharijjamāṇeṇaṃ seya-vara-cāmarāhiṃ uddhuvvamāṇīhiṃ[1] maṅgala-jaya-sadda-kayâloe aṇega-gaṇanāyaga-daṇḍanāyaga-rāīsa-ra-talavara-māḍambiya-koḍumbiya - manti-mahāmanti-gaṇaga-dovāriya-amacca-ceḍa-pīḍhamadda - nagara-nigama- seṭṭhi- seṇāvai -satthavāha -dūya- sandhivāla[2]-saddhiṃ saṃparivuḍe dhavala-mahāmeha-niggae iva gaha-gaṇa-dippanta-rikkha-tārā-gaṇāṇa majjhe sasi vva piya-daṃsaṇe nara-vaī nar'inde nara-vasahe nara-sīhe abbhahiya-rāya-teya-lacchīe dippamāṇe majjaṇa-gharāo paḍinikkhamai.

(62). -*ttā* jeṇ'eva bāhiriyā uvaṭṭhāṇa-sālā, teṇ'eva uvāgacchai -*ttā* sīhāsaṇaṃsi puratthâbhimuhe[3] nisīyai.

(63) -*ttā* appaṇo uttara-puratthime disī-bhāe aṭṭha bhaddâsaṇāiṃ seya-vattha-paccutthuyāiṃ[4] siddh'atthaya-kaya-maṅgalôvayārāiṃ rayāvei, -*ttā* appaṇo a-dūra-sāmante nāṇā-maṇi-rayaṇa-maṇḍiyaṃ ahiya-peccha-ṇijjaṃ mah'aggha-vara-paṭṭaṇ'-uggayaṃ saṇha-paṭṭa-bhatti-saya-citta-tāṇaṃ[5] īhāmiya- usabha- turaya -nara-magara- vihaga- vālaga- kinnara- ruru- sara-bha- camara- kuñjara - vaṇalaya- pauma - laya - bhatti-cittaṃ[6] abbhintariyaṃ javaṇiyaṃ añchāvei,[7] -*ttā* nā-ṇā-maṇi-rayaṇa-bhatti-cittaṃ attharaya-miu-masū-

---

1 uddhuvvamāṇa 'shaken' (*ud+dhū*), dhuvvai § 135.

2 This list of personages may be interpreted variously. rāīsara (*rājeśvara*) Comm.=*yuvarāja*, Jacobi S.B.E. 'kings, princes.' *daṇḍa-nāyaka* 'judges,' Jacobi 'satraps.' talavara 'bodyguards,' J. 'knights.' māḍambiya 'sheriffs.' *pīṭhamarda* 'parasites, companions,' J. 'dancing masters.'

3 purattha 'east' (*purastāt*).

4 paccutthuya—paccutthaya 'covered' (*prati+ava+stṛ*).

5 saṇha 'smooth' (*ślakṣṇa*). tāṇa 'thread' (*tāna*).

6 *īhāmṛga* 'wolf.' *vyāla(ka)* 'snake' -laya, layā=*latā*.

7 añchāvei 'has drawn.'

rag' -otthayaṃ[1] seya-vattha-paccutthuyaṃ sumauyaṃ aṅga-suha-pharisagaṃ[2] visiṭṭhaṃ Tisalāe khattiyāṇīe bhaddâsaṇaṃ rayāvei, -ttā koḍumbiya-purise saddāvei, -ttā evaṃ vayāsī.

(64). "khippām eva, bho Devâṇuppiyā ! aṭṭh'aṅga-mahānimitta-sutt'-attha-dhārae viviha-sattha-kusale suviṇa--lakkhaṇa-pāḍhae saddāveha.

Translation.[3]

(56). Then the Kshatriya Siddhârtha at the time of daybreak called his family servants and spoke thus:

(57). "Now, beloved of the gods, quickly to-day make ready or have made ready in all particulars the outer hall of audience, (see that it be) sprinkled with scented water, cleaned, swept and newly smeared, furnished with offerings of fragrant, excellent flowers of all five colours, made highly delightful through curling, scented fumes of black aloe, the finest *kundurukka* and *turushka*, and burning incense, exquisitely scented with fine perfumes, and turned as it were into a scent-box; and having done all this arrange my throne, and having done this report to me quickly the execution of these orders."

(58). Then the family servants, on being thus addressed by the King Siddhârtha, with glad, pleased and (*so on down to*) enraptured hearts, saluted (*as before down to* 'on their heads.') and politely accepted the words of the command saying: 'Yes master!' Then they left the presence of the Kshatriya Siddhârtha, and went

---

1 attharaya 'coverlet.' (ā+*stṛ*). *masūra*(*ka*) 'pillow.'

2 mauya 'soft' (*mṛduka*), pharisaga (*sparśaka*).

3 The Kalpasūtra was translated by Dr. J. Stevenson, 1848. That translation however is not accurate. The standard translation is that of Hermann Jacobi's Sacred Books of the East Series, vol. XXII, p. 241ff. This has been modified here only to make the text clearer to the student

to the outer hall of audience and quickly they (made ready) in all particulars the outer hall of audience, sprinkled with scented water, cleared (*and so on*) and prepared the throne. Having done this they repaired to the place where the Kshatriya Siddhârtha was, and joining the palms of their hands so as to bring the ten nails together, laid the folded hands on their heads and reported the execution of that order to the Kshatriya Siddhârtha.

(59). Then on the morrow when the night was growing light, when the pale morning disclosed the soft flowers of the full-blown lotuses, and the sun arose; in hue like the red *aśoka*, the open *rottlesia kiṃśuka*, a parrot's bill or the *guñjârdha*, intensely bright like the *bandhu-jîvaka*, like the eyes and feet of a turtle-dove, the cuckoo's scarlet eyes, a mass of China roses or a lump of vermilion, the waker of the lotus pools; and the maker of the day thousand-rayed was shining in his radiance: when in due time the maker of the day had risen and by the blows of his hands the darkness was driven away, and while the inhabited world was, as it were, dipped in saffron by the morning sun,—the Kshatriya Siddhârtha rose from his bed,

(60). and having risen he descended from the footstool, went to the hall for gymnastic exercises and entered it. And with many strenuous exercises such as leaping, massage and wrestling[1] he became thoroughly tired, and then he was anointed with various kinds of fragrant oil, distilled a hundred or a thousand times, which nourished, beautified, invigorated, exhilarated, strengthened and increased all senses and limbs. On an oiled hide he was shampooed with soft and tender palms of the hand and soles of the feet, by clever men who were well acquainted with the best qualities of

[1] Jacobi renders: "jumped, wrestled, fenced and fought."

anointing, kneading and stretching; well trained, skilful, excellent, expert, intelligent and never tiring. When by this fourfold agreeable treatment of the body the king's bones, flesh, skin and hair had been benefited, and his fatigues banished he left the hall for gymnastic exercises,

(61). and having taken his way towards the bathing house, he entered therein. In a pleasant bath-room delightful with many windows adorned with pearls, its floor decorated with a mosaic of jewels and gems, he sat comfortably on a bathing-stool inlaid with arabesques of various jewels and precious stones, and bathed himself with water scented with flowers and perfumes, with tepid water and pure water, according to an excellent method of bathing, combined with healthy exercises. When this healthy excellent bathing with many hundredfold pleasures was over, his body was dried with a long-haired soft scented and coloured towel, he was clad in a new and costly excellent robe, his limbs rubbed with fresh and fragrant *gośirsha* and sandal and adorned with fine garlands and sandal-ointment. He put on jewels and gold, hung (round his neck) necklaces of eighteen, nine and three strings and one with a pendant and adorned himself with a zone. He put on a necklet, rings and charming ornaments for the hair, and encumbered his arms with splendid bracelets and bangles. He was of exceeding beauty. His face was illuminated by earrings, his head with a diadem. His breast was covered, decked and adorned with necklaces, his fingers were gilded with his rings. His fine cloth toga was swinging with pearl pendants. He put on as an emblem of his undefeated knighthood, glittering, well-made, strong, excellent, beautiful armlets, made by clever artists of flawless and costly jewels, gold and precious stones of many kinds. In short, the king was like a Wishing Tree, decorated and adorned. An umbrella, hung with wreaths and garlands of *koriṇṭa* flowers, was held above him. He was fanned with excellent white chowries, while his appearance was greeted with auspicious shouts of victory. Surrounded by many chiefs, judges, princes, bodyguards, sheriffs, heads of families, ministers, chief ministers, astrologers, doorkeepers, counsellors, servants, dancing masters, citizens, traders, merchants, heads of guilds, generals, leaders of caravans, messengers and frontier-guards, he—the lord and chief of men, a bull and lion among men, shining with excellent lustre and glory, lovely to behold like the moon emerging from a great white cloud in the midst of the flock of the planets and of brilliant asterisms and stars—left the bathing house,

(62). entered the outer hall of audience and sat down on his throne with his face towards the east.

(63). On the north-eastern side he ordered eight state chairs, covered with cloth and auspiciously decorated with white mustard, to be set down. Not too far from and not too near to himself, towards the interior of the palace he had a curtain drawn. It was adorned with various jewels and precious stones, extremely worth seeing, very costly and manufactured in a famous town: its soft cloth was covered all over with hundreds of devices and decorated with pictures of wolves, bulls, horses, men, crocodiles, birds, snakes, *kinnaras*, deer, *śarabhas*, yaks, elephants, shrubs and plants. Behind it he ordered to be placed for the Kshatriyāṇī Triśalā, an excellent chair of state decorated with arabesques of various jewels and precious stones, furnished with a coverlet and a soft pillow, covered with a white cloth, very soft and agreeable to the touch. Then he called the family servants and spoke thus:

(64). "Quickly, O beloved of the gods, call the interpreters of dreams who know well the science of prognostics with its eight branches, and are well versed in many sciences besides!"

Māgadhī.] **Extract No. 22.**

Śakuntalā.

Interlude at the beginning of Act VI. (Pischel p. 113; M.W. p. 216). City-superintendent, two policemen and a fisherman.

Policemen. Haṇḍe kumbhilaā! kadhehi, kahiṃ, tae eśe mahā-ladaṇa-bhāśule ukkiṇṇa-ṇām'-akkhale lāakīe aṅgulīae śa-māśādide? [1]

Fisherman. (*Nervously*) Paśīdantu bhāvamiśśā! ṇa hage īdi-śaśśa akayyaśśa kālake.[2]

First Policeman. Kiṃ ṇu kkhu śohaṇe bamhaṇe śi tti kadua laññā de paliggahe diṇṇe? [3]

Fisher. Śuṇudha dāva. Hage kkhu Śakkāvadāla-vāśī dhī-vale.[4]

Sec. Pol. Haṇḍe pāḍaccalā! kiṃ tumaṃ amhehiṃ yādiṃ va-śadiṃ ca puścide? [5]

[**Superintendent.** Sūaa! kadhedu savvaṃ kameṇa. Mā ṇaṃ paḍibandhedha].[6]

---

1 haṇḍe cf. hanta 'go to!'; only used to inferiors. kumbhilaa 'thief' orig. 'crocodile.' ladaṇa=Śaur. radaṇa (M. raaṇa) § 57. -bhāśula=*bhāsura*. ukkiṇṇa=*utkīrṇa*. akkhala=*akṣara*, according to Grammarians should be aśkala or (Hemacandra) aḫkala. [ḫ=jihvāmūlīya]. lāakīe 'royal.' Pischel thought we should read lāa-kelake. śamāśādide (*sam+ā+sad*).

2 akayya (*akārya*) 'crime.' Pischel's text has akajjaśśa, most of his MSS. akajjassa which is Śaur. kālake=*kārakaḥ*.

3 laññā 'by the king.'

4 *Śakrāvatāra, dhīvaraḥ*.

5 *pāṭaccara* or *paṭaccara* 'thief.' yādiṃ text has jādiṃ like the MSS. Pischel Gr. § 236 shows that य should be read in every case. puśeide= =Śaur. pucchido.

6 The Superintendent does not speak Māgadhī. Sūaa 'spy' (*sūc*).

Both. Yaṃ lāutte āṇavedi. Lavehi, le lavehi ! [1]

Fisher. Śe hage yāla-baḍiśa-ppahudīhiṃ maśca-bandhaṇô vāehiṃ kuḍumba-bhalaṇaṃ kalemi.[2]

[Supdt. (*Laughing*) Visuddho dāṇiṃ de ājīvo !]

Fisher. Bhaṭṭake mā evaṃ bhaṇa !

Śahaye kila ye vi ṇindide na hu śe kamma vivajjaṇīake paśumāli kaledi kālaṇā chakkammā-vidule vi śottie.[3]

[Supdt. Tado, tado ?]

Fisher. Adha ekkadiaśaṃ mae lohida-maścake khaṇḍaśo kappide.[4] yāva taśśa udala'bbhantale edaṃ mahā-ladaṇa-bhāśulaṃ aṅgulīaaṃ peskāmi. paścā idha vikkaa'tthaṃ ṇaṃ daṃśaante yyeva gahide bhāvamiśśehiṃ. Ettike dāva edaśśa āgame. Adhuṇā māledha kuṭṭedha vā.[5]

[Supdt. (*Sniffing the ring*) Jāṇua, macchôdara-saṃṭhidaṃ ti ṇatthi saṃdeho. Tadhā aaṃ se vissagandho. Āgamo dāṇiṃ edassa vimarisidavvo. Tā edha rāaülaṃ jeva gacchamha].[6]

Policemen. (*To the Fisherman*) Gaśca le gaṇṭhi-chedaā gaśca.[7]

[Supdt. Sūaa ! idha Go-ura-duāre appamattā paḍivāledha maṃ jāva rāaülaṃ pavisia ṇikkamāmi].

Both. Paviśadu lāutte śāmi-ppaśād'atthaṃ.

[Supdt. Tadhā]. (*Exit.*)

---

1 lāutte contracted from lāaütte=Śaur. rāautto (*rājaputraḥ*), or=Apa. rāauttu, Bihārī rāut (*rājadūta*), vide Grierson, Phonology.

2 yāla 'net.' baḍiśa 'hook.' maśca 'fish.' kalemi=Śaur. karemi.

3 śahaya (*sahaja*). *vivarjanīya*—māli=' *māraṇam*.' kālaṇā=*kāraṇāt* —kammā—long for metre, vidule 'skilled' (in the six occupations). śottie=*śrotriyaḥ*.

4 lohida- 'Roh' Śaur. rohido, M. rohio (?), Apa. rohiu, Hindi rohū khaṇḍaśo kappide (*kalp*) 'cut into pieces.' peskāmi, according to Hemacandra and others this is the correct form. (Pischel Gr. § 324.) According to another authority and the Lalitavigraharāja-nāṭakam it should be peśkāmi. Text has pekkhāmi.

5 vikkaatthaṃ 'in order to sell.' māledha imperat. of māledi=*mārayati*. kuṭṭedha imperat. of kuṭṭedi (*kuṭṭayati*).

6 Jāṇua (*Jānuka*) Policeman's name. vissa=*visra* 'musty'; Comm. *āmiṣa* 'raw flesh.' vimarisidavvo=*vimarṣṭavyaḥ* 'must be investigated.'

7 gaṇṭhi-chedaā 'cut-purse.'

Spy. Jāṇua! cilāadi lāutte.[1]

Jānuka. Ṇaṃ avaśalôvaśappaṇīā khu lāāṇe honti.[2]

Spy. Jāṇua! sphulanti me aggahastā. (*Pointing to the fisherman*) imaṃ gaṇṭhichedaaṃ vāvādeduṃ.[3]

Fisher. Ṇālihadi bhāve akālaṇa-mālake bhoduṃ.[4]

Jān. (*Looking round*) Eśe amhāṇaṃ īśale patte geṇhia lāaśāśaṇaṃ. (*To the fisherman*) Śaülāṇaṃ muhaṃ peskaśi, adhavā giddha-śiālāṇaṃ balī bhaviśśaśi.[5]

[**Supdt.** (*Entering*) Sigghaṃ sigghaṃ edaṃ (*Drops his voice*)].

Fisher. He hade mhi (*in distress*).

[**Supt.** Muñcedha re muñcedha jālôvajīviṇaṃ, uvavaṇṇo se kila aṅgulīaassa āgamo, amha-sāmiṇā jeva me kadhidaṃ].

Spy. Yadhā āṇavedi lāutte. Yama-vaśadiṃ gadua paḍiṇiutte khu eśe. (*Releases the fisherman.*)

Fisher. (*Saluting the Supdt.*) Bhaṭṭake tava kelake mama yīvide! (*Falls at his feet*).[6]

[**Supdt.** Utthehi, utthehi! Eso bhaṭṭiṇā aṅgulīaa-mulla-sammido pāridosio de pasādīkido. Tā geṇha edaṃ] (*Gives the fisherman a bracelet*).

Fisher. (*Receiving it with delight*) Aṇugahide mhi.

Jān. Eśe khu laññā tadhā ṇāme aṇugahide yaṃ śūlādo odālia hasti-skandhaṃ śamālovide.[7]

Spy. Lāutte! pālidośie kadhedi mahāliha-ladaṇeṇa teṇa aṅgulīaeṇa śāmiṇo bahumadeṇa hodavvaṃ ti.[8]

---

1 cilāadi 'is a long time.'

2 'Kings must be approached as occasion offers' (*upa*+*sṛp*).

3 sphulanti 'quiver.' Text phulanti but see Pischel § 311. Similarly § 310 for -hastā (text hatthā). vāvādeduṃ infin. caus. (*vi*+*ā*+*pad*).

4 ṇa+alihadi (*arhati*).

5 śaüla kind of fish (*Śakula*). There are various readings here. Pischel says=*svakulānām*.

6 kelake=kerako the prototype of genitival affixes like -kero -ker -er. yīvide 'life.'

7 odālia (cf. odāra § 75)=*avatārya*. śamālovide past part. caus. (*sam*+*ā*+*ruh*). 'Mounted on the withers of an elephant' denotes elevation to high dignity (MW.). Text has—hatthi-kkhandhaṃ.

8 mahāliha=*mahârha*.

[**Supdt.** Ṇaṃ tassiṃ bhaṭṭiṇo mahāriha-radaṇaṃ ti ṇa paridoso. Ettikaṃ uṇa—].

Both. Kiṃ ṇāma ?

[**Supdt.** Takkemi tassa daṃsaṇeṇa ko vi hiaa-tthido jaṇo bhaṭṭiṇā sumaridŏ tti, jado taṃ pekkhia muhuttaaṃ paidigambhīro vi pajjussua-maṇo āsi].[1]

Spy. Tośide dāṇiṃ bhaṭṭā lāutteṇa.

Jān. Ṇaṃ bhaṇāmi imaśśa maścalī-śattuṇo kidĕ tti (*Looks jealously at the fisherman*).[2]

Fisher. Bhaṭṭakā ido addhaṃ tumhāṇaṃ pi śulā-mullaṃ bhodu.

Jān. Dhīvala! mahattale śaṃpadaṃ me piavaaśśake śaṃvutte'śi kādaṃbalī-śaddhikĕ kkhu paḍhamaṃ amhāṇaṃ śohide iścīadi. Tā śuṇḍikāgālaṃ yeva gaścamha.[3]

(*Exeunt omnes.*)

Māgadhī.] Extract No. 23.

Sthāvaraka (Mṛcch. Act X)

Enters along the roof and in chains.

(*Listens to the proclamation in distress*).

Kadhaṃ apāve Cāludatte vāvādīadi! Hage ṇialeṇa śāmiṇā bandhide. Bhodu! akkandāmi. Śuṇādha, ayyā śuṇādha. Asti dāṇiṃ mae pāveṇa pavahaṇa-paḍivatteṇa Puspa-kalaṇḍaayiṇṇuyyāṇaṃ Vaśantaśeṇā ṇidā. Tado mama śāmiṇā 'maṃ ṇa kāmeśi' tti kadua, bāhu-pāśa-balakkāleṇa mālidā, ṇa uṇa ediṇā ayyeṇa. Kadhaṃ? Vidūladāe ṇa ko vi śuṇādi. Tā kiṃ kalemi? Attāṇaaṃ pāḍemi. (*Reflecting*) Yaï evvaṃ kalemi, tadā ayya-Cāludatte ṇa vāvādīadi. Bhodu. Imādo pāśādabālagga-padolikādo ediṇā yiṇṇa-gavakkheṇa attāṇaaṃ ṇikkhi-

---

1 paidi=*prakṛti*. pajjussua (*paryutsuka*) cf. § 41.

2 maścalī 'fish,' cf. Hindi machlī; Sindhi machaḍī; Marāṭhī māsalī from a popular diminutive of maccha=*matsya*. § 56.

3 mahattale compar. of *mahat-*. kādambalī, *kadamba* 'toddy.' śaddhike 'feast enjoyment' (*sagdhi*). śohide=*sauhṛdam*. śuṇḍikāgāla 'grog-shop.'

vāmi. Balaṃ hage uvalade, ṇa uṇa eśe kula-putta-vihagāṇaṃ vāśapādave ayya-Cāludatte. Evvaṃ yaï vivayyāmi laddhe mae palaloe. (*Throws himself down*) Hī hī! ṇa uvaladĕ mhi. Bhagge me daṇḍa-ṇiale. Tā caṇḍāla-ghośaṃ śamaṇṇeśāmi.

apāve 'sinless.' vāvādīadi, pass. caus (*vi*+*ā*+*pad*). ṇialeṇa 'with a fetter' (*nigaḍa*). mālidā=Ś. māridā. -bālagga- 'dovecot' (?) (*vālâgra*). padolikā (*pratolī*+kā) 'gateway' (*vide* Vogel, J.R.A.S., July, 1906). gav'akkha 'bull's-eye,' 'round window or loophole,' cf. French '*œil de bœuf*' meaning 'bull's-eye,' i.e. 'window.' (Acc. Grammarians should be gavaśka or gavaẖka). uvalade 'done for' (*uparataḥ*). pādave 'tree.' vivayyāmi (text vivajjāmi) (*vi*+*pad*). pala-loe 'the other world.'

Māgadhī.] **Extract No. 24.**

Śakāraḥ (Mṛcch. Act X).

(*Entering in great glee*).

Maṃśeṇa tikkhâmilikeṇa bhatte
śākeṇa śūpeṇa śa-maścakeṇa
bhuttaṃ mae attaṇaaśśa gehe
śāliśśa kūleṇa gulodaṇeṇa.[1]

(*Listening*) Bhiṇṇa-kaṃśa-khaṅkhaṇāe Caṇḍālavāāe śala-śaṃyoe.[2] Yadhā a eśe ukkhālide *vajjha*-ḍiṇḍima-śadde paḍahāṇaṃ a śuṇīadi, tadhā takkemi, dalidda-Cāludattāke *vajjhaṭṭhāṇaṃ* ṇīadi tti.[3] Tā peskiśśaṃ. Śattuviṇāśe ṇāma mama

---

1 bhuttaṃ mae 'I have dined' (*bhuj*). tikkha 'pungent'=*tīkṣṇa*. (Possibly tiẖkha or tiśkha would be better Mg.). āmilika 'acid,' 'tamarind' (*amlikā* cf. H. imlī). bhatte 'food.' 'rice,' *bhakta* cf. H. bhāt. śūpa, would expect śūva cf. rūva. attaṇaaśśa, a later form than attaṇo, § 36. kūla 'food, boiled rice.' gulodaṇa 'treacle porridge' (H. guṛ).

2 śala-saṃyoa 'combination of accents.' (*svara*) 'intonation.' vāā 'speech.' kaṃśa 'goblet, gong' (*kāṃsya* 'brass,' etc.).

3 ukkhālide 'raised.' *khal* 'move or shake,' vajjha 'of execution.' (*vadhya*). Proper Mg. said to be vayyha. The combination *yyha* suggests that Mg. *y* differed from the usual pronunciation of य in the direction of zh. -ṭṭhāṇa acc. Hemacandra should be -stāṇa.

mahante haḷakkaśśa palīdośe hodi.[1] Śudaṃ a mae, ye vi kila śattuṃ vāvādaantaṃ peskadi, taśśa aṇṇaśśiṃ jammantale aḫkhi-loge ṇa hodi. Mae khu viśa-gaṇṭhi-gabbha-paviṣṭeṇa via kīḍaeṇa kiṃ pi antalaṃ maggamāṇeṇa uppāḍide tāha dalidda-Cāludattāha viṇāśe.[2] Śaṃpadaṃ attaṇakelikāe pāśāda-bālagga-padolikāe ahiluhia attaṇo palakkamaṃ peskāmi.[3] (*Does so, and has a look*) Hī, hī, edāha dalidda-Cāludattāha *vajjhaṃ* ṇīamāṇāha evaḍḍhe yaṇa-śaṃmadde, yaṃ velaṃ amhāliśe pavale vala-maṇuśśe *vajjhaṃ* ṇīadi taṃ velaṃ keliśe bhave ?[4] (*Looking again*) Kadhaṃ ! Eśe śe ṇava-baladdake via maṇḍide *dakkhiṇaṃ* diśaṃ ṇīadi.[5] Adha kiṃṇimittaṃ mama-kelikāe pāśāda-bālagga-padolikāe śamīve ghośaṇā ṇivaḍidā, nivālidā a ?[6] (*Looking round*) Kadhaṃ ! Stāvalake ceḍe vi *ṇatthi* idha.[7] Mā ṇāma teṇa ido gadua mantabhede kaḍe bhaviśśadi.[8] Tā yāva ṇaṃ aṇṇeśāmi. (*Descends and comes forward.*)

Servant. (*Catching sight of him*) Bhaṭṭālakā, eśe śe āgade !

Executioners. Ośaladha, dedha maggaṃ, dālaṃ ḍhakkedha,
hodha tuṇhīā,
aviṇaa-tikkha-viśāṇe dusṭa-baille ido edi.[9]

This character is supposed to speak a dialect Śākārī (see

---

1 haḍakka is the usual form ; also haḷaa, haḷaka (in verse) **hṛdaka*.

2 Text akkhi (Pischel § 24). kīḍaa 'insect' (*kīṭaka*). viśagaṇṭhi ? a plant.

3 ahiluhia (*adhi+ruh*). bālagga (*vide* Ex. 23).

4 evaḍḍhe 'so great' (JM. evaḍḍa evaḍḍaga) e- not from *evam*, but from **ayat* (Pisch. § 149, cf. *ayat+tya* **ayattia*—ëttia) vaḍḍha=*vṛddha*. yaṇa-śaṃmadda 'press of people.' pavale=Śaur. pavaro. keliśe=*kīdṛśaḥ*.

5 baladdake 'bull' (cf. *balīvarda*). ? daḫkiṇaṃ.

6 ṇivaḍidā (*ni+pat*). ṇivālidā (*ni+vṛ* caus.).

7 Stāvalake (text ṭhāvalake) (*Sthāvaraka*).

8 mantabhede 'breach of counsel,' 'betrayal.' kaḍe=*kṛtaḥ*.

9 ośaladha (*apa* or *ava+sṛ*). dālaṃ 'door' Śaur. duāraṃ. ḍhakkedha 'shut' from ḍhakkedi 'shuts,' cf. Pāli thaketi from an O. I. root like **sthak*, cf. H. ḍhāknā, ḍhaknā 'cover, shut.' -viśāṇa 'horn.' baïlle 'bull,' Apa. baïllu, Modern, 'bail.' Cāṇḍālī is sometimes spoken of as a separate dialect, and classed as an Apabhraṃśa.

next extract). This passage however appears to be in much the same kind of Māgadhī as spoken by other characters.

Māgadhī.] **Extract No. 25.**

Dialect. Śākārī.

Mṛcchakaṭikam.

(*a*) Act I, v. 18.

cyiṣṭha Vaśanta'eṇie, cyiṣṭha,
kiṃ yāśi, dhāvaśi, palāaśi paskhalantī
vāśū paśīda ṇa maliśśaśi, cyiṣṭha dāva ‖
kāmeṇa dajjhadi hu me hadake tavaśśī
aṅgāla-lāśi-paḍide via maṃśa-khaṇḍe ‖

cyiṣṭha=*tiṣṭha*, Pischel Grammar § 24, and § 217 quotes the commentator Pṛthvīdhara as the authority for the form **ycisṭha,** and in general a weak *y before c;* he also quotes Mārkaṇḍeya for a weak *y* before *c* and *j* in Mg. and Vrācaḍa Apabhraṃśa: Mg. ycilaṃ=*ciram*, yjāā=*jāyā*. The spelling cyiṣṭha may be explained as the substitution of the familiar *cy* च्य for the strange *yc* य्च. At the same time it may be noted that no one knows how 'yciṣṭha' should be pronounced. We cannot be positive how च was pronounced in old Magadha; but if it resembled any modern pronunciation, or any sort of palatal stop with an off-glide, one could more readily understand a weak *y* being heard *after* it.[1] Very probably the य was used to mark a peculiar way of pronouncing च, not amounting to a distinct sound either before or after it. (So the *h* in English *wh* does not represent a separate sound either after *w*, or before *w* as written in old English *hw*, but the surd equivalent of the sonant *w*). The reading of Vararuci's rule XI, 5 (Cowell, p. 179) is doubtful, but it evidently refers to a method of pronouncing च not to the addition of a distinct sound.

---

1 So S. K. Chatterji: 'Origin and development of Bengali Language,' p. 248. against Grierson: 'The Pronunciation of the Prakrit Palatals, J.R.A.S., 1913, p. 391.

paskhalantī (*pra + skhal*). According to the grammarians *skh* should remain. Text pakkhalantī. maliśśaśi = Śaur. marissasi. H. and P. text has ciṭṭha, which is Śaur. dajjhadi 'is burned.' (? dayyhadi). haḍake 'heart,' the prose form is haḍakke (**hṛdaka*) Pischel § 194. tavaśśī = *tapasvī*. lāśi = *rāśi*. maṃśa = *māṃsa*.

Verse 21. Mama maaṇam aṇaṅgaṃ vammahaṃ vaḍḍhaantī
niśi a śaaṇake me ṇiddaaṃ askivantī ।
paśalaśi bhaa-bhīdā paskhalantī skhalantī
mama vaśam aṇuyādā Lāvaṇaśśêva kuntī ॥

Vammaha so in M. and Mg. verses. Śaur. mammadha. (Text has mammaha). ṇiddaā 'sleep,' askivantī = *ākṣipantī*. Kṣ becomes sk. (Text has ākkhivanti, the *ā* is impossible). paśalaśi = *prasarasi*. skh remains. (Text has aṇujādā the Śaur. form.) Lāvaṇaśśa 'of Rāvaṇa.' The student will probably find the characteristic change *l* for *r* the most baulking feature in reading Māgadhī or its dialects.

Verse 23. Eśā ṇāṇakamūśi-kāma-kaśikā maścâśikā lāśikā
ṇiṇṇāśā kula-ṇāśikā avaśikā kāmaśśa mañjūśikā ।
eśā veśavahū śuveśa-ṇilaā veśaṅgaṇā veśiā
eśe śe daśa ṇāmake maï kaḷe ayyāvi maṃ ṇeścadi ॥

ṇāṇaka 'coin.' mūśi = *moṣi-* 'stealing.' kaśikā 'whip.' maśca + aśikā 'fish-eating.' (Text macchā°). lāśikā 'dancer.' ṇiṇṇāśā 'snub-nosed' (*nir + nāsa*), i.e. of low caste. (Text kāmassa = Śaur.). eśe nom. pl. masc. 'these.' śe = Śaur. se 'of her.' maï 'by me.' kaḷa Mg. has also kaḍa and (like Śaur.) kada. (Text, like Northern MSS. kale). (ajjā in Text is Śaur.). ṇĕścadi (*na + icchati*). Text has ṇecchadi.

Māgadhī.] **Extract No. 26.**

Lalita-Vigraharāja-nāṭaka (Act IV).

(Edited Kielhorn, *Indian Antiquary*, vol. xx, 1891).

Two **Turushka** prisoners meet a spy who is a fellow-countryman.

Vandinau: Eśe śe **Śāyambhlīśala**-śivila-ṇiveśe.[1] Edaśśiṃ alaśkiyyamāṇa-payyande kadhaṃ [lā]-ulaṃ yāṇidavvaṃ.[2] (*Purôvalokya*) Vayaśśa eśe ke vi cale[3] vva dīśadi? Tā imādo edaśśa śivilaśśa śalūvaṃ[4] lāulaṃ ca yāṇiśśamha.

Caraḥ: Aścaliyaṃ aścaliyaṃ! Aho **Viggahalāa**-ṇaleśala-śilīṇaṃ avayyandadā.[5] (*Purôvalokya*) Amha-deśīya vva kevi puliśā *peśkiyyandi*. Yāṇe vandīhiṃ edehiṃ huvidavvaṃ.

Vandinau: Bhadda, amhāṇaṃ Tuluśkāṇaṃ deśīye vva tumaṃ *peśkiyyaśi*. Tā kadhehi **Cāhamāṇa**-śivila-śalūvaṃ lāulaṃ ca.

Caraḥ: Śuṇādha le vandiṇo śuṇādha. Hage Tuluśkalāeṇa śāambhalīśalaśśa śivilaṃ peśkiduṃ peśide. Taṃ ca dūśaṃcalaṃ; yado tatthastehiṃ idale puścande vi ṇi[liśkan]de vi a palakīye tti *yāṇiyyadi*.[6] Tadhāvi mae kiṃpi kiṃpi *paccakkhīkadaṃ*.[7]

Vandinau: Aścaliaṃ aścaliaṃ! Kadhaṃ bhadda, tattha uvastidāṇaṃ cadulide aṇuaṃ pi tae laśkidaṃ.[8]

Charaḥ: Śuṇādha le vandiṇo yadhā mae taṃ śivilaṃ ṇilūvidaṃ. Hage khu śili-Śomeśaladevaṃ peśkiduṃ vaññandaśśa śaśtaśśa milide, milia a ettha *paviśiūṇa* bhiśkaṃ paśtiduṃ lagge.[9] Tado yaṃ yaṃ yāṇidaṃ taṃ taṃ tumhāṇaṃ *yahastaṃ*[10] kadhīyadu. Maavāli-*ṇijjhala*-kalāla-kaḍastalā-

---

1 *Sākambharīśvara*: śivila=*śibira*

2 *alakṣyamāṇa-paryante*. Yāṇidavvaṃ=Ś. jāṇidavvaṃ.

3 cale 'spy' (*caraḥ*).

4 Inscription has śśalūvaṃ (*svarūpam*).

5 'boundlessness' (*aparyantatā*). śilīṇaṃ 'of glories.'

6 idale=Śidaro; puścande=pucchanto. yāṇiyyadi should be yāṇīadi. ṇiliśkande=Ś. ṇirikkhanto (*nir+īkṣ*).

7 =*pratyakṣīkṛtam* but cf. bhiśkaṃ laśkidaṃ below.

8 cadulide (?)=**caturite* from *catura* 'in their cleverness.' laśkidaṃ =Ś. lakkhidaṃ.

9 *Someśvaradeva* may be the name of a prince. -paviśiūṇa, a M., JM. or AMg. ending. paśtiduṃ=*prārthayitum*.

10 *yathārtham*. According to the rules should be yadhastaṃ.

ṇaṃ kalindāṇaṃ dāva śahaśśaṃ.[1] Tulaṅgāṇaṃ uṇa laśkaṃ. Ṇalāṇaṃ uṇa *yujjha*-śkamāṇaṃ daha laśkāiṃ ti.[2] Kiṃ vahuṇā yampideṇa ? Taśśa kaḍaaśśa pāśa-stide śāale vi śuśke bhodi.[3] (*Bāhum utkṣipya*) Edaṃ ca taṃ lāulaṃ.[4] (*iti darśayati*).

Vandinau : Śāhu le calā śāhu !

Caraḥ : Ale le vandiṇo cilaṃ khu me ṇia-stāṇādo ṇiśśalidaśśa.[4] Tā hage vaññāmi.[5]

Vandinau : Gaśca le calā gaśca.

(*iti caro niṣkrāntaḥ*).

Vandinau : (*Purato gatvâvalokya*) Taṃ ṇidaṃ lāula-duvālaṃ, tā idha stidā eva ṇia-lāa-ppahāvaṃ payāśemha. (*Punar avalokya : sānandam*) Eśe śe Śāambhalīśale astāṇa-stide pulado dīsadi.

The Māgadhī in this inscription is interesting because it follows more closely than any MS. the rules given by Hemacandra. As the author Somadeva was a contemporary of Hemacandra, it has been suggested that he may have been acquainted with that grammarian, or at least with his grammar. Some errors have been corrected in the inscription itself, nevertheless there remain forms which are not correct according to Hemacandra, e.g. ṇijjhala, yujjha, yahastaṃ, paviśiūṇa. There is no reason to suppose that the stage kept up the correct form of Māgadhī down to the twelfth century, and this probably represents an attempt to carry out the rules for Māgadhī that were traditional among the grammarians, more consistently than usual, in order to make the speech of the Turkī prisoners and spies sound very foreign. It is a curious accident that the

---

1 *mada-vāri-nirjhara.* ṇijjhara is M. which should be ṇiyyhala in Mg.

2 yujjha=*yuddha* is against the dialect. daha for daśa according to Pischel is wrong.

3 kaḍaa 'host.' (*kaṭaka*). śāale 'ocean.'

4 ṇiśśalida p. part from ṇiśśaladi (*niḥ*+*sṛ*).

5 'wander.' **vrajñāmi* in class 9.

latest recorded fragment of Māgadhī is the most archaic in form that has been found.

"Āvantī."] **Extract No. 27.**
and *Dākṣiṇātyā.*

Vīraka and Candanaka (Mṛcch. Act VI).

Vīrakaḥ. Are re are Jaa-Jaamāṇa-Candaṇaa-Maṅgala-Phulla-bhadda-ppamuhā—

kiṃ acchadha vīsaddhā jo so govāla-dārao baddho,
bhettūṇa samaṃ vaccaï ṇaravaï-hiaaṃ a bandhaṇaṃ câvi ||

Ale, puratthime padolī-duāre ciṭṭha tumaṃ. Tumaṃ pi pacchime, tumaṃ pi dakkhiṇe, tumaṃ pi uttare. Jo vi eso pāāra-khaṇḍo, edaṃ ahiruhia Candaṇaeṇa samaṃ gadua avaloemi. Ehi Candaṇaa, ehi. Ido dāva.[1]

Candanakaḥ. Are re Vīraa-Visalla-Bhīmaṅgaa-Daṇḍakālaa-Daṇḍasura-ppamuhā,

āacchadha vīsaddhā turiaṃ jatteha lahu karejjāha
Lacchī jeṇa ṇa raṇṇo pahavaï gottantaraṃ gantuṃ ||[2]

avi a,

ujjāṇesu sahāsu a magge ṇaarīa āvaṇe ghose |
taṃ taṃ johaha turiaṃ saṅkā vā jāae jattha ||[3]
re re Vīraa kiṃ kiṃ darisesi bhaṇāhi dāva vīsaddhaṃ
bhettūṇa a bandhaṇaaṃ ko so govāla-dāraaṃ haraï ||[4]
kass' aṭṭhamo diṇaaro, kassa caüttho a vaṭṭae cando,

---

[1] Śaur. acchadha. M. bhettūṇa, vaccaï. These latter however occur in a verse; gadua below is of the Śaur. type. Ale seems to be a fragment of Mg. out of place here.

[2] visalla=*vi-śalya.*

[3] turiaṃ Ś. turidaṃ. jatteha=Ś. jattedha (*yatadhvam*). karejjāha opt., pahavaï, are all M. in form. ṇaarīa loc. sing. Oblique fem. sing. in -īa is common in M. verses. johaha (*yojayata, anveṣayata*) ? fut. of (Apa.) joedi 'sees.' (*dyu*) or √*yudh* 'to go for.' jāae=JŚ. jāyade. jattha relat. of attha=*atra.* In other dialects generally jahiṃ is used.

[4] darisesi "seest."

chaṭṭho a bhaggava-gaho, bhūmisuo pañcamo kassa ?[1]
bhaṇa kassa jamma-chaṭṭho jīvo ṇavamo tahea sūrasuo
jīante Candaṇae ko so govāla-dāraaṃ harai ?[2]

Vīrakaḥ. Bhaḍa Candaṇaa!
avaharaï kovi turiaṃ, Candaṇaa, savāmi tujjha hiaeṇa
jaha addh'-uīda-diṇaare govālaa-dārao khuḍido.[3]

[Servant. Yādha goṇā, yādha.][4]

Candanakaḥ. Are re, pekkha pekkha.
ohārio pavahaṇo vaccaï majjheṇa rāa-maggassa
edaṃ dāva viāraha kassa kahiṃ pavasio pavahaṇŏ tti.[5]

Vīrakaḥ. Are pavahaṇa-vāhaā! mā dāva edaṃ pavahaṇaṃ vāhehi. Kassa-kerakaṃ edaṃ pavahaṇaṃ? Ko vā idha ārūḍho? Kahiṃ vā vajjaï?

[Servant. Eśĕ kkhu pavahaṇe ayya-Cāludattāha kelake. Idha ayyaā Vaśantaśeṇā ālūḍhā. Puspa-kalaṇḍaaṃ yiṇṇuyyāṇaṃ kilidum Cāludattaśśa ṇīadi.][6]

Vīrakaḥ (*Going up to Candanaka*). Eso pavahaṇa-vāhao bhaṇādi "ajja-Cārudattassa pavahaṇaṃ; Vasantaseṇā ārūḍhā Puppha-karaṇḍaaṃ jiṇṇujjāṇaṃ ṇīadi tti."[7]

---

1 caüttho 'fourth,' Ś. caduttho. chaṭṭho 'sixth' (cf. H. chaṭā). gaho for -ggaho 'planet.' bhaggava 'belonging to Bhṛgu's daughter.' bhūmisuo 'son of the earth'=Mars.

2 tahea=*tathaiva*. sūrasuo 'son of the Sun'=Saturn.

3 savāmi 'I swear.' addh'uīda 'half risen,' Śaur. udida; M. uia (? read udia). khuḍido 'removed' (*khaṇḍitaḥ*)? from a root *khuṭ*. Not the same as Ś. khuḍida 'broken,'=**kṣudita* for *kṣuṇṇa*. (Pischel § 568.)

4 The servant speaks Mg. goṇo 'bull' is the masc. form usual in AMg, Mg. For derivation Pischel suggests **gavaṇa* or **gūrṇa*. The first seems the more probable.

5 ohāria 'covered' (*apa+vṛ*). pavahaṇa 'carriage.' (*pra+vah*). vacca 'goes' (cf. JM. p. 135, n. 4). viāraha 'ascertain' (*vi+car*), pavasio 'set out' (*pra+vas=proṣita*).

6 MSS. and Editions have *ja* and *jja* for Mg. *ya yya*. Mg. kelake =Ā. kerako. puspa (following Hemacandra), MSS. vary. Usual reading puppha. yiṇṇuyyāṇaṃ 'old garden.' Here we have the two Mg. genitives side by side.

7 There is no point in supposing V. mimics the servant's dialect

C. Tā gacchadu.
V. Aṇavaloïdo jjeva.
C. Adha iṃ?
V. Kasssa paccaeṇa?
C. Ajja-Cārudattassa.
V. Ko ajja-Cārudatto? Kā vā Vasantaseṇā, jeṇa aṇavaloïdaṃ vajjaï?
C. Are, ajja-Cārudattaṃ ṇa jāṇāsi, ṇa vā Vasantaseṇiaṃ! jaï ajja-Cārudattaṃ Vasantaseṇiaṃ vā ṇa jāṇāsi, tā gaaṇe joṇhā-sahidaṃ candaṃ ṇa jāṇāsi.[1]

ko taṃ guṇâravindaṃ sīla-miaṅkaṃ jaṇo ṇa jāṇādi?
āvaṇṇa-dukkha-mökkhaṃ caü-sāara-sāraaṃ raaṇaṃ।
do jeva pūaṇīā iha ṇaarīe tilaa-bhūdā a,
ajjāVasantaseṇā, dhamma-ṇihī Cārudatto a.[2]

Notes.—Pṛthvīdhara makes both characters speak Āvantī, of which he gives only the jejune information that it possesses the dental *s*, and *ra*, and is rich in proverbial sayings. Mārkaṇḍeya describes it as a mixture of Śaurasenī and Māhārāṣṭrī. Such indeed appears to be the character of the dialect as given by the MSS. Candanaka however speaks of himself as a Southerner "vaaṃ dakkhiṇatthā avvatta-bhāsiṇo—" 'We Southerners speak indistinctly. So Pischel thought it unlikely that Candanaka spoke Āvantī, but more probable that he spoke Dākṣiṇātyā (Bharata 17. 48. Sāhityadarpaṇa, p. 173. 5). It would appear that this was not very different from Āvantī, and that both were nearly related to Śaurasenī. 'vaaṃ dakkhiṇatthā' however would be 'amhe dakkhiṇaccā' in Śaurasenī.

---

especially as he does not repeat his exact words; naturally he reports to C. in his usual language.

1 jöṇhā 'moonlight.'

2 caü-sāara-sāraaṃ 'containing the essence of the four oceans.' -ṇihī 'treasury.'

Jain Śaurasenī] Extract No. 28.

Pravacanasāra.

(Portions of this were printed with Sanskrit version by R Bhandarkar in Appendix III, (p. 379 ff.) of Report on the Search for Sanskrit Manuscripts in the Bombay Presidency during the year 1883-84. Published 1887. There is a complete edition with several Sanskrit commentaries published at Bombay. Vīra Saṃvat 2438.)

I. (69). Deva-jadi-guru-pūjāsu veva dāṇammi vā susīlesu |
uvavāsādisu ratto suhôvaog'appago appā ||

(70). Jutto suheṇa ādā tiriyo vā māṇuso ya devo vā |
bhūdo tāvadakālaṃ lahadi suhaṃ indiyaṃ viviham ||

(74). Jadi santi hi puṇṇāṇi ya pariṇāma-samubbhavāṇi vivihāṇi |
jaṇayanti visaya-taṇhaṃ jīvāṇaṃ devadantāṇaṃ ||

(75). Te puṇa udiṇṇataṇhā duhidā taṇhāhiṃ visaya-sokkhāṇi |
icchanti aṇuhavanti ya āmaraṇaṃ dukkha-santattā ||

III. (13). Caradi ṇibaddho ṇiccaṃ samaṇo ṇāṇammi daṃsaṇamuhammi |
payado mūla-guṇesu ya ajo so paḍipuṇṇa-sāmanno ||

(18). Havadi va ṇa havadi bandho made hi(ṃ) jīve'dha kāyaceṭṭhammi |
bandho dhuvam uvadhīdo idi savaṇā chaḍḍiyā savvaṃ ||

(19). Ṇa hi ṇiravekkho cāū ṇa havadi bhikkhussa āsaya-visuddhī |
avisuddhassa ya citte kahaṃ ṇu kamma-kkhayo vihiū ||

The cerebral *ṇ* is used initially whereas AMg. JM. manuscripts prefer initial *n* (dental). The letter *ya* is used as in other Jain MSS.

This Prakrit contains words and forms that are quite foreign to ordinary Śaurasenī—but found in Māhārāṣṭrī or Ardha-Māgadhī. Perhaps some of the Śaurasenī forms which are allowed by Hemacandra, but never found in the dramas, are derived from Digambara Texts. (Pischel § 21.)

(69). veva. Editor suggests yeva. Sanskrit-version *caiva*. The MS. seems to have fluctuated in the use of *ya* and *va*. dāṇammi loc. as in M. suhôvaog'appago =*śubhopayog-ātmako*.

(70). ādā=*ātmā*, i.e. **ātā*, cf. AMg. āyā; JM. attā. tiriyo 'animal' (*tiryak*).

(74). *devadāntānām*.

(75). tanhā=taṇhā. This is merely an orthographical peculiarity; so is the spelling *khk* for *kkh*.

III. (13). ṇāṇammi 'in knowledge.'

(18). uvadhīdo abl. of uvadhi (*upadhi*). idi=*iti*. savaṇā =*śramaṇāḥ*, chaḍḍiya should be chaḍḍida (Pischel § 291)=*chardita* cf. Ś. vicchaḍḍida, M. vicchaḍḍia, AMg. JM. vicchaḍḍiya.

(19). cāū=*tyāgo* JM. cāo. The ending *ū* (cf. vihiū) is exceptional and probably wrong, the mistake being due to the similarity of *u* and *o* in Jain MSS. Bombay Edition has cāyo and vihio.

Bhāsa.] **Extract No. 29.**

Svapna-Vāsavadattam (Act IV, p. 29).

Praveśakaḥ.

Enter the Jester.

Jester. (*Gleefully*) Diṭṭhiā *tattahodo* Vaccha-rāassa abhippeda-vivāhamaṅgala-ramaṇijjo kāḷo diṭṭho. Ko ṇāma edaṃ jāṇādi—tādise *vayaṃ* aṇattha-saḷiḷāvatte pakkhittā uṇa ummajjissāmo tti.[1] Idāṇiṃ pāsādesu vasīadi, *andeura-digghiāsu hṇāīadi*, *paḷama-maüra-suumārāṇi* modaa-khaj-

[1] tattahodo should be tattha. § 45. maṅgaḷa. Cerebral ḷ is written throughout for the dental. This is common in MSS. written in S. India. vayaṃ Śaur. has amhe, Dākṣinātyā vaaṃ (also allowed in Śaur. by Vararuci and Mārkaṇḍeya), AMg. vayaṃ, Pali vayaṃ. ummajjissāmo 'we shall emerge.'

jaāṇi khajjīanti tti aṇ-Acchara-saṃvāso Utturakuru-vāso mae aṇubhavīadi.[1] Ekko khu mahanto doso, mama āhāro suṭṭhu ṇa pariṇamadi, suppacchadaṇāe *sayyāe* ṇiddaṃ ṇa labhāmi, *jaha* vāda-soṇidaṃ abhido via vattadi tti pekkhāmi.[2] Bho suhaṃ *ṇâmaya*-paribhūdaṃ akallavattaṃ ca.[3]

Enter a Maidservant.

Maid. Kahiṃ ṇu khu gado *ayya*-Vasantao ? (*Stepping round*) *Ahmo* eso Vasantao. (*Approaches*) *Ayya* ! Vasantaa ! Ko kāḷo tumaṃ aṇṇesāmi.[4]

Jester. (*With a leer*) Kiṃ ṇimittaṃ, bhadde ! maṃ aṇṇesasi ?

---

1 andeura. anteura is correct (as on p. 24) but MSS. often give -nd for -nt, so "Saundalā" for Sauntalā. This was probably due to the influence of Apabhraṃśa in which the change is common. hṇāīadi. Śaur. ṇhāīadi. The MS. has regularly **hṇ** and **hm** for *ṇh, mh*. At first sight this looks like a sign of antiquity; for *h* here represents *s* and *hṇā* seems nearer *snā* than *ṇhā*. The spelling *hm, hṇ* however is found in texts, where *ṇh, mh* is well established as correct. Pali forms like amhe, nahātako (=*snātako*) show that the inversion is ancient. Moreover the difference between *e.g.*, bamhaṇo and (as in Bhāsa) bahmaṇo is not very great to the ear. So *hṇa, hma* may be only *orthographical* variations. paḷama=*parama*. No apparent reason for *l* or *ḷ* here. maüra for mahura (=*madhura*). This appears to be a mistake, p. 6 has mahurā. suumārāṇi=°rāiṃ. Neut. Plural in *-āṇi* occurs in AMg. JM. JŚ. not in M. or Śaur. In Pali it can be *-āni* as in Skt.

2 sayyāe (=*śayyāyām*) M. AMg. JM. sejjāe, Mg. śeyyāe. Here again double *yy* for double *jj*, as in ayyaütta, might be taken as a sign of antiquity. Hemacandra allows *yya* for *rya* in Śaur. The spelling is occasionally found in South Indian MSS. Most write only a circle य○य *a*○*a* which, says Pischel, either allows a choice between *yya* and *jja*, or is intended to express a sound between the two. (Pischel § 284.) In the case of Skt. *yya* there is no authority for Śaur. having anything but *jja*. jaha is regular in M. (Śaur. jadhā).

3 ṇâmaya- *āmaya* 'indigestion' should be āmaa in Śaur. If it is not a mistake, it is an archaism. kalla-vatta 'breakfast.'

4 ayya, see note on sayyāe above. Ahmo usual spelling ammo, see note on hṇāīadi above. Telang's edition of the Mālatī-mādhavam has the spelling ahmo. Another reading here is amme, p. 10 has ammo.

Maid. *Ahmāṇaṃ* bhaṭṭinī bhaṇādi—avi *hṇādo* jāmāduo tti.[1]

Jester. Kiṃ ṇimittaṃ bhodī pucchadi ?

Maid. Kim aṇṇaṃ ? sumaṇa-vaṇṇaaṃ āṇemi tti.

Jester. *Hṇādo tatta*bhavaṃ. Savvaṃ āṇedu bhodī vajjia bhoaṇaṃ.

Maid. Kiṃ ṇimittaṃ vāresi bhoaṇaṃ ?

Jester. Adhaṇṇassa mama koiḷāṇaṃ akkhi-parivaṭṭo via kukkhi-parivaṭṭo saṃvutto.[2]

Maid. Īdiso evva hohi.

Jester. Gacchadu bhodī. Jāva ahaṃ vi *tattahodo* saāsaṃ gacchāmi.[3]

Exeunt.

(*Enter* Padmāvatī *with retinue and* Vāsavadattā *wearing Avanti dress.*)

Maid. Kiṃṇimittaṃ bhaṭṭi-dāriā Pamada-vaṇaṃ āadā ?

Padmā. Haḷā, *tāṇi* dāva sehāḷiā-*guhmaāṇi* pekkhāmi kusumi*dāṇi* vā ṇa ve tti.[4]

Maid. Bhaṭṭi-dārie ! *tāṇi* kusumid*āṇi* ṇāma, pavāḷ'-antaridehiṃ via mottiā-ḷambaehiṃ āid*āṇi* kusumehiṃ.

Padmā. Haḷā ! jadi evvaṃ, kiṃ dāṇiṃ viḷambesi ?

Maid. Teṇa hi imassiṃ siḷā-vaṭṭae muhuttaaṃ *upa*visadu bhaṭṭi-dāriā. Jāva ahaṃ vi kusumâvacaaṃ karemi.[5]

Padmā. *Ayye* ! Kiṃ ettha *upa*visāmo ?

Vāsava. Evvaṃ hodu.

(*They both sit down.*)

[The words in italics are not normal Śaurasenī.]

---

1 jāmāduo § 60. 2 kukkhi 'belly.'

3 jāva is the ordinary form. *Ya* does not appear here. ahaṃpi would be better.

4 guhmaa (*gulmaka*) AMg. Ś. Mg. gumma § 48. There seems no reason for the spelling with hm. In the previous Act "guhmadu" represents *gumphadu*, where the inversion is not archaic.

5 *śilā-paṭṭaka* 'stone slab.' (On p. 36, silā-paṭṭaka). uvavisadu is correct Śaur. So correctly uvaradā, p. 40. avacaaṃ, no *ya* appears here.

Translation.

Jester. Ha. ha! How good to see the delightful time of the auspicious and welcome marriage of His Highness the King of the Vatsas. Who could have known that after being hurled into such a whirlpool of misfortune, we should rise again to the surface. Now we live in palaces, we bathe in the tanks of the inner court, we eat dainty and delicious dishes of sweetmeats—in short I am in Paradise, except that there are no nymphs to keep me company. But there is one great drawback. I do not digest my food at all well. Even on the downiest couches I can not sleep, for I seem to see the Wind and Blood disease circling round—Bah! there is no happiness in life if you are full of ailments, or without a good breakfast.

Maid. Wherever has the worthy Vasantaka got to? *why here he is.* Oh, Master Vasantaka, what a time I have been looking for you.

Jester. And why were you looking for me, my dear.

Maid. Our queen says, "hasn't our son-in-law finished his bath?"

Jester. Why does she want to know?

Maid. So that I may bring him a garland and unguents of course.

Jester. His Highness has bathed. You may bring everything except food.

Maid. Why do you bar food?

Jester. Unfortunate that I am, like the rolling of cuckoo's eyes..my stomach is like that.

Maid. May you ever be as you are!

Jester. Off with you! I will go and attend on His Highness.

Maid. What has brought your ladyship to this pleasure-garden?

Padmāvatī. My dear, I want to see if the *seoli* clusters have flowered or not.

Maid. Yes, princess they have with blossoms like pendants of pearls interset with coral.

Padmāvatī. If that is so, my dear, why do you delay?

Maid. Wont your ladyship sit on this stone-bench for a moment, while I gather some flowers?

Padmāvatī. Dear lady, shall we sit here?

Vāsavadattā. Let us do so.

EARLY PRAKRIT.

Extract No. 30.

Aśoka].

Fourth Rock Edict.

Western dialect from Girnar and Eastern from Dhauli. For details about the text see Hultzsch: Corpus Inscriptionum Indicarum. Vol. I. A synoptic view of all six versions is given in Woolner: Aśoka Text and Glossary. The translation follows Hultzsch. The old Brāhmī script did not mark the doubled consonants.

Girnar. Atikātaṃ aṃtaraṃ bahūni vāsasatāni vaḍhito eva prāṇārambho vihiṃsā ca bhūtānaṃ ñātisu asaṃpratipat brāmhaṇasramaṇānaṃ asaṃpratipatī.

Dhauli. Atikaṃtaṃ aṃtalaṃ bahūni vasa-satāni vaḍhite va pānālaṃbhe vihisā ca bhūtānaṃ nātīsu asaṃpaṭipati samanabābhanesu asaṃpaṭipati.

In times past, for many hundreds of years, there had ever been promoted the killing of animals and the hurting of living beings, discourtesy to relatives (and) discourtesy to Brāhmaṇas and Śramaṇas.

Atikātaṃ=*atikrāntam*. vaḍhito=*vardhito* cf. Pali vaddhito. nāti=*jñāti* Pali ñāti. *sampratipatti* 'proper recognition.'

Girnar. Ta aja devānaṃ priyasa Priyadasino rāño dhaṃmacaraṇena bherīghoso aho dhaṃmaghoso vimānadasaṇā ca hastidasaṇā ca agikhaṃdhāni ca aññāni ca divyāni rūpāni dasayitpā janaṃ.

Dhauli. Se aja devānaṃ piyasa Piyadasine lājine dhaṃmacalanena bhelighosaṃ aho dhaṃmaghosaṃ vimānadasanaṃ hathīni agikaṃdhāni aṃnāni ca diviyāni lūpāni dasayitu munisānaṃ.

But now, in consequence of the practice of morality on the part of King Devānāmpriya Priyadarśin the sound of drums has become the sound of morality, showing the people representations of aerial chariots, representations of elephants, masses of fire and other divine figures.

aho from an aorist **abhot* (Kern *abhavat*). Others have taken it in the sense of "or rather" cf. *athavā* Apa. ahavai. -tpā, -tu=Skt. *-tvā*, *darśayitvā*. hathīni acc. plur. masc. taken from the neuter declension. The meaning of *agni-skandha* 'masses of fire, may be bonfires or radiant beings.'

Girnar. Yārise bahūhi vāsasatehi na bhūtapuve tārise aja vaḍhite devānaṃ priyasa Priyadasino rāño dhaṃmānusaṣṭiyā anārambho prāṇānaṃ avihisā bhūtānaṃ ñātīnaṃ saṃpatipatī brahmaṇasamaṇānaṃ saṃpaṭipatī mātari pitari susrusā thairasusrusā.

Dhauli. Ādise bahūhi vasasatehi no hūtapuluve tādise aja vaḍhite devānaṃ piyasa Piyadasine lājine dhaṃmānusathiyā anālaṃbhe pānānaṃ avihisā bhūtānaṃ nātisu saṃpaṭipati samanabaṃbhanesu saṃpaṭipati mātipitusususūsā vuḍhasusūsā.

Such as they had not existed before for many hundreds of years, thus there are now promoted, through the instruction in morality on the part of King Devānāmpriya Priyadarśin, abstention from killing animals, abstention from hurting living things, courtesy to relatives, courtesy to Brāhmaṇas and Śramaṇas, obedience to mother and father, obedience to the aged.

thaira=*sthavira*, Pali thera. vuḍha=*vṛddha*, Pali vuḍḍha or vuddha.

Girnar. Esa añe ca bahuvidhe dhaṃmacaraṇe vaḍhite vaḍhayisati ceva devānaṃ priyo Priyadasī rājā dhaṃmacaraṇaṃ idaṃ.

Dhauli. Esa aṃne ca bahuvidhe dhaṃmacalane vaḍhite vaḍhayisati ceva devānaṃ piye Piyadasī lājā dhaṃmacalanaṃ idaṃ.

In this and many other ways is the practice of morality promoted. And King Devānāmpriya Priyadarśin will ever promote this practice of morality.

Girnar. Putrā ca potrā ca prapotrā ca devānaṃ priyasa Priyadasino rāño vadhayisaṃti idaṃ dhaṃmacaraṇaṃ āva saṃvaṭakapā.

Dhauli. Putā pi ca natipanati ca devānaṃ piyasa Piyadasine lājine pavaḍhayisaṃti yeva dhaṃmacalanaṃ imaṃ ākapaṃ.

And the sons, grandsons and great-grandsons of King Devānāmpriya Priyadarśin will promote this practice of morality, until the æon of destruction.

Āva saṃvaṭa-kapā=*yāvat saṃvarta-kalpāt*. ākapaṃ=*ā-kalpam*. nati-panati (*naptṛ-pranaptṛ*).

Girnar. Dhaṃmamhi sīlamhi tisṭaṃto dhaṃmaṃ anusāsisaṃti.

Dhauli. Dhaṃmasi sīlasi ca ciṭhitu dhaṃmaṃ anusāsisaṃti.

Abiding by morality and by good conduct they will instruct (people) in morality.

ciṭhitu gerund from a present *ciṭhati.

Girnar. Esa hi sesṭe kaṃme ya dhaṃmānusāsanaṃ.

Dhauli. Esa hi seṭhe kaṃme yā dhaṃmānusāsanā.

For this is the best work viz., instruction in morality.

Girnar. Dhaṃmacaraṇe pi na bhavati asīlasa. Ta imamhi athamhi vadhī ca ahīnī ca sādhu.

Dhauli. Dhaṃmacalaṇe pi cu no hoti asīlasa. Se imasa aṭhasa vaḍhī ahīnī ca sādhu.

And the practice of morality is not for one who is devoid of good conduct. Therefore promotion and not neglect of this object is meritorious.

Girnar. Etāya athāya idaṃ lekhāpitaṃ imasa athasa vadhi

yujaṃtu hīni ca mā locetavyā. Dbādasavāsābhisitena devānaṃ priyena Priyadasinā rāña idaṃ lekhāpitaṃ.

Dhauli. Etāye aṭhāye iyaṃ likhite imasa aṭhasa vaḍhī yujaṃtū hīni ca mā alocayisū. Duvādasavasāni abhisitasa devānaṃ piyasa Piyadasine lājine yaṃ idha likhite.

For the following purpose has this been caused to be written, that they should devote themselves to the promotion of this practice and that they should not approve the neglect of it.

This was caused to be written by King Devānāmpriya Priyadarśin when he had been anointed twelve years.

yujaṃtu imperat. 'let them devote themselves to, carry on. mā alocayisu 3. plur. aor. of ālocayati 'let them not countenance'; locetavyā (Girnar) is fut. part., the construction seems to have been mixed. Dbādasa 'twelve' cf. *tp* for *tv*. Pronounced as an implosive *d* eventually disappeared leaving only *b*. Such is the origin of the Prakrit terms bārasa, bāraha Hindi bārah, etc.

Pali] **Extract No. 31.**

Jātaka 308.

(Fausbøll Edn., Vol. III, p. 25. Trans. Francis and Neile. Vol. III, p. 17.)

Java-sakuṇa-jātakaṃ.

Atīte Bārāṇasiyaṃ Brahmadatte rajjaṃ kārente Bodhisatto Himavanta-padese rukkha-koṭṭha-sakuṇo hutvā nibbatti. Ath-'ekassa sīhassa maṃsaṃ khādantassa aṭṭhi gale laggi, galo uddhumāyi, gocaraṃ gaṇhituṃ na sakkoti, kharā vedanā vattanti.

Notes.—*Vārāṇasyām*=AMg. Vāṇārasīe. **Brahma**, Pkt. bamha. **kārente** causal participle, Ś. karente is active. **rukkha°**-"woodpecker." rukkha so in M. Ś., etc.=Vedic *rukṣa* "tree" doubtlessly related to *vṛkṣa* whence M. JM. vaccha. (Pischel § 320). **hutvā**=Ś. bhavia, AMg. hŏttā. **nibbatti** "was born again" aor. (*nir+vṛt*) from nibbattati=Ś. ṇivvaṭṭadi. **atha**=Ś adha. **sīha** so in M. (§ 65). **laggi** "stuck" aor.

from laggati. **ud-dhumāyi** 'was blown up, swelled up.' pass. aor: from uddhumāyati=*uddhmāyate*. **gaṇhituṃ**=Ś. geṇhiduṃ. **sakkoti**=Ś. sakkuṇoti. JM. sakkai, sakkei. **vattanti**=Ś. vaṭṭanti.

Atha naṃ so sakuṇo gocara-pasuto disvā sākhāya nilīno "kin te samma dukkhatīti" pucchi. So tam atthaṃ ācikkhi "Ahan te samma etaṃ aṭṭhiṃ apaneyyaṃ, bhayena te mukhaṃ pavisituṃ na visahāmi, khādeyyāsi pi man" ti. "mā bhāyi samma, nâhan taṃ khādāmi, jīvitaṃ medehîti."

Notes.—naṃ 'him.' pasuto 'intent on' seeking (food)=*prasita*. **disvā**=*dṛṣṭvā*, AMg. dissā, dissa dissaṃ. **Sākhāya** cf. M. loc. mālāa. nilīno "perched" past part. pass. of nilīyati cf Ś. ṇilīamāṇa. **samma** "friend, good sir"? from *samyak*. **ācikkhi** "told" ācikkhati (*ā+khyā* reduplicated)=Amg. āikkhai. **apaneyyaṃ** "I would remove" Ś. would be avaṇeaṃ, AMg. avaṇejjā. **visahāmi** (*vi+sah*) "dare."

So "sādhu" ti taṃ passena nipajjāpetvā "ko jānāti kiṃ p'esa karissatīti" cintetvā yathā mukhaṃ pidahituṃ na sakkoti tathā tassa adharoṭṭhe ca uttaroṭṭhe ca daṇḍakaṃ ṭhapetvā mukhaṃ pavisitvā aṭṭhikoṭiṃ tuṇḍena pahari. Aṭṭhi patitvā gataṃ. So aṭṭhiṃ pātetvā sīhassa mukhato nikkhamanto daṇḍakaṃ tuṇḍena paharitvā pātento nikkhamitvā sākhagge nilīyi.

Notes.—**passa**=Ś. pāsa. **nipajjāpetvā** gerund of causal from nipajjati (*ni+pad.*) **pidahituṃ** infin. from pidahati 'shuts' ((*a*)*pi+dhā.*) **nilīyi** 'perched' see nilīno above.

Sīho nīrogo hutvā ekadivasaṃ vana-mahisaṃ vadhitvā khādati. Sakuṇo "vīmaṃsissāmi nan" ti tassa uparibhāge sākhāya nilīyitvā tena saddhiṃ sallapanto paṭhamaṃ gātham āha:

Akaramhase te kiccaṃ yaṃ balaṃ ahuvamhase,
migarāja namo ty-atthu, api kiñci labhāmase.

Notes.—**vīmaṃsissāmi** fut. of vīmaṃsati "examine, try" (*mīmāṃsate*). **paṭhama**=Pkt. paḍhama. **akaramhase** imperfect (or aorist) ātm. **ahuvamhase** the same from bhavati. **ty-atthu**=(*iti+astu*). **labhāmase** imperative ātm

Taṃ sutvā sīho dutiyaṃ gātham āha:

Mama lohita-bhakkhassa niccaṃ luddāni kubbato
dant'antara-gato santo taṃ bahuṃ yaṃ hi jīvasîti

Taṃ sutvā sakuṇo itarā dve gāthā abhāsi:

Akataññuṃ akattāraṃ katassa appaṭikārakaṃ
yasmiṃ kataññutā n'atthi niratthā tassa sevanā.
Yassa sammukha-ciṇṇena mittadhammo na labbhati
anusuyyam anakkosaṃ sanikaṃ tamhā apakkame ti.
Evaṃ vatvā so sakuṇo pakkāmi.

Notes.— **-bhakkha** 'feeding on.' **kubbanto** pres. part. of karoti. **luddāni** 'cruelties.' (*rudra-*). **abhāsi** 'spoke' aor. of bhāsati. **kataññu** 'grateful' (*kṛtajña*). **-ciṇṇa** 'performed' (**cīrṇa*) used as p.p.p. to carati "a deed done in a person's presence, so, a personal kindness." **sanikaṃ** 'quickly.' Sometimes means 'slowly' like *śanaiḥ*: original meaning 'gently, softly.' **tamhā** (*tasmāt*) is used adverbially in Ś.

Pali]. **Extract No. 32.**

Jātaka 339.

(Fausbøll. Vol. III, p. 126. Trans. Vol. III, p. 23.)

Bāverujātakaṃ.

Atīte Bārāṇasiyaṃ Brahmadatte rajjaṃ kārente Bodhisatto mora-yoniyaṃ nibbattitvā vuddhim anvāya sobhagga-patto araññe vicari. Tadā ekacce vāṇijā disā-kākaṃ gahetvā nāvāya Bāveruraṭṭhaṃ agamaṃsu. Tasmiṃ kira kāle Bāveruraṭṭhe sakuṇā nāma n'atthi. Āgatâgatā raṭṭha-vāsino taṃ kūp'agge nisinnaṃ disvā "passath' imassa chavivaṇṇaṃ gala-pariyosānaṃ mukhatuṇḍakaṃ maṇi-guḷaka-sadisāni akkhīnîti" kākam eva pasaṃsitvā te vāṇijake āhaṃsu: "imaṃ ayyo sakuṇaṃ amhākaṃ detha, amhākaṃ hi iminā attho, tumhe attano raṭṭhe aññaṃ labhissathā" ti. "Tena hi mūlena ganhathā" ti. "Kahāpaṇena no dethā" ti. "Na demā" ti. Anupubbena vaḍḍhetvā "satena dethā" ti vutte "amhākaṃ esa bahûpakāro, tumhehi pana saddhiṃ mettī hotū" ti kahāpaṇasataṃ gahetvā adaṃsu.

vuddhim anvāya "attaining full growth" gerund (*anu*+*i*) formed by analogy with māya from mi, instead of *anvetvā. **ekacce** 'certain' (*eka-tya-*). **disā-kākaṃ** 'foreign crow.' **agamaṃsu**, 3, plur. aor. "went." **Kira**=*kila*. The Bāveru kingdom was evidently on the sea, in a country where birds were supposed to be scarce, probably up the Persian Gulf. **āgatâgatā** "passers by, spectators." **kūpa** 'mast.' **nisinnaṃ** 'perched'=JM. nisiṇṇa. **passatha**, 2nd plur. imperat. "look at." **-pariyosānaṃ** "at the end of" (*paryavasāna*) "termination." **ayyo**, perhaps we should read ayyā "Sirs" =Ś. ajjā. **Kahāpaṇa** "a coin, here probably of silver." **mettī** "friendship." **adaṃsu**, aor. "they gave."

Te taṃ gahetvā suvaṇṇa-pañjare pakkhipitvā nānappakārena macchamaṃsena c'eva phalāphalena ca paṭijaggiṃsu. Aññesaṃ sakuṇānaṃ avijjamānaṭṭhāne dasahi asaddhammehi samannāgato kāko lābhagga-yasagga-ppatto ahosi. Punavāre te vāṇijā ekaṃ mayūra-rājānaṃ gahetvā yathā accharāsaddena vassati pāṇippahārasaddena naccati evaṃ sikkhāpetvā Bāveruraṭṭhaṃ agamaṃsu. So mahājane sannipatite nāvāya dhure ṭhatvā pakkhe vidhūnitvā madhura-ssaraṃ nicchāretvā nacci.

phalāphala "wild fruit." Pali often lengthens a vowel when a word is repeated in a compound, so khaṇḍākhaṇḍaṃ "in pieces," kiccākiccāni "all sorts of duties." **paṭijaggiṃsu**, aor. paṭi-jaggati "watch over, look after" (*prati*+*jāgṛ*). **samannāgato** "endowed with" (*sam*+*anu*+*ā*+*gam*): the equivalent of this is found in Buddhist Sanskrit. **yasagga** "height of glory. **puna-vāre** "the next time." **accharā** "snapping of the fingers." **vassati** "screams" √*vāś*. They had trained it to scream at the snapping of the fingers and to dance at the clapping of the hands. **dhure** "on the prow.', **ṭhatvā**, M. JM. ṭhāiūṇa, AMg. JŚ. ṭhiccā. **nicchāreti** "emit, utter" causal of niccharati (*niś*+*car*).

Manussā taṃ disvā somanassa-jātā "etaṃ ayyo sobhaggapattaṃ susikkhita-sakuṇa-rājānaṃ amhākaṃ dethā "ti āhaṃsu. "Amhehi paṭhamaṃ kāko ānīto, taṃ gaṇhittha, idāni etaṃ mora-rājānaṃ ānāyimha, etaṃ pi yācatha, tumhākaṃ raṭṭhe sakuṇaṃ nāma gahetvā āgantuṃ na sakkā" ti. "Hotu ayyo, attano raṭṭhe aññaṃ labhissatha, imaṃ no dethā" ti mūlaṃ vaḍḍhetvā sahassena gaṇhiṃsu. Atha naṃ satta-ratana-vicitte pañjare ṭhapetvā macchamaṃsa-phalāphalehi c'eva madhu-lāja-sakkharā-pānakâdīhi ca paṭijaggiṃsu. Mayūrarājā lābhagga-yasagga-ppatto jāto. Tassâgatakālato paṭṭhāya kākassa lābhasakkāro parihāyi, koci naṃ oloketuṃ pi na icchati. Kāko khādaniya-bhojaniyaṃ alabhamāno 'kākā' ti vassanto gantvā ukkārabhūmiyaṃ otari.

āhaṃsu aor. "they said." **gaṇhittha** 2, plur. "you took." **ānāyimha** "we have brought." **sakkā** "it is possible." Sometimes this can be explained as the plural of sakko, 'able' (=*śakyaḥ*), but it is often indeclinable, and Pischel derived from *śakyāt* § 133. "Really it is impossible to come with a bird in your country." **ṭhapetvā**=AMg. ṭhāvettā, JM. ṭhavittā, ṭhaviūṇa, ṭhaviya, Ś. ṭhāvia, ṭhavia. **lāja** "fried corn." **paṭṭhāya** "from" lit, "setting out from" (*pra+sthā*), so ajjapaṭṭhāya "from this day forth." **parihāyi** "fell off." **khādaniyaṃ** "what can be chewed, hard food." **bhojaniyaṃ** "soft food." In verse we find khajjabhojjaṃ. **'kākā' ti vassanto** "crying caw,caw." **ukkārabhūmi** "dunghill," AMg. uccāra°. **otari** "settled on."

Pali]. **Extract No. 33.**

Mahāvaṃsa, Bk. VII.

Conquest of Ceylon.

(Dines Andersen's Reader, p. 110. Geiger's trans. p. 55.)

The Buddha at his decease informed Indra that Vijaya son of King Sīhabāhu had gone to Laṅkā with seven hundred followers, and asked that he and his followers should be carefully protected. Indra handed over the guardianship of Laṅkā to Viṣṇu.

V. 6. Sakkena vuttamatto so Laṅkam āgamma sajjukaṃ
paribbājaka-vesena rukkhamūlam upāvisi.

7. Vijaya-ppamukhā sabbe taṃ upecca apucchisuṃ ;
"Ayaṃ bho ko nu dīpo ?" ti. "Laṅkādīpo" ti abruvi.

V. 6. "vutta p.p.p. from vatti "he speaks" so in JM. AMg. **-matta** (*mātra*), Pkts. have more commonly -metta. AMg. -mitta. **āgamma** gerund of āgacchati. **sajjukaṃ** "quickly" derived from *sadyaḥ*. **vesena** "in the disguise" (of a *parivrājaka*, wandering ascetic).

V. 7. **-ppamukhā** 'with Vijaya at their head,' i.e. 'Vijaya and his followers.'

V. 8. "Na santi manujā ettha, na ca hessati vo bhayaṃ"—
iti vatvā kuṇḍikāyaṃ te jalena nisiñciya

9. Suttañ ca tesaṃ hatthesu laggetvā nabhasâgamā,
dassesi soṇirūpena paricārika-yakkhinī.

10. Eko taṃ vāriyanto pi rājaputtena anvagā
"gāmamhi vijjamānamhi bhavanti sunakhā" iti.

11. Tassā ca sāminī tattha Kuveṇī nāma yakkhinī
nisīdi rukkha-mūlamhi kantantī tāpasī viya.

12. Disvāna so pokkharaṇiṃ nisinnaṃ tañ ca tāpasiṃ
tattha nahātvā pivitvā c'ādāya ca muḷālayo—

13. Vāriñ ca pokkhare heva so vuṭṭhāsi, tam abruvi :
"bhakkho si mama, tiṭṭhā" ti, āḷhābaddho va so naro.

14. Parittasuttatejena bhakkhetuṃ sā na sakkuṇi
yāciyanto pi taṃ suttaṃ nâdā yakkhiniyā naro.

15. Taṃ gahetvā suruṅgāyaṃ rudantaṃ yakkhinī khipi,
evam ekekaso tattha khipi sattasatāni pi.

V. 8. **hessati,** fut. from bhavati (*havissati) bhavissadi is also common.

V. 9. **suttaṃ,** e.g. as a protection against evil spirits. **agamā,** aor. "vanished"; also agami, agacchi, agamasi, etc. **dassesi** "there appeared," aor. cf. dasseti=*darśayati*. **soṇi** "bitch."

V.10. **vāriyanto,** partic. of vāriyati pass. of vāreti "forbid," caus. of vuṇāti. **anvagā** "followed." **sunakhā** "dogs" (*śunakāḥ*)—"only where there is a village."

V.11. **Kantantī** "spinning."

V.12. **disvāna,** gerund=disvā, also passitvāna. **muḷālayo,** acc. plur. "lotus shoots" (*mṛṇālī*).

V.13. **So.** Reader has sā but it was the man who came out of the tank not the yakkhinī. **āḷhâbaddho** "fast bound." āḷhaka is a tethering post (*ārdhaka*).

V.14. **sakkuṇi** aor. sakkuṇāti 'is able," also asakkhi from sakkati. **paritta-sutta** "protection thread," i.e. "thread charm" or "magic thread." **nâdā**=na adā "he did not give."

V.15. **khipi** "hurled."

V.16. Anāyantesu sabbesu Vijayo bhayasaṅkito
naddhapañcâyudho gantvā disvā pokkharaṇiṃ subhaṃ

17. Apassa-m-uttiṇṇapadaṃ hasantiñ c'eva tāpasiṃ,
"imāya khalu bhaccā me gahītā nū" ti cintiya;

18. "Kiṃ na passasi bhacce me bhoti tvam" iti āha taṃ,
"kiṃ rājaputta bhaccehi, piva nahāyā" ty-āha sā.

19. "Yakkhinī tāva jānāti mama jātin" ti nicchito
sīghaṃ sanāmaṃ sāvetvā dhanuṃ sandhāy' upāgato.

20. Yakkhim ādāya gīvāya nārāca-valayena so
vāmahatthena kesesu gahetvā dakkhinena tu

21. Ukkhipitvā asiṃ āha: "bhacce me dehi dāsi, taṃ
māremîti," bhayaṭṭhā sā jīvitaṃ yāci yakkhinī:

22. "Jīvitaṃ dehi me sāmi, rajjaṃ dassāmi te ahaṃ,
karissām' itthikiccañ ca aññaṃ kiñca yathicchitaṃ"

23. Adūbhatthāya sapathaṃ so taṃ yakkhim akārayi,
"Ānehi bhacce sīghan" ti vuttamattā va sā nayi.

24. "Ime chātā" ti vuttā sā taṇḍulādi viniddisi
bhakkhitānaṃ vāṇijānaṃ nāvaṭṭhaṃ vividhaṃ bahuṃ

25. Bhaccā te sādhayitvāna bhattāni vyañjanāni ca
rājaputtaṃ bhojayitvā sabbe câpi abhuñjisuṃ.

V.16. **anāyanta** "not coming." **naddha** "fastened, equipped with." **apassa**—"where he saw no footstep of any man coming forth," -m- is a sandhi consonant. **bhaccā** "servants" (*bhṛtyāḥ*). **bhoti** "Lady."

V.19. **sa-nāmaṃ** "his name." **sāvetvā,** gerund. caus. of suṇoti. **sandhāya** "making ready, drawing," also sandhetvā, sandahitvā, from sandahati, sandheti (*sam + dhā*).

V.20. **nārāca** "a weapon." **valaya-** "noose."

V.21. **bhayaṭṭhā**=*bhaya-sthā*.

V.22. **-kiccaṃ** (*kṛtyam*) so in Ś.

V.23. **adūbhatthāya.** "that he might not be betrayed." **sapathaṃ** "oath."

V.24. **chātā** "hungry" (*psāta*) § 39. **viniddisi** "showed" (*vi + nir + diś*).

Old Prakrit.] **Extract No. 34.**

Hāthīgumphā Inscription.

This Inscription is in one of the Udayagiri caves 19 miles from Cuttack. A corrected text was published by Bhagwānlāl Indrajī in the Proceedings of the Sixth International Congress of Orientalists at Leiden, 1883, Part III, p. 135. Since then the text has been edited by Mr. Jayaswal on the basis of new impressions including the casts and estampages in the Patna Museum. This revised text will be found in the Journal of the Bihar and Orissa Research Society, 1917, 1918 and 1927. The supposed date in a Mauryan era has been found untenable. It is written in Old Brāhmī characters and has been assigned to the 2nd century B.C.[1] The inscription gave a summary of Khāravela's reign year by year. Unfortunately it is very fragmentary. As is the case with Aśoka's inscriptions, double consonants are written single.

(1) Namo Arahaṃtānaṃ. Namo sava-Sidhānaṃ. Verena (or Airena) mahārājena Mahāmeghavāhanena Ceti-rāja-vaṃsa-vadhanena pasathasubha-lakhanena catur-aṃta-luṃṭhita-gunôpagatena Kaliṅgâdhipatinā Siri-Khāravelena paṃdarasa-vasāni Siri-Kaḍāra-sarīravatā kīḍitā kumāra-kīḍakā.

---

[1] Vincent Smith, 'Early History of India,' 2nd Edition. Notes on pages 38, 40, 187 and 196. Fleet, J.R.A.S. 1910, p. 242 and p. 824.

Salutation to the Arhats. Salutation to all the Siddhas. Śrī Khārvela the overlord of Kaliṅga, the heroic (or Aira), Mahārāja Mahāmeghavāhana, furtherer of the royal house of the Cedis, possessing lauded and auspicious marks, endowed with the quality of having pillaged the four ends (of the earth), for fifteen years played princely games with a body like that of Śrī-Kaṭāra.

For discussion of the proper names see Jayaswal's articles cited above. pasatha=*praśasta*. Jayaswal's last reading is luṭhita but the anusvāra may be there, so =luṇṭhita 'pillaged.' paṃdarasa cf. Pali pannarasa, Pali. AMg. JM. paṇṇarasa, Apa. paṇṇaraha, H. pandrah, etc. It is noteworthy that the *d* should occur so early. Kaḍāra used to be read kumāra.

(2) Tato lekha-rūpa-gaṇanā-vavahāra-vidhi-visāradena sava-vijāvadātena nava-vasāni Yova-rājaṃ pasāsitaṃ.

Then for nine years he enjoyed power as heir-apparent, being proficient in writing, currency (?), accounting and the rules of procedure and accomplished in all the sciences.

Meaning of rūpa is doubtful, probably not "painting." J. takes *vyavahāra* and *vidhi* separately "municipal law and dharma injunctions." *sarva-vidyā-avadāta* the number varies from 4 to 64. yova-rājaṃ=*yauvarājyam*. *praśāsitam*.

(3) Sampuṇa-catuvīsati-vaso tadāni vadhamāna-sesayo Venabhi-vijayo tatiye Kaliṅga-rāja-vaṃsa-purisa-yuge mahārājā-bhisecanaṃ pāpunāti.

Having completed twenty-four years then having been prosperous in his boyhood, a conqueror like Vena, obtained in the third generation of the Kaliṅga dynasty consecration as a mahārāja.

The readings are not quite clear. *vardhamāna-śaiśavaḥ*.

(4) Abhisita-mato ca **padhama**-vase vāta-vihata-gopura-pā-kāra-nivesanaṃ paṭisaṃkhārayati Kaliṅga-nagari(ṃ), Khi-bīra-isi-tāla-taḍāga-pāḍiyo ca baṃdhāpayati savûyyāna-paṭisaṃṭhapanaṃ ca kārayati: panatīsāhi sata-sahasehi pakatiyo raṃjayati.

As soon as he was anointed in his first year he repaired Kaliṅga city, of which the gates, city-walls and dwellings had been damaged by a storm, and he had constructed the embankment to the tank of the Rishi Khibīra, and he had all the gardens put in order: with thirty-five lakhs he pleased the people.

Padhama Pali paṭhama, Ś. ete paḍhama. Khibīra was formerly understood as 'royal camp' cf. *śibira*. "Khibīra Rishi" is due to Mr. Jayaswal. pāḍi (pāli) 'dam, dike.' The thirty-five lakhs J. takes to refer to the population, more probably it represents the expenditure.

(5) **Dutiye** ca vase acitayitā Sātakaṇiṃ pacchima-disaṃ haya-gaja-nara-radha-bahulaṃ daṃḍaṃ paṭhāpayati. Kañha-beṃnā gatāya ca senāya vitāsitaṃ Musika-nagaraṃ.

And in the second year, disregarding Śātakarṇi he sent into the west a numerous army of horse, elephants, infantry and chariots. And with his army having reached the Kṛṣṇāveṇā he terrified the city of Musika.

Read aciṃtayitā. The condition of the rock often makes it uncertain whether an *anusvāra* was written or not. ? For -beṃnā *read*-benāṃ.

(6) **Tatiye** ca puna vase gandhava-veda-budho dampa-nata-gīta-vādita-saṃdaṃsanāhi usava-samāja-kārāpanāhi ca kīḍāpayati nagariṃ.

In the third year again versed in the science of music he amused the city by exhibitions of *dampa* (?) dancing, singing and music and by arranging fêtes and shows.

The meaning of dampa is doubtful. nata=*narta*. vādita=*vāditra*. usava i.e. ussava=*utsava*.

The inscription continues up to the thirteenth year of the reign. There are however so many gaps in the text that it is often difficult to interpret the remaining words or letters. In the eighth year he gave trouble to the king of Rājagṛha—(**Rāja-gaha**-napaṃ pīḍāpayati)[1]—who apparently deserted his

1 J. now reads Rājagahaṃ upapīḍayati.

army and made off to Mathurā. In the twelfth year he caused great consternation among the people of Magadha(—**Magadhā-naṃ** ca vipulaṃ bhayaṃ janeto)—made his elephants drink of the Ganges, and made the king of Magadha bow at his feet—(*Magadhaṃ* ca rājānaṃ pāde va(n)dāpayati).

Late Prakrit.

Apabhraṃśa] **Extract No. 35.**

From the Bhavisatta-kaha of Dhanavāla edited by Hermann Jacobi. 1918. Sandhi III 52. Bandhudatta sets out on a journey. Leaving the Kurujangal he goes S.E. to the sea. Builds ships, abandons many hundreds of bulls and buffaloes and sets sail with five hundred excellent merchants.

1 aggeya-disaĕ malhanti janti/Kurujaṅgalu mahi-maṇḍalu muanti.

2 laṅghanti viyaṇa-kāṇaṇa palaṃva/pura-gāma-kheḍa kav-vaḍa-maḍaṃva.

3 Jauṇā-nai-salilu samuttarevi/jala-duggaĭ thala-duggaĭ sarevi.

4 ann'anna-desa-bhāsaĭ niyanta/rayaṇāyare velāulaĭ patta.

5 lakkhiu samuddu jala-lava-gahīru/sappurisa va thiru gam-bhīru dhīru.

6 āsīviso vva visa-visama-sīlu/velā-mahalla-kallola-līlu.

7 diṭṭhaĭ viulaĭ velāulāĭ/kaya-vikkaya-raya-vayaṇāulāĭ.

8 dhamm'attha-kāma-kaṅkhira-suhāĭ/suviyaḍḍha-vayaṇa-vila-yā-muhāĭ.

9 tahi ṭhāivi jalajantaĭ kiyāĭ/pariharivi vasaha-mahisaya-sayāĭ.

10 jalajantā-kamm'antaru karevi/karaṇaĭ piya-vayaṇahĭ saṃ-varevi.

11 vahaṇahĭ ārūḍha mahāpahāṇa/vaṇivarahā sayahĭ pañcahĭ samāṇa.

1 *āgneya-diśā* S.E. Read malhanta 'sporting' Deśī word. muanti **mucanti* for muñcanti.

2 *vijana-*, *pralamba*, *kheṭa* 'village' *karvaṭa*; **maḍamba* or **maṭamba* (?).

3 samuttarevi 'crossing' gerund.

4 niyanta 'observing.' *ratnākare, velākūla* 'shore.'

6 *āśīviṣa* 'snake.' mahalla=maha+alla.

7 *vipulāni. Kraya-vikkraya-rata-vacanākulāni.*

8 kaṅkhira means *kāṅkṣin. suvidagdha.* vilayā (*vanitā*) Deśī.

9 ṭhāivi for *sthitvā jala-yantra* 'ship.'

11 *mahā-pradhānāḥ.*

Notice the weakness of the finals, the merging of the accusative with the nominative, and the frequency of non-Sanskritic words.

INDEX OF EXAMPLES.

[This index comprises most of the examples given in Part I, and of the words explained in Part II.]

A

a, ‘and,’ § 3.
aaṃ, ‘this,’ § 110. (AMg. ayaṃ).
aiṇīa, ‘led beyond,’ § 125.
aṃsi, AMg., ‘I am,’ § 64. cf. mhi.
aṃsu, ‘tear.’ §§ 40, 64. Also assu. H. ā̃sū.
akaaṇṇua, ‘ungrateful,’ p. 132, v. 83.
akaṇḍa, ‘unexpected,’ p. 105, n. 5.
akayya, Mg. (*akārya*), p. 177, n. 2.
akariṃsu, aor., ‘they did,’ § 133.
akāsī, AMg., ‘he did,’ § 133.
akkhala, Mg., ‘letter,, p. 177, n. 1.
akkhi, ‘eye,’ § 40, Pb. akkh. H. ā̃kh. cf. acchi.
agaḍa, ‘a well,’ p. 135, n. 2.
aggala, ‘bolt,’ p. 148, v. 19.
aggahattha, ‘finger,’ p. 113, v. 4.
aggi, ‘fire,’ § 36, 62, 88. Pb. agg. H. āg.
aggha, ‘valuable,’ § 56.
aṅgulīaa, ‘ring,’ p. 102, n. 6.
accanta, ‘excessive,’ § 44.
acchai, ‘stays,’ § 60, p. 153, n. 9.
accharā, ‘nymph,’ § 39.
acchariaṃ, ‘wonderful,’ §§ (?), 58. Also accharīam.
acchi, ‘eye,’ § 39. cf. akkhi.
acchīiṃ, acchīṇi, M. plur., § 92.
acchera, M. =accharia, § 76.
ajja, (1) ‘to-day,’ § 44. Apa. ajju. Pb. ajj. Old H. āju. H. āj. (2) = *ārya*, § 50.
ajjuā, ‘lady,’ p. 109, n. 7.
ajjaütta, ‘gentleman,’ § [illegible]
ajjhatthiya, [illegible]
ajjhavasida, ‘determined,’ p. 95, n. 8.
aṭṭhāe, AMg., ‘on account of,’ p. 159, n. 1.
aṭṭhi, ‘bone,’ § 38.
aṇajjanto, ‘not being known,’ p. 135, n. 9.
aṇavayagga, AMg., ‘endless,’ p, 158, n. 1.
aṇavaraya, JM., ‘incessant,’ p. 141. n, 2.
aṇasaṇa, ‘fasting,’ p. 158, n. 10.
anahiaa, ‘heartless, p. 129, v. 64.
aṇahiṇṇa, ‘ignorant,’ § 36.
aṇāiya, AMg., ‘without beginning,’ p. 158, n. 1.
aṇiada, ‘uncertain,’ p. 99, n. 6.
aṇugejjha, Ś., ‘to be favoured,’ § 53.
aṇudiahaṃ, ‘day by day,’ § 27.
aṇurāa, ‘affection,’ § 9.
aṇuvvaya, AMg., ‘ordinance,’ p. 157, n. 4.
aṇeṇa, ‘by this,’ § 110.
aṇṇa, other,’ §§ 48, 111.
aṇṇuṇṇa=aṇṇoṇṇa ‘one another,’ § 73.
aṇṇesaṇā, ‘search,’ § 48.
aṇṇesidum, p. 94, n. 5.
attae, AMg., ‘son,’ p. 159, n. 2.
attā, ‘self,’ §§ 36, 100. cf. appā.
attiā, ‘mother,’ p. 122, (c).
attha, (1) ‘here,’ § 45 (*atra*).
(2) -*artha*, § 45.
(3) ‘weapon,’ § 56 (*astra*).
atthi, (1) ‘is,’ (*asti*), §§ 38, 132.
(2) ‘bone,’ cf. aṭṭhi.
(3) -arthī, JM.
adidhi, ‘guest,’ §§ 11, 14.
adda, ‘wet, p. 122, n. 3.
addhii, ‘anxiety,’ p. 140, n. 3.
adha, ‘then,’ § 14.
adhaṇṇadā, Ś., ‘misfortune,’ p. 100 n. 2.
antakkaraṇa, ‘conscience,, § 51.
andhāra, Apa., ‘darkness,’ p. 77.
andhāria, ‘darkened,’ § 82.
apavagga, JM., ‘final beatitude,’ p. 147, n. 1.
appa, ‘small,’ § 37.
appā, ‘self,’ §§ 36, 100. H. āp. cf. attā.
appatta, ‘unobtained,’ p. 126, v. 3.
appia (1) ‘not dear,’ Ś. 148.
(2) ‘sent,’ JM., p. 148, v. 23.
abīe, AMg., ‘without a second,’ p. 157, n. 1.
abbhantara, ‘interior,’ § 43.

abbhahia (=*abhy-adhika*), p. 121 (*e*).
amiaṃ, 'nectar,' p. 114, v. 2.
amejjha, 'impure,' p. 142, n. 9.
amhaiṇ, 'of us,' M., AMg., JM., § 107.
amhakera, 'our,' § 76.
amhe, 'we,' §§ 47, 106.
ariha, 'worth,' § 57.
alasī, 'common flax', § 23.
alia, 'in vain,' § 67.
alihadi, Mg. =*arhati*. p. 179. n. 4.
avaṇīda, 'taken away,' § 125.
avatthā, 'condition,' § 38.
avara, 'other' § 17. H. aur. Romani (w)aver.
avarajjhai, passive, *apa*+*rādh*, § 125.
avaraṇha, 'afternoon,' § 52.
avaratta, AMg., 'latter half of night,' p. 157, n. 2.
avaricida, 'stranger,' p. 103 n. 1.
avassaṃ, 'necessarily,' § 49.
avaṅga, 'corner (of eye),' p. 128, v. 61.
avi, 'also,' § 17.
asamatthaa, 'unable,' p. 124 (*a*).
asesa, 'all,' § 20.
asoga, § 11.
assa, (1) 'of him,' § 110.
(2) 'horse,' § 49. cf. M. āsa.
assu, 'tear,' § 64. cf. amsu.
aha, 'then,' § 14. Ś. adha.
ahakaṃ, OMg., "I" p. 74.
ahara, 'lower,' p. 128, v. 63.
ahighāa, 'smitten,' p. 128, v. 61.
ahiṇava, 'new,' § 13.
ahiṇṇāṇa, 'token,' p. 102, n. 3.

Ā

āada, 'arrived,' § 2.
ā(y)ava, 'heat,' p. 165, n. 1.
āāsa, (1) 'trouble,' p. 113, n. 7.
(2) 'sky,' p. 125 (*b*).
āāredi, 'invites,' p. 113, n. 9.
āiṭṭha, JM., 'commanded,' p. 142, n. 1.
āihĩ, Apa., 'in the beginning,' § 93.
āuso, AMg., 'long-lived one,' p. 162, n. 4.
āojja, JM., 'drum?' p. 142, n. 7.
āohaṇa, 'battle,' p. 142, n.
āgada, Ś. = **āada**, § 2.
āgantum, JM., 'having come,' p. 135, n. 9.
āgāra, AMg., 'house,' p. 157, n. 5.
āgāsa, AMg., JM. = āāsa, § 11.
ācāria, 'teacher,' § 58.
āḍhatta, 'begun—applied,' § 125, pp. from āḍhaī.
āḍhappai, caus. pass. ā+*dhā*, § 135 (*c*).
āṇatta, 'ordered,' § 125.
āṇavedi, 'orders,' § 36.
āṇia, 'brought,' § 125.
āṇīda, Ś., 'brought,' § 125.
āṇesu, 'bring,' § 116.
āṇe, (ṇa āṇe) 'I (don't) know,' p. 120 (*c*).
ābhioia, ābhiogiya, AMg., 'of the state?' p. 157, n. 9.
āmărisa, 'impatience, § 57.
āraddha, 'begun,' § 12
ārabbhai, ārambhadi, 'is begun,' § 125.
āruhai, 'mounts,' § 125.
āliddha, 'embraced,' p. 128, v. 61.
ālekkha, 'picture,' p. 96, n. 3.
āvajjia, JM., 'poured out,' ā+*vṛj*, p. 151, n. 3.
āvatta, 'turned round,' p. 114, v. 6.
āveia, 'announced,' p. 137, n. 5.
āsa, 'horse,' = **assa**.
āsa, acc. plur., AMg., § 92.
āsĭ, 'was,' § 133.
āsīdadi, Ś. 'sits down,' § 125.
āhaü, Apa., 'battle,' p. 77.
āhaṃsu, AMg., 'they said,' § 133. Also āhu.
āhevacca, AMg., 'overlordship,' p. 156, n. 5.

I

i=*iti*, p. 148, v. 10.
ia=*iti*, p. 123, (*e*).
iaṃ, 'this,' § 110.
ikkhu, 'sugar-cane,' § 40. cf. ucchu.
icchai, 'promises,' JM., p. 140, n. 4.
icche, 'I desire,' ātm., § 115.
iddhi, AMg., 'increase,' p. 158, n. 6.
iṇaṃ, 'this,' § 71.
itthī, 'woman,' p. 96, n. 1.
idha 'here,' § 28.
indaāīlammi, 'in magic,' p. 125 (*b*).
imīse, AMg. = imīe, 'of this,' fem., § 110.
iścaśe, Mg., 'desirest,' § 115.
isi, 'sage,' § 60.
iha, 'here,' § 28. = **idha**.

Ī

īdisa, 'like this,' § 70.
īsīsi, 'gently,' p. 119 (*a*).
īhāmiya, 'wolf,' p. 172, n. 6.

U

ua, 'lo!,' M., p. 115, v. 4.
uaa, 'water,' § 10.
uatthia (=*upa-sthita*), p. 130, v. 78.
uaroa, 'ill-will,' p. 148, v. 10.
uahi, 'ocean,' p. 126, v. 56.
uahīu, M., abl., § 93.
uida, 'fitting,' p. 107, n. 2.
ukkara, 'multitude,' p. 106, 10.
ukkiṇṇa, 'scattered,' p. 177, n. 1.
ukkhaa, 'rooted up,' p. 133, v. 85.
ukkhitta, 'thrown up,' p. 128, v. 63.
uggama, 'rising,' § 34.
uggāhihi, 'will sing,' p. 132, v. 84.
uccoḍa, 'withering?' p. 112 (*a*).
ucchu, M., 'sugar cane,' §§ 40, 70. cf. Ś. ikkhu. H. īkh. E.H. ūkh. Mar. ūs. Bg. ākh.
ujjala, 'blazing,' § 42.
ujjāṇa, 'garden,' p. 109, n. 11.
ujjua, 'straight,' §§ 15, 68.
ujjoviya, 'lighted up,' p. 161, n. 14.
ujjhida, (JM., ujjhiya), 'left behind,' p. 141, n. 11.
uṇa, 'but,' § 3.
uṇha, 'hot,' § 47. Mar. ūn. G. ūn(h)ū.
uṇhāla, Apa., 'summer,' p. 77.
utta, 'spoken,' § 125.
uttiṇṇa, 'traversed,' § 125.
utthaṅgia, M., 'supported,' p. 126, v. 56.
utthedu, 'let him stand up,' p. 109, n 8.
uppala, 'lotus,' § 34.
uppīḍa, 'bursting out,' p. 126, v. 3.
ubbheiya, 'erect,' p. 142, n. 2.
ummilla, 'opened,' p. 129, v. 64.
ummuha, 'looking up,' § 46.
ure, 'on the breast,' p. 129, v. 76.
ullavida, 'shouted out,' p. 105, n. 12.
uvaaraṇa, 'aid,' § 17.
uvacchandido, 'coaxed,' p. 102, n. 15.
uvajjhāa, 'teacher,' § 17, 44.
uvaṭṭhavei, AMg., 'prepares,' p. 158, n. 5.
uvarāa, 'colouring,' p. 113, n. 4.
uvari, 'above,' § 17.
uvalevaṇa, 'smearing,' p. 112, n. 4.
uvasappissaṃ, 'I will creep up.' p. 111, n. 4.
uvasampajjai, AMg., 'gets to,' -ittāṇaṃ, absol., p. 159, n. 4.
uvahāra, 'oblation,' p. 112, n. 5.
uvāiya, JM., 'offering,' p. 140, n. 4.
uvālahissaṃ, 'I will reproach,' p. 95, n. 9.
uvvatta, 'turned over,' p. 126, v. 56.
uvvigga, 'anxious,' § 42.
usu, AMg., 'arrow,' § 70.
ussāsa (M. ūsāsa) 'sigh,' § 41.
uhaa, 'both,' p. 113, n. 5.

Ū

ūsava, 'festival,' § 41, 63.
ūsāsa=ussāsa.

E

eassiṃ, 'in this,' § 47.
eāvatthaṃ, 'In this state,' p. 122 (*c*).
e(y)ārūva, AMg., 'of this form,' p. 157, n. 2.
ei, 'goes,' § 12.
ekka, 'one,' § 15, 112. JM., ega.
ettāhe, M., p. 131, v. 80.
ettha, 'here,' § 70.
edi, 'goes,' §§ 12, 132. cf. ei.
edihāsia, 'legendary,' § 61.
enti, 'they go,' § 132.
erāvaṇa, § 61.
erisa, 'like this,' §§ 24, 70.
evaḍḍhe, Mg., 'so great,' p. 182, n. 4. (evaḍḍa, JM.).
evvaṃ, 'thus,' § 68.
eso, 'this,' § 110.

O

oāsa, M., 'space,' p. 126, v. 3.
oiṇṇa, 'descended,' § 125. Also odiṇṇa.
oṇavia, 'bent down,' § 25.
otthaya, 'covered with,' p. 171, n. 15.
odaria, 'having descended,' § 122, Mg., odalia.
olagga, JM., 'followed,' p. 136, n. 9.
oviya, 'decorated,' p. 171, n. 16.
osaria, 'gone off,' p. 120 (*b*).
osaha, 'herb,' AMg., osaḍha, § 20.
oharia, 'lopped,' p. 128, v. 61.

K

kaa, 'done,' § 125. JM., kaya, § 60. Ś. kada and kida.
kaa-ggaha, 'hair-seizing,' p. 129, v. 64.
Kaanta, 'Fate,' p. 111, n. 10.
kaalī-hara, 'plantain-house,' p. 94, n. 6.
kayāi kayāvi, AMg., 'sometime,' p. 157, n. 1.
kai, 'poet,' p. 115, v. 3.
kaima, M., (=*katama*), § 69.
kae, 'for the sake of' p. 122 (*a*).
kao, JM.AMg., 'whence,' Ś. kado, p. 165, n. 2.
kakkoḷa =*kaṅkoṭa*, § 16.
kaṅkamaa, JM., 'like a heron's bill,' p, 136, n. 11.
kaṅkhia, 'desired,' p. 124 (*a*) *kāṅkṣita*.
kacchabha, AMg., 'tortoise, § 19.
kajja, 'to be done,' § 50, 137.
kajjai, AMg., 'is done,' § 135. *Note*.
kaḍaa, 'JM., 'fetter,' p. 141, n, 7.
kaḍakkha, 'side glance,' p. 124 (*h*).
kaḍua, 'bitter,' p. 99, n. 5.
kaḍhia, 'boiled,' Ś. kaḍhida, § 42.
kaṇaa, 'gold,' p. 113, n. 6.
kaṇakkaṇia, 'resounding,' p. 123(*d*).
kaṇaïlla, AMg., 'parrot' from Deśī kaṇa, p. 78.
kaṇṭha, 'neck,' § 35.
kaṇṇa, 'ear,' § 48.
kaṇha, = *kṛṣṇa*, § 47.
kattava, (Bhāsa), 'to be done,' p. 75.
kattuṃ, (Bhāsa), 'to do,' p. 75.
kada, see kaa.
kadama, kadara, 'which?' §§ 69, 111.
kadhaissaṃ, 'I will relate,' § 134. Also kadhissaṃ, M. kahissaṃ.
kadhaṃ, Ś., 'how?' § 14. M. kahaṃ.
kadhida, 'told,' § 11.
kadhiduṃ, 'to tell,' § 136.
kadhedu, 'let him tell,' §§ 11, 14, 75.
kadhesu, 'tell,' § 116.
kanta, 'gone,,' § 125 (*kram*).
kandalilla, 'sprouting,' p. 77.
kappa, 'age, etc.,' § 37.
kappaḍiya, JM., 'pilgrim,' p. 135, n. 10.
kamala, 'lotus,' p. 96, n. 9.
kamalā,=*Lakṣmī*, p. 124 (*h*).
kammagara, JM., 'workman,' p. 139, n. 5.
kammaggiṇo, JM. (*karmāgneḥ*), § 93.
kammi, M., 'in what?' p. 129, v. 76.
karaṇa, Apa., 'cause,' p. 77.
karaṇijja, (Ś. karaṇīa), 'to be done,' § 137.
karaṇḍaa, 'basket,' p. 100, n. 11.
karia, (Bhāsa), 'having done,' p. 75.
kariduṃ, 'to do,' § 112.
karittā, AMg., 'having done,' § 122.
karissaṃ, 'I will do,' § 134.
karīadi, 'is done,' § 135.
karīadu, 'let it be done,' p. 108, n. 5.
karedi, 'does,' § 128.
karenta, 'doing,' § 102.
karemāṇa, AMg., 'doing,' p. 157, n. 2.
karesu, 'do,' § 116.
kalama, 'rice,' p. 114, n. 9.
kalemi, Mg., 'I do,' p. 178, n. 2.
kalevara, 'body, § 18.
kallākalliṃ, 'every morning,' p. 162, n. 6.
kavala, 'mouthful,' § 18, p. 120 (*b*).
kāvala, Apa., 'lotus,' § 25.
kavalia, 'eaten,' p. 111 (*f*).
kavāḍa, 'door-panel,' p. 113, n. 6.
kavva, 'poetry,' § 50.
kasaṇa, 'dark,' p. 128. v. 63.
kaha, **kahaṃ**, 'how?' p. 114, v. 2, § 14.
kahā, 'story,' p. 132, v. 84.
kahiṃ, 'where,' p. 93, n. 1.
kahissaṃ, 'I will tell,' § 134.
[illegible], § 38
kaum, [illegible],' § 121.
(2) AMg., 'having done,' § 136.
kāūṇa, M., 'having done,' § 122.
kāduṃ, Ś. Mg., 'to do,' §§ 63, 121, 136.
kāmāe=*kāmyayā*, § 48.
kāredi, caus., 'has done,' § 128.
kāreduṃ, infin., § 136.
kālake, Mg., 'doer,' p. 177, n. 2.
kālaṇā, Mg.=*kāraṇāt*, p. 178, n. 3.
kāhaṃ, 'I will do,' § 134.
kiṃ uṇa, 'what then?,' § 3.
kiṅkiṇī, 'bell,' p. 123 (*d*).
kiccā, AMg., 'having done,' p. 159, n. 7.
kiṇai, 'buys,' § 131.
kida, 'done,' § 11.

kilanta, 'weary,' § 57.
kilittha, 'afflicted,' § 125.
kilinna, 'moistened,' § 57.
kilitta, 'prepared,' § 59.
kilissai, M., 'is afflicted,' § 125.
kivina, 'wretched,' § 60.
kiśśa, OMg.=kīsa, p. 74.
kissa, (Bhāsa)=kīsa, p. 75.
kīdisa, 'of what sort ?' § 70.
kīrai, 'is done,' § 135.
kīsa, 'why ?' p 97, n. 2.
kuo, JM., 'whence,' p. 151, n. 1.
kukkhi, Ś. **kucchi**, M., 'belly,' § 40. kucchīo, AMg., abl., § 93. kucchiṃsi' loc., § 93.
kujjā, AMg., 'he may do,' § 133.
kuttedi, Mg , 'has cut,' p. 178, 5.
kuḍila, 'crooked,' § 16.
kuḍumba, 'household,' § 16.
kuṇai, 'does,' § 131, p. 124(*a*).
kuṇamāṇe, AMg., 'doing,' p. 156, n. 5.
kuddho, J.M., 'angry, p. 140, n. 8.
kuppadi, 'is angry,' § 125.
kumbhaṇḍa, 'white gourd,' p. 105, n. 5.
kumbhilaa, Mg., 'thief,' p. 177, n. 1.
kullā, 'canal,' p. 122(*a*).
kuṽara, Apa., 'prince,' p. 77.
kuvia, JM., 'angry,' p. 141, n. 11.
kuvida, 'angry,' § 125.
kuvvaṃ, AMg., 'doing,' § 103.
kuvvamāṇe ātm., p. 158, n. 9.
kera, 'to be done,' § 76.
keria, 'belonging to,' p. 111, n. 8.
kerisa=kīdisa, § 24, 70. Mg., keliśe.
kelake, Mg., 'belonging to,' p. 179, n. 6.
kevali, AMg., 'possessing absolute knowledge,' p. 157, n. 3.
kesarilla M.=(*kesara*+illa), p. 77.
kesesu, (Mg. keśeśu), § 21.
ko, 'who,' § 110.
koila, 'cuckoo,' p. 124(*g*).
koñca, 'crane,' § 35.
komudī (M. komuī), 'moonlight,' § 61.

KH

khaa, (1) 'hurt—a wound.' Ś. khada, § 125, p. 110(*b*).
(2) 'dug,' § 125. Ś. khaṇida.
khaia, (Ś khacida), 'inlaid,' p. 121(*a*).
khagga, 'sword,' § 34.
khajjai, 'is eaten,' § 135(*a*).
khaṇṇa, 'dug,' § 125. AMg., JM., khatta.
Khattia=*Kṣatriya*, § 40.
khammai, 'is dug,' § 135(*d*).
khavia, 'exhausted, p. 127, v. 14.
khāi, Apa.=khāai, 'eats,' § 127.
khāma, 'thin,' p. 109, n. 2.
khāra, 'alkali,' p. 122 (*b*).
khijjai, 'is wasted,' § 125.
khiṇṇa, 'wasted,' § 125. cf. khīṇa.
khitta, 'thrown,' § 40, 125.
khippai, is thrown,' § 135, p. 130, n. 7.
khippām eva, AMg., 'quickly,' p. 158, n. 5.
khividuṃ, 'to throw,' § 136.
khīṇa, 'wasted,' § 40. H. chīn
khu, 'particle,' § 74.
khujja, 'hump-back,' §§ 6, 34.
√**khel**, √khel ('play') §§ 6, 22.

G

gaa (Ś **gada**), 'gone,' §§ II, 125.
gaaṇa, 'sky' (*gagana*), p. 113, n. 1.
gaammi=*gate*, § 92.
ga(y)ava(y)a, JM., 'aged,' p. 148, v. 14.
gaīnda, 'lord of elephants,' § 81.
gaccha, (1) 'go,' § 116. Kash. gats.
(2) JM., "school-sect," p. 148, v. 23.
gacchāhi, AMg., 'go,' § 116.
gacchia, (Bhāsa), 'having gone,' p. 75.
gacchittae, AMg., inf., § 136.
ganthi, 'knot,' § 55.
gaṇḍo, 'night-watchman ?' p. 134, n. 3.
gaṇhadi, (Bhāsa), 'seizes,' § 70 *d*.
gantā, AMg., 'having gone,' § 122.
gantuṃ, 'to go,' §§ 121, 136. Also gacchiduṃ, gamiduṃ.
gamissadi, 'will go,' § 134.
gamīadi, Ś. passive, 'is gone,' § 119. M. gammai, §§ 119, 125.
garala, 'poison,' p. 112(*b*).
garua, 'heavy,' § 71.
garukka JM., 'full of,' p. 148, v. 13.
Garuḍa, Ś.=Garuḷa, M. Galuḍa, Mg., § 22.
gallakka, 'crystal,' (*galvarka*) § 50.
gaviṭṭha, 'sought,' § 125 (gavesai).

gahavai, 'house-holder,' p. 111, n. 8.
gahia (Ś. **gahida**), 'seized,' § 125.
gahium, M. inf., § 136, note.
gāi, 'sings,' § 127.
gāma, 'village,' § 45. cf. § 25 end.
gāmilla, AMg., 'peasant,' p. 78.
gāravia, JM., 'highly esteemed,' p. 147, v. 5, from M., AMg., JM., gārava=M.Ś. gorava=*gaurava*.
gijjai, 'is sung,' § 135, p. 142, n. 5.
giṇhium, AMg., 'to seize,' § 136, note.
giddha, 'vulture,' § 60. Pb. giddh. H. gīdh.
gimha, 'summer,' § 47. Mār. dialect, gīm.
giha, AMg., 'house,' p. 164, n. 7.
gīa, 'sung,' § 125.
guttha, 'strung,' p. 123 (*f*).
gumma, 'bunch,' § 48.
gejjha=*grāhya*, §§ 70, 137.
geṇhai, (Ś. **geṇhadi**) 'seizes,' §§ 52, 131. geṇhia, gerund., p. 107, n. 4. geṇhium (Ś. geṇhidum), inf., § 136. geṇhidavva, § 137.
geha, JM., 'house,' p. 164, n. 7.
goilla, AMg.=*gomat*, p. 78.
goccha, M., 'bush,' § 71.
goṭṭhī, JM., 'society,' p. 148, v. 23.

GH

ghaḍanta, 'joining with,' p. 127, v. 6.
ghaḍāvehi, 'have fashioned,' p. 112, n. 3.
gharā, M.AMg., abl. 'from home,' § 92.
ghariṇī, 'wife,' p. 105, n. 13.
ghettuṃ, M. 'to seize,' §§ 19, 136.
ghettūṇa M., 'having seized,' p. 133 v. 14. cf. geṇhia.
gheppai, 'is seized,' § 135.

C

caai, M., 'abandons,' § 125.
caüro, 'four,' § 112. causu. loc. § 112.
cakka, 'wheel,' § 45. Apa. cakku. Sindhi caku. Pb. cakk. H. cāk.
cakkamai, JM., 'goes in circles,' p. 134, n. 4.
cakkavaṭṭi, 'emperor,' p. 105, n. 13.
cakkhusā, 'with the eye,' § 104.
caṅga, 'beautiful,' p. 123 (*e*).
caccara, 'square,' p. 136, n. 10.
caḍāvia, 'having placed on p. 135, n. 12.
catta, 'abandoned,' § 119.
cattāri, 'four,' § 112.
caḍukka, Ś. (caükka M.), 'square,' § 38. H. cauk.
caḍussamudda. 'four oceans,' § 51.
cammāraa, 'leather-worker,' § 82. H. camār.
cāī, JM., 'generous,' p. 147, v. 5.
Cāṇakka, § 43.
Cāuṇḍa, § 25.
cāva, 'bow,' p. 121 (*e*).
cia, 'like,' p. 114, v. 3; p. 129, v. 75.
ciñcaia, 'adorned,' p. 142, n. 4.
ciṭṭhai, M. (Ś. **ciṭṭhadi**). Mg. ciṣṭhadi, 'stands,' § 7.
ciṭṭhittae, AMg., inf., § 136.
ciṇai, 'collects,' § 131.
ciṇijjai, pass., § 135.
ciṇedi, Ś. 'collects,' §§ 128, 131. cf. ciṇai (*cinoti*).
ciṇha, 'mark,' § 52.
citta (1) 'bright,' § 45.
(2) 'heart,' 123 (*e*).
cittaara, 'painter,' p. 123 (*e*).
cittaphalaam, 'picture tablet,' § 5.
cindha=ciṇha, § 52.
cimmai, passive *ci*, § 135.
cilāadi, Mg., 'delays,' p. 179, n. 1.
civvai=cimmai.
cīadi, passive *ci*, § 135.
cuṇṇa, 'lime,' p. 114, n. 3. H. cūnā, (*cūrṇa*) 'powder,' p. 153, n. 8.
cumbia, 'kissed,' p. 119 (*a*).
cūa (Ś. **cūda**), 'mango,' p. 113, n. 5.
ceiya, AMg., 'sacred,' p. 163, n. 6.
coria=*caurya*, § 58.

CH

cha, M. AMg., 'six,' § 6, § 112.
chaccaraṇa, 'six footed,' § 34.
chaṭṭha, 'sixth,' § 6.
chaṇa, 'festival,' p. 131, v. 81.
channa, 'hidden,' p. 103, n. 5.
chammuha, 'six-faced,' § 46.
chāā, 'colour,' etc., p. 109, n. 6; p. 102, n. 2.
chāṇe (?), p. 131, v. 81.
chāva, AMg., 'child, etc.' Pali chāpa=*śāba*, § 6.
chāhā, 'shadow,' p. 114, n. 2.
chijjai, 'is split,' p. 121 (*a*).
chiṇṇa, 'cut,' §§ 125, 130.

chindai, (Ś. chindadi), 'cuts,' § 130.
chuhai, JM., 'throws,' p. 136, n. 6.
chuhā, M., 'hunger,' § 39.
chea, 'a cut,' p. 128, v. 62.
cheettā, AMg., 'having cut,' p. 158, n. 10.
chettuṃ, 'to cut,' § 136.
chettūṇa, M. JM., 'having cut,' p. 158, n. 10.

J

jaï, (Ś. also. **jadi**), 'if,' § 1.
Jaüṇā, Apa.=*Yamunā*, p. 77.
Jāüṇā=*Yamunā*, § 25.
jakkha=*yaṣka*, p. 140, n. 4.
jaccāṇa, *gen. plur.*, 'genuine,' p. 123 (c).
jaṇṇa, 'sacrifice,' § 36.
jadhā (M. jaha. Mg. yadhā). 'as,' §§ 1, 14.
jappia, 'babbled,' § 37.
jampia, JM., 'said,' p. 141, n. 9.
jampimo, 'we speak,' § 69.
jambu, § 35.
jammai, 'is born,' § 135 (a).
jammantara, 'another birth,' § 80.
jalai, 'blazes,' p. 122 (b).
jaladda, 'running with water,' p. 123 (b).
jalaṇa, 'flames,' p. 125 (b).
jasa, 'glory,' p. 125 (b).
jaha=jadhā, §§ 14, 68.
jāa (Ś **jāda**), 'born, child,' § 125.
jā(y)a, JM., 'quantity,' p. 134, n. 5.
jāadi 'is born,' § 125.
jāṇae *ātm.* 'knows,' § 115.
jāda Ś. child,' p. 102, n. 7=jāa.
jāmādua, 'son-in-law.' § 60.
jālāula, 'mass of flames,' p. 148, v. 17.
jia(Ś. **jida**), 'conquered,' § 125. Also jitta.
jiṇai, M., 'wins,' §§ 125, 131.
jiṇṇa, 'old,' p. 109, n. 11.
jibbhā, AMg., 'tongue,' § 54. H. jībh.
jivvai, 'is conquered,' § 135.
jīhā, 'tongue,' § 54.
juai, 'young women,' p. 121 (e).
juarāo, 'heir apparent,' § 99, note.
juala, 'pair,' § 9. AMg. juvala, p. 158, n. 10.
jugucchā, 'disgust,' § 39.
jugga, 'pair,' § 36.
jujjadi, 'is joined,' §§ 119, 129, 135.
jujjha, 'battle,' p. 140, n. 7. Pb. jujjh. H. jūjh.
juñjai, 'joins,' § 125.
jutta, 'joined,' §§ 34, 125.
jūdiaro, 'gamester,' p. 109, n. 10.
jeuṃ, 'to win,' § 136.
jeva, jevva, § 68.
jo, 'who,' § 110.
joïsara, 'magician,' p. 105, n. 10.
joehi, 'harness, p. 109, n. 12.
jogi=*yogī*, § 1.
jogga, 'fit,' § 43.
joṇhā, 'moonlight,' p. 122 (b). dat. joṇhāa, § 94.
jovvaṇa, 'youth,' §§ 15, 61, 68.

JH

jhaṇajhaṇanta, 'jingling,' p. 123(d).
jhāi, 'reflects,' § 127.
jhāṇa, 'meditation,' p. 108, n. 6.
jhīṇa=khīṇa, § 40.

ṬH

ṭhāi, 'stands,' § 127.
ṭhāduṃ, 'to stand,' § 136.
ṭhāvettā, AMg., 'having made to stand,' p. 159, n. 2.
ṭhāhihi, 'will stand,' § 134.
ṭhia, (Ś. **ṭhida**), 'stood,' §§ 12, 38, also thia.
ṭhii, (Ś. **ṭhidi**), 'standing-state,' § 38. Also thii.

Ḍ

ḍakka, 'bitten,' § 125.
ḍajjhamāṇa, JM., 'burning,' p. 141, n. 8.
ḍasai, 'bites,' § 125.
ḍoya, 'clapper ?' p. 142, n. 3.

ḌH

ḍhakkedi, 'shuts,' p. 182, n. 9.
ḍhaṅka, 'crow,' § 7.

Ṇ

ṇaa, 'bent,' § 125, (Ś. ṇada).
ṇaaṇa, 'eye,' §§ 7, 20. H. Pb. nain. S. neṇu.
ṇaara, 'city,' § 9. nayara, JM., p. 134, n. 1.
ṇaïa, 'having led,' § 122.

ṇaissadi, 'will lead,' § 134.
ṇaṃ, (1) 'him,' § 110.
(2) 'now,' p. 97, n. 5.
ṇakkha, 'nail,' § 15.
ṇaccaṇa, 'dancing,' p. 120 (*b*). (**nṛtyana*).
ṇajjai, 'is known,' § 135, n.
ṇattaa, 'drama,' § 43.
ṇaṭṭha (1) 'lost,' § 125.
(2) 'placed,' p. 135, n. 2.
ṇatthi, 'isn't,' § 83.
ṇamayam, 'meekness,' p. 147, v. 7.
ṇamejja, 'may bend,' p. 127, v. 14.
ṇarinda, 'king,' § 81.
ṇavara, 'only,' p. 133, v. 86.
ṇavari, 'thereupon,' p. 132, v. 82.
ṇavahī, Apa.=(*namanti*), § 25.
ṇaha=ṇakkha, § 13.
ṇāa, 'known,' § 125.
ṇāagu, Apa. (=*nāyakaḥ*), § 10.
ṇāuṃ, 'to know.' § 136. ṇāūṇa, absol., p. 151, n. 1. [Jain MSS., vary in the use of initial ṇ and n].
ṇādha (M ṇāha), 'protector,' § 14.
ṇāhaṃ, 'not I,' § 83.
ṇia, (1) 'own,' AMg., niyaya, p. 107, n. 3 (*nija-ka*).
(2) 'led,'=ṇīa, § 125. AMg. niya.
ṇiatta, 'returned,'=ṇivutta.
ṇiattaissadi, fut. caus., § 134.
ṇiattāidum, caus., inf. § 136.
ṇiattihii, fut. caus., p. 132, v. 84.
ṇiala, 'fetter,' p. 181.
√ṇikkam 'go out,' § 38.
ṇikkiva, 'cruel,' p. 120 (c).
ṇikkhitta, 'placed,' p. 113,' n. 5.
ṇikkhivia, 'having thrown down,' p. 93, n. 2.
ṇikkhividuṃ, inf., § 40.
ṇiccala, 'still,' § 38. Mg. ṇiścala.
ṇijja, 'to be blamed,' p. 148, v. 13.
ṇijjida, 'vanquished,' p. 96, n. 1.
ṇijjhāidā, 'looked at, p. 110, n. 1.
ṇijjhāanti, 'they look at,' p. 114 n. 7.
ṇiṭṭhavaṇa, 'inflection,' p. 148. v. 11.
ṇiṇṇa, 'low,' § 46.
ṇidiṭṭha, 'informed,' p. 105, n. 13.
ṇiddaa, 'pitiless,' p. 128, v. 63.
ṇiddāati, 'sleeps,' p. 114, n. 8.
ṇiddālu, 'sleepy, p. 77.
ṇiddha=siṇiddha, § 47.
ṇipphala, 'fruitless,' § 38.
ṇibbandha, 'perseverance,' § 45.
ṇibbhiṇṇa, 'burst open,' p. 106, n. 11.
ṇilāḍa, 'forehead,' p. 129, v. 64. H. lilār.
ṇirūvaissaṃ, 'I will investigate,' p. 96, n. 8.
ṇivadanta, 'falling down,' p. 96. n. 10.
ṇivaṇṇa, 'entered,' p. 135, n. 9.
ṇivaha, 'multitude,' p. 113, n. 4..
ṇivutta, 'returned,' § 60. Apa ṇivuttu. H. lauṭ.
ṇivesāvia, 'made to enter,' p. 136, n. 13.
ṇivvavijjjaü, 'let it be poured out,' p. 130, v. 76.
ṇiv-vāvedi, 'pours out,' § 120.
ṇivviggha, 'without hindrance,' p. 108, n. 6 (*nirvighna*).
ṇivviṇṇa, 'disgusted, p. 99, n. 2.
ṇivvuo, 'finished, etc. p, 120 (*d*).
ṇivvūḍha, 'accomplished,' p. 128, v. 62.
ṇisagga, 'nature,' p. 123, (c).
ṇisāmenti, AMg.
ṇisiara, 'fiend,' p. 129, v. 64.
ṇihaa, (Ś. ṇihada), 'struck down,' p. 133, v. 85.
ṇihaṇiuṃ, JM., 'to bury,' p. 136, n. 3.
ṇihasa, M., 'rubbing,' § 19.
ṇihāa, 'smashed,' p. 133, v. 85.
ṇihuda, (M. nihua) 'secret, etc.' § 60.
ṇīa (S. **ṇīda**), 'led.' § 125, cf. ṇia, [v. 78.
ṇīsāmaṇṇa, 'absolute,' p. 130,
ṇīsāsa, 'sigh,' p. 122 (*a*) (*niḥśvāsa*).
ṇīsasiūṇa, 'sighing,' p. 141, n. 9.
ṇīsesa, 'entire,' p. 147, v. 1.
ṇūṇaṃ, 'now,' § 7, 20
ṇe, 'they,' § 110.
ṇe(y)a=*naiva*, p. 148, v. 13.
ṇeuṃ, 'to lead,' § 136.
ṇeura, 'anklet,' p. 121, (*a*).
ṇeuriilla=(nūpura)—?), p. 78.
ṇĕcchadi. 'does not wish,' § 83.
ṇeṇa, 'by this,' § 110.
ṇedaṃ=*nu*+*etad*, § 83, p. 106, n. 8.
ṇedi, 'leads,' § 127.
ṇeha, 'affection,'=siṇeha § 47.
ṇehii, 'will lead,' § 134.
nomāliā, 'fresh jasmine,' § 75.
ṇhāa, 'bathed,' § 125.
ṇhāi, 'bathes,' § 125.
ṇhāṇa, 'bathing,' §§ 30, 47.

T

taï, loc. 'in thee,' § 107.
taï, Apa., 'thee,' § 107.
tae, 'by thee,' § 106.
tao, (1) =**tado**.
(2) 'three,' AMg., § 112.
taṃ, (1) 'him, her, it,' § 108.
(2) 'thou,' M., § 107.
taṃsi, loc. AMg., § 109.
takkissadi, fut., § 134.
takkemi, 'I guess,' § 45. Pb. takk-. H. tāk-, 'gaze.'
takkhaṇaṃ, 'at that time,' p. 102, n. 14.
tacca, 'meritorious,' p. 163, n. 8.
taḍa, 'edge,' p. 136, n. 5.
taṇua, 'small,' p. 133, v. 86.
taṇhiāe, abl., § 94.
tatta, (1) 'heated,' § 125.
(2) =*tattva*, p. 115, v. 2.
tatto, 'from thee,' § 107.
tattha, 'there,' § 45.
tado, 'then,' §§ 11, 109.
tadhā, 'so,' § 14.
tambola=*tāmbūla*, § 71.
tammi, loc. 'in that,' § 109.
talavara, 'chief,' p. 156, n. 5.
tavaṇa, 'heating,' p. 122 (*b*).
tavida=tatta, 'hot,' § 125.
tassa, 'of him,' § 45.
tahiṃ,=tassiṃ, § 27.
tā, 'so,' § 109 p. 93, n. 4.
tāe, 'of, by her,' § 108.
tāo, abl. AMg., § 109.
tāva, 'fever,' § 17.
tāsa, M.=tassa, § 109.
ti, 'thus,' § 74.
tikhutto, AMg., 'thrice,' p. 164, n. 8.
tiṇṇi, 'three,' § 112. Pb. tinn.
tiriccha, 'oblique,' § 74. H. tirchā.
tissā, M., 'of her,' § 109.
tīrai, 'is accomplished,' § 135, p. 123, n. 7. Also tīrae, § 115.
tīsaṃ, 'thirty,' p. 159, n. 6.
tīse, AMg., 'of her,' § 109.
tīsu, 'in three,' § 112.
tui, 'in thee,' § 107.
tue, 'with thee,' § 106.
tujjha, 'to, or of thee,' § 107, p. 129, v. 76 (=**tuhyam* for *tubhyam*). H. tujh (ko).
tuṭṭa, 'broken,' § 125.
tuṭṭai, is broken,' § 125.
tuṭṭha, 'pleased,' § 125.
tuṇṇāo, tuṇṇāgo, JM., 'beggar?' p. 134, n. 2.
tubbhe, AMg., 'you,' § 107.
tumammi, M., 'in thee,' §§ 106, 107.
tume, AMg., 'thou,' § 107.
tumma, M., 'of thee,' § 107.
tumhakera, 'your,' § 76.
tumhārisa, 'like you,' § 24.
tumhe, 'you,' § 106.
turukka, 'incense,' p. 169, n. 1.
tulla, 'equal,' p. 122 (*a*).
tuvara, 'hasten,' § 57.
tuvatto, 'from thee,' § 107.
tussadi, 'is pleased,' § 125.
tuha, 'of thee,' § 106.
tuhaṃ, 'thee,' § 107.
tuhū, Apa., 'thou,' § 107.
tūra, JM., 'musical instrument,' p. 140, n. 1.
tūlilla,=(*tūla*+illa), p. 77.
tebbho, AMg., 'from those,' § 109.
teyasā, AMg.=*tejasā*, § 104.
tella, 'oil,' §§ 15, 61, 68.
tevaṭṭhi, 'sixty-three,' p. 156, n. 4. Also tesaṭṭhi.
tti=ti, § 74.
ttha, 'ye are,' § 132.

TH

thaṇa, 'breast,' § 38.
thala, 'surface,' p. 113, n. 6.
thavai, 'architect,' p. 139, n. 3.
thia, 'stood,' =ṭhia, § 38. Ś. **(thida)**.
thii(Ś. thidi), =ṭhii.
thuvvai, 'is praised,' § 135.
theo=thevo, JM., 'little,' p. 139, n. 8; p. 147, v. 7.
thero, 'elder,' § 82.
thora, 'large,' § 71.

D

daïa, 'having given,' § 127.
daṃsaissaṃ, 'I will show,' § 127.
daṃsadi, 'bites,' § 125.
daṃsaṇīa, daṃsaṇijja, 'worth showing,' § 137.
daṃsida, (1) 'shown,'
(2) 'bitten,' § 125.
daṃseduṃ, inf., § 136.
dakkhiṇa, 'right, south,' § 40.
dakkhiṇā, 'fee,' p. 105, n. 10.
dacchaṃ, M. AMg., 'I will see,' § 134. dacchāmi, p. 130, v. 77. dacchimi, dacchimmi, p. 133, v. 85.

daṭṭhavva, 'to be seen,' p. 131, v. 81.
daṭṭhuṃ, 'to see,' § 136, p. 131, v. 80.
daḍha, 'firm,' § 60.
daddha, 'burnt,' § 125.
dappulla, =*darpin*, p. 78.
dara, 'a little,' p. 128, v. 62.
dalayai, dalai, AMg., 'gives,' p. 165, n. 1.
dalidda, 'poor,' § 26.
davāvia, 'made to give,' p. 137, n. 4.
dahi, 'curd,' p. 114, n. 9.
dahiduṃ, 'to burn,' § 136.
dāissaṃ, 'I will give, § 134.
dāuṃ, 'to give,' § 136.
dāḍhā, 'tusk,' § 65, p. 128, v. 63.
dāṇiṃ, 'now,' § 74.
dādavva, to be given,' § 137.
dābai, 'heats,' p. 120 (*c*).
dāmaguṇa, 'festoon,' p. 113, n. 2.
dārao, 'boy,' p. 111, n. 5.
dālaṃ, Mg., 'door,' p. 182. n. 9.
dāva,=*tāvat*, § 3.
dāvaggi, 'forest fire,' p. 124 (*h*).
dāvijjau, 'let it be demanded,' p. 125 (*b*).
dāham, 'I will give,' § 134.
dāhiṇa, = dakkhiṇa, p. 124 (*a*), p. 146, n. 3.
dia, 'twice-born,' § 42, p. 148, v. 11.
diara=*devara*, § 72.
diaha, 'day,' § 9.
dikkhā, 'consecration,' p. 105, n. 9.
dijjadi, 'is given,' § 119.
diṭṭha, 'seen,' § 125.
diṭṭhi, 'sight,' §§ 38 60. Sindhi diṭhi. Pb. ḍiṭṭh. H. dīṭh.
diṭṭhiā=*diṣṭyā*, § 95.
diḍha, 'firm,' § 60. cf. daḍha.
diṇa, 'day,' p. 109, n. 5.
diṇṇa, 'given,' § 125, p. 109, n. 5, p. 121 (*e*).
dimmuha, 'facing the quarters,' §§ 35, 46.
dihi, M., 'firmness,' (*dhṛti*) § 19.
dīadu, 'let it be given,' p. 105, n. 1.
dīva, 'lamp,' § 17. H. diyā.
dīsai, 'appears,' p. 127, v. 14. Ś. dīsadi, § 125.
dīhāuṃ, 'long-lived,' § 103.
duāra, 'door,' § 57.
dukkha, 'trouble,' § 51.
duggaü, Apa,=*durgama*, p. 77.
duggada, 'poor,' p. 113, n. 7.
duccarida, 'wickedness,' § 38.
duṭṭha-gaṇḍo, JM., 'suffering from a virulent sore,' p. 134, n. 3.
duṇṇimitta, 'bad omen,' p. 96, n. 2.
duttara, 'invincible,' § 38.
duddha, 'milk,' § 34. Pb. duddh. H. dūdh.
dubbhai, 'is injured,' § 134.
dubbhejja, 'impervious,' p. 113, n. 6.
duria, 'sin,' p. 147, v. 1.
duruhittā, AMg., 'having mounted,' p. 157, n. 9.
dullaha, 'difficult,' § 50, Also dulaha, § 79.
duvāra, 'door,' § 57.
duvārio, 'door-keeper,' p. 114, n. 8.
duvālasa, AMg., 'twelve,' p. 157, n. 4.
duve, 'two,' § 112.
duvvinīda, 'ill conducted,' § 125.
dussaha, 'intolerable,' § 51.
duhā kāuṃ, 'having split,' p. 136, n, 11.
dūa, 'messenger,' p. 157, n. 6.
dūijjamāṇe, AMg,, 'wandering,' p. 157, n. 6.
dūsa, 'robe,' p. 169, n. 6.
dūsaha,=dussaha, § 51, 63, 79.
de,=*te*, § 3.
deula, 'temple,' § 82.
dejjā, 'he might give,' AMg. § 133.
dedi, Ś., 'gives,' §§ 125, 127.
devattāe=*devatvāya*, § 92, ii.
devāṇuppiya, AMg., 'beloved of the gods,' p. 158, n. 7.
devī, 'goddess, queen,' Declension § 91.
devvaṇṇaa 'soothsayer,' p. 105, n. 13.
desaḍaa,=*dêsa*, p. 78.
desi, 'givest,' § 127.
do, 'two,' § 112. Also doṇṇi, gen. doṇha(ṃ), ins. dohiṃ; loc. dosu(ṃ).
doggacca, 'poverty,' p. 118, v. 76.
dosaḍa,=doṣa, p. 78.
dohaḷa, 'longing,' § 23.

DH

dhaya, JM., 'flag,' p. 142, n. 2.
dhaṇāla, AMg. 'wealthy,' p. 77.
dhamma,=*dharma*, § 48.
dhammia, 'juggler,' p. 94, n. 1
dharia, 'waited,' p. 141, n. 13.

dhāi, dhāaī, 'places,' § 127.
dhāridum, 'to support,' § 136.
dhīdā, Ś. 'daughter,' § 74. JM., dhīyā. cf. dhūdā.
dhua, 'agitated,' p. 127, v. 20.
dhuaṃ, 'certainly,' p. 117, v. 42.
dhuṇai, 'shakes,' § 131.
dhuṇijjai, 'is shaken,' § 135.
dhuvai, 'washes,' § 129. Also dhuvei § 128.
dhuvvai, 'is shaken,' § 135.
dhūdā, (M. dhūā, JM., dhūyā), 'daughter,' § 19, p. 141, n. 12. Also Ś. duhidā.
dhūmāi, 'smokes,' p. 116, v. 13.
dhūva, incense,' p. 169, n. 1.
dhoadi, 'washes,' § 129. AMg., dhovai, dhovei.

N

navalla, AMg.=*nava*, p. 78.
niya, Apa.=*nīta*, p. 77.
niyaḍilla, AMg.=*nikṛtimat*, p. 78.

P

paaḍa, (M.) 'evident,' JM., payaḍa, p. 148, v. 17.
paaṭṭa, 'set out,' § 125. paatta, p. 130, v. 76. payatta, JM., p. 136, n. 1.
paavi, 'path,' p. 118, v. 107.
payāī, 'foot-soldier,' p. 141, n. 1; p. 136, v. 20.
paāsei, 'reveals,' § 2.
paī, (1) 'towards,' (*prati*) p. 153, n. 9. cf. paḍi.
(2) 'husband,' (*pati*) p. 130, v. 78.
paiṇṇa, 'scattered,' § 125.
paīdi, Mg., 'nature,' p. 180, n. 1.
paüñjai, 'uses,' § 125.
pautta, (1) 'used,' § 125, p. 102, n. 2 (*prayukta*).
(2) 'set forth,' p. 97, n. 1, (*pravṛtta*).
paüttha, 'exiled,' § 125.
paüma, 'lotus,' §§ 36, 57.
paüra, (1) 'abundant,' § 9 (*pracura*).
(2) 'of the city,' JM.=Ś. pora, p. 148, vv, 1, 2.
paoṭṭha, 'courtyard,' p. 114, n. 1.
pakka, 'cooked,' § 42.
pakkhalantī, 'stumbling,' p. 184.
pakkhiyaṃ, AMg., 'fortnightly,' p. 157, n. 1.
pagāra, JM., 'kind,' p. 137, n. 4.
pagāsa, AMg., 'clear,' p. 168, n. 6.
pagāsento, JM., 'revealing,' p. 134, n. 2.
paccaa, 'trust,' p. 103, n. 6.
paccakkha, 'visible,' p. 110, n. 2.
paccācakkhidum, 'to repulse,' p. 101, p. 11.
paccāṇīda, 'restored,' § 125.
paccutthuya, AMg., 'covered,' p. 172, n. 4.
paccupanna, AMg., 'present,' p. 163, n. 5.
paccūse, 'at dawn,' p. 99, n. 8.
pacchā, afterwards,' § 38.
pajjatti, 'sufficiency,' p. 153, n. 6. Also pajjattiā, p. 122, (*c*).
pajjalai, 'blazes,' p. 116, v. 13.
Pajjuṇṇa=*Pradyumna*, § 46.
pajjussua, 'excited,' § 41, p. 180, n. 1.
pajjharāvedi, 'makes ooze,' § 40. p. 106, n. 10.
paṭṭa, 'bandage—"*putty*"' p. 134, n. 3.
pattha, 'eminent,' p. 171, n. 9.
paṭṭhavei, 'sends,' p. 152.
paḍa, 'cloth" § 15.
paḍāā, M.Ś. 'flag' (*patākā—paṭākā*), § 16. cf. § 20. AMg. JM., paḍāgā. JM. also paḍāyā. Paiś. patākā. Pischel § 218.
paḍi,=*prati*, § 20.
paḍia, (Ś.paḍida), 'fallen,' § 20.
paḍikkante, AMg., 'confessed,' p. 159, n. 7.
paḍijāgaramāṇe, AMg., 'keeping vigil,' p. 157, n. 1.
paḍiṭṭhāvida=*pratiṣṭhāpita*, p. 105, n. 8.
paḍiṭṭhia, 'established,' p. 125 (*b*).
paḍivajjadi 'attains,' § 125.
paḍivaṇṇa, 'attained,' § 125, p. 138, v. 83.
paḍivesia, 'neighbour,' p. 111, n. 8.
paḍihāi, (Ś. paḍihāadi), 'seems,' § 127.
paḍihāra, JM., 'door-keeper,' p. 147, v. 2.
paḍhaṇa, 'reading,' § 16.
paḍhama, 'first,' § 20.
paḍhium, 'to read,' p. 115, v. 2.
paḍhīadi, 'is read,' § 58.
paṇaa, 'confidence,' p. 103, n. 3.
paṇai, 'beloved,' p. 118, v. 76; 'attached,' p. 148, v. 15.
paṇamāmi, 'I salute,' p. 107, n. 1.

paṇamaha, 'revere,' p. 125 (*b*).
paṇasa, (Ś. phaṇasa),' bread-fruit,' § 6.
pannattaṃ, AMg., 'perceived,' p. 157, n. 3.
paṇha, 'question,' § 47.
patāria, 'seduced,' p. 101, n. 10.
patta, (1) 'wing, leaf,' § 45.
(2) 'obtained,' § 125.
patteya, 'alone,' p. 142. n. 11.
'severally,' p. 152, n. 11.
patthaṇā, 'request' p. 95, n. 2.
patthara, 'stone,' p. 103, n. 6.
patthia, 'set out,' p. 126, v. 57. Ś. patthida, p. 94, n 4.
padolika, 'gateway, p. 181.
panti or paṃti, 'row,' § 35, p. 114, n. 5.
pabodhiāmi, 'am awakened,' p. 99, n. 10.
pabbhaṭṭha, 'slipped off,' p. 102, n. 8.
pabhāda, 'morning,' p. 109 n. 8, 9.
pamada, 'pleasure,' p. 106, 4.
pamhala, AMg., ' downy,' p. 171, n 5.
paramatthado, 'really,' p. 102, n. 2.
parassiṃ=*parasmin*, § 111.
parahua, 'cuckoo,' p. 169, n. 7.
pariyāga, AMg,, 'wandering,' p. 158, n. 10.
parikamma, 'toilet,' p. 100, n. 5.
parriggaha, 'wife,' p. 102, n. 2.
pariccaia, 'having abandoned,' p. 95, n. 6.
pariccatta, 'abandoned,' p. 127, v. 20.
pariṇāīdavva, 'to be made to marry,' p. 105, n. 4. pariṇedavva, p. 105, n. 14.
pariṇīda, 'married,' § 125.
pariluppamāṇa, JM., 'being destroyed,' p. 142, n. 9.
parivvājaa, 'mendicant,' § 50, p 121 (*b*).
parisā, AMg., 'community,' p. 157, n. 7.
parissaadi, 'embraces,' § 49.
pariharia, 'avoiding,' p. 96, n. 8.
paruṇṇa, 'cried out,' p. 131, v. 76.
parokkha, 'invisible,' p. 106, n. 3.
palattaṃ, 'cried,' p. 131. v. 79.
palāa, M., JM., 'fled,' § 125. M. palāia. Ś. palāida, p. 184, n. 1. JM., also palāṇa.
paliovama, AMg., 'myriad, a very long period,' p. 159, n. 8.
palobheuṃ, 'to allure,' p. 135, n. 1.
palohida, 'greedy,' p. 114, n. 9.
pallattha, 'surrounded, etc.,' § 50.
pallī, 'hamlet,' p. 148, v. 17.
palhatta, 'brought to nought,' § 52, p. 133, v. 85. cf. H. palṭā. Mar. pālaṭ.
palhāyaṇijja, AMg., 'refreshing,' p. 170. n. 7.
pavaṃga, 'monkey,' § 37.
pavañca, 'display,' § 111 (*e*).
pavaṭṭai, 'occurs,' § 125.
pavasanta, 'living abroad,' p. 118, v. 94.
pavahaṇāhiṃ, loc. Mg., § 92.
pavāṇa, Apa.=*pramāṇa*, p. 77.
paviṭṭha. 'entered,' p. 100, n. 2; p. 93, n. 9
pavutta, 'arisen,' § 125.
pavvaa, 'mountain,' p. 127, v. 94.
pavvaia, 'entered the Order,' JM., p. 142, n. 12 (*pravrajita*).
pavvaittae, inf. AMg., p. 158, n. 2.
pasammai 'is soothed,' p, 127, n. 6.
[paśalaśi, Mg., 'goest forward,' p. 184, v. 21].
pasādīkida, 'presented,' p. 110, n. 7.
pasīda, 'be quiet,' p. 95, n. 1.
[paśtiduṃ, Mg., to request,' p. 187. n. 2.
paha, 'path,' p, 123, (*f*).
paharanta, 'attacking,' p. 96, n. 1.
pahāda=pabhāda, p. 100, n. 4
pahāva, 'power,' p. 106, n. 3.
pahuí (Ś. pahudi), 'beginning,' § 12. cf. AMg., pahuḍi and pabhii.
pahuttaṇaṃ, 'power,' p. 102, n. 10.
pāa, 'foot,' p. 122, n. 4.
pāyacchitta, 'expiation,' p. 164, n. 4.
pāikka, 'foot-soldier,' § 82.
pāua (Ś. pāuda). 'Prakrit,' § 12, p. 115, v. 2.
pāuṃ, 'to drink' (Ś. pāduṃ), § 136.
pāüṇiūṇa, 'putting on,' p. 135, n. 8. [n. 10.
pāüṇittā, 'fulfilling,' AMg., p. 158,
pāubbhavitthā, 'appeared,' AMg., p. 163, n. 4.
pāusa, JM., 'rains, p. 151, n. 7.
pāga, AMg.. 'refined,' p. 170, n. 6.
pāḍaccale, Mg., thief,' p. 177, n. 5.
pādava, 'tree,' p. 99, n. 3.
pārāvaṇa, 'pigeon,' p. 169, n. 7.
pāriyāya, JM., 'coral tree,' p. 140, n. 5.

pāridosia, 'reward,' § 11. Mg., pālidośia.
pāvai, pāvedi, 'obtains,' § 125.
pāsa, 'side,' § 49.
pāsāda, 'palace,' p. 114, n. 5.
pāhuṇaya, JM., 'guest.' p. 136, n. 4.
pi=*api*, § 74.
pia, 'dear,' § 9.
piaaṇa, 'lover,' p. 124 (*a*).
piussiā, 'paternal aunt,' § 74.
pikka, 'ripe,' § 69=pakka.
piṭṭei, 'crams,' p. 119, v. 171.
piṇiddha, 'put on,' p. 171, n. 11.
pidā, Ś. 'father,' (M. piā), declension, § 97; gen. piduṇo, piuṇo.
piya, Apa.=*pīta*, p. 77.
piyāra. [illegible] p. 77.
pivai, [illegible] § 125.
pīḍhamadda, 'parasite,' p. 172, n. 2.
pīṇaṇijja, AMg., 'pleasing,' p. 170, n. 7.
pīsei, pīsedi, 'crushes,' § 65.
pucchai, pucchadi, 'asks,' § 60.
puṭṭha, (1) 'asked,' § 125 (*pṛṣṭa*).
(2) 'touched,' AMg., § 125 (*spṛṣṭa*).
(3) 'back,' JM. (*pṛṣṭha*). Guj. pūṭh. Sindhi puṭhi.
puṇṇa (1) 'full,'
(2) 'meritorious,' § 48.
putta, 'son,' § 2; declension, § 86.
puttakidao, 'fosterchild,' p. 102, n. 14.
puttaliā, 'statue,' p. 106, n. 10.
puppha, 'flower,' § 38. O.H. puhup. H. phup.
purattha, 'East,' p. 172, n. 3
purisa, 'man,' § 71.
purisakkāra, 'man's strength,' AMg., p. 165, n. 3.
Purūravā, § 104.
puliśa, Mg., 'man,' § 92.
puloedi, 'looks at,' § 69; pres. past. puloanto, § 102; fut. puloissaṃ, § 134.
puvvaratta, AMg., 'first part of the night,' p. 157, n. 2.
puvvāṇupuvviṃ, AMg., 'in succession,' p. 157, n. 6.
puvvilla, AMg., 'previous,' p, 78.
puścide, Mg.=pucchido 'asked,' p. 177; n. 5.
puhavī, (Ś. puḍhavī), 'earth,' p. 130, v. 78.
peccha, 'see!' § 40.
pecchai, 'sees,' p. 126, v. 57.
pecchae, ātm. § 115.
pecchissaṃ, M., 'I will see,' § 118.
pekkhadi, 'sees,' §§ 40, 81.
pekkhissaṃ, fut., § 134. Apa. pekkhihimi.
pemma, 'affection,' §§ 15, 68; declension: § 98. pemā, p. 133, v. 86.
peranta, 'limit,' § 76.
pesida, 'sent,' p. 94, n. 3.
pesei, 'sends,' p. 140, n. 6.
peskāmi, Mg., 'I see,' p. 180, n. 4.
pokkhara, 'lotus,' §§ 38, 71. H. pokhar, 'tank.'
poṭṭha, 'belly,' p. 119, v. 171.
popphalī, 'areca nut,' § 74.
pomma, 'lotus,' §§ 36, 82. cf. paüma.
posaha, AMg., 'fast-day,' § 74, p. 157, n. 1. Pali uposatha.

PH

phaṃsa, 'touch,' §§ 38, 49, 64.
phagguṇa, 'the month,' § 37.
phaḍiha, 'crystal.' Also phaḷiha, §§ 19, 38, p. 113, n. 5.
phaṇasa=paṇasa, § 6.
pharisaga, AMg., 'soft,' p. 173, n. 2 (**sparśaka*).
phāsa, AMg., =phaṃsa, § 63.
phurantaa, 'manifest,' p. 124 (*g*)
phusai, AMg., 'touches,' § 38.

B

baïlla, Mg., 'bull,' p. 184, n. 9. Apa. baïllu. H., etc., bail.
bajjhai, 'is bound,' § 135.
baḍiśa, Mg., 'hook,' p. 178, n. 2.
baddha, 'bound,' § 125.
bandhai, 'binds,' § 125.
bappha, 'steam,' p. 96, n. 10.
bamhaṇa=*brāhmaṇa*, § 52.
balakkāra, 'violence,' § 34.
baladdaka, Mg., 'bull,' p. 182, n. 5.
balā, 'perforce,' p. 113, n. 9.
baliaṃ, 'more strongly,' p. 120 (*c*).
bahiṇiā, 'sister,' p. 110, n. 5.
bahiṇī, 'sister,' § 19.
bahuphala, 'fruitful,' § 5.
bārasa, 'twelve,' p. 142, n. 2. M. Apa. bāraha. H. bārah. cf. § 24.
bāha, 'tear,' p. 96, n. 10.
bāhirilla, AMg., 'external,' p. 78.
bihei, 'fears,' §§ 125, 132.

bīa, bīya, AMg., JM., 'second,' p. 148, v. 19.
bujjhai, 'is wakened,' § 125. cf. Pb. bujjh.
būyā, AMg., 'might say,' § 133.
bola, 'speech,' p. 136, n. 8. cf. H. bolnā.
bolanti, 'they pass,' p. 126, v. 57.
bolīṇa, 'passed,' p. 132, v. 83.

BH

bhaavaṃ, 'blessed,' declension, § 103.
bhai, 'hire,' p. 162, n. 6.
bhaühā, Apa.=bhamuhā, 'eye-brow,' p. 77.
bhaṃvaṇa, Apa.=*bhramaṇa*, p. 77.
bhakkhanti, 'they eat,' p. 114, n. 9.
bhagga, 'broken,' p. 141, n. 6.
bhajjai, 'is broken,' § 135.
bhajjanta, 'being broken,' p. 128, n. 62.
bhajjā, 'wife,' p. 147, v. 3.
bhañjai, 'breaks,' § 130.
bhaṭṭa, 'lord,' declension, § 97; gen. bhaṭṭino.
bhaṭṭidāraa, 'crown prince,' § 60.
bhaṭṭha, 'dropped,' § 125.
bhaṇaï, Apa, 'speaks,' p. 77.
bhaṇādi, 'speaks,' § 132. Also bhaṇedi, §§ 128, 132; passive bhaṇīadi. § 135, n.
bhaṇiū, Apa., Nom. Sing. p. 77.
bhaṇḍāra, Apa., 'store-room,' p. 77.
bhatta, 'food-rice,' p. 181, n. 1.
bhattā, 'husband,' declension, § 97; gen. bhattuno.
bhadda, 'blessed,' § 45. H. bhalā through. Apa. *bhallaü. cf. M., AMg., alla, 'wet,'=Ś. adda (*ārdra*).
bhamara, 'bee,' p. 119 (*a*). H. bhaürā.
bhamāida, 'agitated,' p. 113, n. 2.
bhamiū, Apa., Nom. Sing. p. 77.
bhamira, AMg., wandering, p. 78.
Bharaha, § 19.
bhavaṃ,=*bhavān* declension, § 103.
bhavittā, bhavittāṇaṃ, AMg., 'having been,' § 122.
bhavissaṃ, 'I will be,' § 134.
bhavīsa, Apa.,=*bhaviṣya*, p. 77.
bhaveaṃ, 'I might be,' § 129.

bhāa, 'part,' p. 112, n. 5.
bhāadi, 'fears,' §§ 125, 132.
bhāi, 'shines,' p. 112 (*g*). Ś. bhādi, § 127.
bhāillaga, AMg.,=*bhāgin*, p. 78.
bhāiṇejja, 'sister's son,' p. 156, n. 2.
bhādu-saa, '100 brothers,' § 60.
bhiuḍi, 'frown,' p. 129, v. 64 AMg., bhiguḍi.
bhijjai, 'is split,' § 135, p. 126, v. 56.
bhiṇṇa, 'split,' § 125.
bhindai, 'splits,' §§ 125, 130.
bhīa, bhīda, 'frightened,' § 125.
bhujjai, 'is enjoyed,' § 135. Ś. bhuñjīadi.
bhuñjadi, 'enjoys,' § 125, 130.
bhutta, 'enjoyed,' § 125.
bhumaā, 'brow,' p. 129, v. 64.
bhūa, bhūda, 'become,' § 125.
bhettuṃ, 'to split,' § 136.
bhoaṇa, 'meal,' § 9.
bhottuṃ, 'to enjoy,' § 136.
bhodi, 'becomes,' §§ 4, 11, 75, 127. M. hoi.

M

maa, (1) 'dear,' p. 99, n. 3; p. 124 (*g*). (*mṛga*). Also mia.
(2) 'intoxication, etc.' p. 109, n. 2. (*mada*).
(3) 'dead,' § 125. (*mṛta*). Also mua, muda.
(4) 'made of' (=*maya*), p. 117, v. 11. Also maia.
maagala, JM., 'elephant,' p. 140, n. 9.
maaṇijja, AMg., 'invigorating,' p. 170, n. 1.
maarahara, 'sharks' home,' p. 132, v. 83.
maalañchaṇa, 'moon,' p. 106, n. 9.
maï, loc., 'in me,' § 106.
maï, Apa., 'by me,' § 107.
-maia=*maya*.
maï, 'doe,' p. 120 (*b*).
maüa, 'tender,' p. 112 (*a*), p. 126, v. 3.
maüla, 'bud,' § 71.
maülanta, 'budding,' p. 128, v. 62.
maüli, 'head,' § 61.
maüra=mora, § 82.
mae, 'by me,' § 106.
maṃsūiṃ, maṃsūṇi, AMg., 'moustaches,' § 93.

makkaḍa, 'ape,' p. 119, v. 171.
magga, 'road,' § 45.
magganta, 'demanding,' p. 111, n. 9. H. māg-nā.
maccha, 'fish,' § 56, p. 126, v. 56.
macchara, 'envy,' § 39, p. 148, v. 10.
majjāra, Ś. 'cat,' § 67. M. maṃjāra.
majjida, 'swept,' p. 112, n. 4.
majjha (1) 'middle,' § 44.
(2) M. 'of me,' § 107.
majjhaārammi, 'in the middle,' p. 115, v. 3.
majjhaṇṇa, 'midday,' § 74, majjhaṃdiṇe, 'at mid-day,' p. 99, n. 3; also majjhaṇha, § 52.
majjhima, 'middle,' § 69.
maṭṭiā, 'earth,' § 55. H. maṭṭī, miṭṭī.
maṇasā, ins., § 104.
maṇīṇa, 'of gems,' p. 123(c).
maṇīsi, 'clever,' p. 124(h).
maṇussa, 'man,' § 49. AMg., maṇūsa, § 63.
maṇojja, 'charming,' § 36.
maṇoradha, Ś. 'wish,' § 14. M. **maṇoraha**.
maṇḍalagga, 'scimitar,' p. 128, v. 61.
maṇṇe, 'I think,' § 115.
-matta=-metta, p. 119, n. 81.
madda, 'crushing,' p. 100, n. 6.
mamaṃ, M., AMg., JM., 'me,' § 107.
mammadha, Ś. 'love' (M. vammaha), § 25.
marai, maradi, 'dies,' § 125.
maragaa, M. (S. **maragada**), 'emerald,' § 12, p. 105, n. 1; p. 115, v. 6.
malliā, 'jasmine,' p. 113, n. 2.
masāṇa, 'cemetery,' § 47.
maśca, maśçalī, Mg., 'fish,' p. 178, n. 2; p. 180, n. 9.
mahaṃ, 'of me,' p. 130, v. 77.
mahao, AMg., =*mahataḥ*, § 103.
mahalla, AMg. 'great,' p. 78.
mahasi, 'desirest,' § 113(c).
mahārāo, 'great king,' declension, § 99, n.
mahālaya, AMg., 'great,' p. 77.
mahāliha, Mg., 'precious,' p. 179, 8.
mahilā, 'woman,' p. 129, v. 75.
mahuara, 'bee,' p. 121(d).
mahūsava, 'great festival,' § 81.
māilla AMg=*māyāvin*, p. 78.
mādā, Ś. **māā**, M. 'mother,' declension, § 97.
māriduṃ, 'to strike,' § 136.
mālā, 'garland,' declension, § 91.
māliśśaśi, 'wilt strike,' § 134.
miaā, 'hunting,' p. 99, n. 2.
miaṅka, 'moon,' p. 106, n. 10.
miṃja, AMg., 'marrow,' p. 162, n. 3.
midhuṇā, Ś. 'pairs,' § 92.
mittea=*maitreya*, § 72.
milāṇa, 'faded,' § 57. [16.
misimisinta, 'shining,' p. 171, n.
missa (M. mīsa), 'mixed,' § 49.
mua, muda, 'dead,' § 125.
muai, 'releases,' § 130, p. 182, v. 115.
muiṅga, 'drum,' p. 142, n. 7.
mukka, 'released,' § 125.
muccai, 'is released,' § 135.
mucchia, 'stunned,' p. 126, v. 56.
AMg., 'greedy,' p. 158, n. 1.
mujjhai, 'is perplexed,' § 125.
muñcai, **muñcadi**, 'releases,' §§ 125, 130. Also muñcedi, § 128; passive muñcīadi, § 135, n.
mutthi, 'handful,' p. 114, n. 3. JM., mutthiga, p. 142, n. 12.
muṇai, 'knows,' Pāli munāti, p.
muṇāla, 'lotus fibre,' § 60.
mutta, 'urine,' p. 142, n. 9.
muddha, 'foolish'' (*mugdha*), p.
muddhā, 'head,' declension, § 98,
mulla, 'value,' § 50.
muha, 'face,' § 13.
muhala, noisy, § 26.
mūlāhi, M.=*mūlāt*, § 92. [§ 134,
moāvaissasi, 'will make release.'
moāvia, 'having made to release,' p. 121 (b).
moāvedi, 'makes release,' § 128.
moggara, 'hammer,' § 71. Bg. mugur.
moccham, mocchihimi, 'I will release,' § 134, p. 130, v. 76.
mottā, 'pearl,' p. 127, n. 6.
mottum, 'to release,' § 136.
mora, 'peacock,' § 82, p. 120 (b).
mōlla, 'price,' § 71. H. mol.
mha, 'we are,' §§ 30, 132. Also mho.
mhi, 'I am,' §§ 30, 132.

R

raa, 'gratified,' § 125.
raia, 'formed,' p. 141, n. 4.

rakkhāghara, 'prison,' p. 107, n. 7.
racchā, 'highroad,' § 44.
raṇṇa, 'jungle,' § 74. Abl. AMg. raṇṇāu, § 92.
raṇṇadaa,=*araṇya*, p. 78.
raṇṇā, 'by the king,' § 99.
rattiṃ, 'during the night,' p. 99, n. 7.
ramai, 'delights.' § 125.
ramahī, Apa., '(thou) delightest' p. 77.
rasāala, 'lower world,' § 9.
rassi, 'ray,' § 47.
ravai, 'weeps,' § 125.
rahasa, 'force' (*rabhasa*), p. 123 (*f*).
rahassa, 'secret,' § 49.
rāā, 'king,' declension, § 99.
rāiā, 'mustard,' p. 119, v. 128.
rāī, 'road,' p. 99, n. 4.
rāīsara. 'prince,' p. 156, n. 5.
rāesi, 'royal sage,' § 80.
riccha, 'bear,' §§ 39, 60.
rittattaṇa, emptiness, p. 124 (*h*).
riddhi, 'increase,' § 58.
risi=*ṛṣi*, § 60. AMg., plur. risao, § 93.
ruai, 'weeps,' § 125.
ruia, 'bright,' § 125.
ruccai, ruccadi, 'is made bright,' § 125, 129.
rujjhai, 'is obstructed,' § 135.
ruṭṭha, 'angered,' § 125.
rundhedi, 'obstructs,' p.p.p. ruddha, § 125; passive, rubbhai.
rumbhai, 'supports,' p. 132, v. 82.
ruvai, 'weeps.' Also rovai; passive ruvvai, § 125.
rusai, 'is vexed,' § 125.
rudhira, 'red,' § 13.
rūva, 'form,' § 17. (M. rūa, § 9.)
rehā, M. 'lines,' § 94.
rehai, M. 'shines,' p. 115, v. 4.
roadi, 'weeps,' § 125, p. 111, 7.
rodadi, rovai, ruai. ruvai; fut., rodissaṃ, roccham, § 134; pass., rodīadi, § 135; inf. rottuṃ, § 136.

L

laā (Ś. ladā), 'creeper,' § 12.
Lacchī=*Lakṣmī*, p. 123 (*c*).
laṭṭhi, 'stick,' p. 122 (*a*); p. 121, v. 14.
laddha, 'taken,' §§ 34, 125; inf. laddhum, § 136; passive labbhai, labbhadi, § 134. Also lambhīadi, § 135.
lambira, AMg., 'hanging' p. 78.
lahai, 'takes,' § 125.
lahasu, 'take,' p. 107, n. 2.
lahua, 'light,' § 13.
lahuṃ, 'quickly,' p. 103, n. 2.
lahe, 'I take,' ātm., § 115.
laheaṃ, opt., p. 100, n. 7.
lāakīya, Mg., 'royal.' § 165, n. 1.
lāūle, Mg., 'palace,' § 82.
lāutte, Mg., =*rājaputraḥ*, p. 178, n. 1.
lia, 'attached to,' § 125. Also līna
litta, 'smeared,' p. 134, n. 3 (*lip*).
libbhai, 'is licked,' § 135.
lihai, (1) 'licks,' § 125.
(2) 'writes,' p.p.p. lihida. Ś 'painted,' p. 112, n. 5.
lukka, 'sticking to,' p. 117, v. 49.
luddha, 'hunter,' p. 99, n. 8.
luppai, 'is robbed,' § 125.
lekkha, 'list,' p. 137, n. 5.
loa, M. 'world,' § 9. Apa. lou. § 73. AMg., JM., loga, § 11; *loc.* logaṃsi, § 92.
loadi, Mg., 'shines,' § 129.
loṇa. 'salt,' § 75. Sindhi lūṇu. H. lūn.
loya, 'plucking out hair,' p. 142, n. n.
loluva, 'greedy,' p. 120 (*d*), (=*lolupa*).
lohāra, 'blacksmith,' § 82.
lohida, Mg., '*rohū*,' p. 178, n. 4.

V

va=*iva*, p. 120, n. 4.
vaassa, 'companion,' § 49.
vayāsi, AMg., 'spoke,' p. 157, n. 8.
vaiyara, JM., 'story,' p. 135, n. 7.
vaïra, M. 'hostile,' § 61.
vae, AMg., 'herd,' p. 162, n. 5.
vakkala, 'bark,' § 37.
vakkha, 'breast,' p. 113, n. 6.
vaggaṇa, 'jumping,' p. 170, n. 5.
vaggurā, AMg., 'crowd,' p. 164, n. 6.
vaccai, 'goes,' p. 135, n. 4.
vaccha, (1) 'child,' § 3 (*vatsa*).
(2) 'tree' (*vṛkṣa*).
(3) 'breast,'=vakkha.
vacchā, 'girl,' p. 107, n. 4.
vajja, 'adamant,' p. 113, n. 6.
vajjadi, 'wanders, § 129.
vajjanti, 'is sounded,' p. 142. n. 7.
vajjia, 'excepting,' p. 96, n. 9.

vajjha, 'victim,' p. 181, n. 3.
vaññāmi, Mg., 'I wander,' p. 187, n. 8.
vaṭṭadi, 'twines,' § 45.
vaṭṭi, 'wick,' p. 169, n. 2.
vaṭṭe, opt. of vaṭṭadi, § 117.
vaṭṭhida, 'engaged in,' § 74.
vaḍa, 'fig-tree,' § 15. AMg., vadha, § 19.
-vaḍāa, 'flag,' p. 142, n. 3.
vaḍḍhida, 'increased,' pp. 95, 6.
vaṇijja, Apa, 'trade,' p. 77.
vatta, 'leaf,' p. 90, n. 10; pp. 120, 3; p. 127, v. 6.
vattiā, 'paint brush,' p. 94, n. 6. cf. H. battī, 'wick.'
vattuṃ, 'to speak,' § 136.
vattehāmi, 'I will perform,' § 134.
vaddhāvaṇaaṃ, AMg., 'birth ceremony,' p. 140, n. 5.
Vappaīrāa, § 34.
vammaha, M., 'love,' § 25, p. 184, v. 21.
variṭṭha, 'choicest, p. 123 (*b*).
varisa, 'rain,' § 57.
valia, 'turned round,' p. 123 (*f*).
vavadesi. 'pretending,' p. 103, n. 5.
vavasissaṃ, 'I will decide,' p. 101, 5.
vasantūsava, 'spring-festival,' § 81.
vasaha, 'bull,' § 60.
vasahi, 'dwelling,' § 19=vasai.
vasā, 'by force of,' § 92.
-vaha, 'path,' p. 127, v. 14.
vahai, 'carries,' § 125.
vahia, 'rapturously gazed at,' p. 16, n. 6.
vahū, bride, § 13; declension, § 91.
vāai, 'blows,' p. 124 (*a*) Ś. vāadi.
vāasa, 'crow,' p. 114, n. 9.
vāi, M=vāai, § 127.
vāu, 'wind' declension, § 90.
vāḍāaṇa, 'window'; p. 114, n. 6.
vāmaddaṇa, 'massage,' p. 170, n. 5.
vālaga, AMg., 'snake,' p. 172, n. 6.
vāvādīadi, 'is destroyed,' p. 181; inf., vāvādeduṃ, p. 179, n. 3.
vāharanta, 'calling,' p. 113, n. 4.
vāharesu, 'summon,' p. 152, n. 9.
vāhi, 'illness,' p. 141, n. 10.
vāhiria, 'outside,' p. 136, n. 1.
vi=*api*, § 3, § 74.
via, 'like,' p. 93, n. 5.
viaṇā, 'pain,' § 72.
viambhidaṃ, 'exploit, p. 106, n. 7.
viala, 'lame,' p. 100, n. 7.
vialia, M., 'vanished,' p. 131, v. 79.
vialida, Ś., p. 109, n. 6.
viiṇṇa, AMg., 'bestowed,' p. 156, n. 5.
viuha, 'learned,' § 9.
viesa, 'abroad,' p. 118, v. 76.
vioa, 'separation' § 9.
vikkaa, 'sale,' p. 178, n. 5.
viggha, 'obstacle,' § 36.
vighaṭṭha, 'eaten up,' p. 141, n. 10.
vicchaḍḍa, 'liberality, p. 142, n. 8.,
vijju, 'lightning,' p. 148, n. 10.
vijjuliā, 'lightning,' § 23.
vijjhai, 'wounds,' p. 124 (*a*)
Viṃjha. § 35.
viḍahara (?), p. 152, n. 2.
vidhappai, 'has arranged,' § 135.
viṇajjai, 'is perceived,' p. 132, v. 82.
viṇadida, 'puzzled,' p. 108, n. 6.
viṇodemi, 'I divert,' p. 111, n. 3.
viṇṇatta, 'reported,' § 125, p. 105, n. 10.
viṇṇavīadi, 'is reported,' § 125, p. 107, n. 3.
viṇṇavei, (Ś. viṇṇavedi), 'reports,' § 125; inf. viṇṇāduṃ, p. 106, n. 1; p.p. viṇṇāvida, 105 n. 2.
viṇṇāda, 'understood,' § 125.
vitthareṇa, 'in full,' p. 105, n. 6.
vidduma, 'coral,' p. 127, v. 6.
vipphoḍao, 'pimple,' p. 99, n. 11.
vibbhala, 'agitated,' § 54.
vimukka, 'unloosed,' p. 126, v. 3.
vimuha, 'indifferent,' p. 118, v. 76.
vimhaa, 'astonishment,' § 47.
vimhaṇijja, AMg., 'nourishing, p. 170, n. 7.
vimharia=vīsaria, p. 121 (*d*).
vivajjai, 'perishes,' p. 135, n. 3.
vivarā, 'awry,' p. 133, v. 85.
vivujjhadi, 'awakes,' p. 109, n. 7.
visaṃghaḍanta, 'dispersing,' p. 118, v. 115.
visalla, 'pointless,' p. 188, n. 2.
vissa, 'musty,' p. 178, n. 6.
vissāma, 'rest,' p. 100, n. 7.
vihatthimitta, AMg., 'measure of a span,' § 69.
vihalia, 'trembling,' p. 136, n. 7.
vihāṇa, 'mannēr,' p. 135, n. 3.
vihādi, 'shines,' § 127.
vihi, 'performance,' p. 105, n. 9.
vihu, 'moon,' p. 148, v. 19.
vīaṇa, 'fanning,' p. 156, n. 5.

vīsaṃ, 'twenty,' § 112.
vīsamasi, 'takest rest,' p. 117, v. 49.
vīsasadi, 'trusts,' p. 103, n. 4.
vīsaria, 'forgotten,' p. 121 (*d*).
vīsā=vīsaṃ, § 112.
vīhattha, 'loathsome,' p. 129, v. 75.
vuccai, 'is said,' § 135.
vuḍḍha, 'grown,' § 55.
vuṭṭa, 'finished,' p. 99, n. 11.
vuttanta, 'news,' § 60.
vutthaṃ, 'dawned,' p, 131, v. 80.
vubbhai, 'is carried,' § 135.
vūḍha, 'carried,' § 125.
vūha, 'order of battle,' p. 141, n. 4.
veyaṇa, AMg., 'wages,' p. 162, n. 6.
veaṇā, 'pain,' p. 108, n. 1.
vecchaṃ, 'I shall know,' § 134.
vejja, 'learned,' § 61.
veḍha, 'enclosure,' p. 127, v. 14.
veḍhia, 'enclosed,' p. 127, v. 14.
vediā, 'raised seat,' etc., p. 113, n. 5.
vedissaṃ=vecchaṃ, § 134.
verulia, 'cat's eye,' § 58.
vehavvaṃ, 'widowhood,' p. 130, v. 78.
vo, 'you, of you,' §§ 106, 107.
vocchaṃ, 'I will speak,' § 134.
vojjha, 'to be carried,' § 137.
voḍhuṃ, 'to carry,' § 136.
vŏttuṃ, 'to speak,' § 136.
voliya, JM., 'passed,' p. 141, n. 8. M. bolīṇa.
volo, JM., 'cry.' cf. M. bolo, 'speech,' p. 136, Ś. n. 8.

S

sa, (1) 'with,' (*sa*).
(2) 'own' (*sva*), p. 107, n. 6.
saa, (Ś. sada. AMg., saya. Mg., śada), 'hundred, §§, 12, 112, p. 156, n. 4.
saaḍa, 'cart,' (Mg., śaaḷa) § 16.
saaḍiā, 'toy cart,' p. 110, n. 8.
saāsa, 'presence,' p. 94, n. 7.
saüntalā, p. 100, n. 2.
saṃlehaṇā, AMg., 'final mortification,' p. 159, n. 6.
saṃsaida, 'questioned,' p. 101, n. 6.
sakkai, sakkei, 'is able,' p. 135, n. 5.
Sakkada, 'Sanskrit, § 11.
sakkā, 'able,' § 133.
sakkāra, 'favour,' p. 137, n 3.
sakkuṇomi, 'I can,' § 131.
saṅkalā, 'chain'' § 19. Also saṅkhalā, siṅkhalā, § 35. Mar. sā̃khal. H. sīkar. Bg. śikal.
saṃkhasutti, 'mother of pearl,' p. 115, v. 4.
saṃkhāa, 'coagulated,' p. 128, v. 63.
saṃkhoha, 'shock,' p. 126, v. 3.
saṃghia, 'applied,' p. 128, v. 61.
sacca, 'true,' § 44.
saccavia, 'verified,' p. 121 (*e*).
sacchāha, 'of the same hue,' p. 114. n. 2.
sajoī, AMg.=Sajyotiṣam, § 104.
sajja, 'ready,' p. 140, 7.
sajjha, 'practicable,' § 53.
saṃjhā, 'twilight,' § 44.
saṇha, 'smooth,' p. 172, n. 5.
saṇṇia, 'made a sign,' p. 136, n. 8.
saṇṇihie, 'in vicinity,' p. 134, n. 5.
satta, (1) 'seven.'
(2) 'nature, etc.' (*sattva*).
satthaa, 'troop,' p. 124 (*a*).
satthia. 'weapon,' p. 152, n. 7.
sada, **Ś.**, 'hundred.' M. saa, § 12. 112.
sadda. 'sound,' § 34. Pb. sadd. H. sād.
saddāla, AMg., '*śabdavat*,' p. 77.
saddāvia, 'summoned,' p. 136, n. 12. [n. 4.
saddāvettā, AMg., gerund., p. 148,
saddhasa, 'panic,' p. 96, n. 5.
[śaddhike, Mg., 'feast,' p. 180, n. 3.
saṃtappadi, 'is in distress,' p. 110, n. 3.
saṃtāva, 'anguish,' p. 95, 3.
saṃdattha, 'bitten through,' p. 128. v. 63.
saphala, 'fruitful,' § 5.
sapphala, 'of good results,' p. 134, n. 14.
sabbhāva, 'good nature,' § 34, p. 101. n. 7.
samaa, 'contract,' p. 101, n. 10; 'doctrine,' p. 162, n. 2.
samagga, 'complete,' p. 141, n. 3.
samannāgaya, AMg., 'provided with,' p. 159, n. 4.
samappida, 'consigned,' p. 96, n. 3; imperat. samappehi, p. 110, n. 5.
samāḍhatta, 'begun,' p. 139, n. 4.
samāṇe, AMg., pass. part. 'being,' p. 159, n. 3.
[śamālovide, Mg., 'mounted,' p. 179, n. 7.

samāsattha, 'consoled,' § 125.
samikkha, AMg., 'discovers,' p. 143, n. 1.
samuggaa, 'box,' p. 94 n. 6.
samucchida, 'elevated,' § 45.
samudāāra, 'address,' p. 101 n. 7.
samudda, 'ocean,' § 45.
samuppajjitthā, AMg., 'occurred,' p. 157, n. 2.
samuppehiyāṇaṃ, AMg., 'perceiving,' p. 143, n. 1.
samullasanta, 'brilliant,' p. 113, n. 5.
saṃpai, JM., 'now,' p. 139, n. 1.
saṃpadatta, 'bestowed,' p. 137, n. 1.
saṃpehei, AMg., 'reflects,' p. 164. n. 3; gerund saṃpehettā, p. 158, n. 3.
sambalayaṃ, JM., 'stores,' p. 153, n. 7.
sambhariūṇa, 'remembering,' p. 132, v. 84.
samma, AMg., 'right,' p. 157, n. 1.
sammajjia, 'swept,' p. 168, n. 4.
saraa, 'autumn,' p. 153, n. 5.
Sarassadī, § 11.
sarisa, 'like,' § 24.
[śala, Mg., 'accent,' p. 181, n. 2.
salāhā, 'praise,' § 57.
savaṇa, Apa.=*Śramaṇa*, p. 77.
savaṇa, 'ear.' p. 123. (*f*).
savattī, 'co-wife,' § 36. H. saut. Mar. savat.
savara=*śabara*, § 18.
savva, 'all,' § 50. H. sab.
savvaṇṇu, 'omniscient,' § 69.
savvāṇaṃ, 'of all,' § 111. AMg. savvesiṃ.
sasahara, 'moon,' p. 124 (*g*).
sasimuhī, 'moon-faced,' p. 123 (*d*).
sassirīadā, 'loveliness,' p. 113, n. 8.
sahattha, 'own hand,' § 49.
sahara=*śaphara*, § 13.
sahassa, 'thousand,' § 49.
sahāü, Apa., 'nature,' p. 77.
sahāsa, Apa., 'thousand,' p. 77.
sahī, 'friend,' § 13.
sāaṃsamae, 'in the evening,' p. 105, n. 3.
sāadaṃ, Ś 'welcome,' § 49. Mg., śaadaṃ, § 11.
[śāala, Mg., 'ocean,' p. 187, n. 6.
sāuṇia, 'fowler,' p. 99, n. 8.
sāo, 'from his own,' p. 164, n. 7.
sārikkha, 'like' (M. sāriccha), §§ 40, 66.
Sālavāhaṇa, § 23.
sāhai, 'tells,' § 125; imperat. sāhasu, p. 130, v. 76; gerund. AMg. sāhettā, p. 153. n. 10.
sāhaṇīa, 'praiseworthy,' § 49.
sāhavo, 'saints,' § 93.
si, '(thou) art,' § 132.
siyā, AMg., 'may be,' § 133.
siāla, 'jackal,' § 60. H. syāl.
siṃha, siṃgha, 'lion,' § 65.
sikkhāvaiya, AMg., 'precept,' p. 157, n. 4.
sikkhida, 'learnt,' § 40.
sijjhai, 'is fulfilled,' § 125; fut. AMg., p. 159, n. 9.
siñcai, 'pours,' § 125.
siñjā, 'jingle,' p. 123 (*d*).
siṭṭha, 'told,' § 125, p. 139, n. 6.
siṇiddha, 'sticky,' etc., § 47.
siṇeha, 'affection,' § 47. cf. ṇeha.
sitta, 'sprinkled,' § 125, p. 112, n. 4.
siri,=*śrī*, § 68.
siviā, AMg., '*palki*,' p. 158, n. 8.
[śivila, Mg., 'camp,' p. 186, n. 1.
sihāla,=*śikhāvat*, p. 77.
sīsa, 'head,' p. 113, n. 1.
sīha, M., 'lion.' cf. siṃha, § 65. Apa. sīhu, § 73.
sīhu, M., 'rum,' p. 122 (*c*).
sua, (1) 'heard,' § 125.
(2) 'parrot (*śuka*).
suai, 'sleeps,' § 132.
suandhi, 'fragrant,' p. 112, n. 5.
suia, 'cleaned,' p. 168, n. 4.
suidavva, 'to be slept,' p. 99, n. 7.
sukkha, 'dry,' § 38. Pb. sukkā. H. sūkhā. Bg. śukā.
sujjhai, 'is purified,' § 125.
suṭṭhu, 'well,' § 38.
suṇai, 'hears,' § 131. Ś suṇādi, § 132; gerundive suṇidavva, § 137; passive, suṇīadi § 135, n.
suṇaī, Apa, 'hears,' p. 77.
[śuṇḍikāgāla, Mg., 'grog-shop,' p. 180, n. 3.
suṇṇa, 'empty,' p. 102, n. 6. Pb. sunnā. H. sūnā.
suṇedi, 'hears,' §§ 125, 128, 131. cf suṇai.
suṇhā, 'daughter-in-law,' p. 118, v. 107.
sutta (1) 'asleep,' §§ 34, 125.
(2)=*sūtra*.
suttaa, AMg., 'belt,' p. 171, n. 10.
suda, Ś. 'heard,' § 125. cf. sua.
suddha, 'purified,' § 125.

sundaraara, 'more beautiful,' p. 121, (*a*).
sumaraṇa, 'memory,' p. 122, (*a*).
sumaradi, 'remembers,' § 57, Also sumaredi, § 128. (M. bharai, p. 132, v. 84); caus. part. sumarāvida, p. 101, n. 3.
summai, 'is heard,' § 135 (*d*).
suvai, 'sleeps,' § 125.
suvahuṃ, 'very much,' p. 135, n. 12.
suviṇa, 'dream,' p. 140 n. 5.
suvo, 'to-morrow,' § 57.
suvvai, 'is heard,' § 135.
sussūsaissaṃ, 'I shall wait upon,' § 134.
suhaa, 'fortunate,' p. 122, (*a*).
sūaa, 'spy,' p. 177, n. 6.
sūida, JM., sūiya, 'shown,' p. 140, n. 5.
se, (1) AMg., 'he.' Mg., śe, § 109.
(2) 'him,' AMg.
(3) '**his**,' M., AMg., Ś., § 109.
(4) 'her,' AMg., (Mg. śe gen.).
(5) 'they, them,' AMg. (Mg. śe), § 109.
sea, (1) 'sweat' (*sveda*).
(2) AMg., seya, 'white,' p. 156, n. 5 (*śveta*).
(3) AMg. seyaṃ, 'better,' p. 158, n. 2 (*śreyas*).
sela, 'rock,' p. 121, (*b*).
sehāliā, 'vitex,' p. 106, n. 10.
so, 'he,' § 108.
soa, (1) 'grief' (*śoka*).
(2) JM. soya, 'washing,' p. 135, n. 2 (*śauca*).
soavva=suṇidavva, § 137.
souṃ, 'to hear,' § 136, p. 103, v. 2.
sokkha, 'happiness,' § 43.
soccā, AMg., 'having heard,' p. 157, n. 8.
soṇhā=suṇhā, p. 118, v. 107.
sottia=*śrotriya*, p. 114, n. 8. Mg. śottie, p. 178, n. 3.
sottuṃ, 'to sleep,' § 136.
sodavva=soavva, § 137.
sodhaṇīa, 'to be purified,' p. 101, [n. 4.
somma, 'good sir,' §§ 48, 61.
sovai, sovadi, 'sleeps,' § 132.
sovāṇa, 'stairs,' p. 114, n. 5,
sohagga, 'auspicious,' p. 113, n. 4.

H

haa, **hada** (1) 'struck,' § 125
(2) 'taken,' § 125. cf. hia.
hage, AMg., 'S.,' §§ 11, 107. Apa. haũ, § 107.
haṭṭha, 'delighted,' p. 157 n. 8.
hadakka, Mg.. 'heart.' p. 182, n. 1.
haṇai, 'kills.' § 125.
hattha, 'hand,' § 38.
haddhī, 'alas,' p. 93, n. 1.
hammai, , is killed, ' § 135 (*d*).
harida, 'green,' p. 112, n. 4.
haridum, 'to take,' § 136.
harisa, 'joy,' § 57.
havissadi, 'will be,' § 4. Mg. haviśśadi.
hasira, AMg., laughing, p. 78.
hasedi, 'laughs,' § 128.
hia, **hida**, 'taken,' § 12. cf. haa.
hiaa, 'heart.' §§ 9, 60; abl. § 92. H. hiā.
hio, 'yesterday,' § 58.
hiṅgulaa, 'cinnabar,' p, 169, n. 7.
hutta, 'facing,' p. 108 (c) p. 133, v. 85.
huvai, M.=hoi.
huvissaṃ (Mg. huviśśaṃ), 'I shall be,' § 134.
hūa, 'become,' § 125. cf. bhūa. H. hūā.
hoi, 'becomes,' §§ 4, 129. cf. huvai. Ś. bhodi.
houṃ, 'to be,' p. 121 (*e*); gerund. houṇa, § 122.
hojjā, AMg., 'might be,' § 133.
hottam, 'being,' p. 131, v. 80.
hotthā, AMg., 'was,' p. 156, n. 1.
homi, 'I am,' § 129, hosi, 'thou art.'
hossaṃ=havissaṃ, § 134.
hohii, 'it will be,' § 134.

STUDENTS' BIBLIOGRAPHY.

[This list is intended to assist the student to extending his knowledge of Prakṛit, and to serve as a guide to College Libraries.]

Prakrit. A. Grammars, etc.

(1). **Pischel** (Dr. Richard). **Grammatik der Prakrit-Sprachen.** ["*Grammar of the Prakrit Languages.*"] Forms one volume (Band 1, Heft 8) of the Grundriss der Indo-Arischen Philologie und Altertumskunde. Strassburg, 1900. 500 pages. Price £1-16*s*.

[Deals with Jain Prakrits, Dramatic Prakrits, Paiśācī and Apabhraṃśa. A monument of industry and sound scholarship. A student who has worked through this "Introduction," should be able to make use of this work of reference, without any knowledge of German, by studying the *examples* given. The book contains an index of more unusual and special forms.]

(2). A complete **Index** to Pischel's Grammar has been published by Don. M. de Zilva **Wickremasinghe** in the **Indian Antiquary.** [Is sold separately.]

(3). **Jacobi** (Dr. Hermann). **Ausgewählte Erzählungen in Māhārāshṭrī,** zur Einführung in das Studium des Prākṛit. ["Selected Narratives in Māhārāṣṭrī as an introduction to the study of Prakrit."] Leipzig, 1886.

[As regards the classification of Prakrits, and in some details of derivation this book is no longer up to date. For Jain Māhārāṣṭrī it gives a concise account (in German) of Phonetics and Grammar, 86 pages of Selections, and a Vocabulary (Prakrit-Sanskrit-German). Nos. V. and IX of the Selected Narratives have been annotated and translated in this "Introduction"; also portions of No. III to illustrate Ardha-Māgadhī.]

(4). **Cowell** (Professor E. B.). The **Prākṛta-Prakāśa,** or the Prākṛt Grammar of **Vararuci** with the commentary (Manoramā) of Bhāmaha .....with notes, an English Translation and index of Prākṛt words; to which is prefixed a short introduction to Prākṛt Grammar. Second Issue. London, 1868.

[Unfortunately Bhāmaha's commentary on the XIIth Section, which deals with Śaurasenī has been lost, and many of the sūtras are "obscure and corrupt." The corresponding rules in Hemacandra's work are given in an Appendix, "but even these leave many difficulties unexplained." Bhāmaha has sometimes misunderstood Vararuci.]

(5). **Hemacandra** (*vide* page 79).

(*a*) **Siddha-hema-candra** (Adhyāya VIII deals with Prakrit), edited by **Pischel,** Parts I and II. Halle, 1877, 1880, with translation and notes. (*German.*)

(6). (*b*) **Deśīnāmamālā,** edited by **Pischel.** Bombay, 1880.

(7). **Hœrnle.** The **Prākṛta-Lakṣaṇam** or Caṇḍa's Grammar of the Ancient (Ārsha) Prākṛt. Calcutta, 1880.

[Ārṣa=AMg., not as Hœrnle stated=AMg.+M.]

(8) **Bühler.** Edition of **Prākṛta-lakṣmīḥ.**

"The Pāiyalachchhī Nāmamālā, a Prākrit Kosha by Dhanapāla. Edited with critical notes, an introduction and a glossary by George Bühler." Gottingen, 1878.

B. **Texts.** *Māhārāṣṭrī.*

(9). **Hāla. Saptaśatakam.** (*Vide* p. 73.)

(*a*) Edited by Weber. Leipzig, 1881.

[Vocabulary in German.]

(*b*) Kāvyamālā Series No. 21. Edited by Durgaprasad and Parab. Bombay, 1889.

[With Sanskrit commentary.]

(10). **Setubandha** or Rāvaṇavaha. (*Vide* p. 72.)

(*a*) Kāvyamālā Series No. 47. Edited by Śivadatta and Parab. Bombay, 1895.

[With Sanskrit version and commentary.]

(*b*) Edited by Siegfried Goldschmidt. Strassburg, 1880.

[With German translation and vocabulary.]

(11). **Gaüḍavaho,** ed. Sh. P. Paṇḍit. Bombay, 1887.

[Bombay Sanskrit Series XXXIV. Revised edition.]

Dramatic Prakrits.

[It is unnecessary to enumerate editions of Sanskrit Plays. Many will be familiar to the student, others he will find in Schuyler's Bibliography. Very few editions give a correct or consistent Prakrit text. This is mainly due to corruptions in the MSS.]

(12). **Karpūramañjarī** of Rājaśekhara.

Critical edition with Vocabulary by **Dr. Sten Konow.** Translation and Introduction by **Prof. C. B. Lanman.**

[Harvard Oriental Series, Vol. 4. This play is also in the K. M. Series No. 4, edited by Durgaprasad and Parab. Bombay, 1887.]

(13). **Śakuntalā**, ed. **Pischel**. Kiel, 1877.

[Follows the Bengal version, edited with a sounder knowledge of Prakrit than Monier Williams' edition of 1867.]

(14). **Mṛcchakaṭikam, ed. Goḍabole.** Bombay, 1896. (Bombay Sanskrit Series).

[Other editions—Stenzler, 1847. Rama Maya Śarma Calcutta, 1829. Hiranand and Parab., 1902. The last has been quoted in the extracts, as it is much used by students. Translation. Dr. A. W. Ryder, Harvard Oriental Series, Vol. 9.]

(15). **Ratnāvalī.** A second text of this, with a Prakrit-Sanskrit glossary by **Capeller,** is given in Böhtlingks Chrestomathie, p. 290 ff. St. Petersburg, 1877.

Ardha-Māgadhī.[1]

(16). **Banarsi Das Jain. Ardha-Māgadhī Reader.** Panjab University Oriental Publications. Lahore, 1923. Price Rs. 3.

(17). **Kalpasūtra** (Kappasutta), ed. **Jacobi**, Leipzig, 1879.

[Translated by Jacobi, S.B.E., XXII, *vide* p. 71, and p. 161, n. 3.]

(18). **Āyāraṅgasutta,** ed. Jacobi. London, 1882. (Calcutta edn., Saṃvat 1936).

[The first *aṅga* and the most archaic. Important for prose.]

(19). **Sūyagaḍaṅgasutta,** ed. Bombay. Saṃvat 1936.

[Second *aṅga*. Important for verse.]

(20). **Uvāsagadasāo,** ed. **Hœrnle.** Calcutta, 1890. (Bibliotheca Indica).

[Seventh *aṅga*, contains narratives. Both text and commentary are edited critically.]

(21). **Svāmi-Ratna-Chandra. Ardha-Māgadhī Dictionary.** (AMg.—Eng. H. Guj.). Indore. 2 Vols. are out, 1923, 1927.

---

[1] The whole of the AMg. canon was published at Bombay some ten years ago.

Jain Māhārāṣṭrī.

(22). **Āvaśyaka,** Erzählungen, ed. Ernst **Leumann.** Heft 1 Leipzig, 1897.

See also No. 3 above, **Jacobi.**

(23). **Kālakācārya**-caritam, ed. **Jacobi** (*vide.* p. 139). Z. D. M. G. Vol. 34 (1880), p. 262.

(24). **Kakkuka** Inscription. (Extract No. 17, p. 134.)

Jain Śaurasenī.

(25). **Pavayaṇasāra** by Kundakundācārya, ed. Manohar Lal, Bombay, 1912.

(26). **Kattigeyāṇupekkhā** by Kārttikeyasvāmin, ed. Bhandarkar.

(27). **Davvasaṃgaha** of Nemicandra, ed. Sarat Chandra Ghosal, Arrah (India), 1917.

(28). **Gommaṭasāra,** ed. Gajadhar Lal, Calcutta.

Paiśācī. (*Vide* p. 68-69.)

Pali.

[It is only necessary to mention a few books useful to the student who does not make a special study of this language.]

Grammars, etc.

(29). **Müller, E.** A simplified grammar of the Pali language. London, 1884. (Trübner.)

[There is a short grammar by Frankfürter with selections and vocabulary. A better grammar is that of M. Duroiselle.]

(30). **Childers,** R. C. Dictionary of the Pali Language. Fourth Impression. London, 1909.

Texts and Translations.

(31). **Jātakas.** edited by **Fausboll.** Trübner. 7 vols. London, 1877.

(32). ,, *translated* by various hands, edited by **Cowell and Rouse.** Cambridge, 1895.

[With these the student can make a good start without a teacher.]

(33). **Andersen** (Dines). Pali Reader. Copenhagen.

(34). **Mahāvaṃsa,** *edited* **Turnour,** translated **Geiger.**

(35). Publications of the **Pali Text Society.**

Old Prākrit.

The material is scattered. For **Aśoka's** Edicts the student may consult 34–36.

(36). **Senart.** Les inscriptions de Piyadasi. 2 Vols. Vol. II, trans. Grierson I.A.

The first volume of the Corpus Inscriptionum Indicarum. Aśoka's Edicts edited by Cunningham is difficult to obtain—and needs revision.

(37). **A. C. Woolner. Aśoka Text and Glossary.** (Panjab University Oriental Publications) Lahore, 1924.

(38). **Hultzsch. Corpus Inscriptionum Indicarum.** Vol. I (Aśoka's Inscriptions) New edition. 1925.

(39). **Franke** (Professor O.) "Pali and Sanskrit," 1902.
[German. *Vide* p. 74, n. 2.]

(40). **Lüders.** "Fragments of two Buddhistic dramas."
[German. *Vide* p. 72, p. 78.]

Late Prakrit. *Apabhraṃśa.*

Hemacandra. *Vide* No. 5 above.

(41). **Piṅgala-**chandaḥsūtra or Prākṛta-Piṅgala-sūtra. Kāvyamālā series No. 41, ed. Śivadatta and Parab.
[A critical edition is needed.]

(42). **Dhaṇavāla. Bhavisattakaha.** ed. Jacobi (with introd. and vocabulary), 1918.

Modern Languages.

(43). **Bloch** (Jules). **La formation de la langue marathè.** Paris, 1920.

(44). **Turner, (R.L.). Gujarātī Phonology J.R.A.S., 1921.**

(45). **Chatterji,** (S.K.) **Origin and Development of Bengali Language.** Calcutta, 1926.

Published by the University of the Panjab, Lahore and printed by P. Knight, Baptist Mission Press, Calcutta.